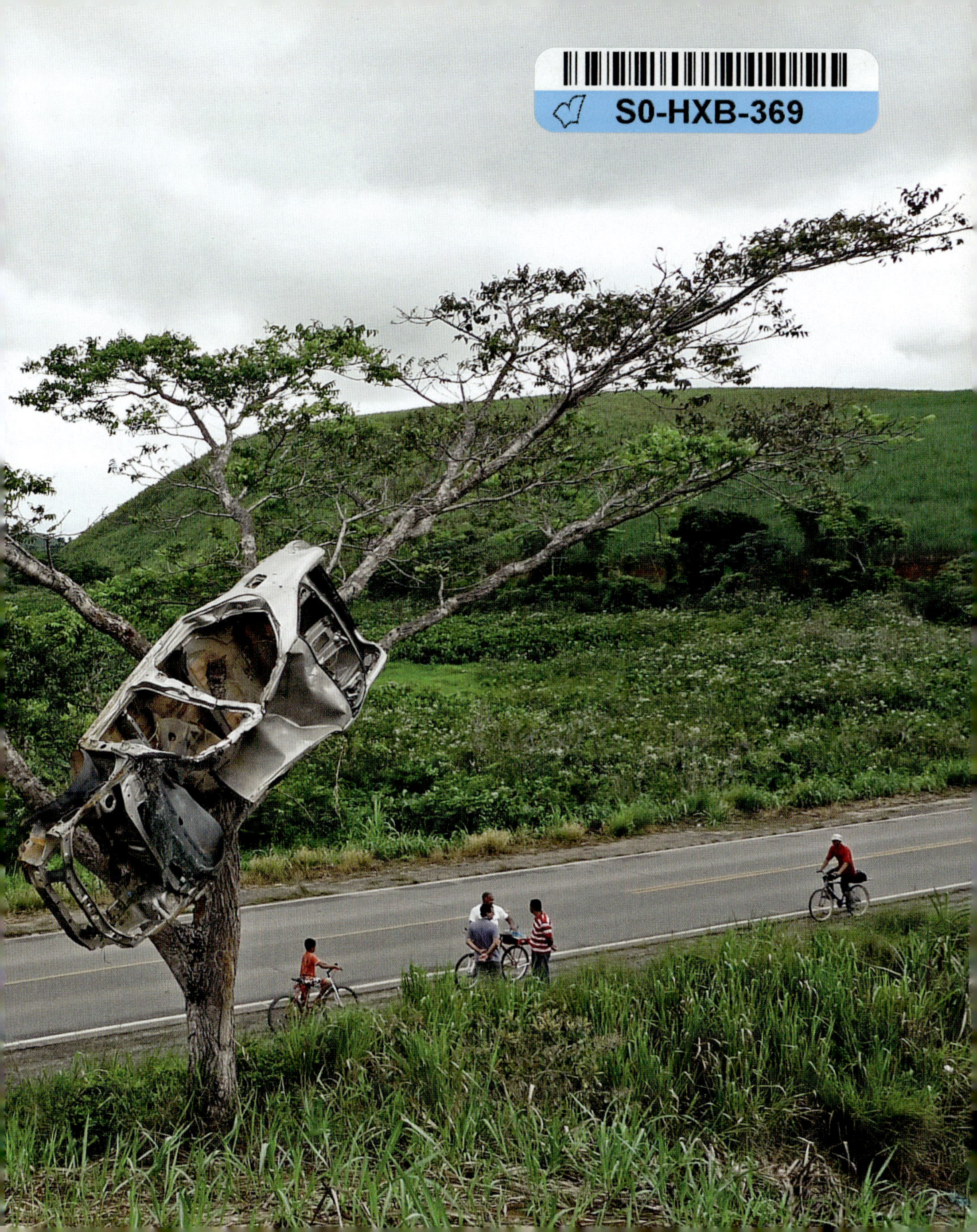

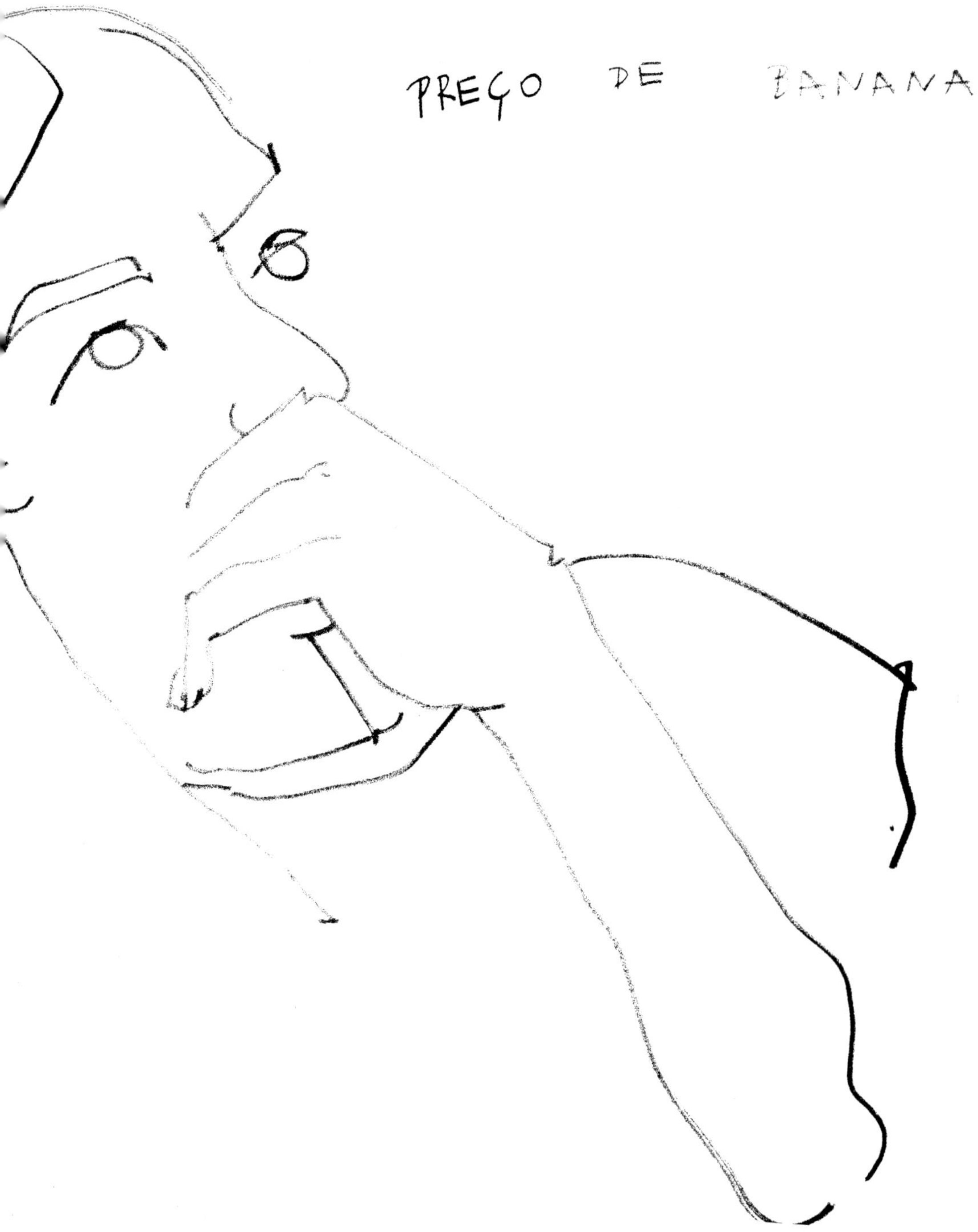
PREÇO DE BANANA

CARLITO CARVALHOSA

NICE TO MEET YOU

CHARTA

PARA MARI, MARIA E CECÍLIA, SEMPRE

pg. 2 Mari Stockler, *Preço de banana*, 1996

CONTENTS/SUMÁRIO

A SOMA DOS DIAS

PINACOTECA DO ESTADO DE SÃO PAULO, 2010
PROJETO OCTÓGONO, CURADORIA IVO MESQUITA
1400M² DE TNT 20G. EM DUAS ESPIRAIS
16M DE ALTURA X 14X14M
BARRA DE ALUMÍNIO, ALTO-FALANTES, MICROFONES
AMPLIFICADORES, LAPTOPS, INTERFACE DE ÁUDIO
2 PERFORMANCES DE PHILIP GLASS
20 PERFORMANCES DE ALUNOS DA ESCOLA
DE MÚSICA DO ESTADO DE SÃO PAULO

The Sum of Days

Pinacoteca do Estado de São Paulo, 2010

Projeto Octógono, curated by Ivo Mesquita
1400m² of TNT 20g. in two spirals
16m h x 14m x 14m
Aluminum bar, loudspeakers, microphones,
amplifiers, laptops, audio interface
2 performances by Philip Glass
20 performances by students of São Paulo State Music School

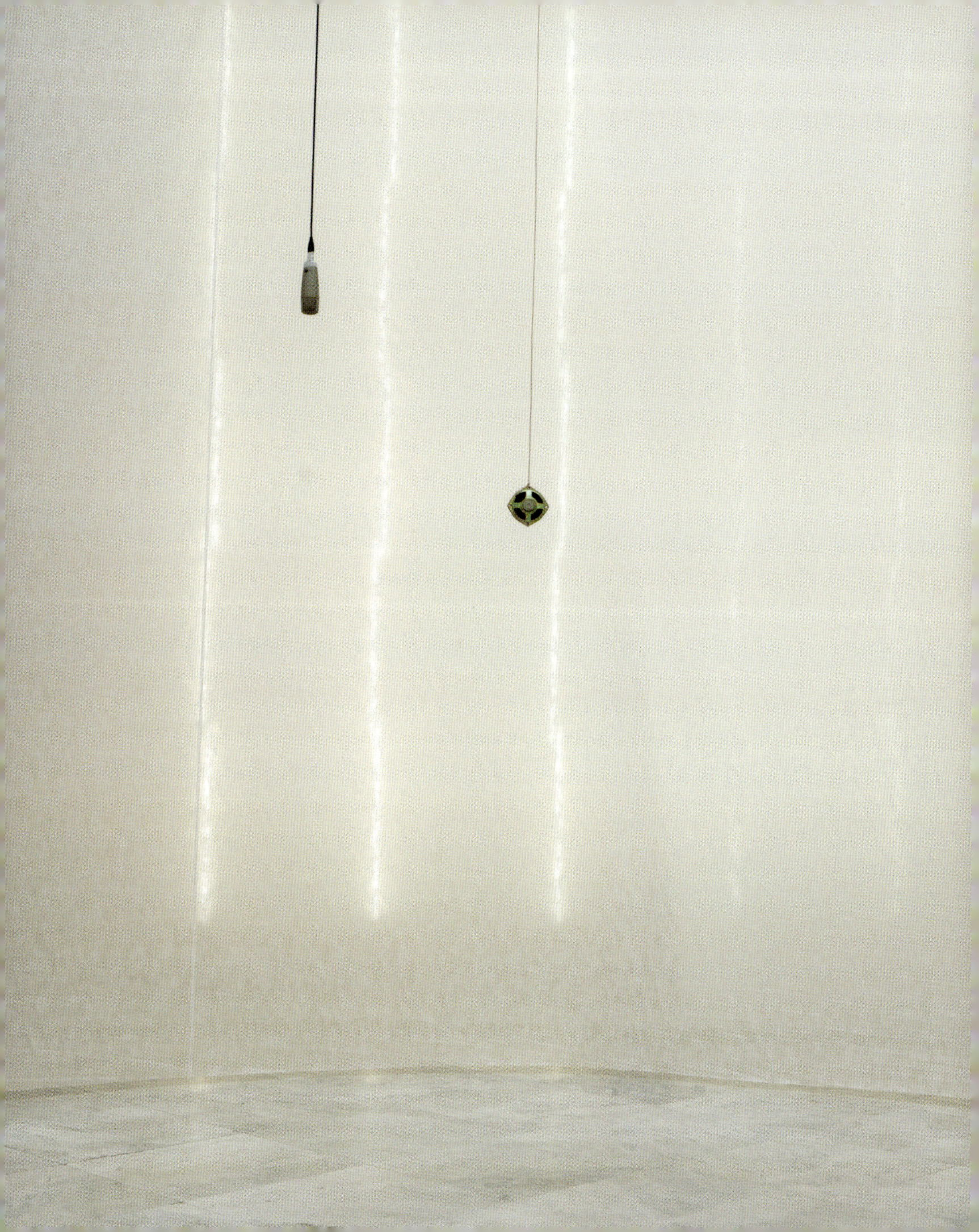

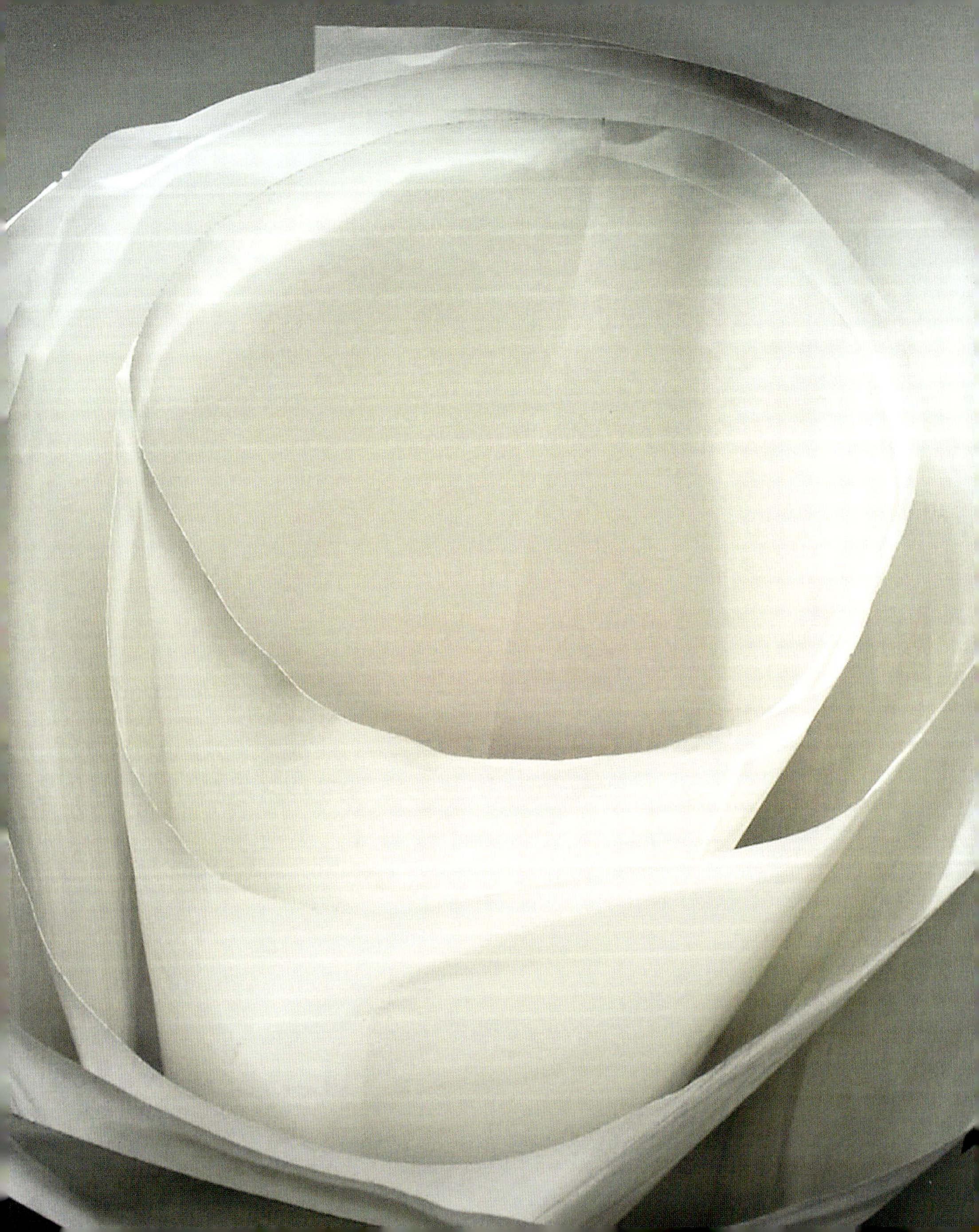

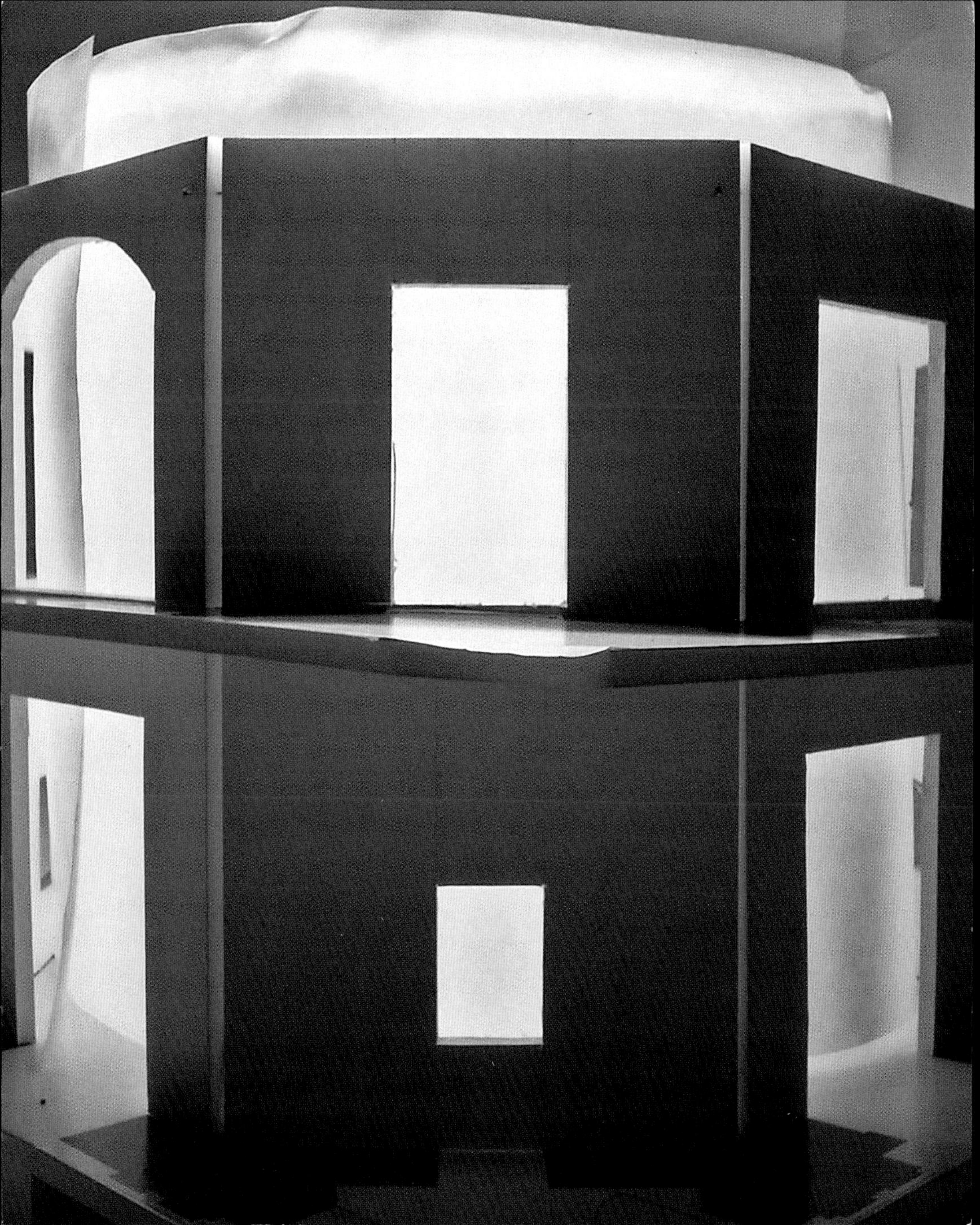

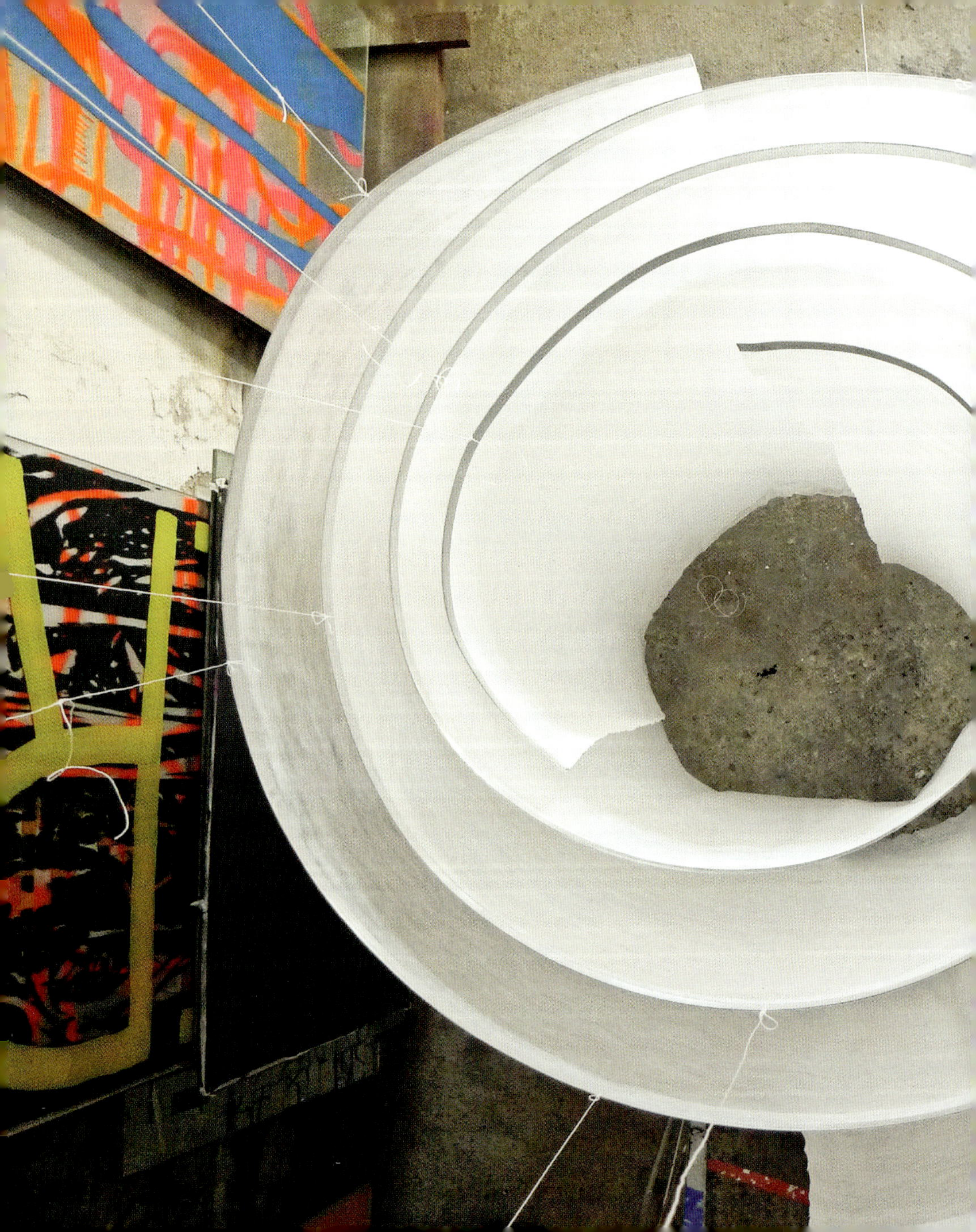

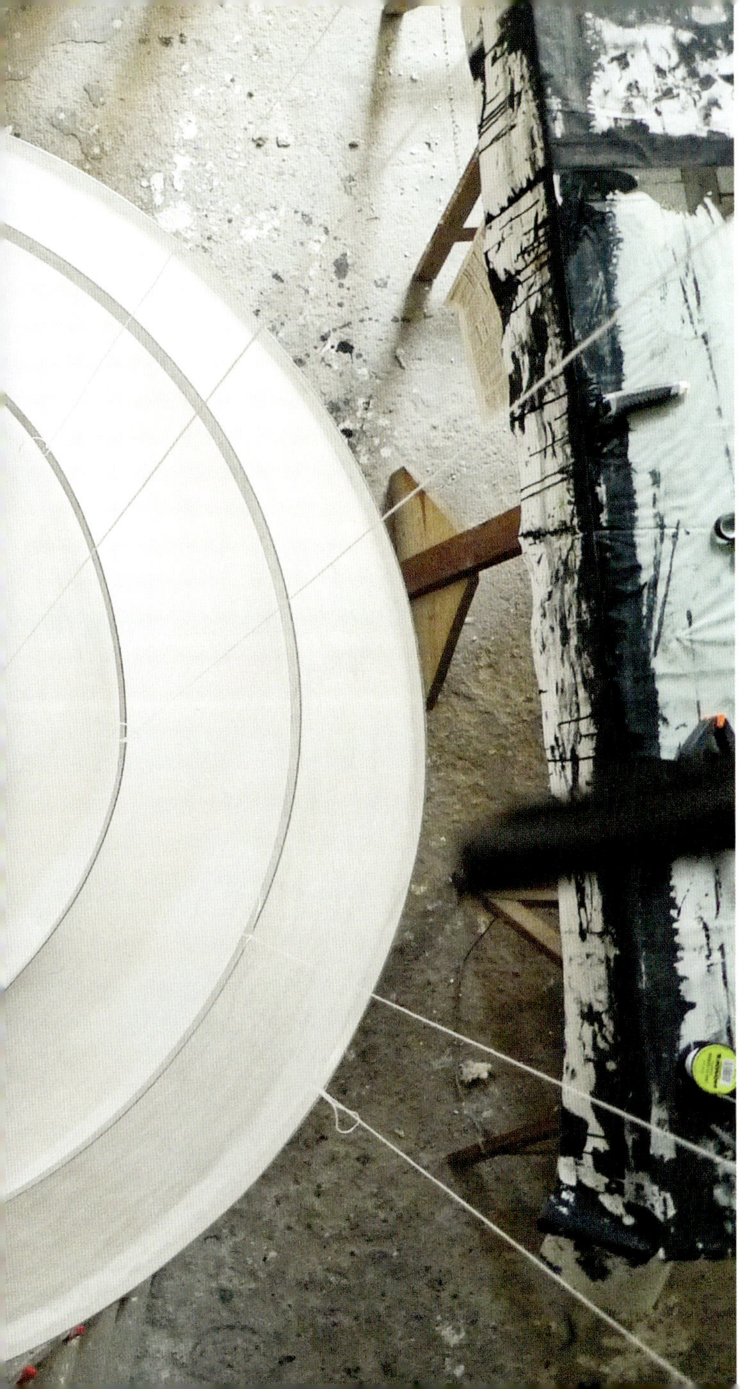

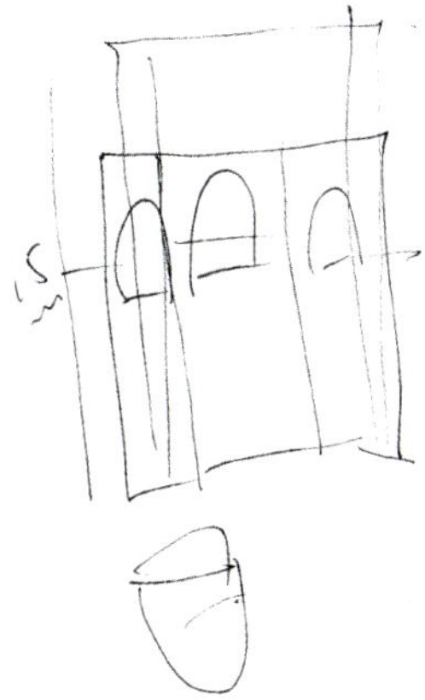

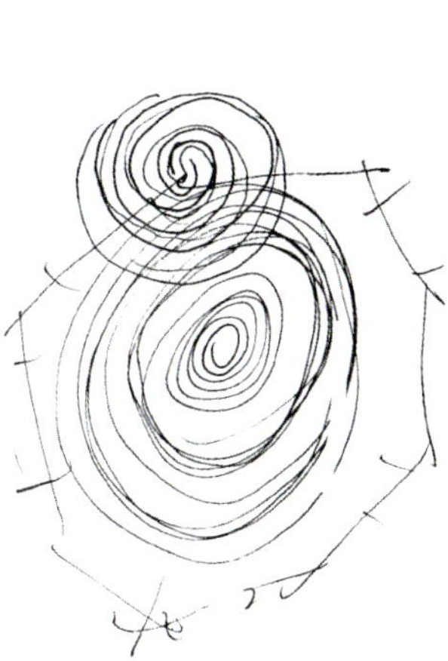

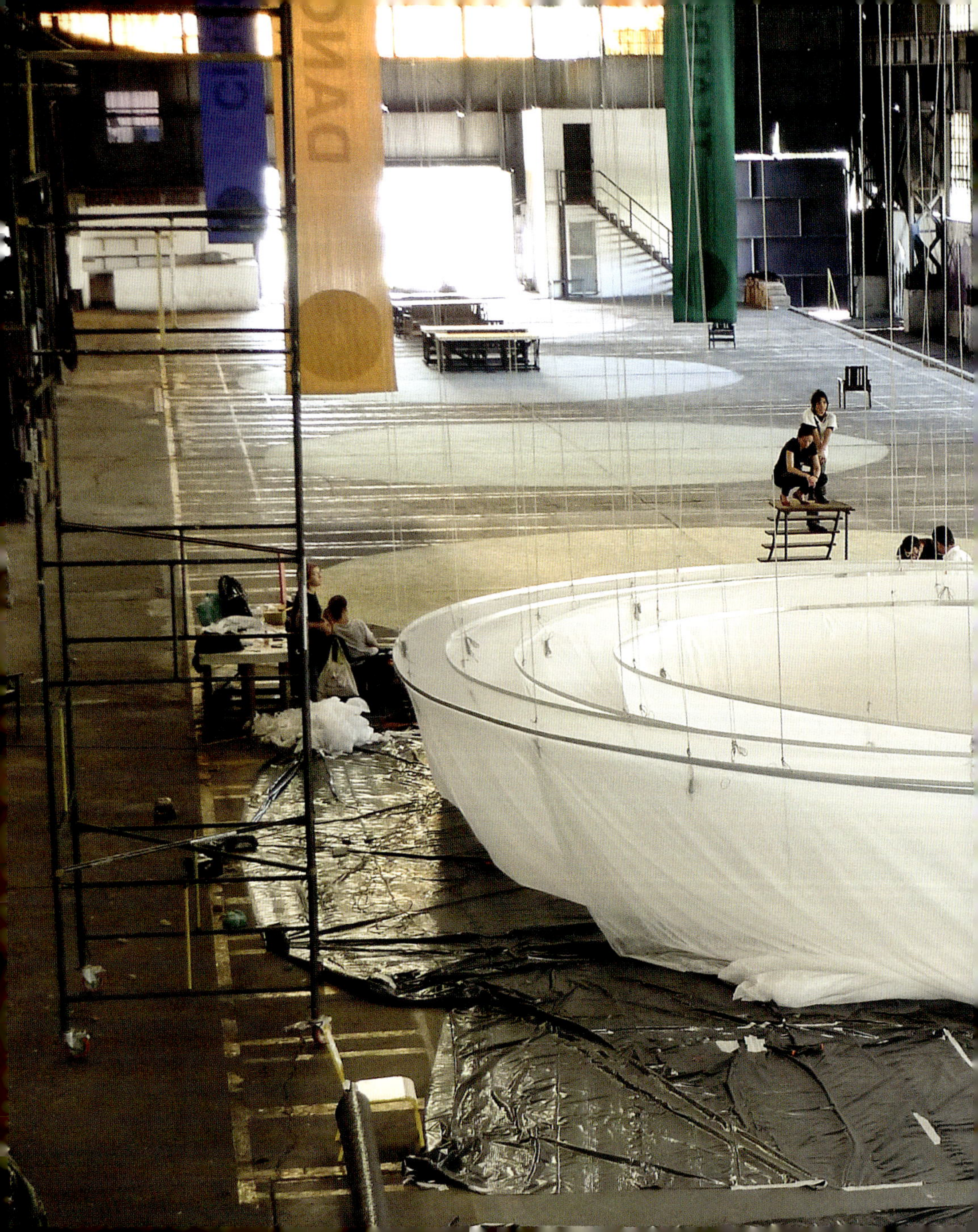

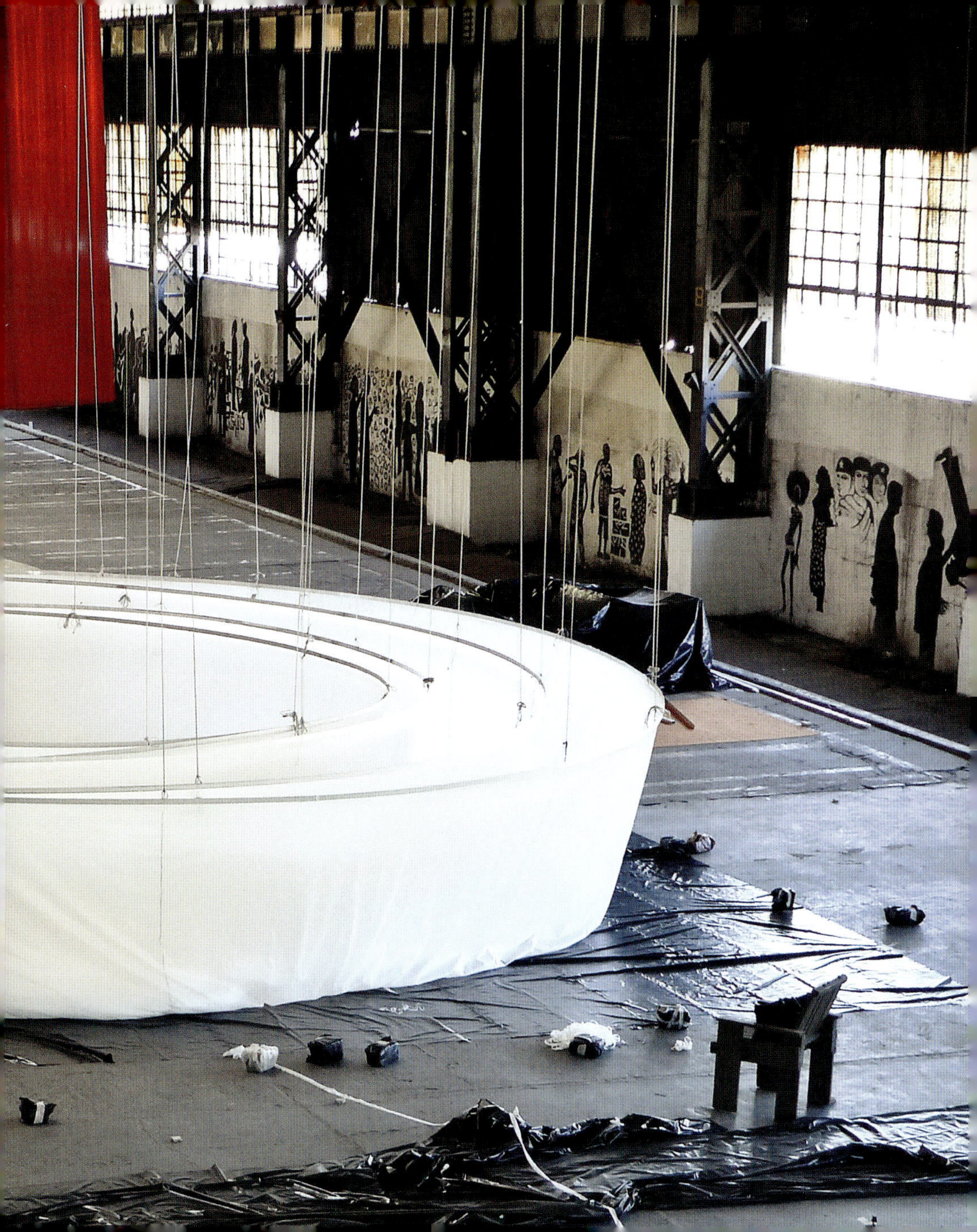

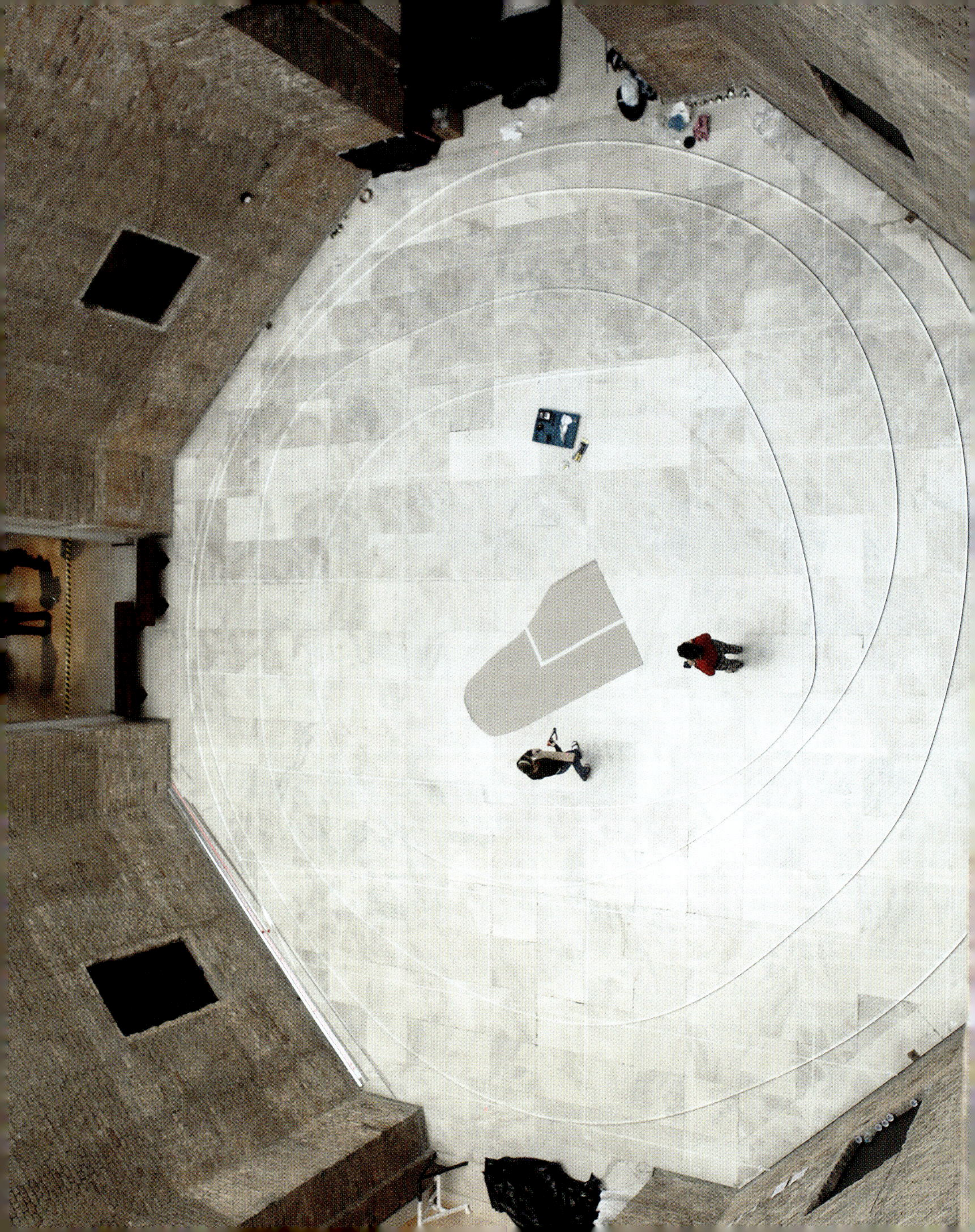

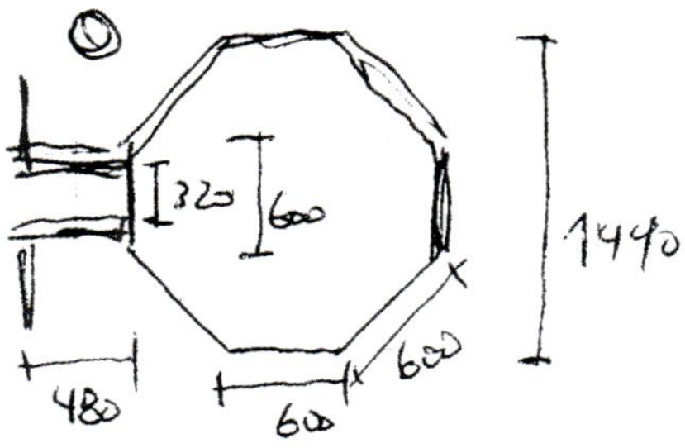
320
600
1440
480
600
600

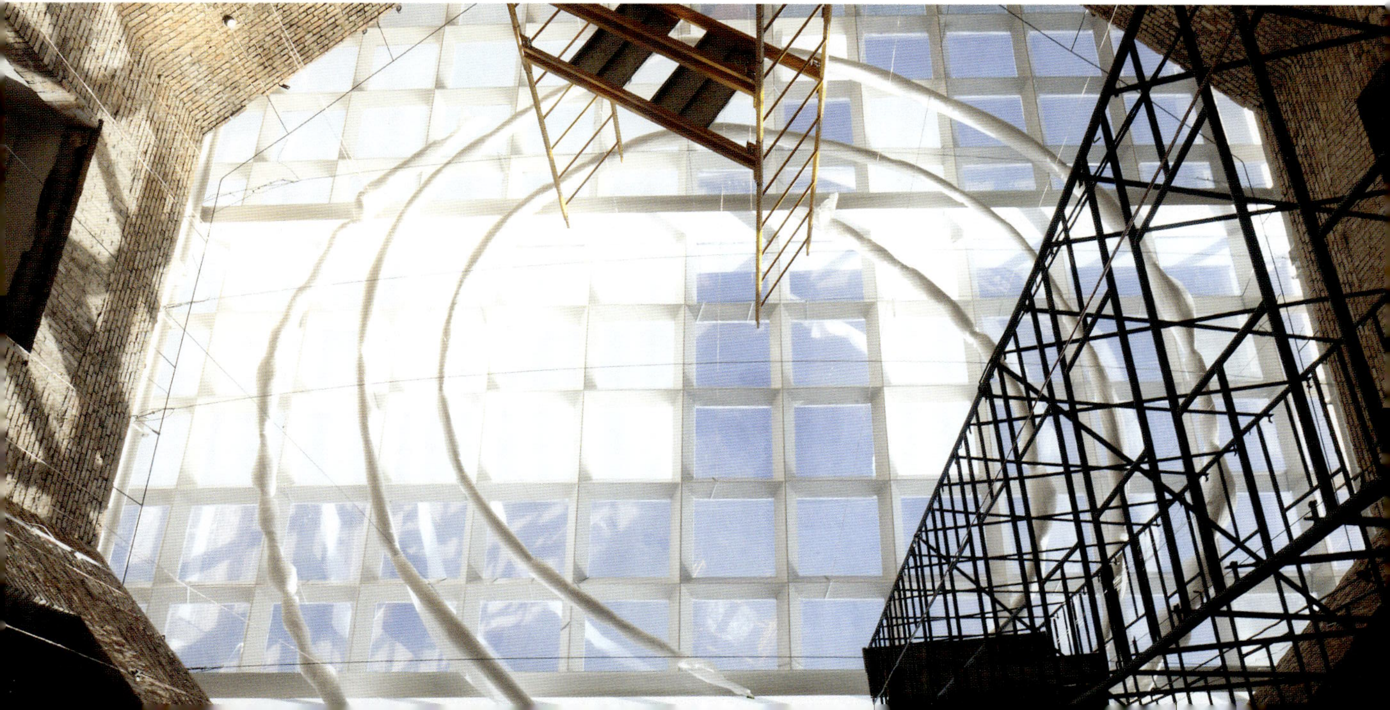

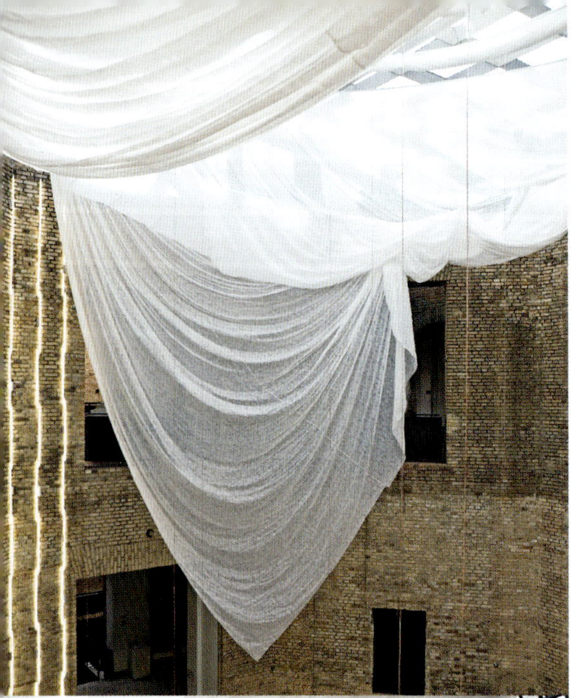

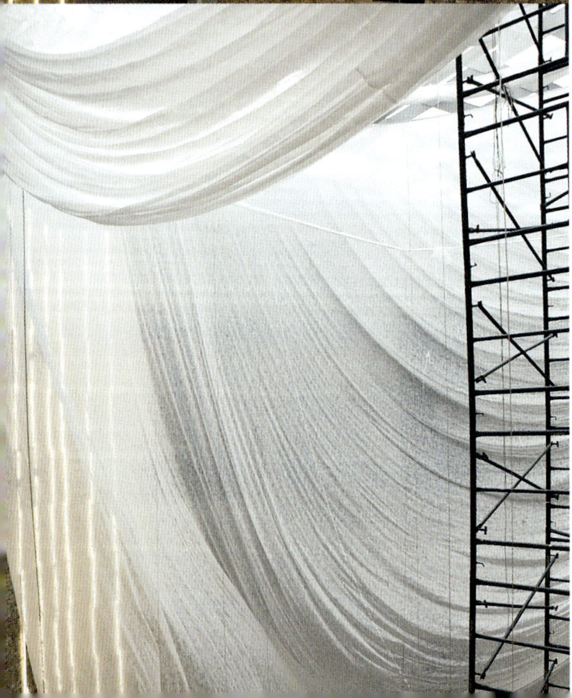

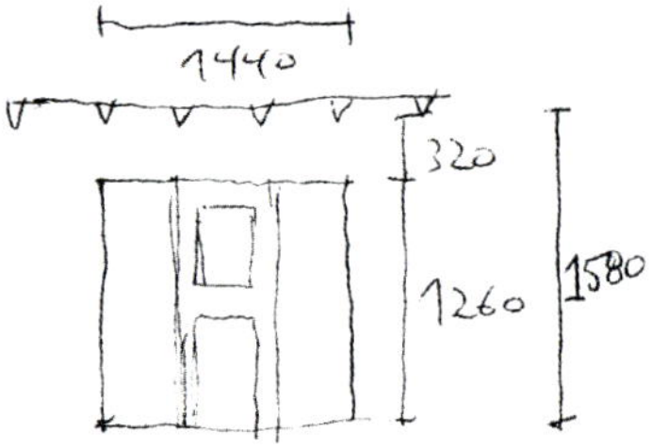
1440
320
1260
1580

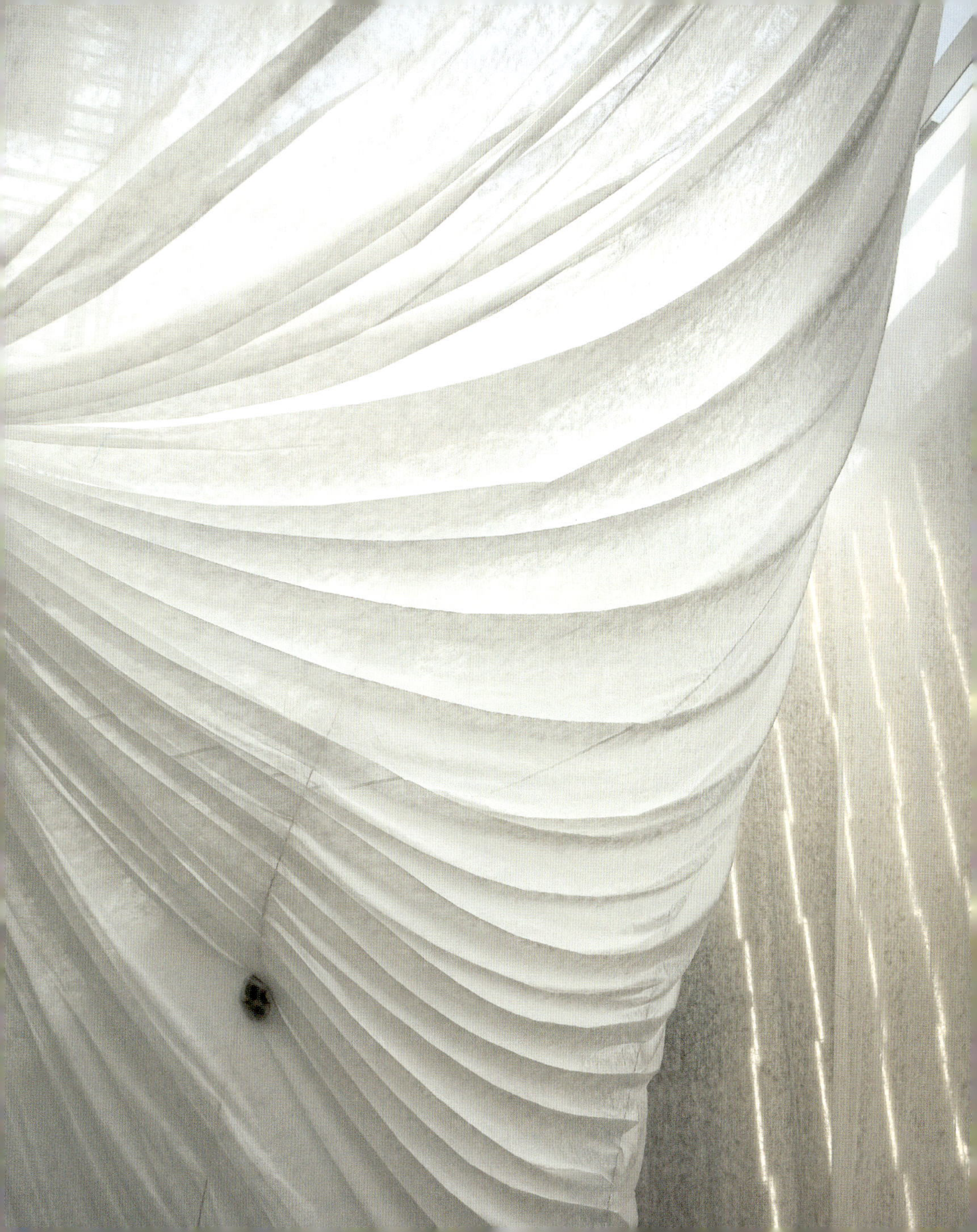

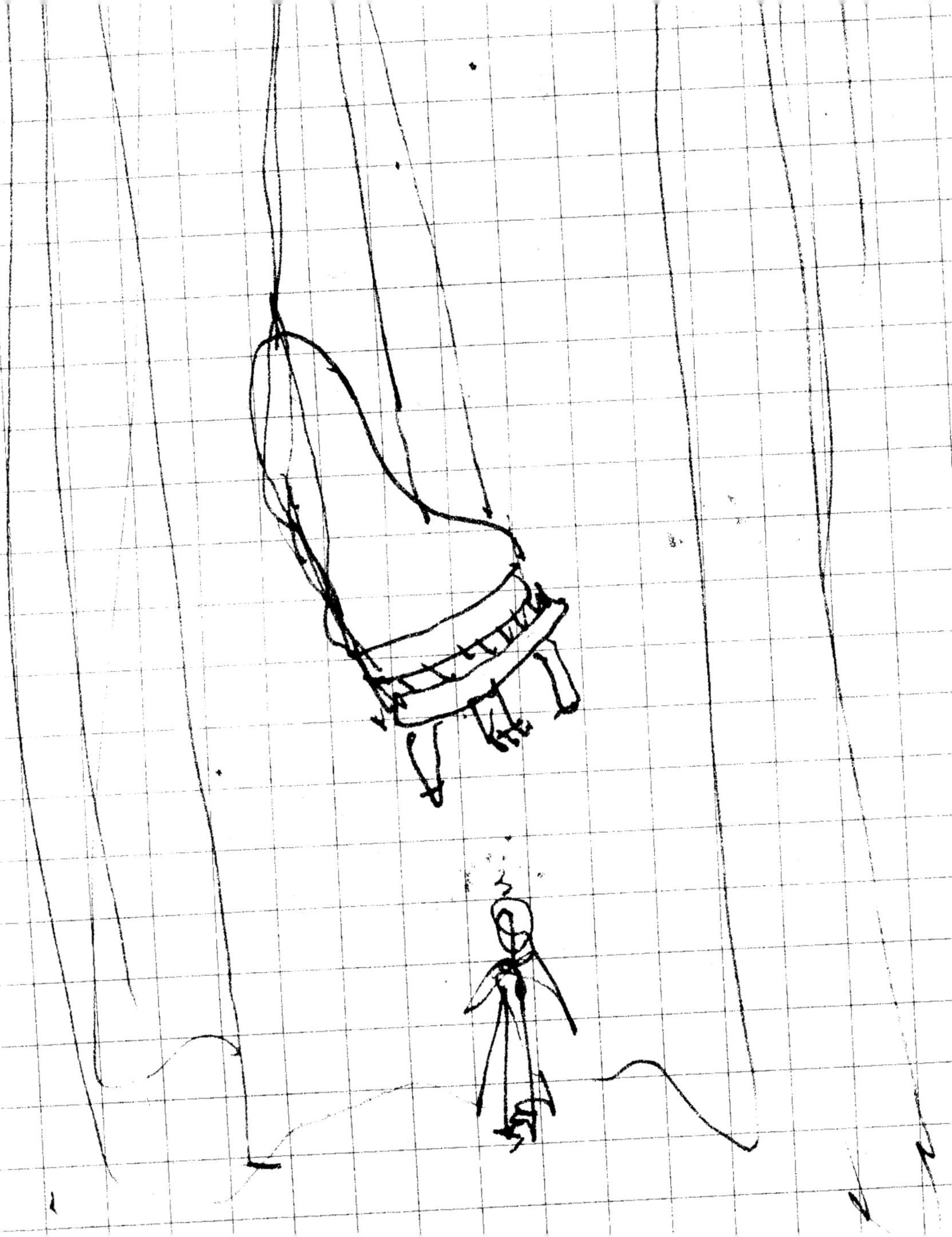

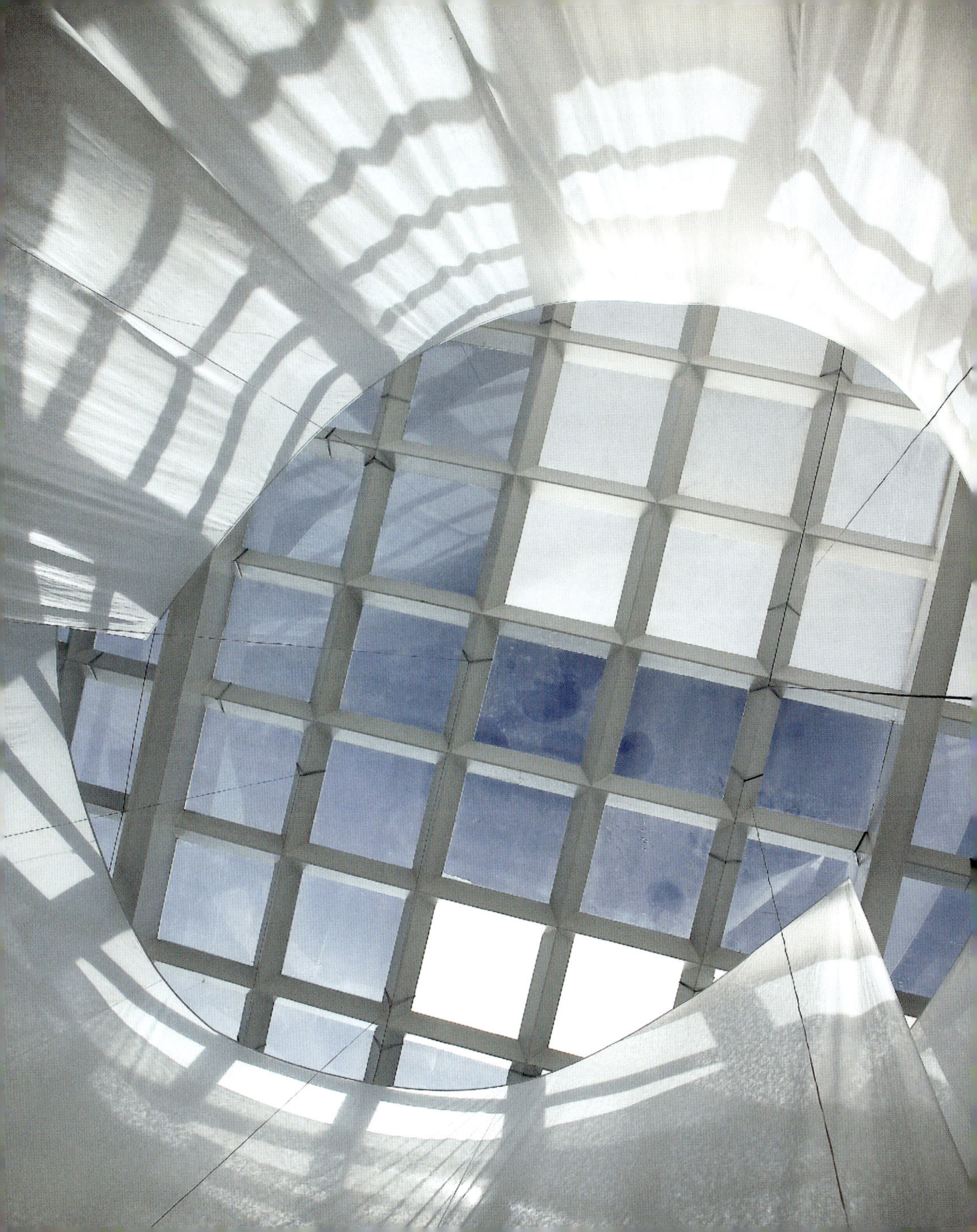

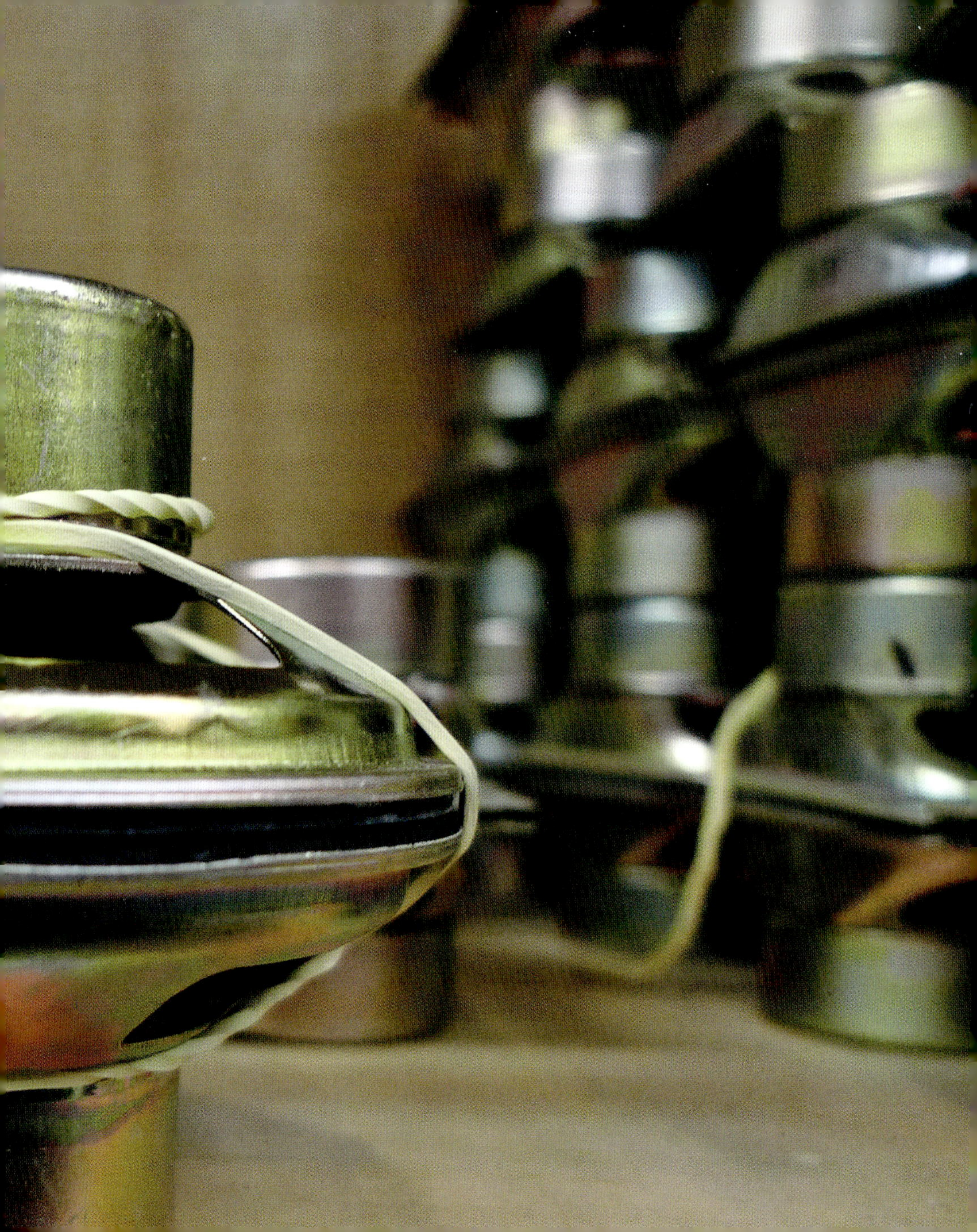

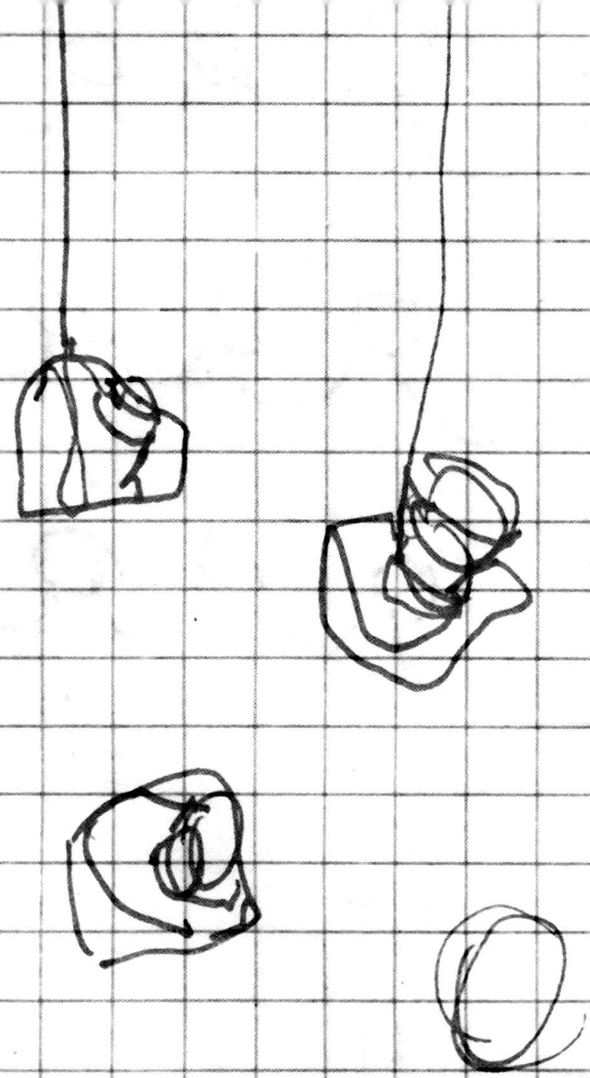

June 10

— EXT. 7173

2 | 7 EXT 55541 Noronda

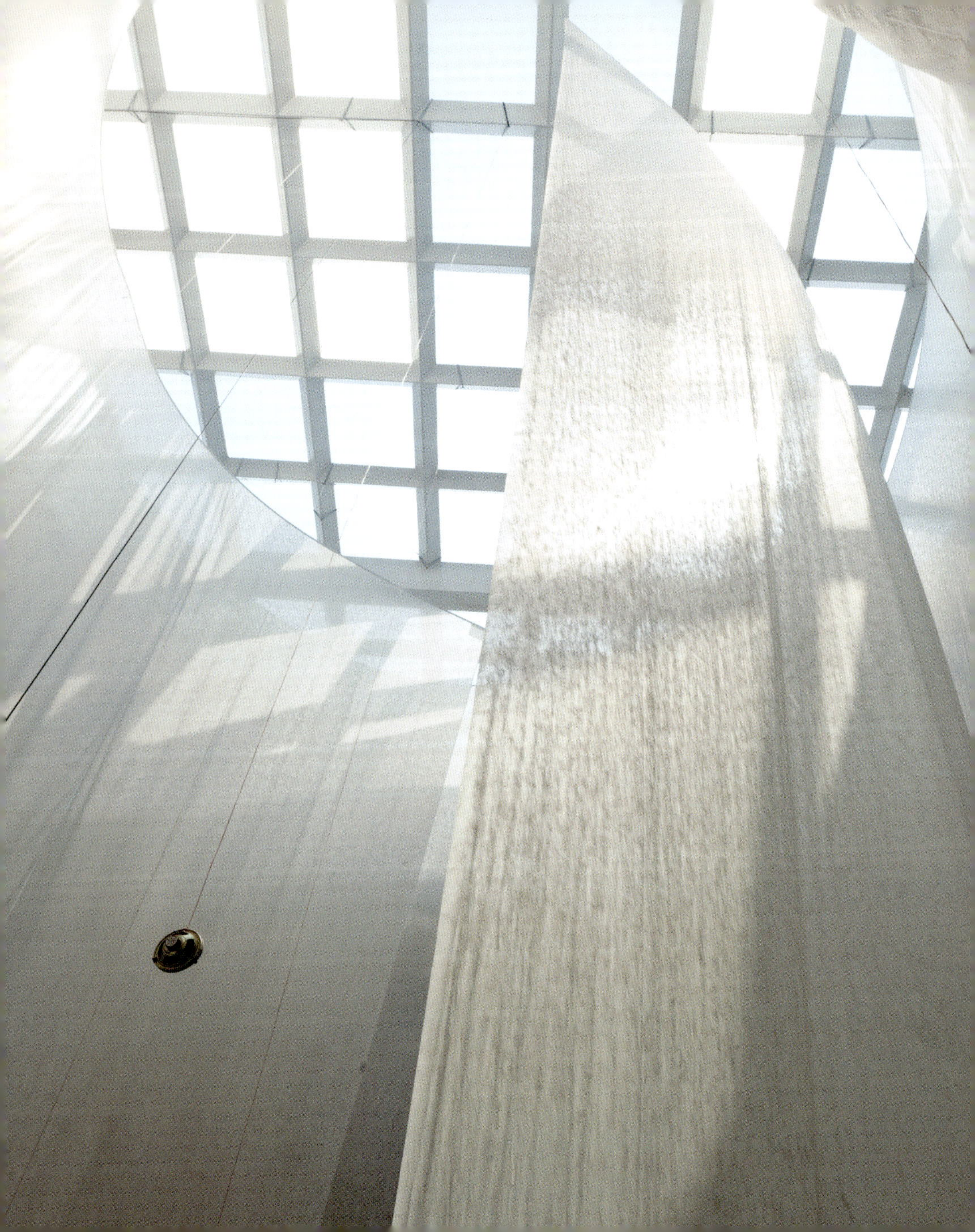

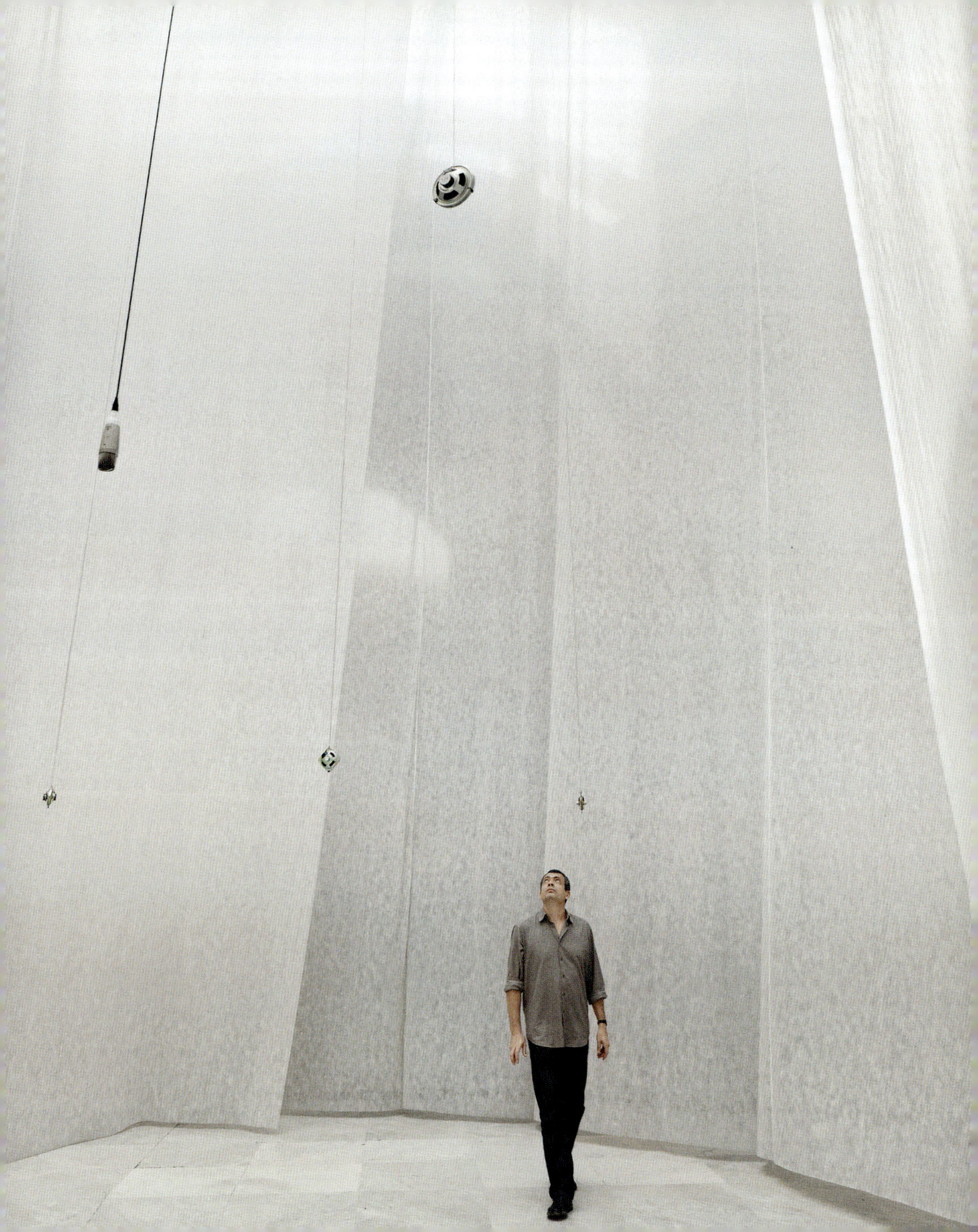

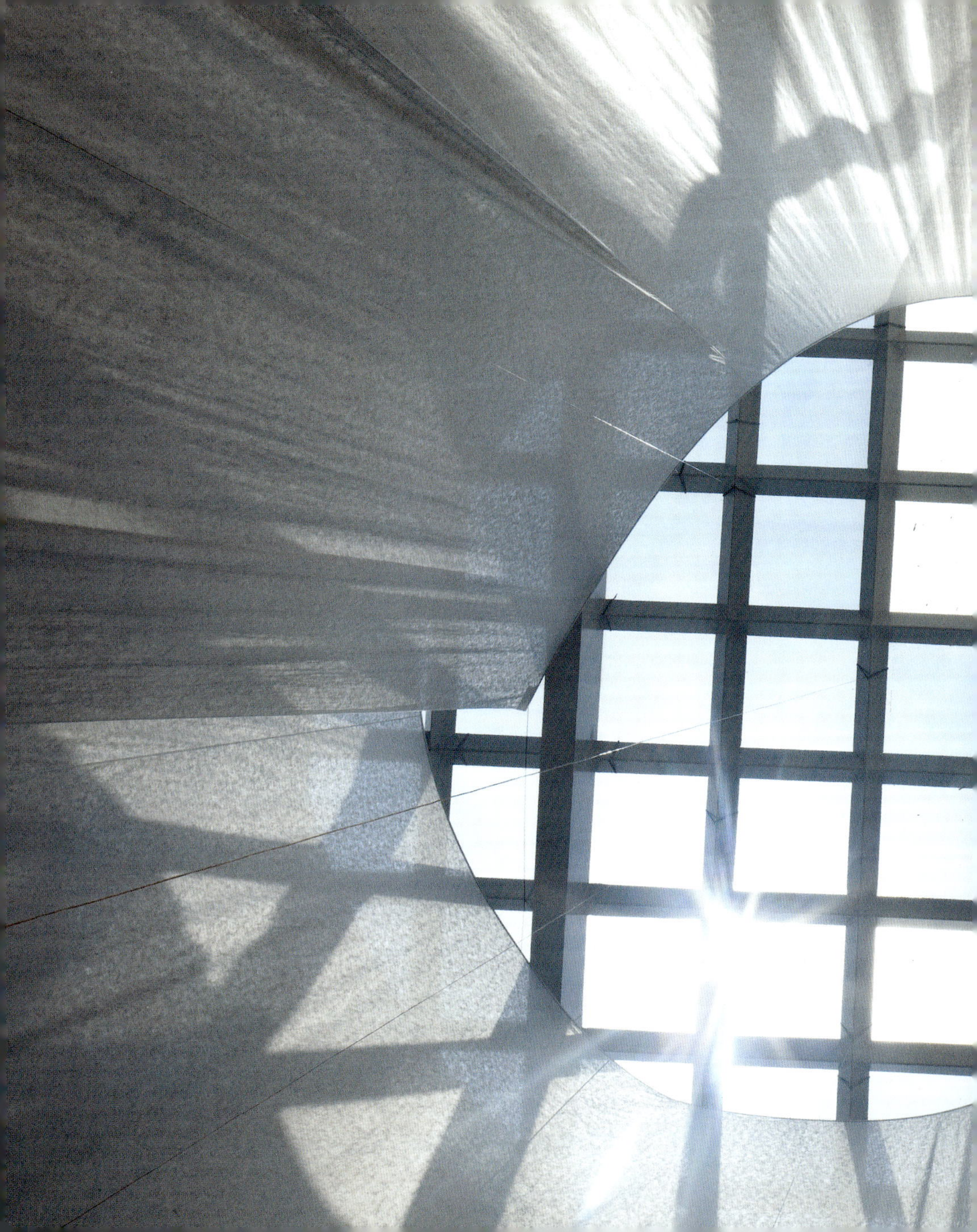

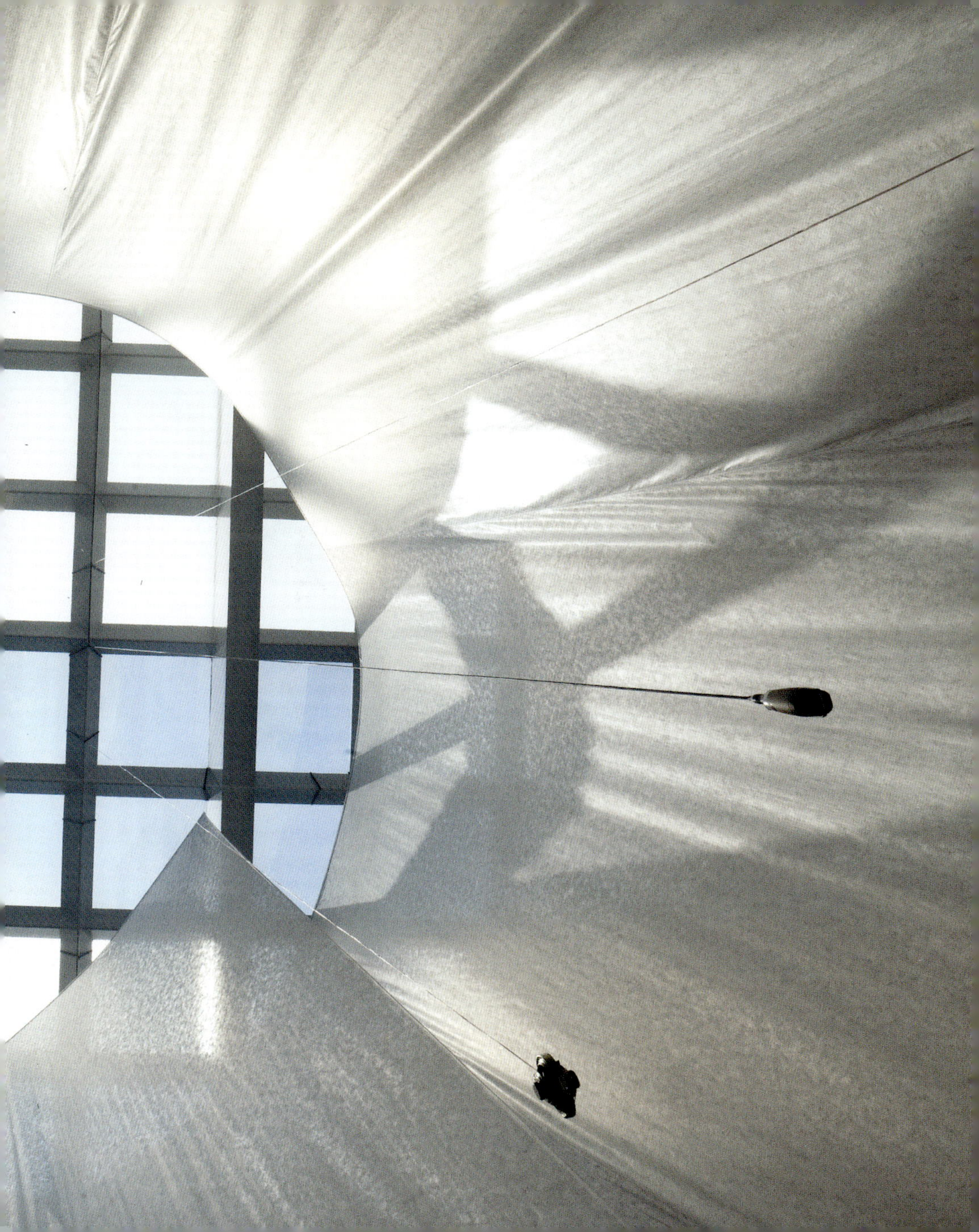

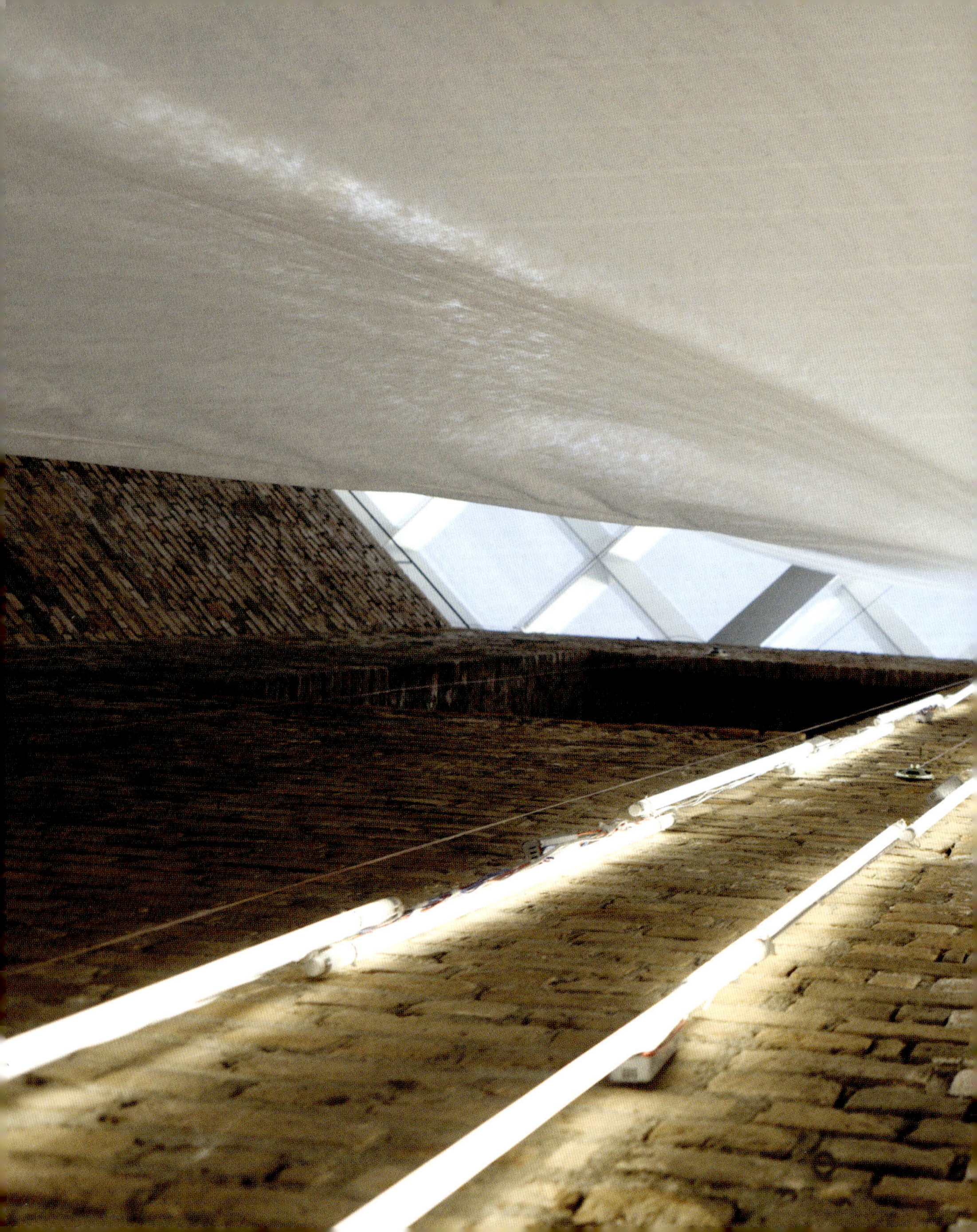

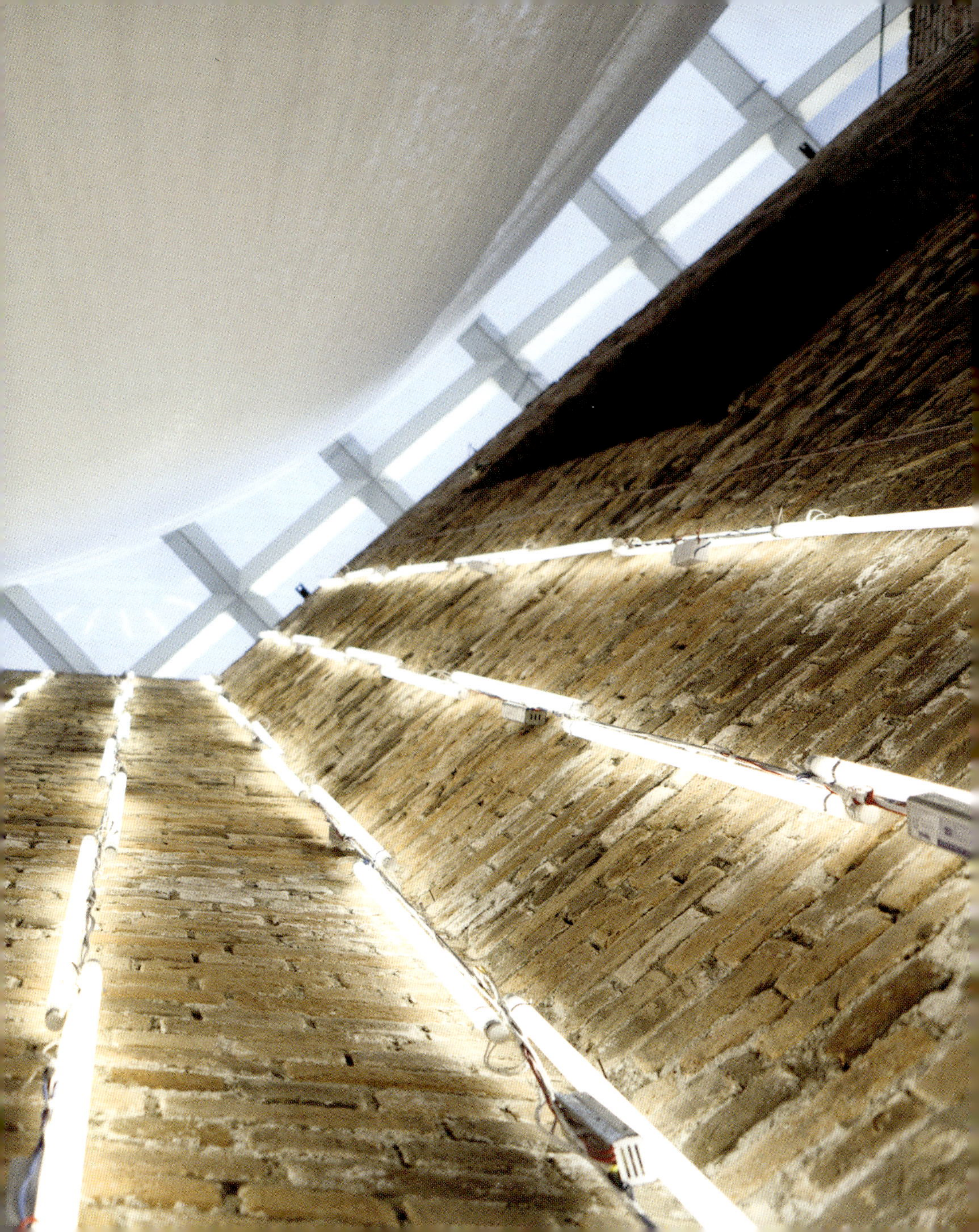

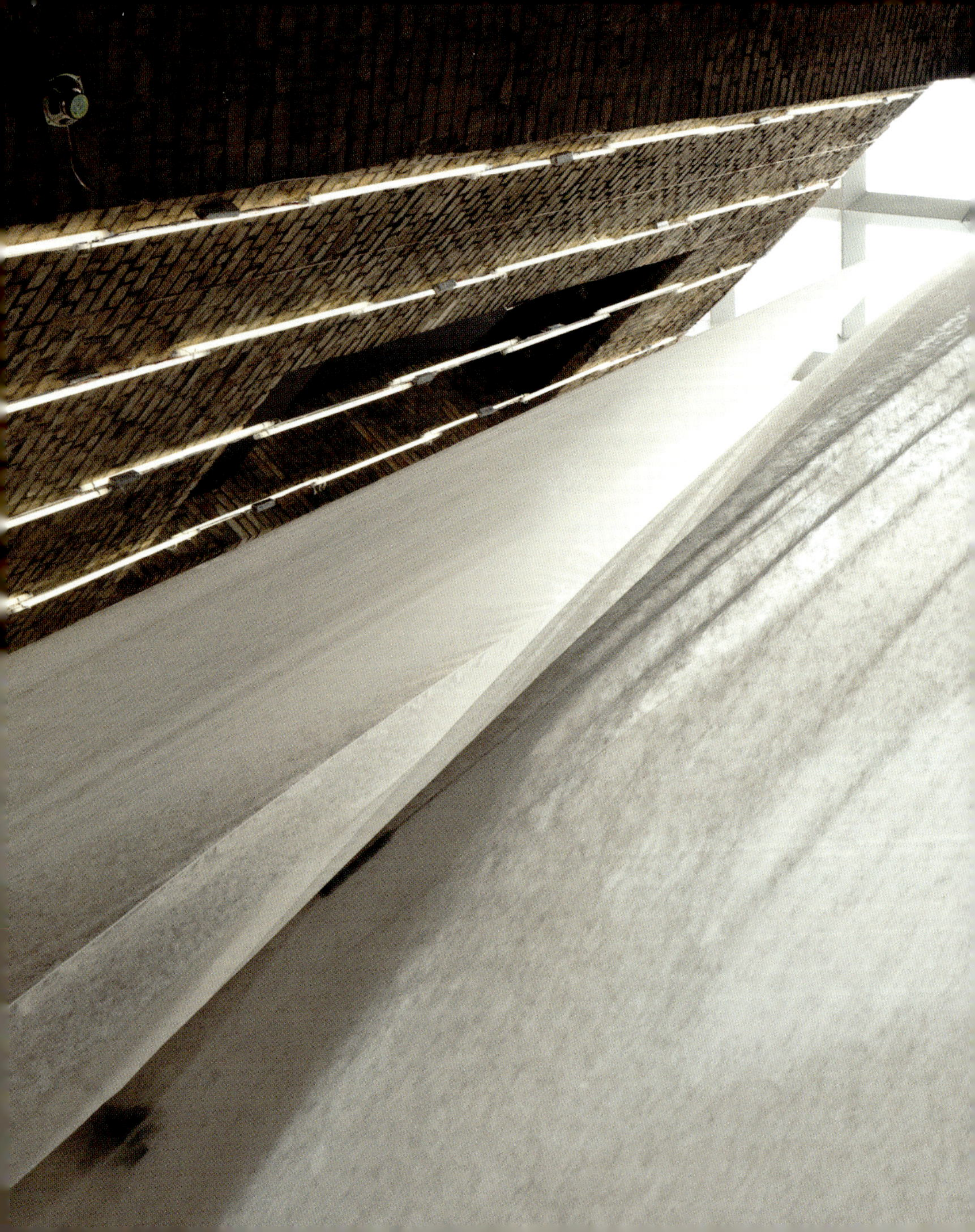

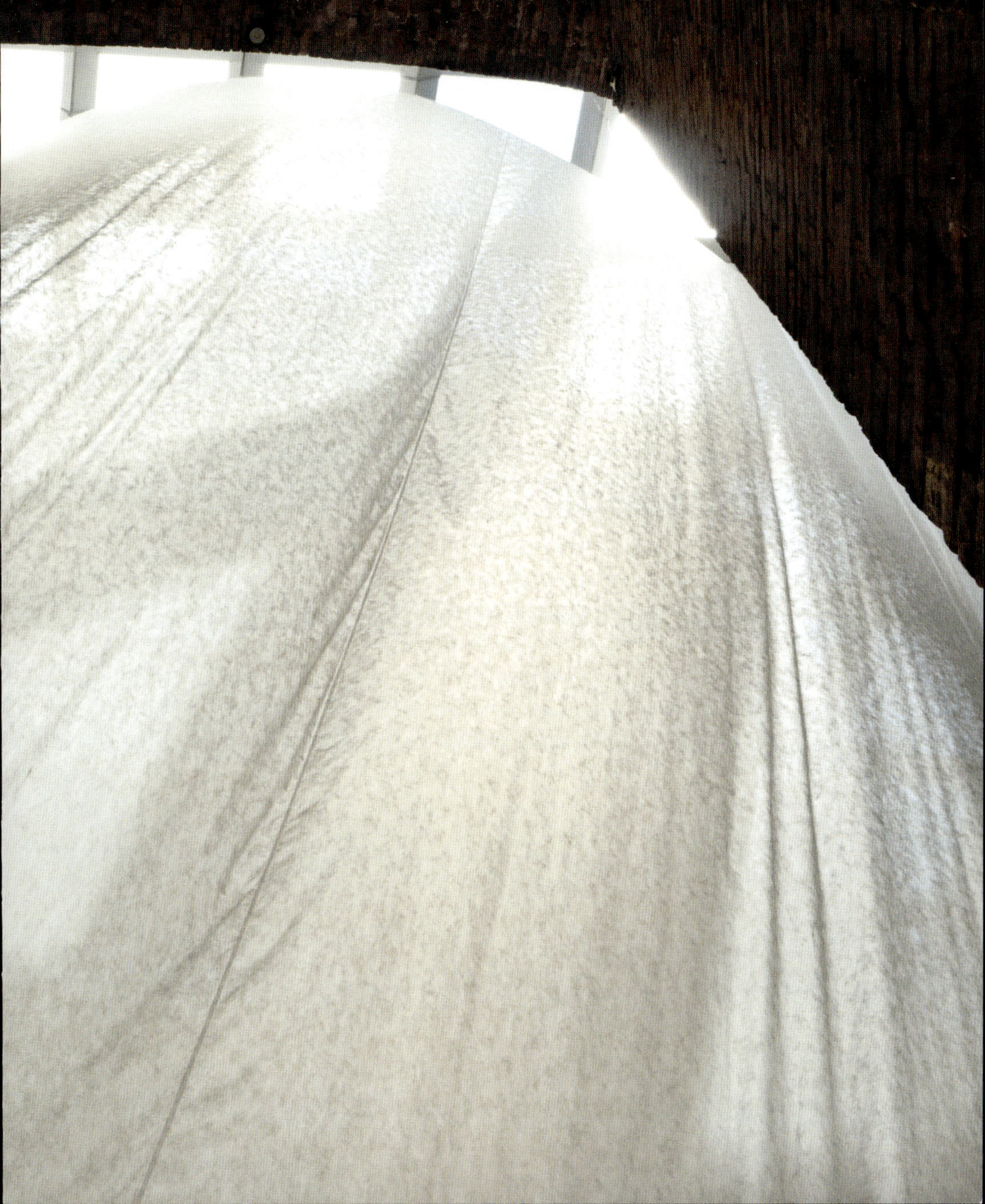

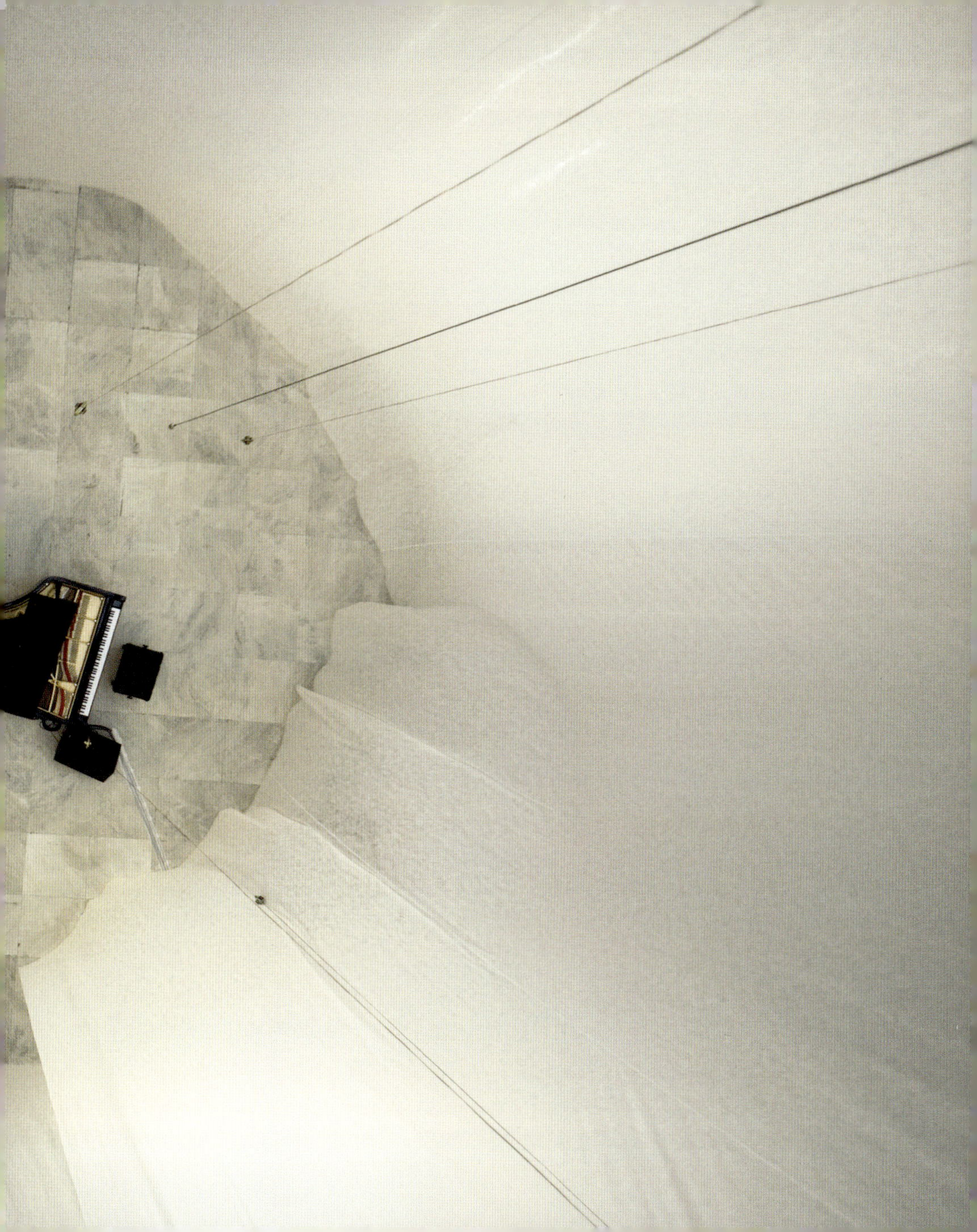

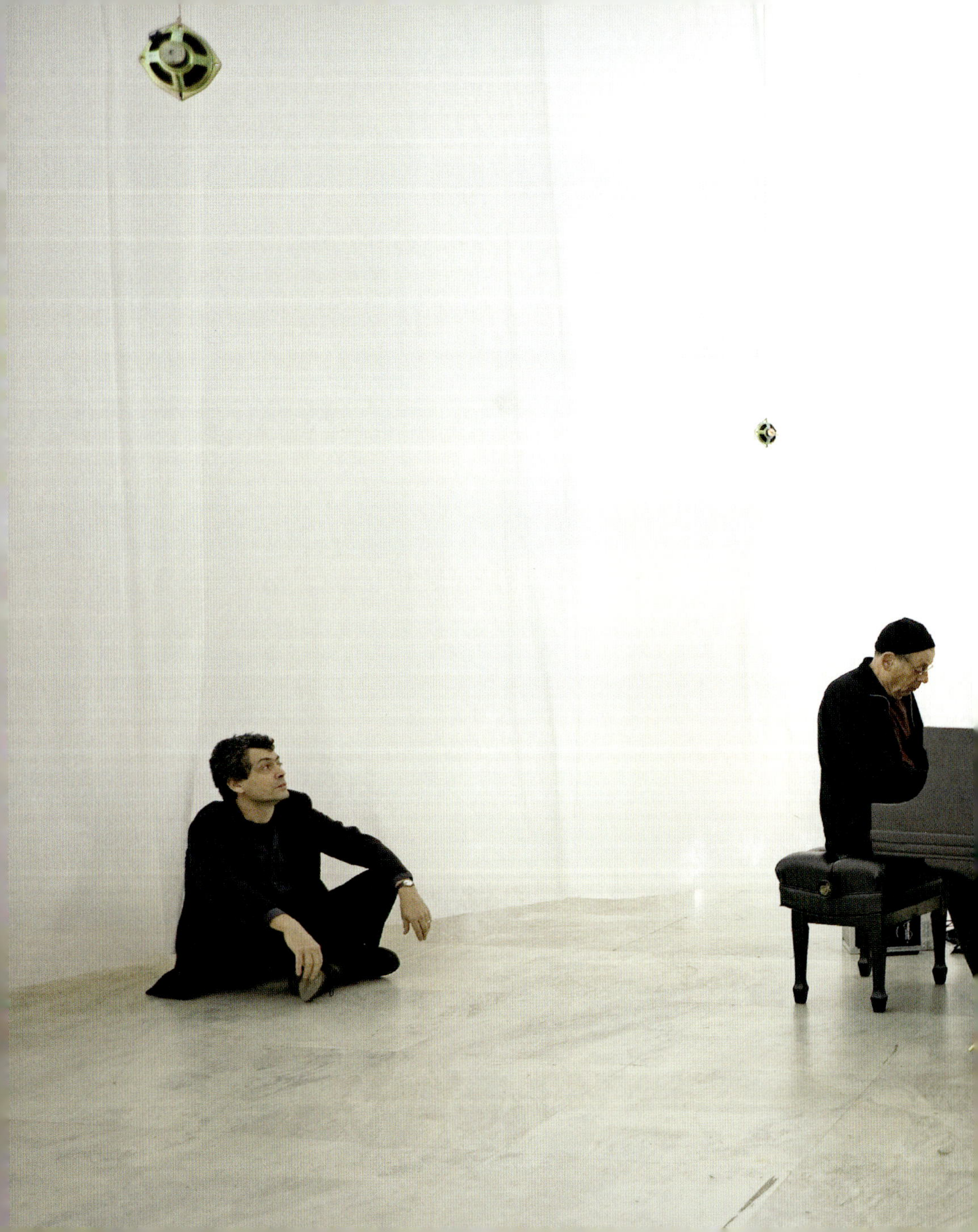

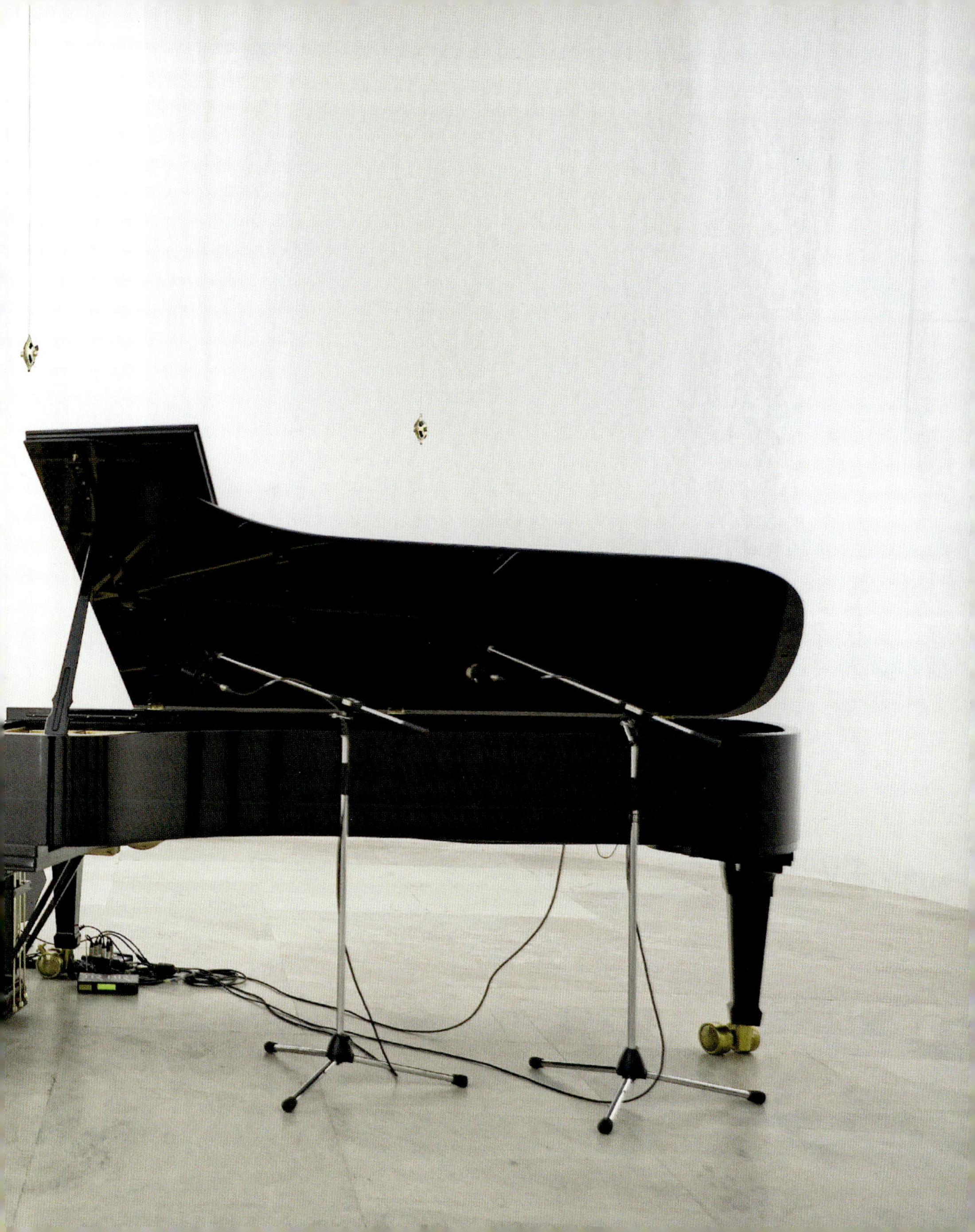

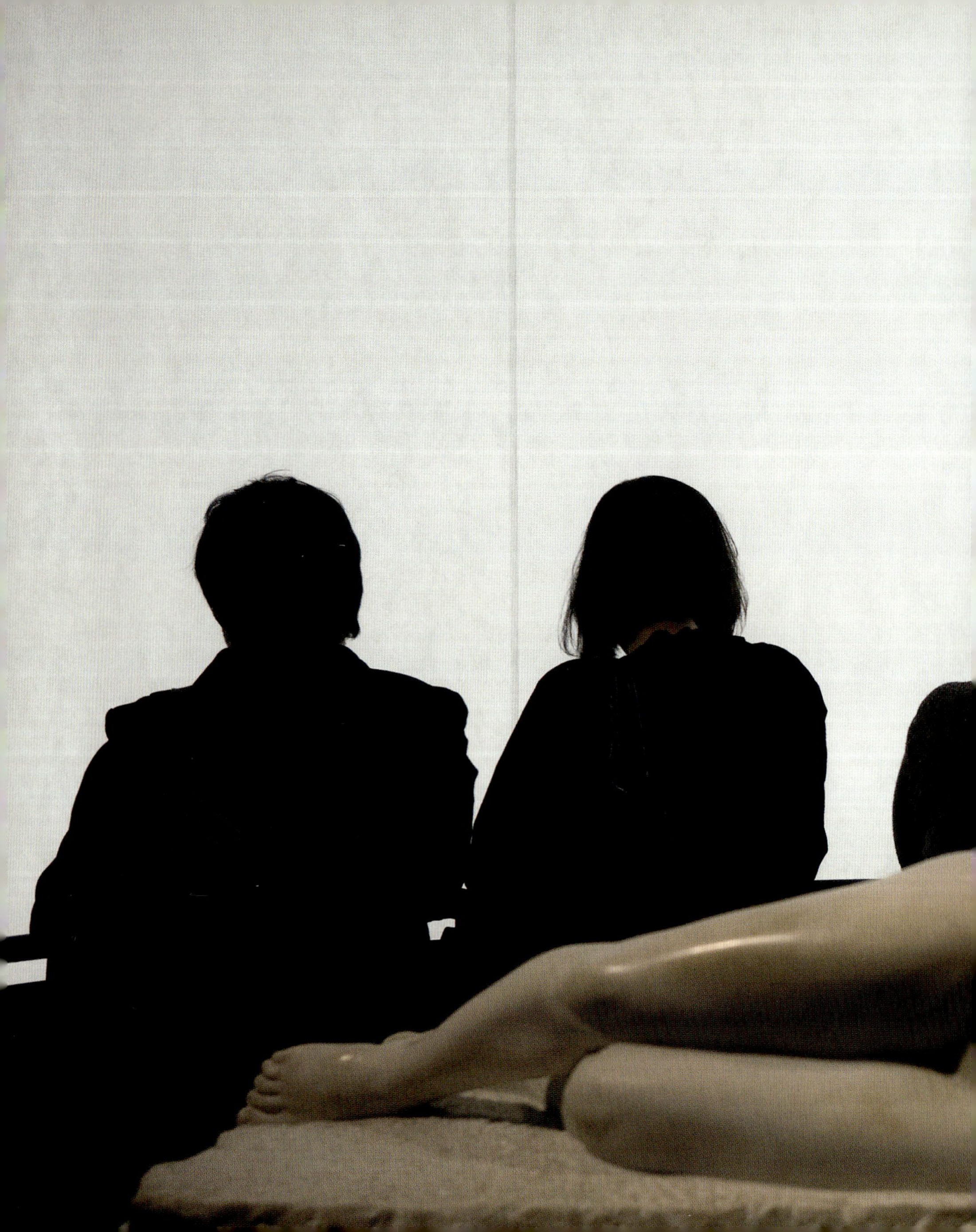

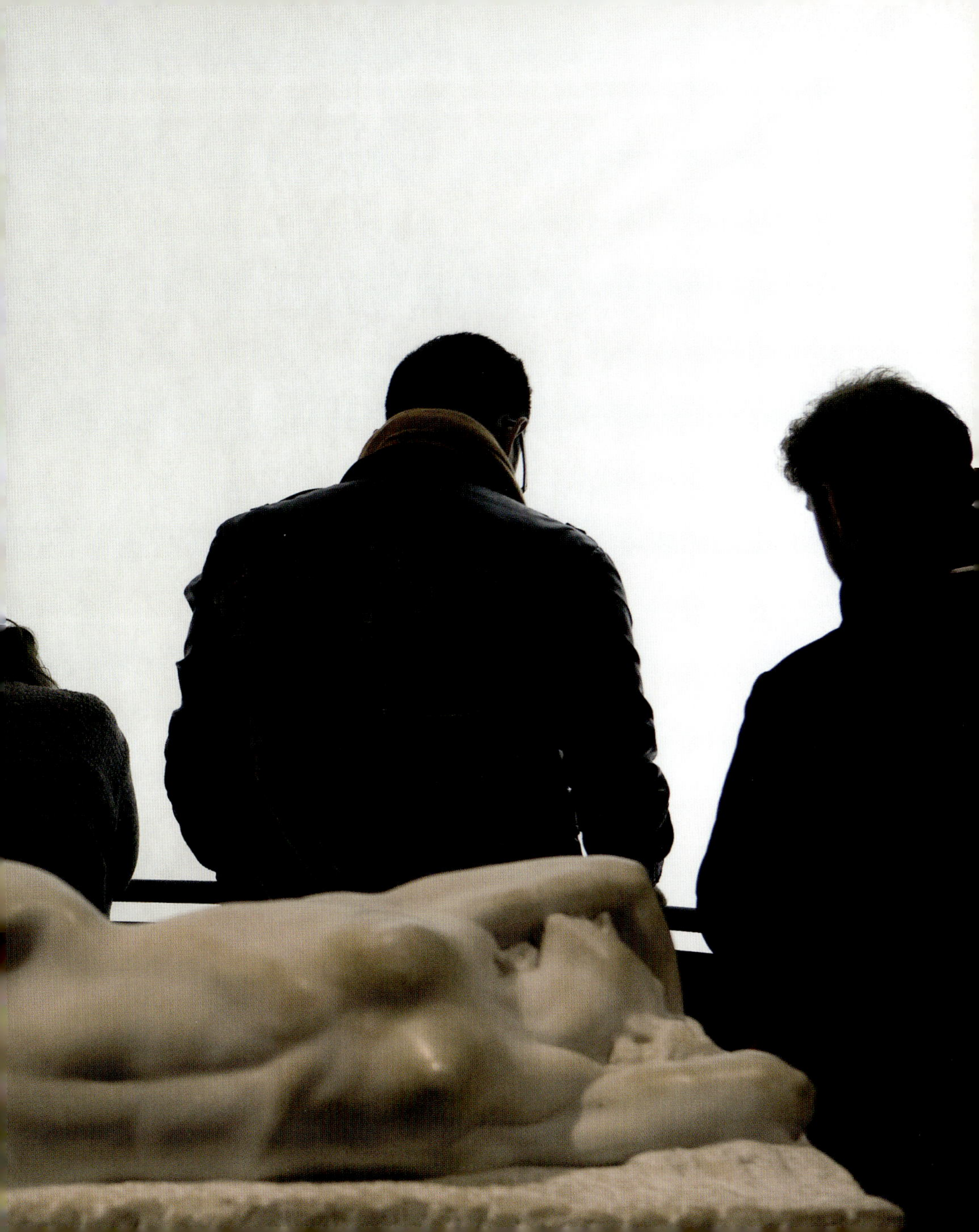

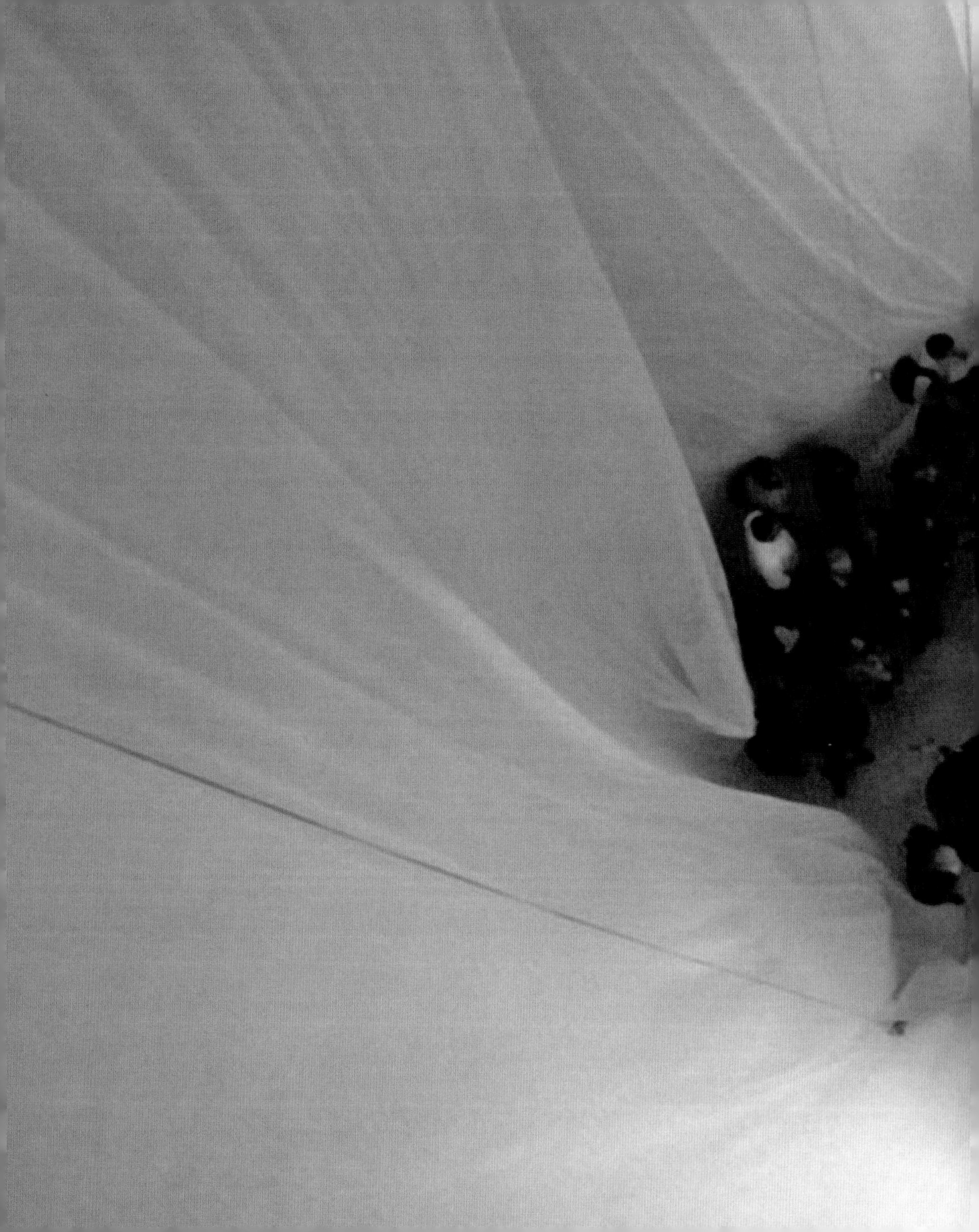

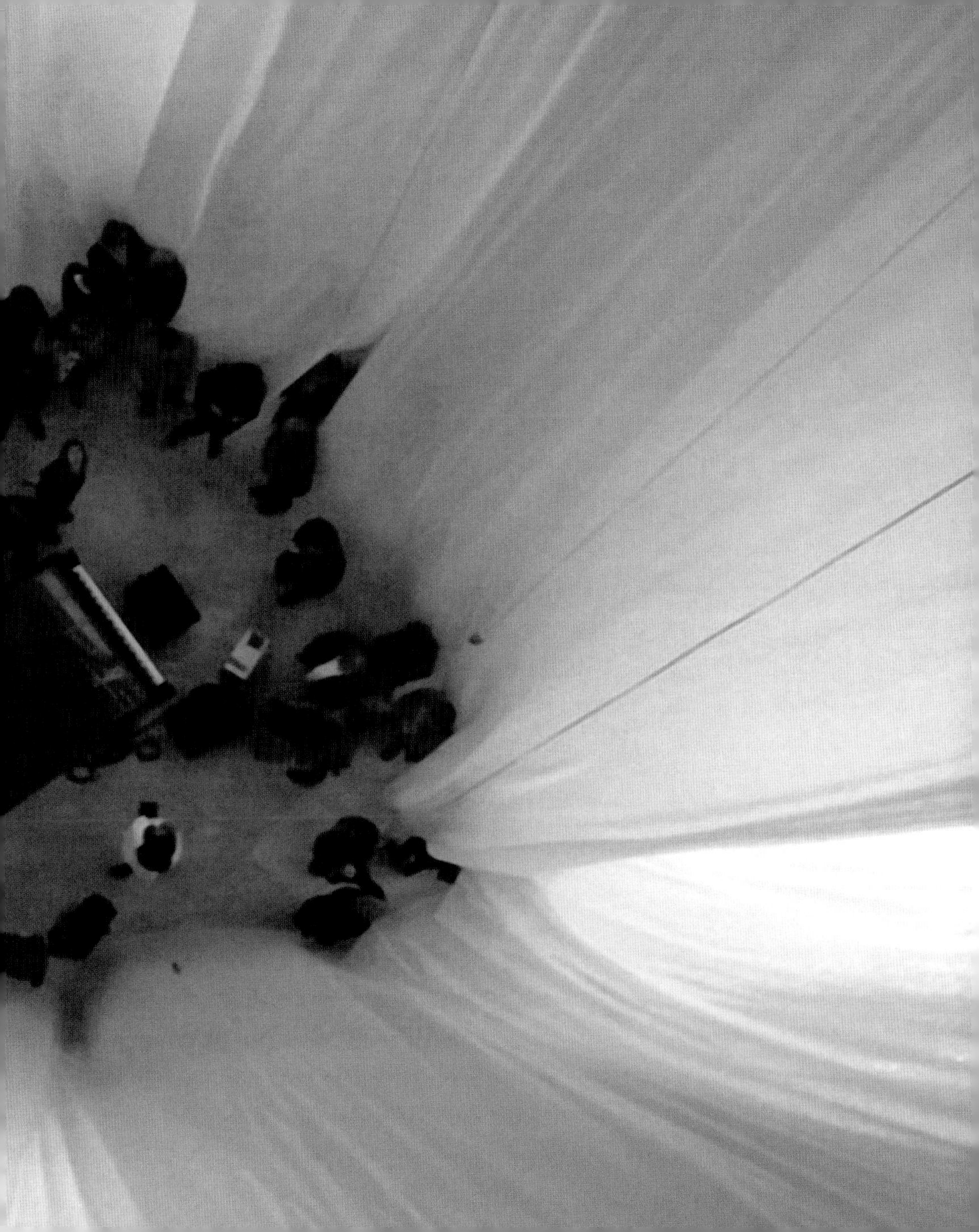

MELHOR ASSIM

ESPAÇO CULTURAL SOSO+, SÃO PAULO, 2010
CURADORIA DANIEL RANGEL
5M DE ALTURA, 14,2M X 8,2M
[redacted] 344 LÂMPADAS T8, 32W, 4100°K
NO TETO, [redacted] CHÃO E PAREDES
DE UMA ANTIGA SALA COMERCIAL
NO CENTRO DE SÃO PAULO

That's Better

Espaço Cultural SOSO+, São Paulo, 2010

Curated by Daniel Rangel
5m h, 14.2m x 8.2m
344 T8 fluorescent lights, 32w, 4100°k
on the ceiling, floor and walls from an old
commercial room in downtown São Paulo

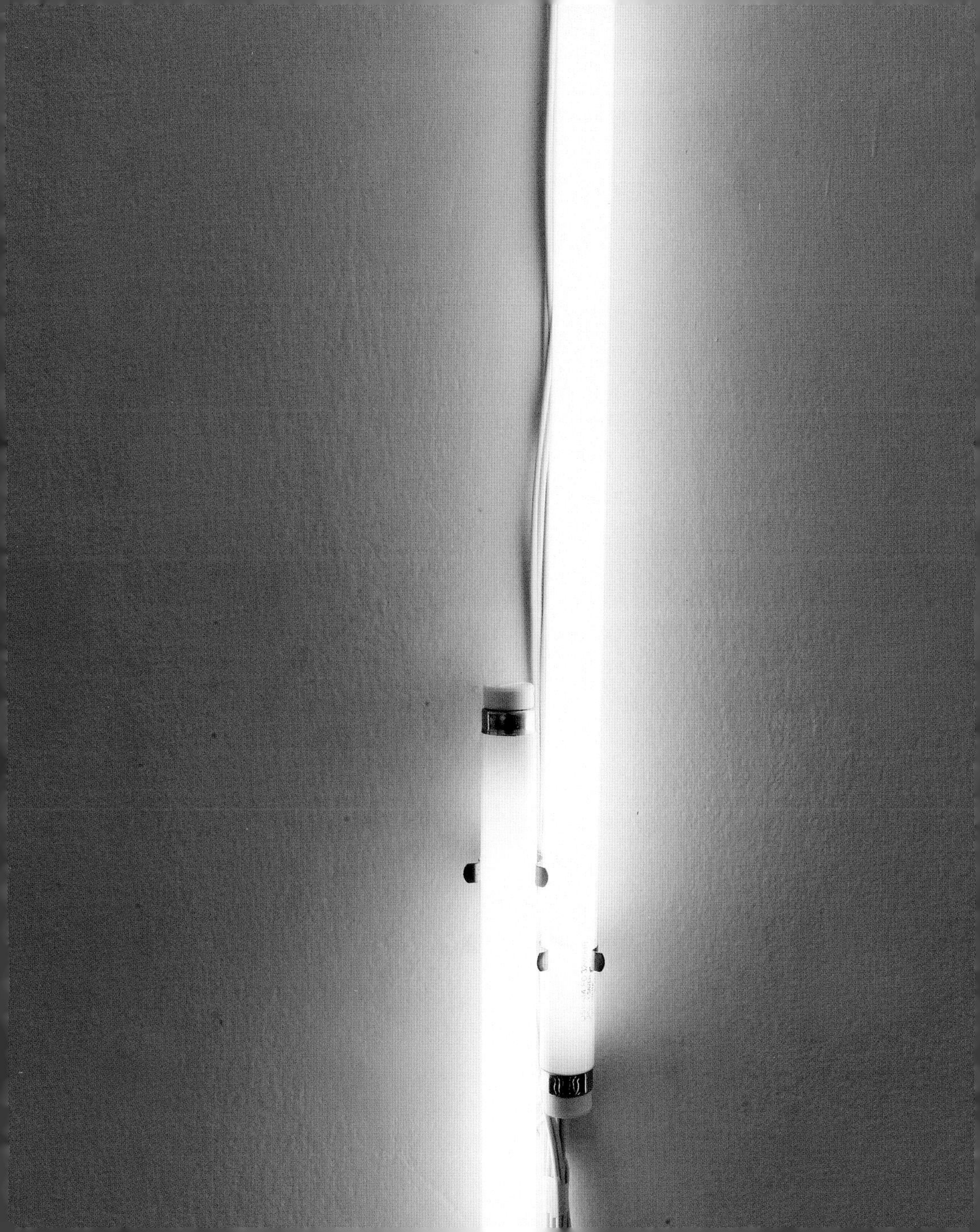

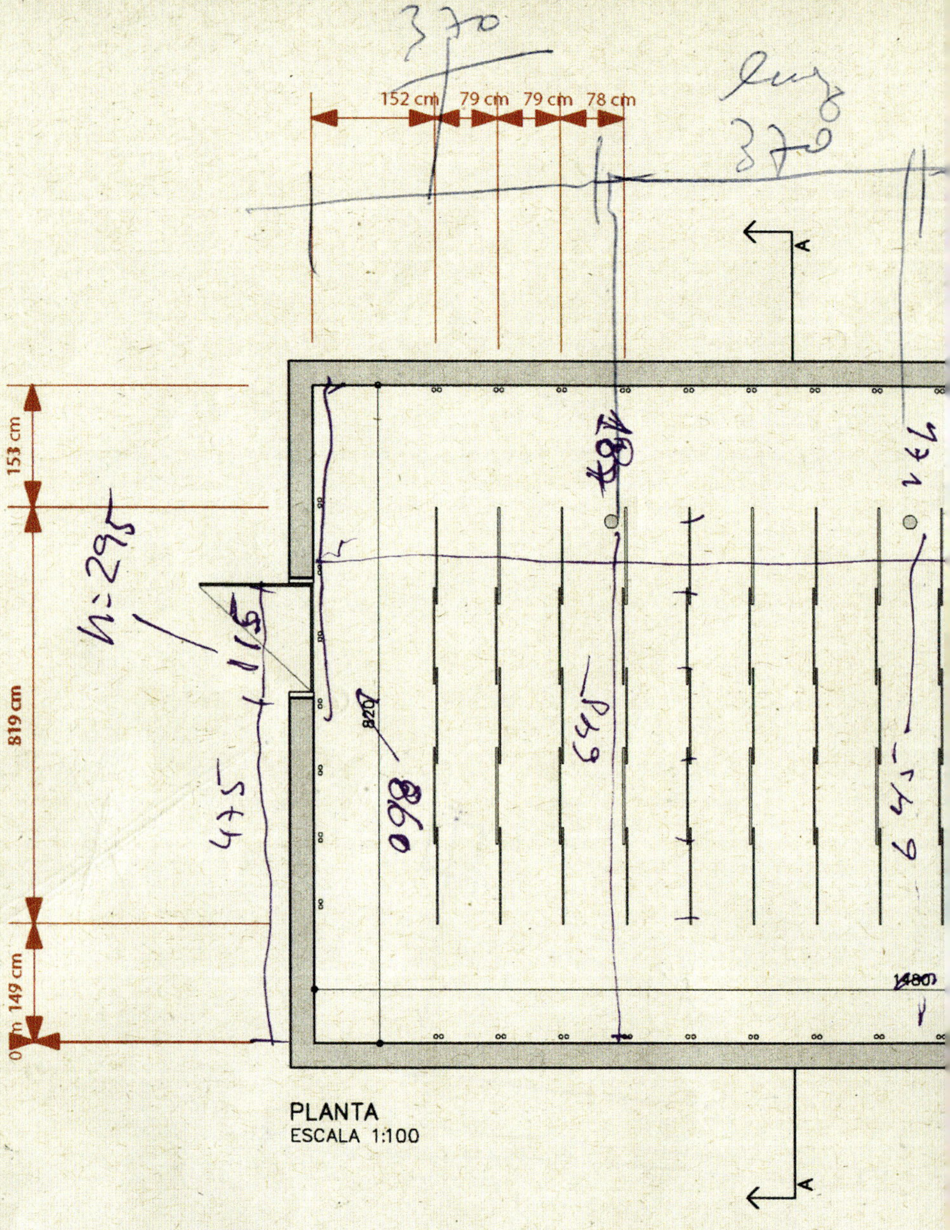

PLANTA
ESCALA 1:100

10 = 10 m

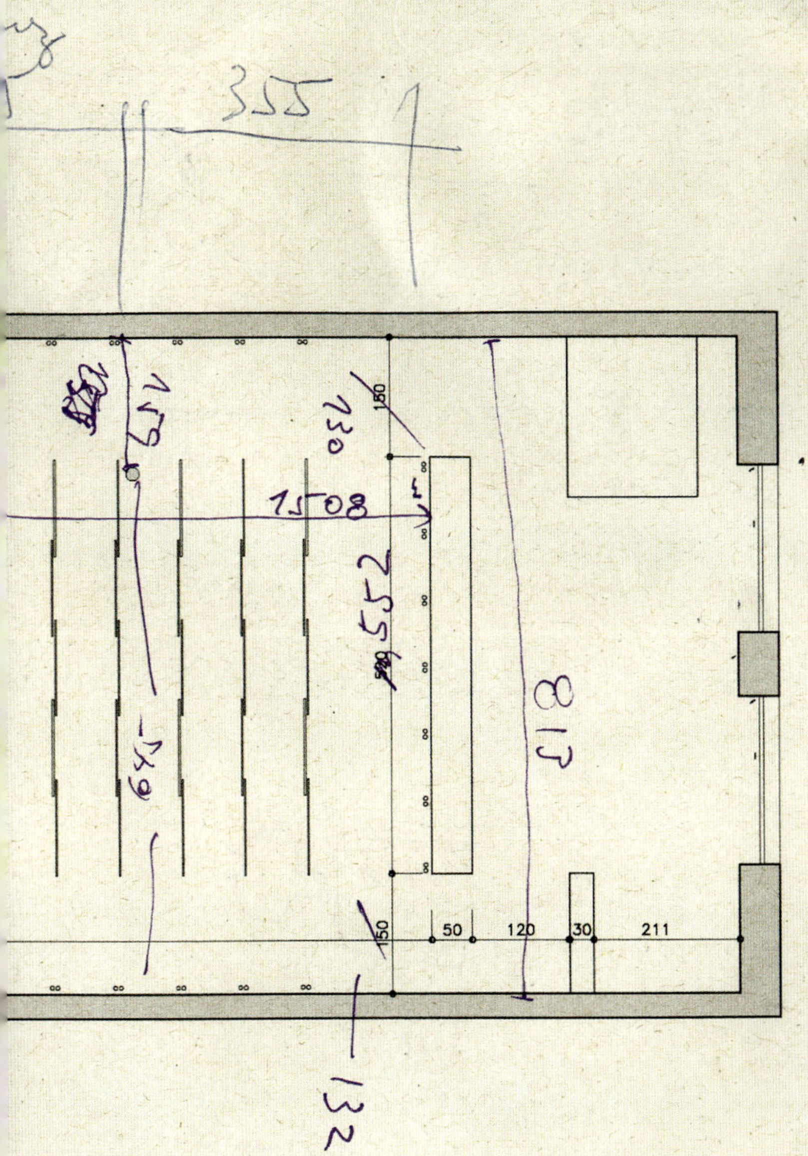

355
1508
150
150
50
120
30
211
132

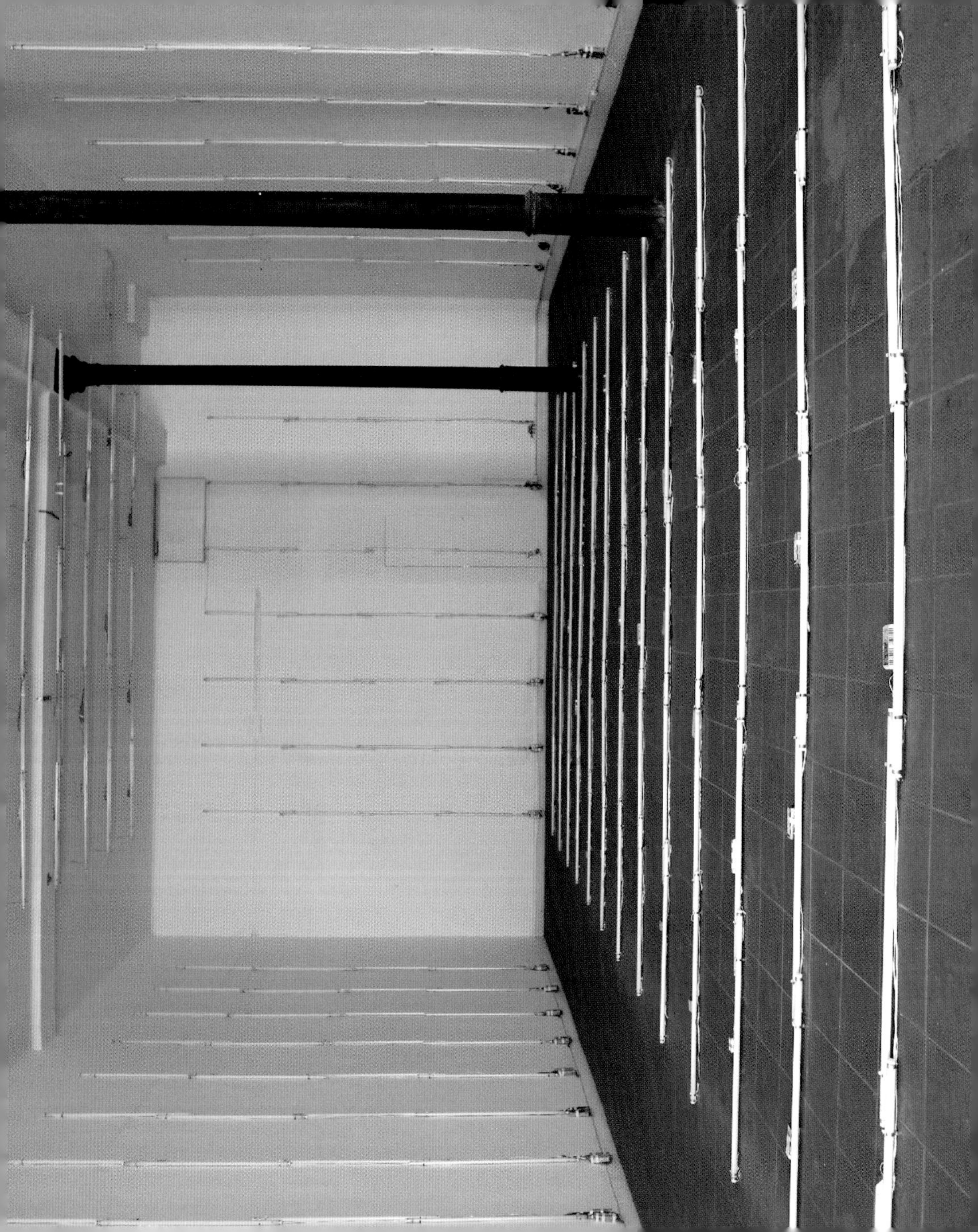

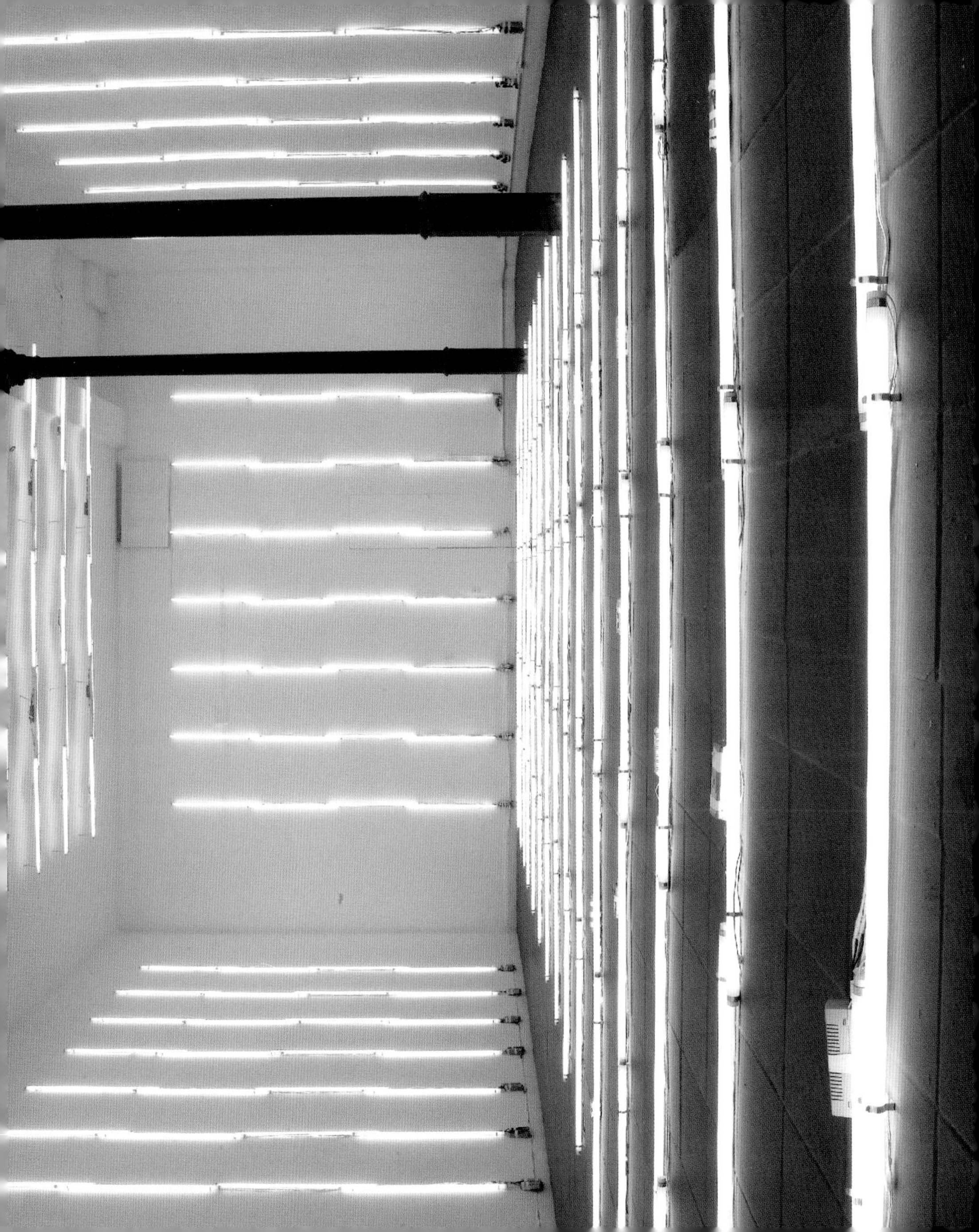

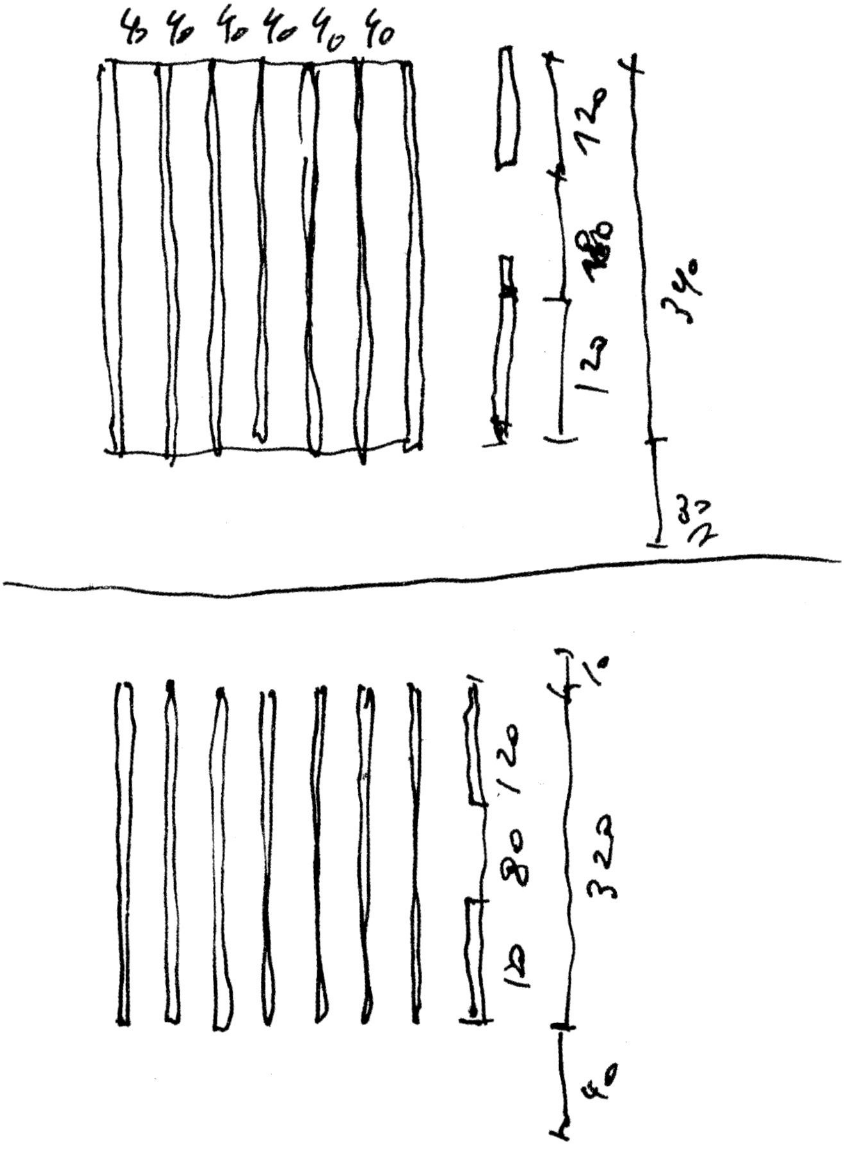
40 40 40 40 40 40
120
80
120
340
120
80
120
320
10
40

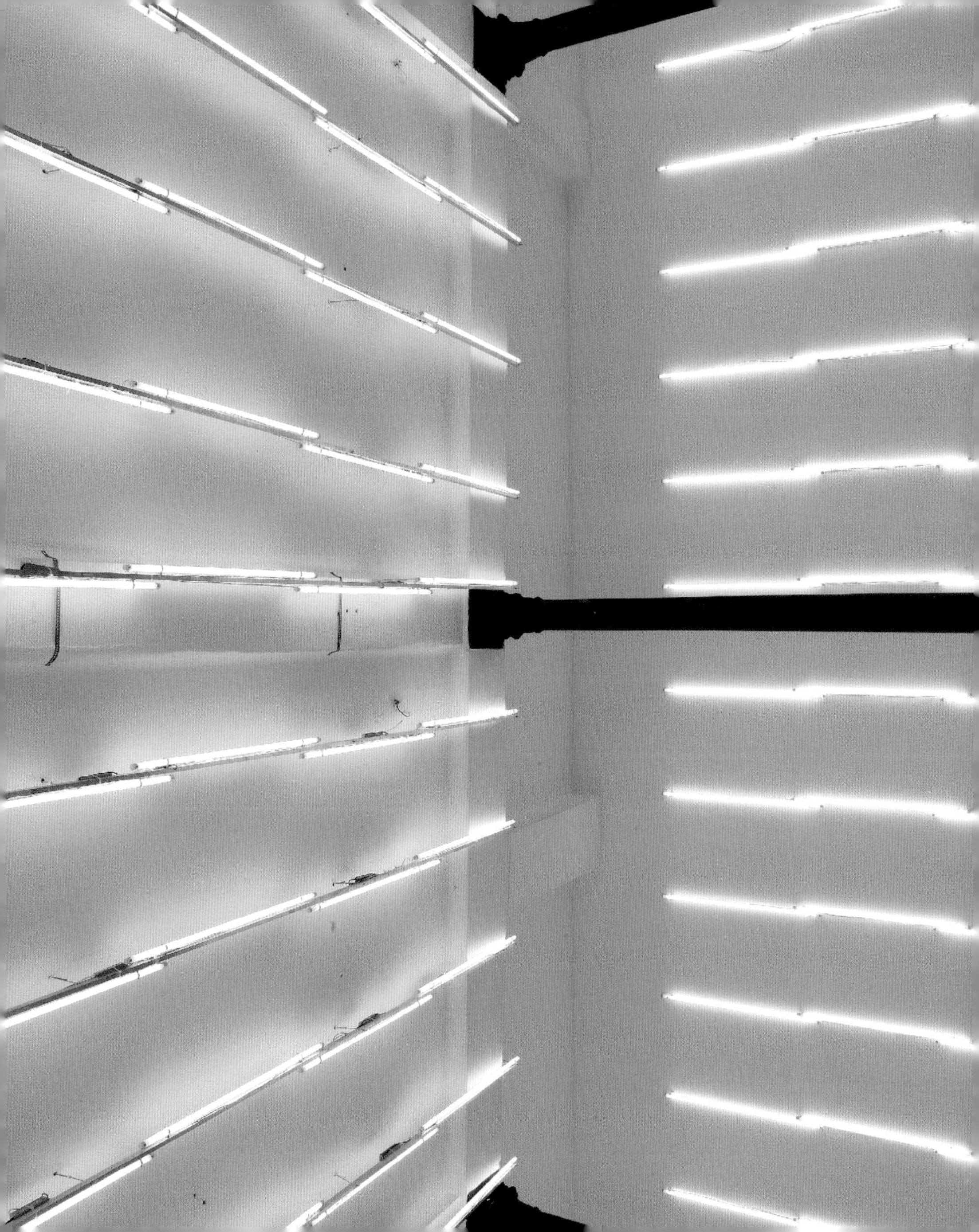

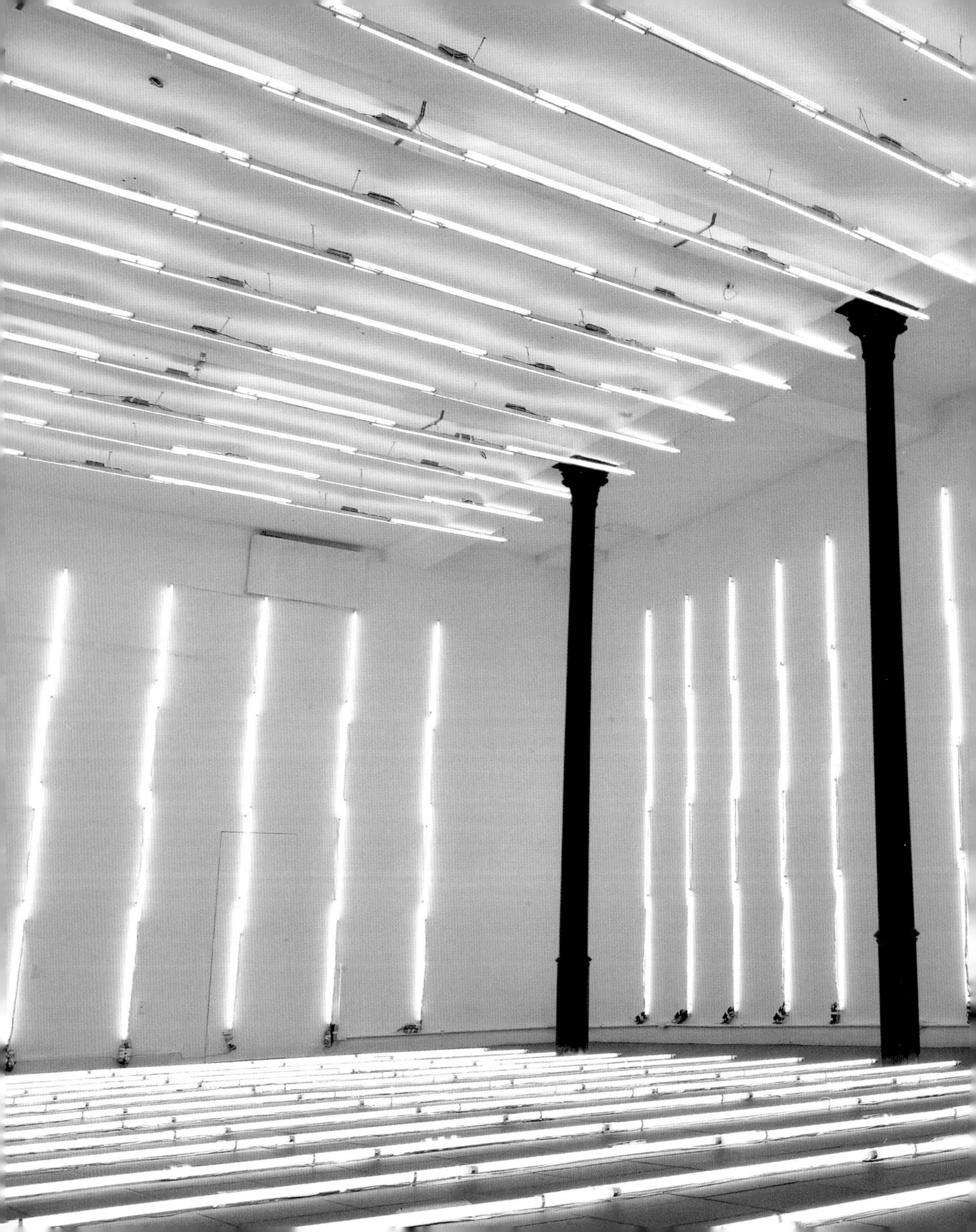

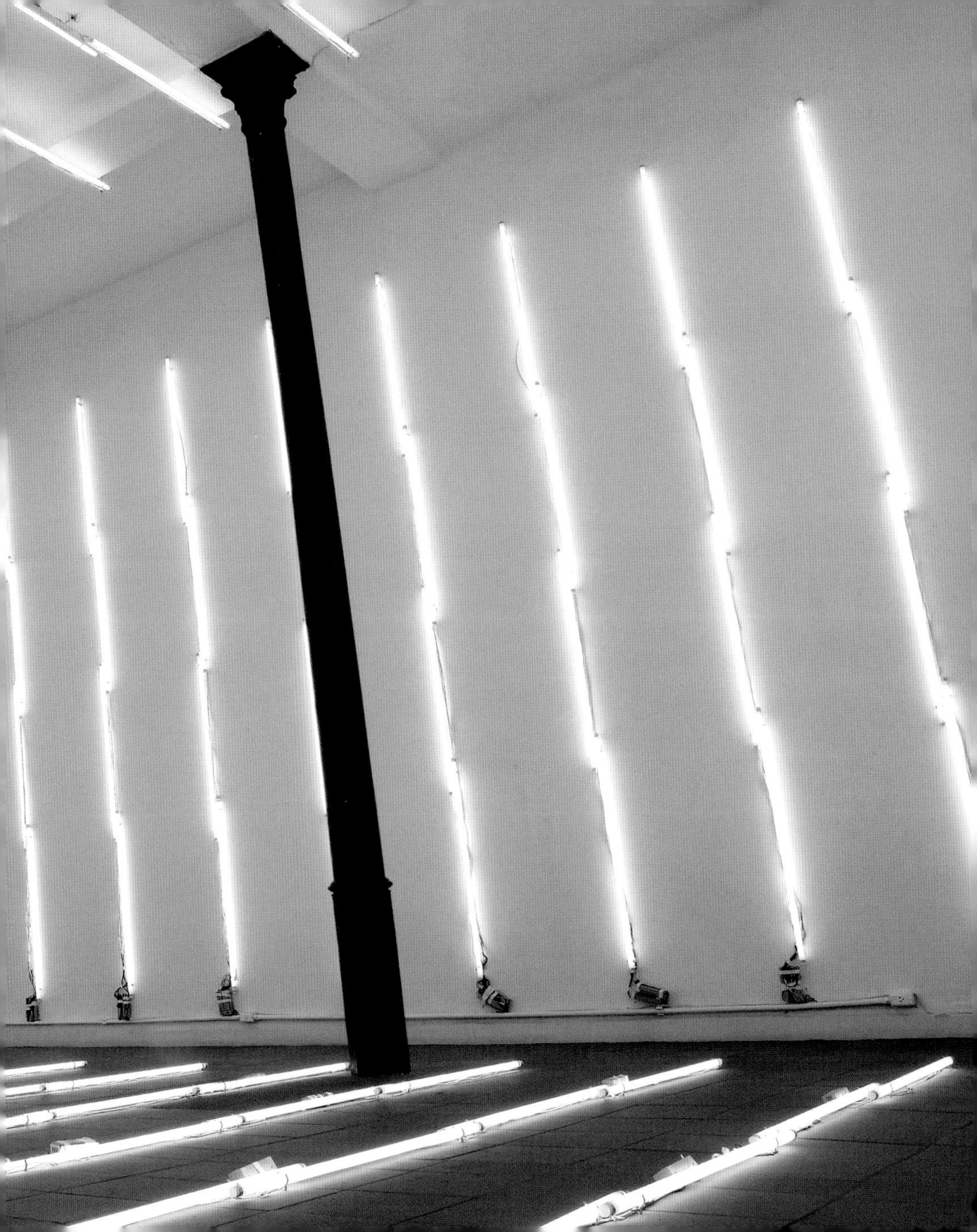

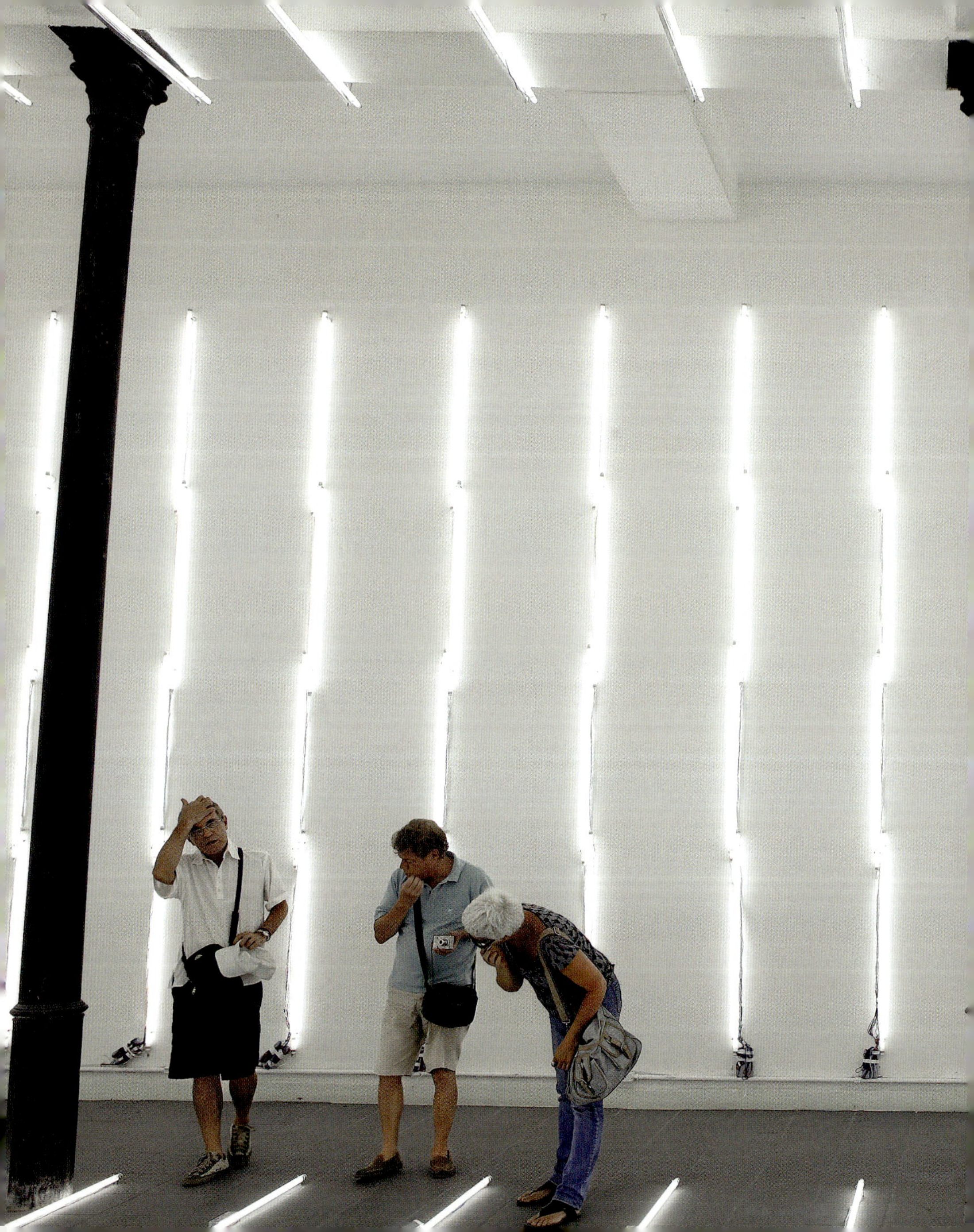

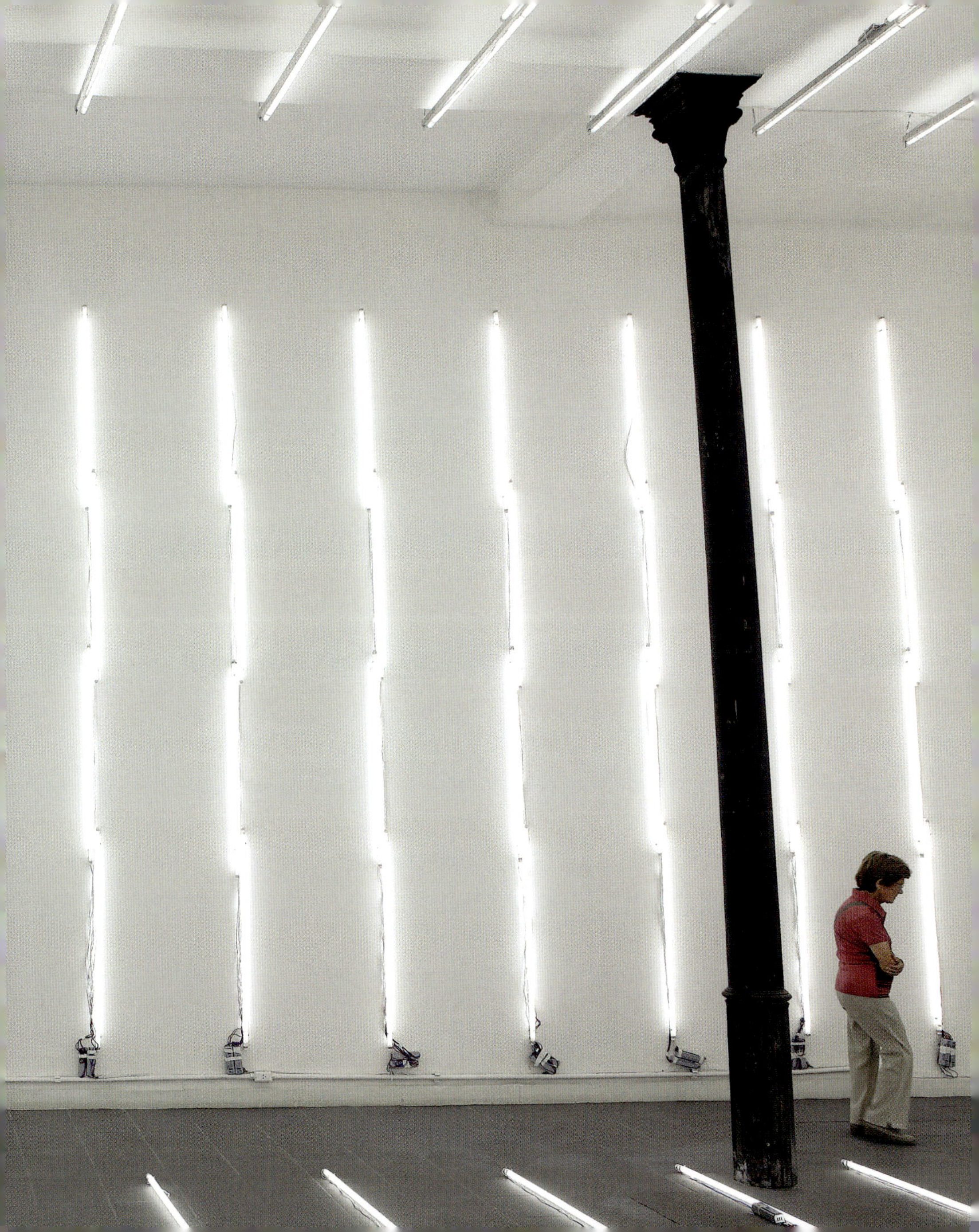

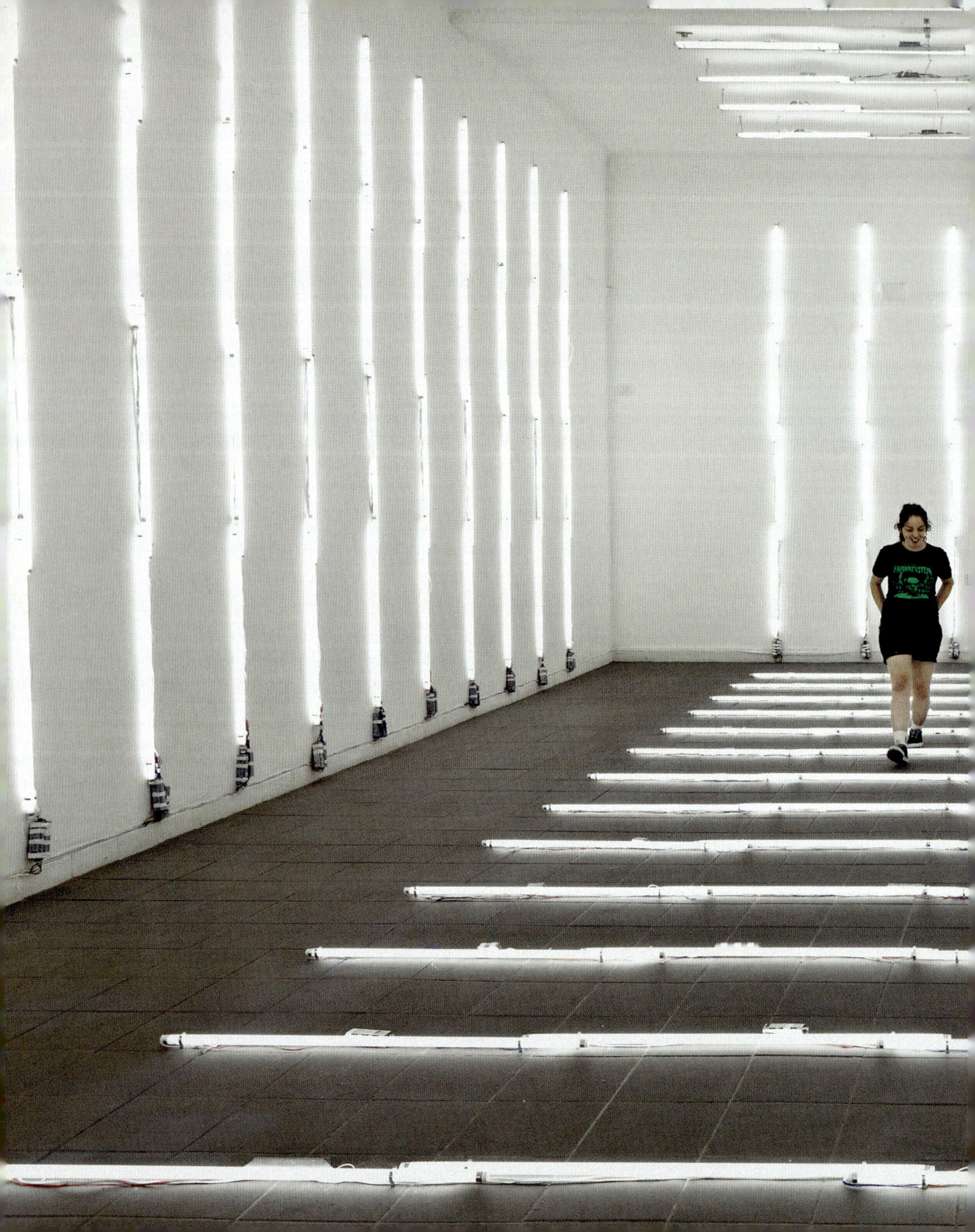

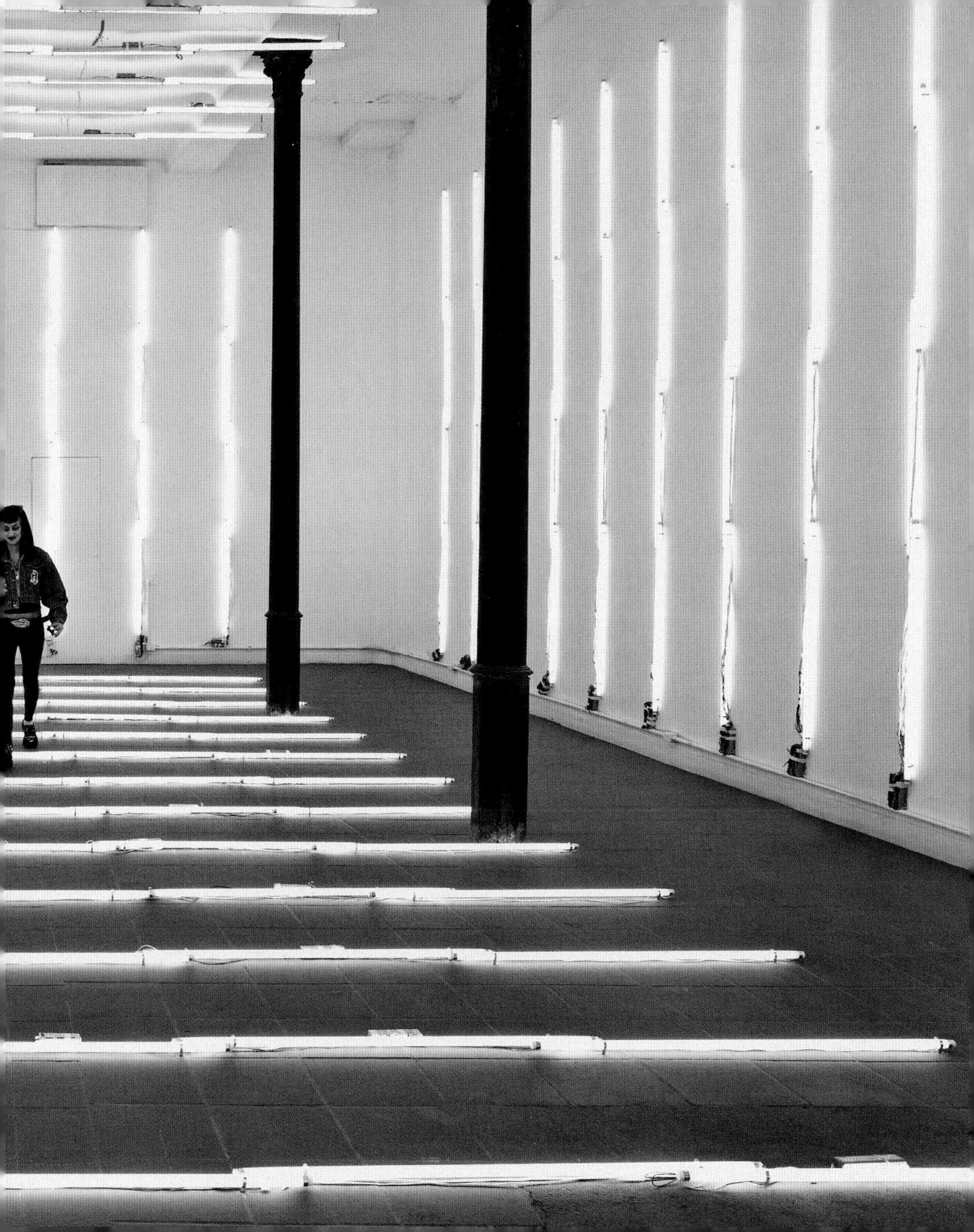

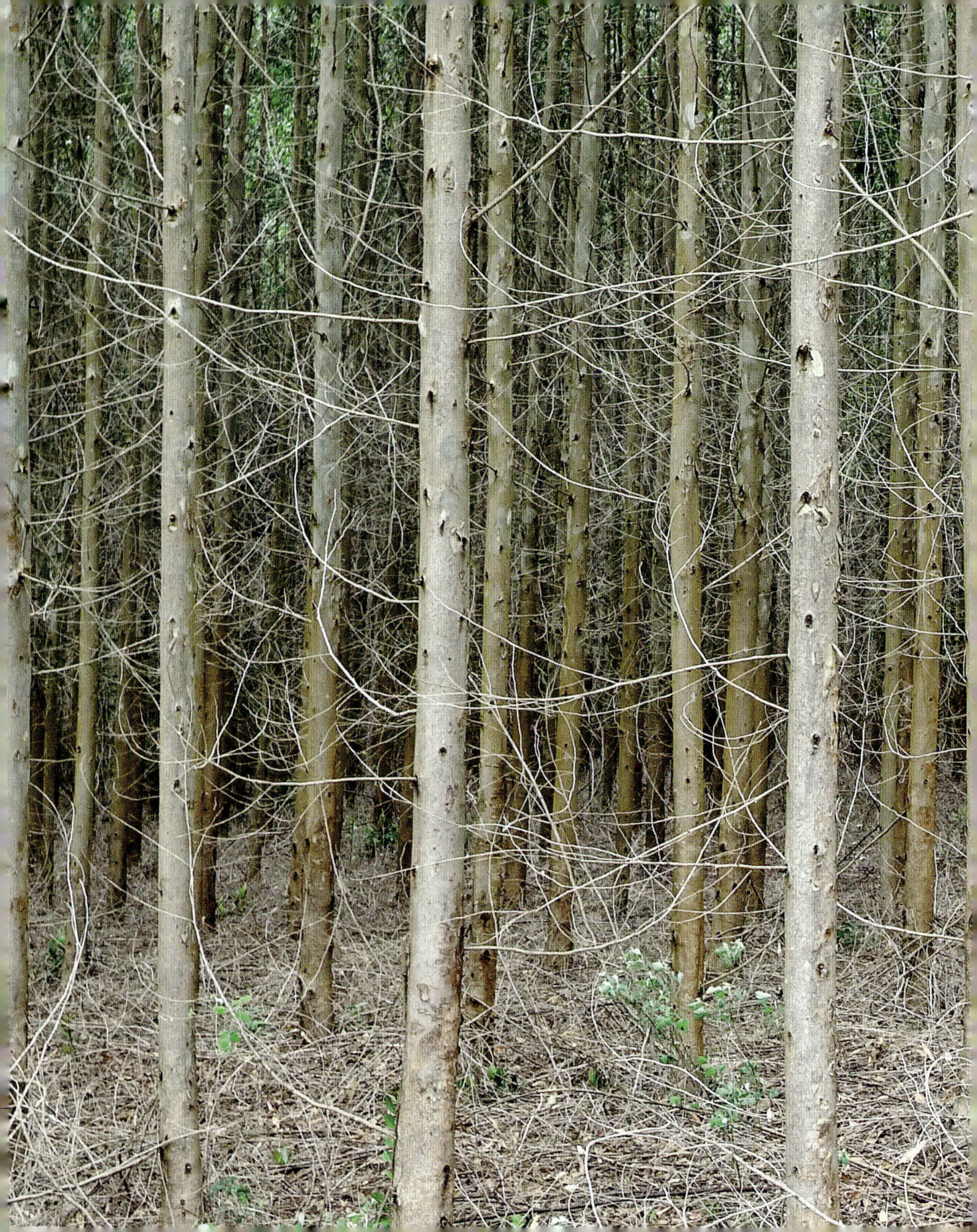

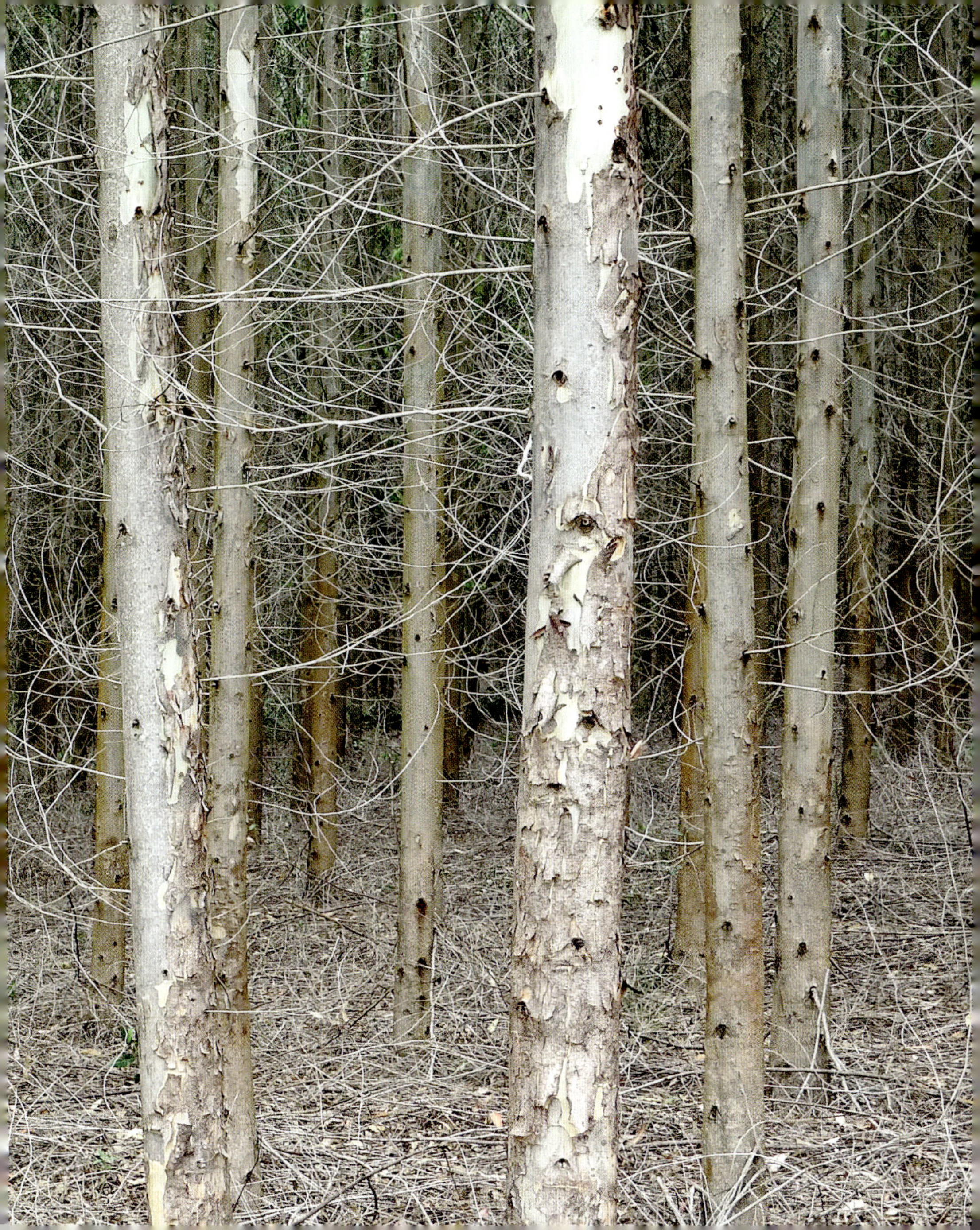

VOCÊ TEM RAZÃO

MUSEU DA CASA BRASILEIRA, SÃO PAULO, 2009
CURADORIA AGNALDO FARIAS
9M DE ALTURA, 29M X 7M, MADEIRA E AÇO
TRÊS POSTES PENDURADOS EM 4 POSTES,
TODOS USADOS POR ANOS E JÁ
DESCARTADOS.

OS POSTES ESTÃO PENDURADOS DE PONTA-CABEÇA. HÁ NO BRASIL O HÁBITO DE SE PINTAR O PÉ DAS ÁRVORES E DOS POSTES DE CAL. PARA CIMA, O BRANCO FORMA UM HORIZONTE DE POSTES MERGULHADOS NO CÉU.

You're Right

Museu da Casa Brasileira, São Paulo, 2009

Curated by Agnaldo Farias
9m h, 29m x 7m, wood and steel
Three telephone poles hung from four telephones poles,
they had been used for years and had already been discarded.
The telephone poles are hung upside-down. In Brazil there is a habit
of painting the base of tree trunks and telephone poles with whitewash.
Upwards, the white forms a horizon of telephone poles diving into the sky.

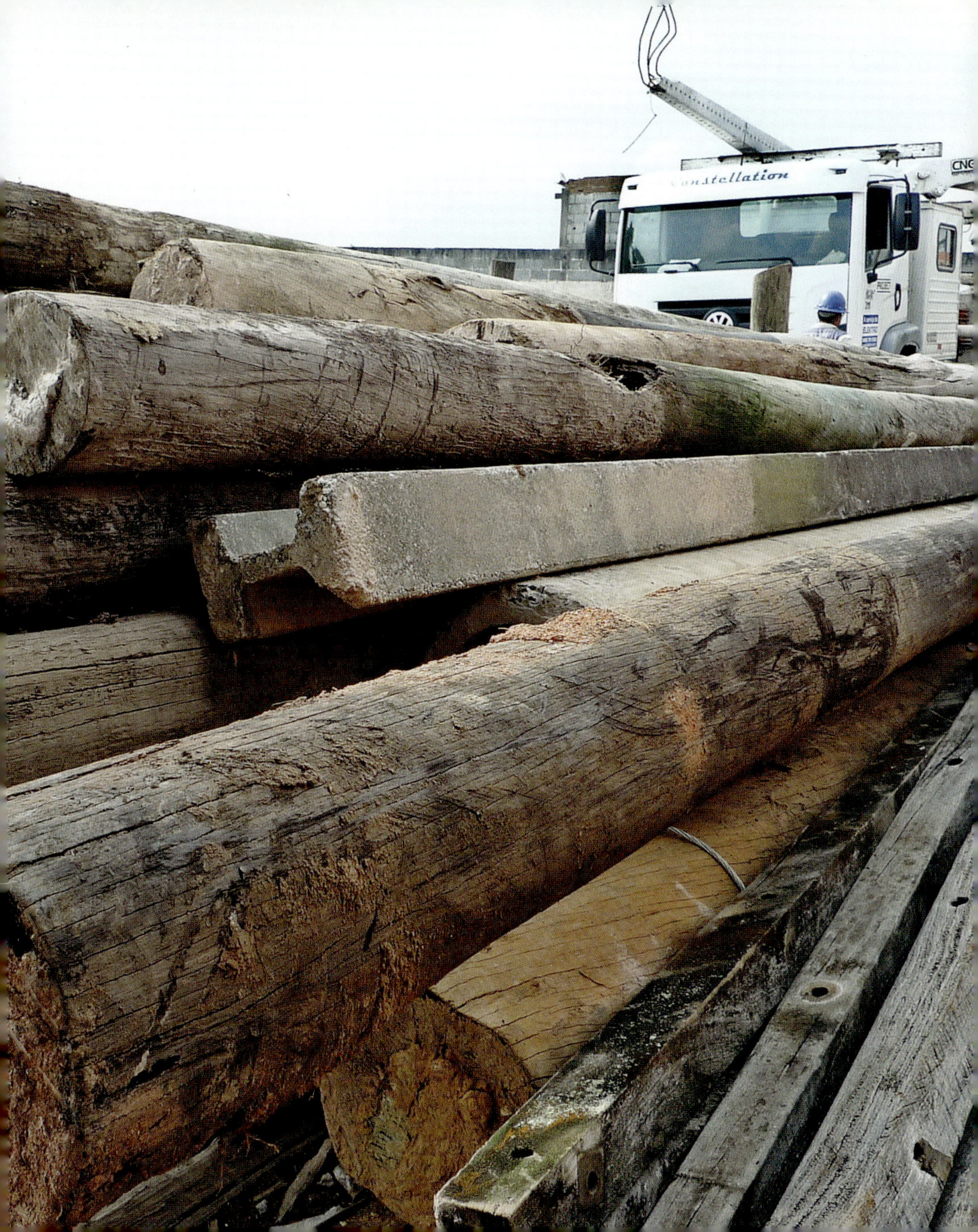
Constellation
CNG

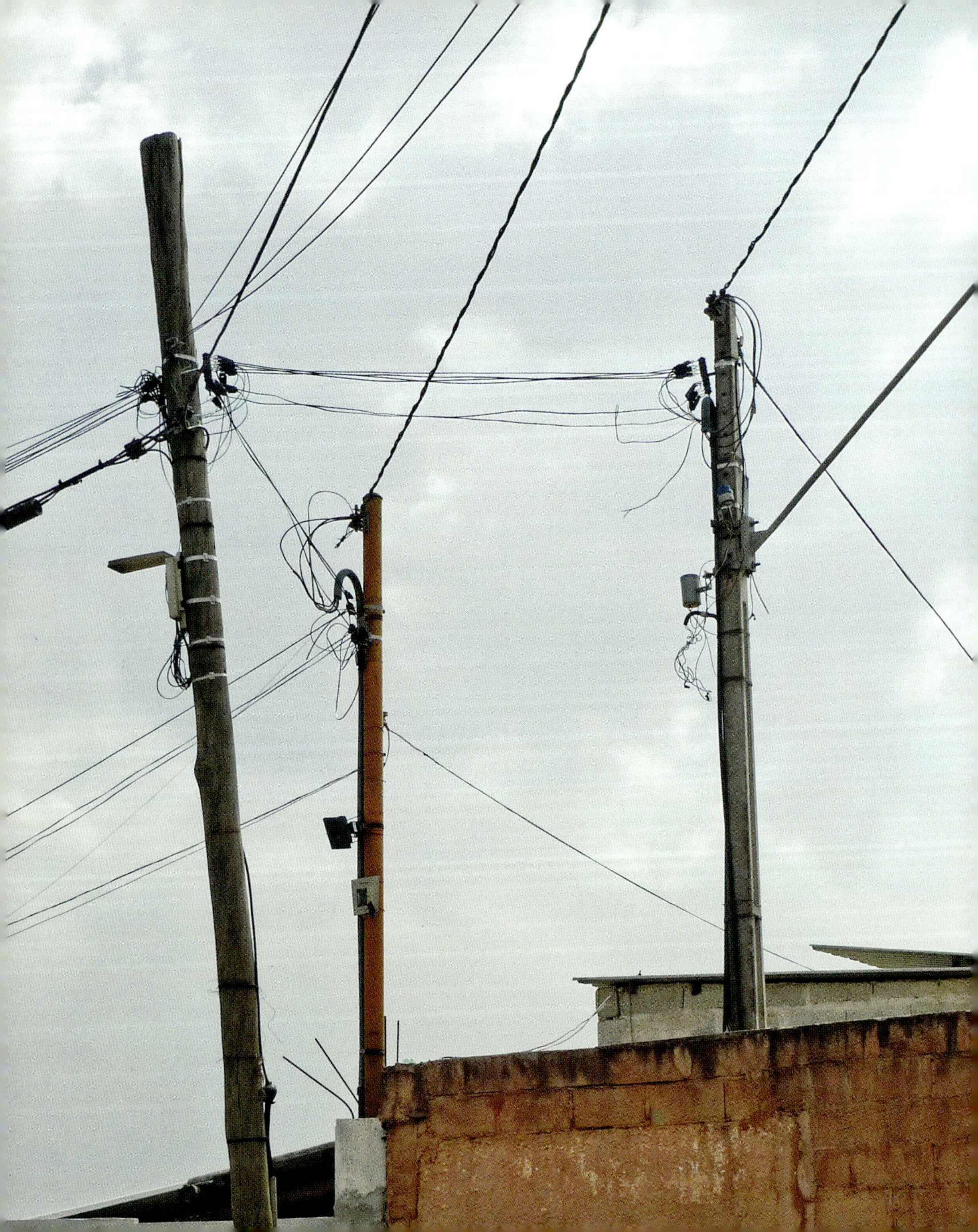

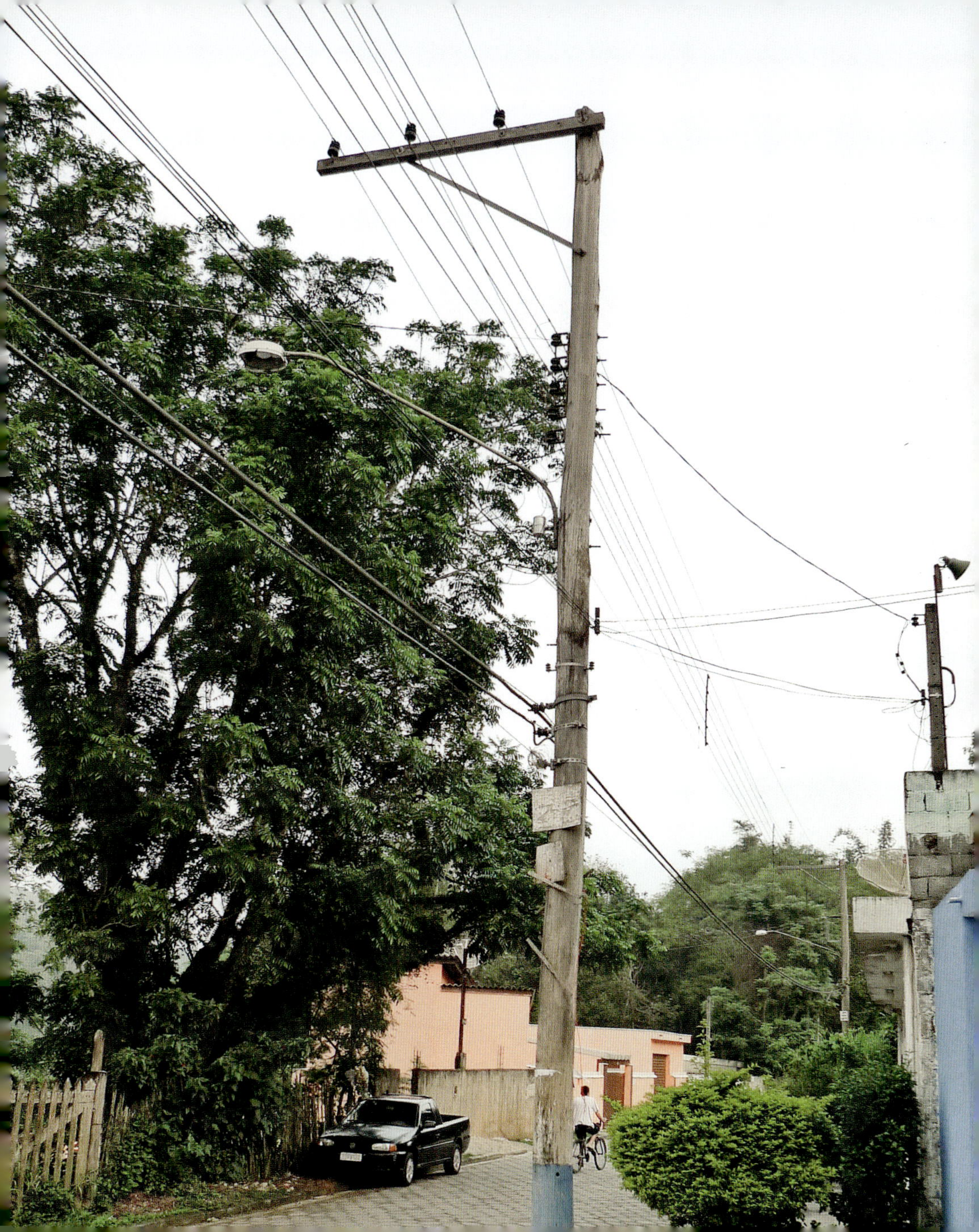

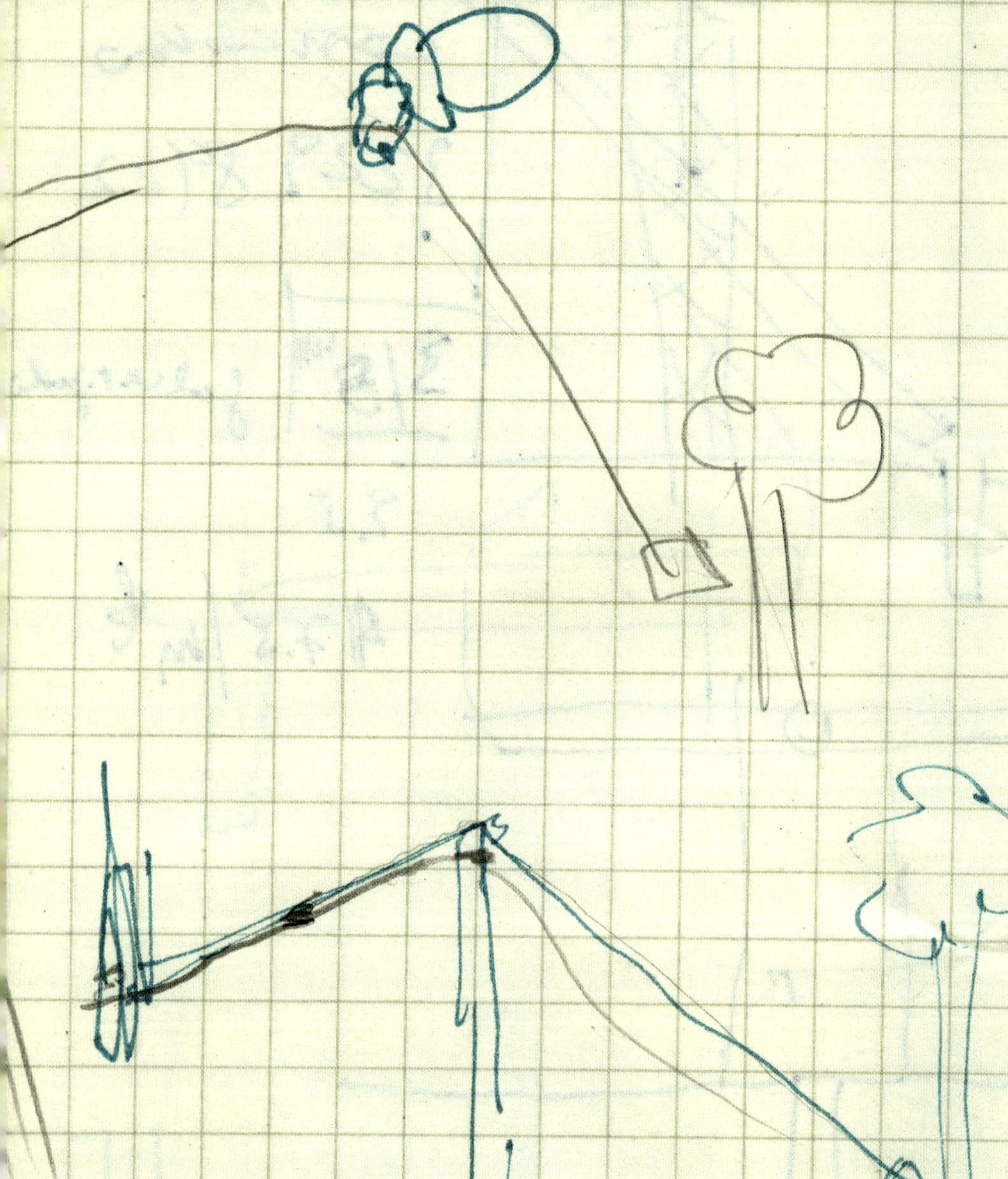

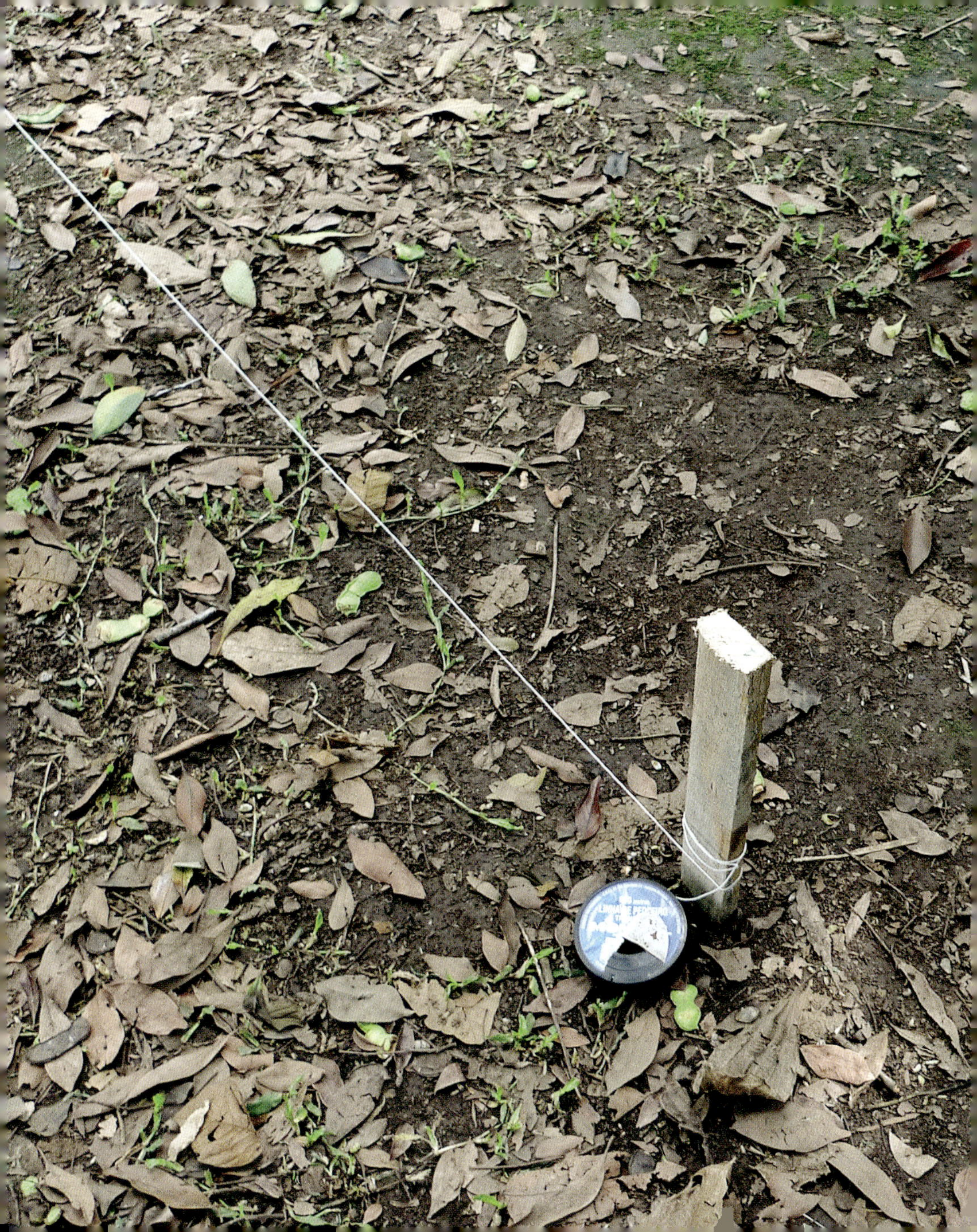

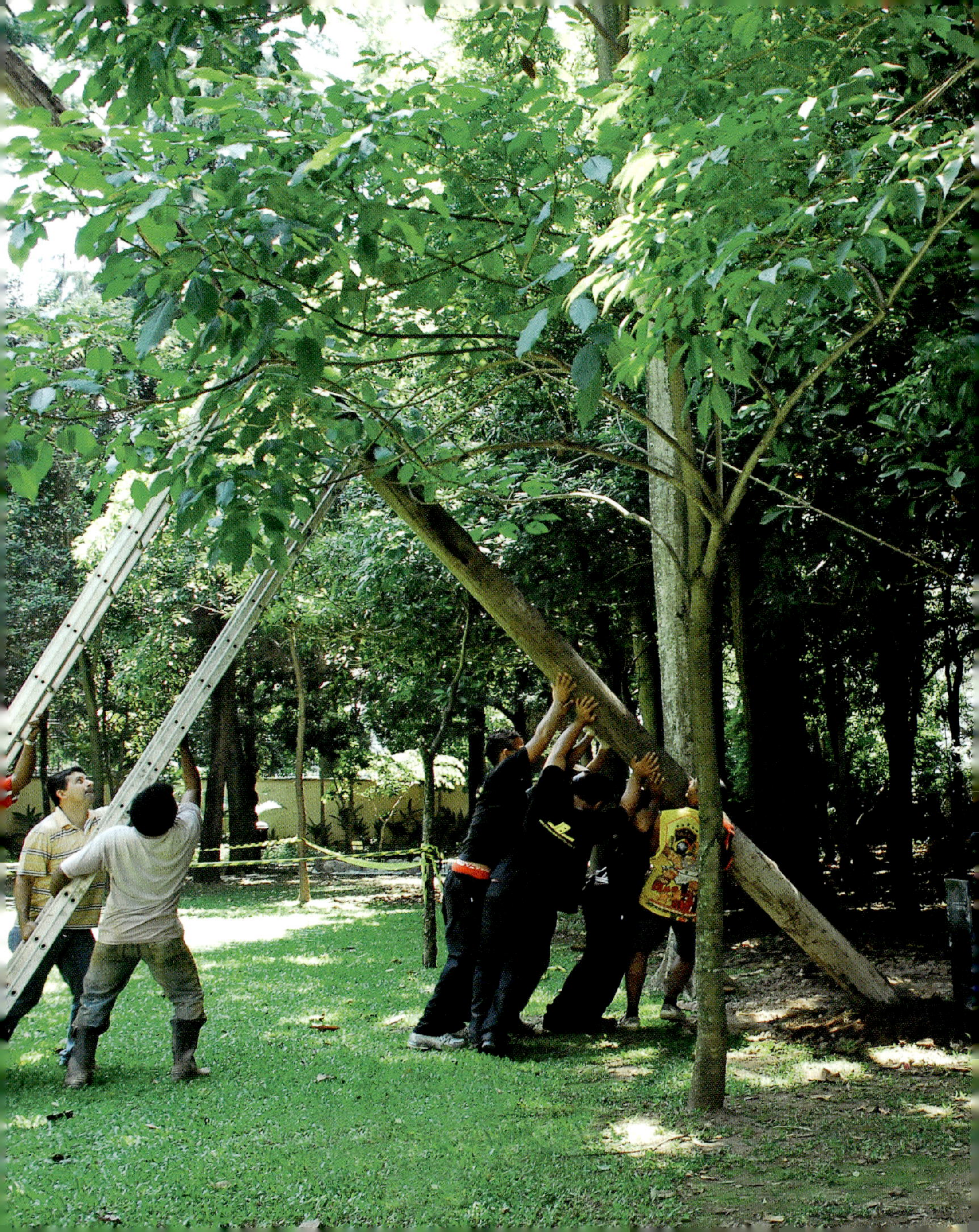

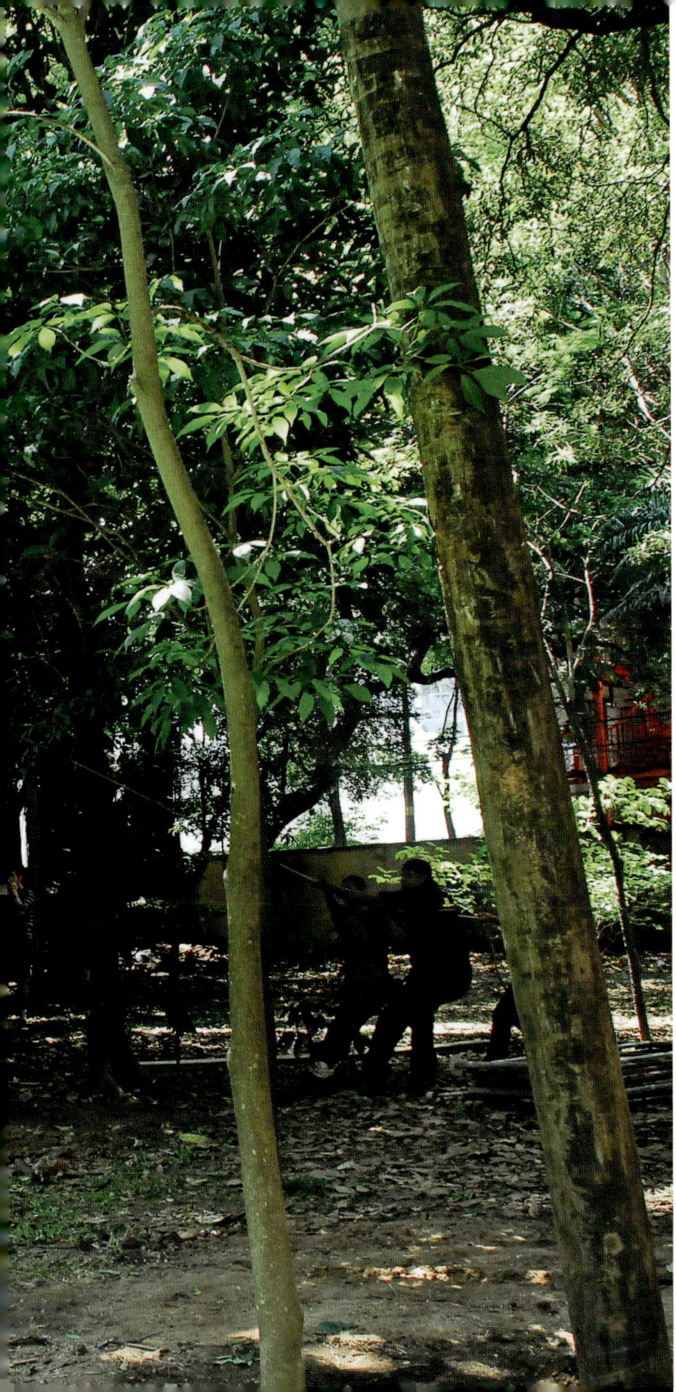

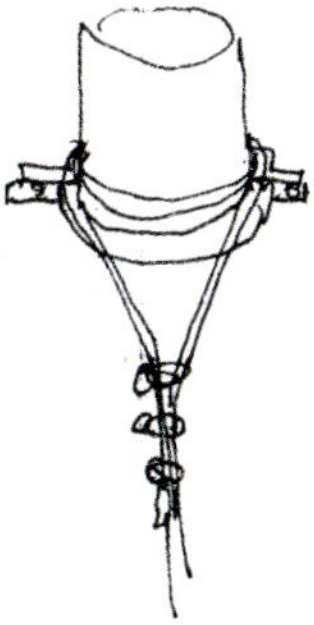

VOCÊ TEM RAZÃO
FIAT LUX
INÚTIL PAISAGEM
TÁ QUALE PRONTO
(A) ÚLTIMA VOLTA
(DE) PONTA CABEÇA

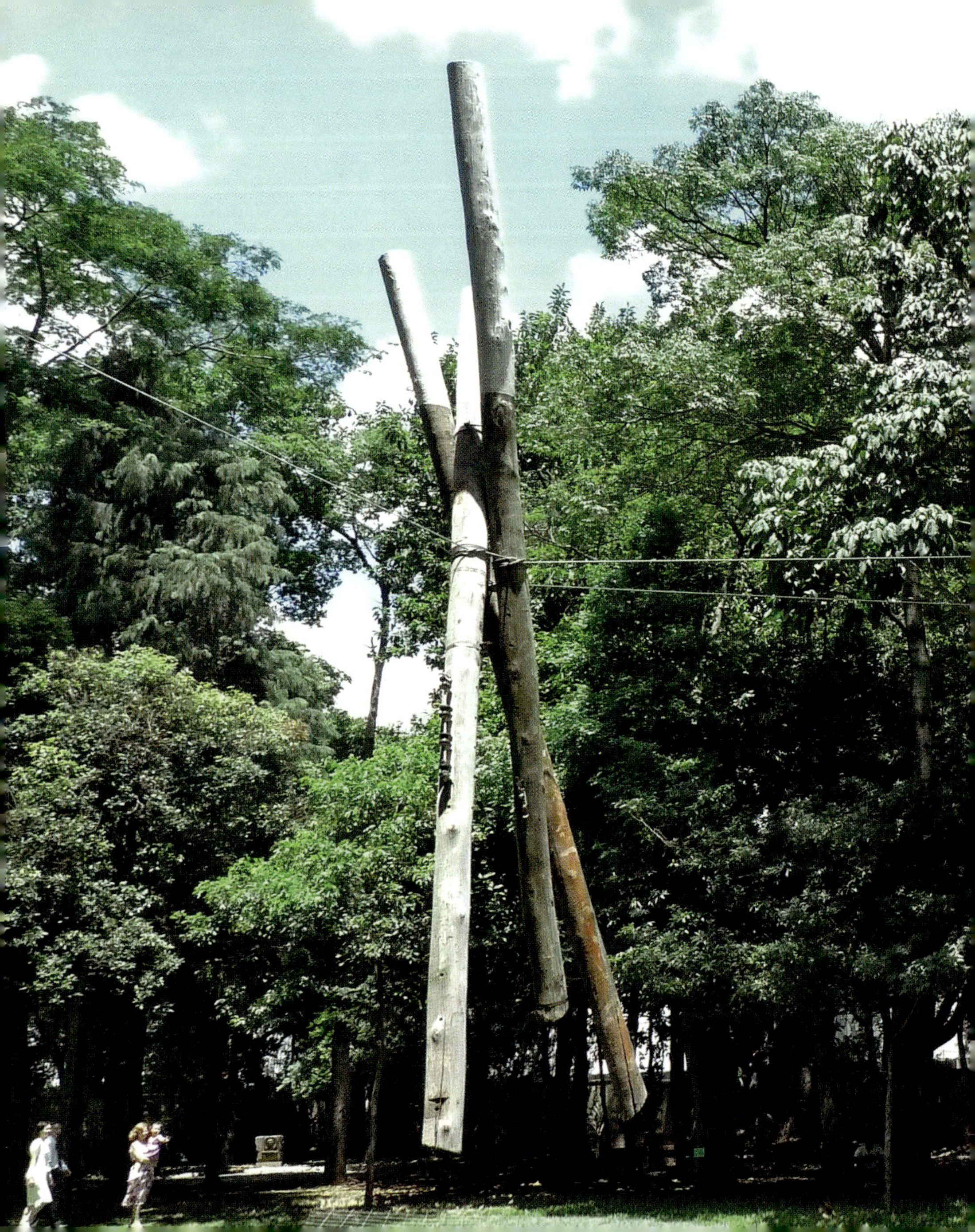

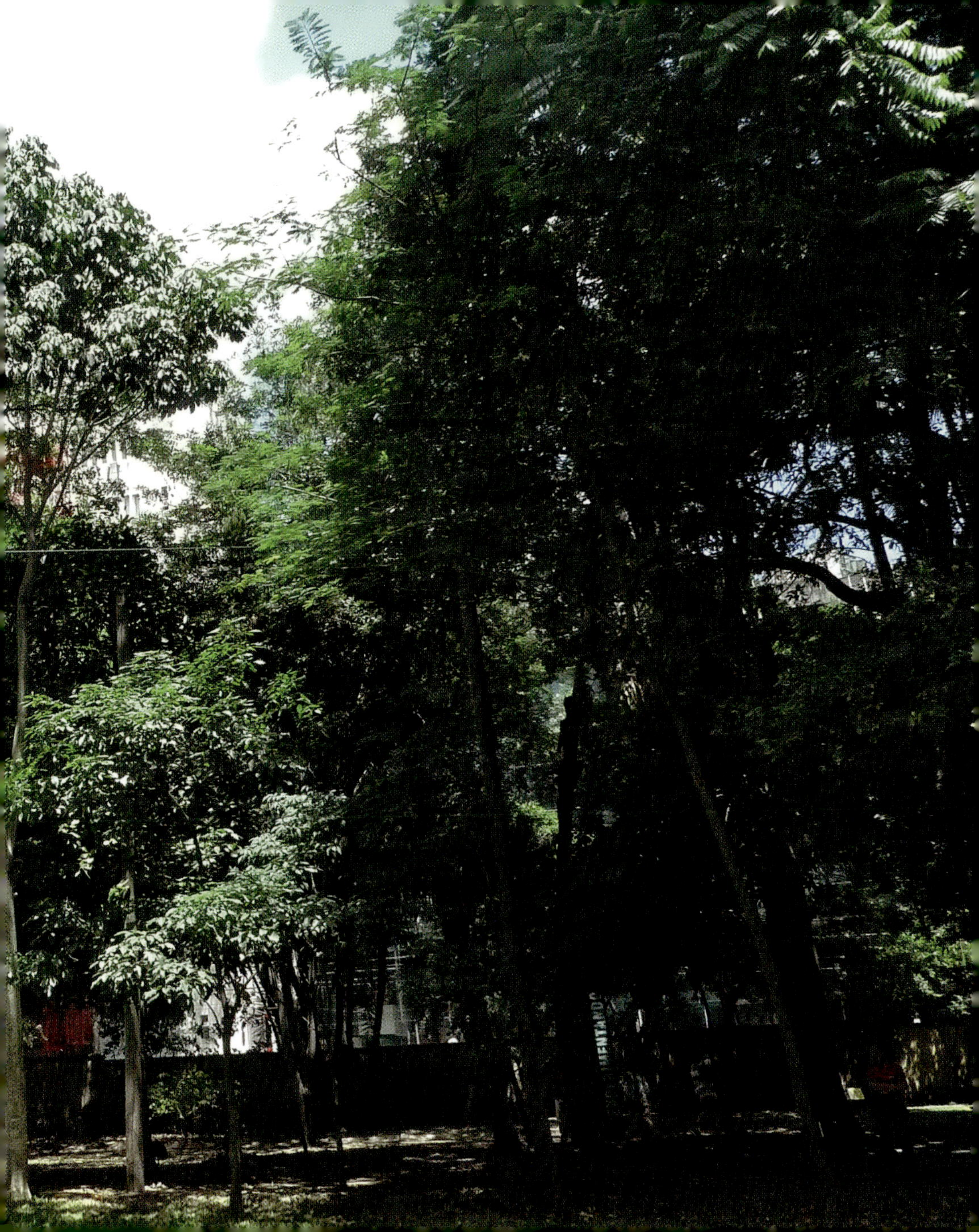

PAISAGEM
GIANCARLO
jornalista
DR. PEDRO MAMEDE VAZ
TRÊS EM UM
PINTURA
(Homenagem, ao
TOMBAMENTO
LATIN AMERICAN ABSTRACTION

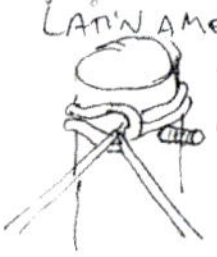

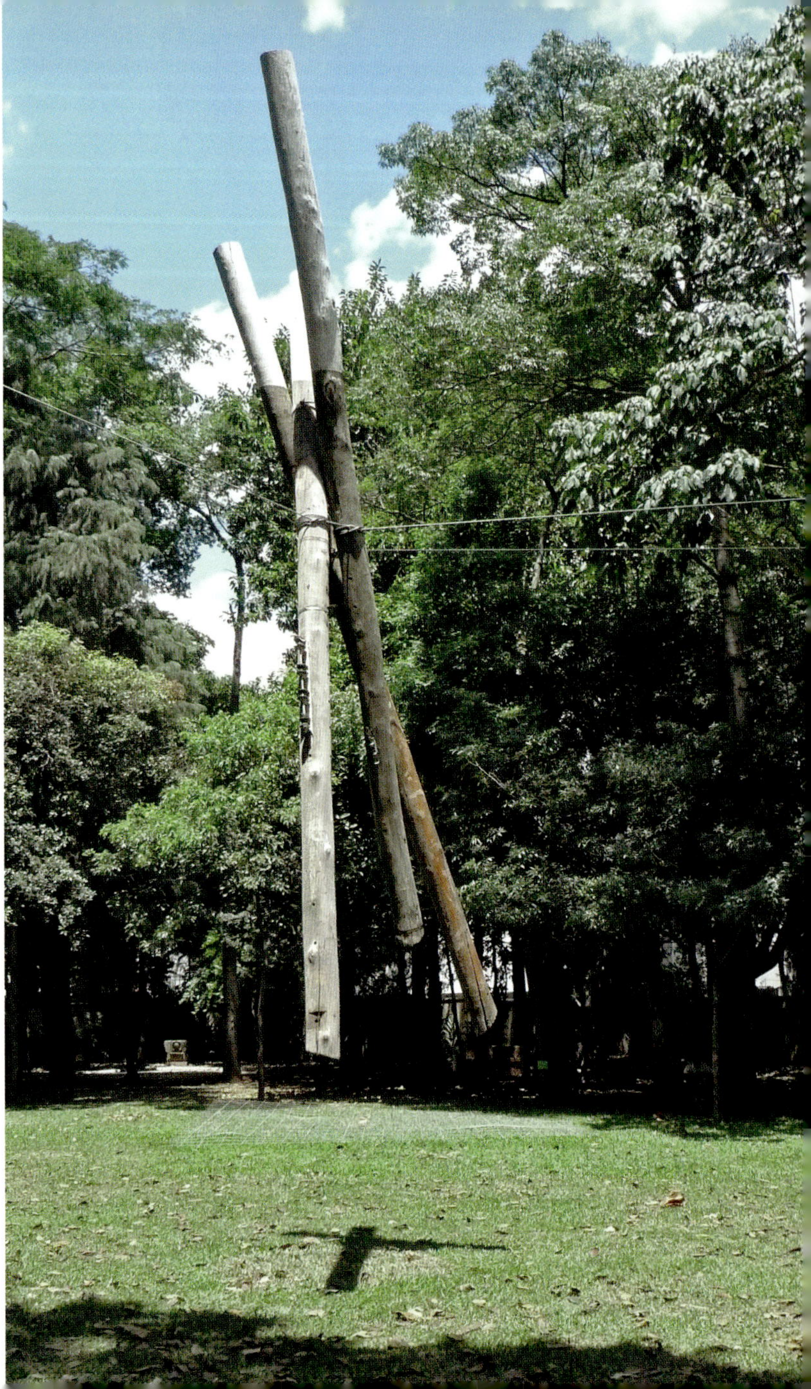

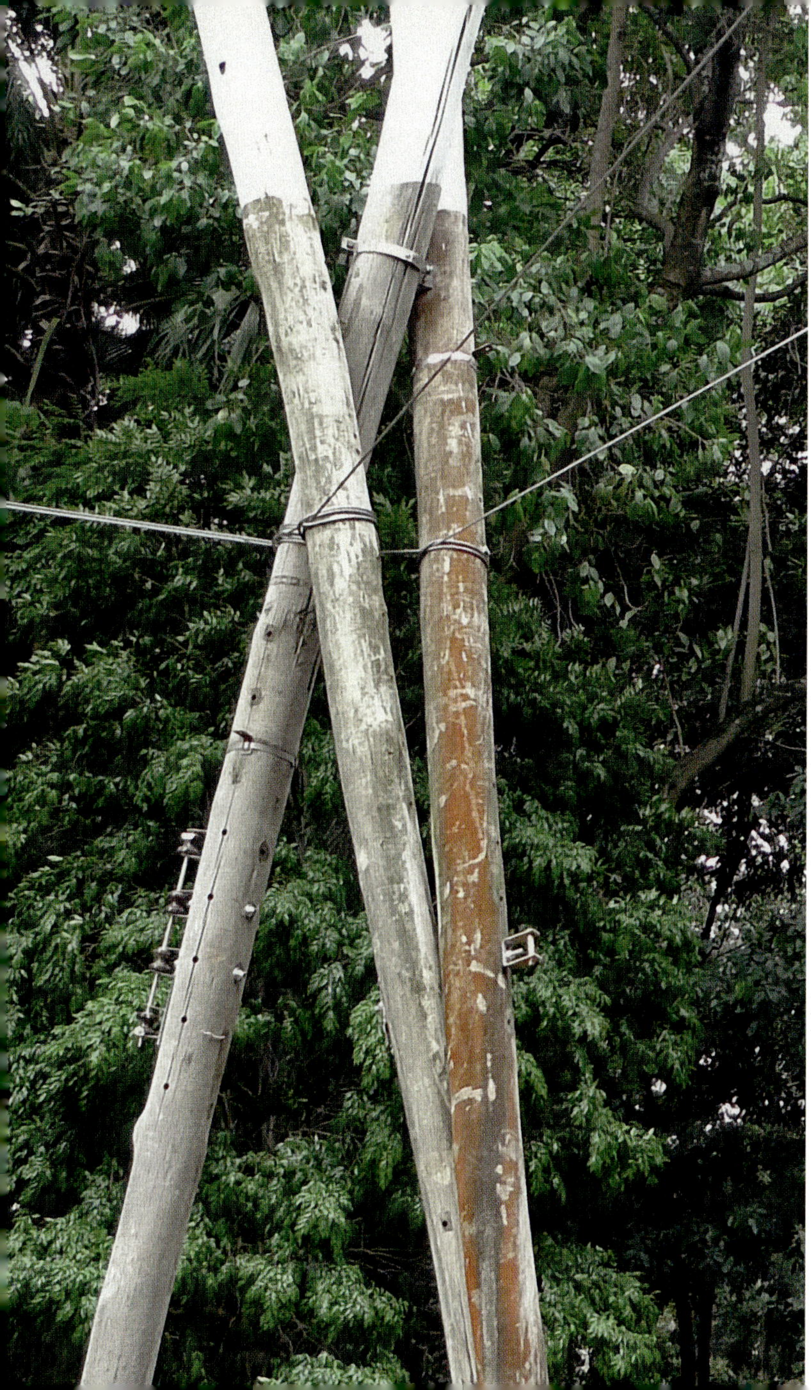

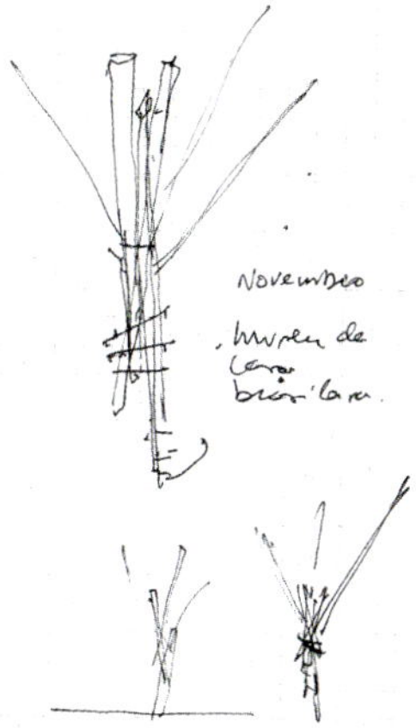
Novembro

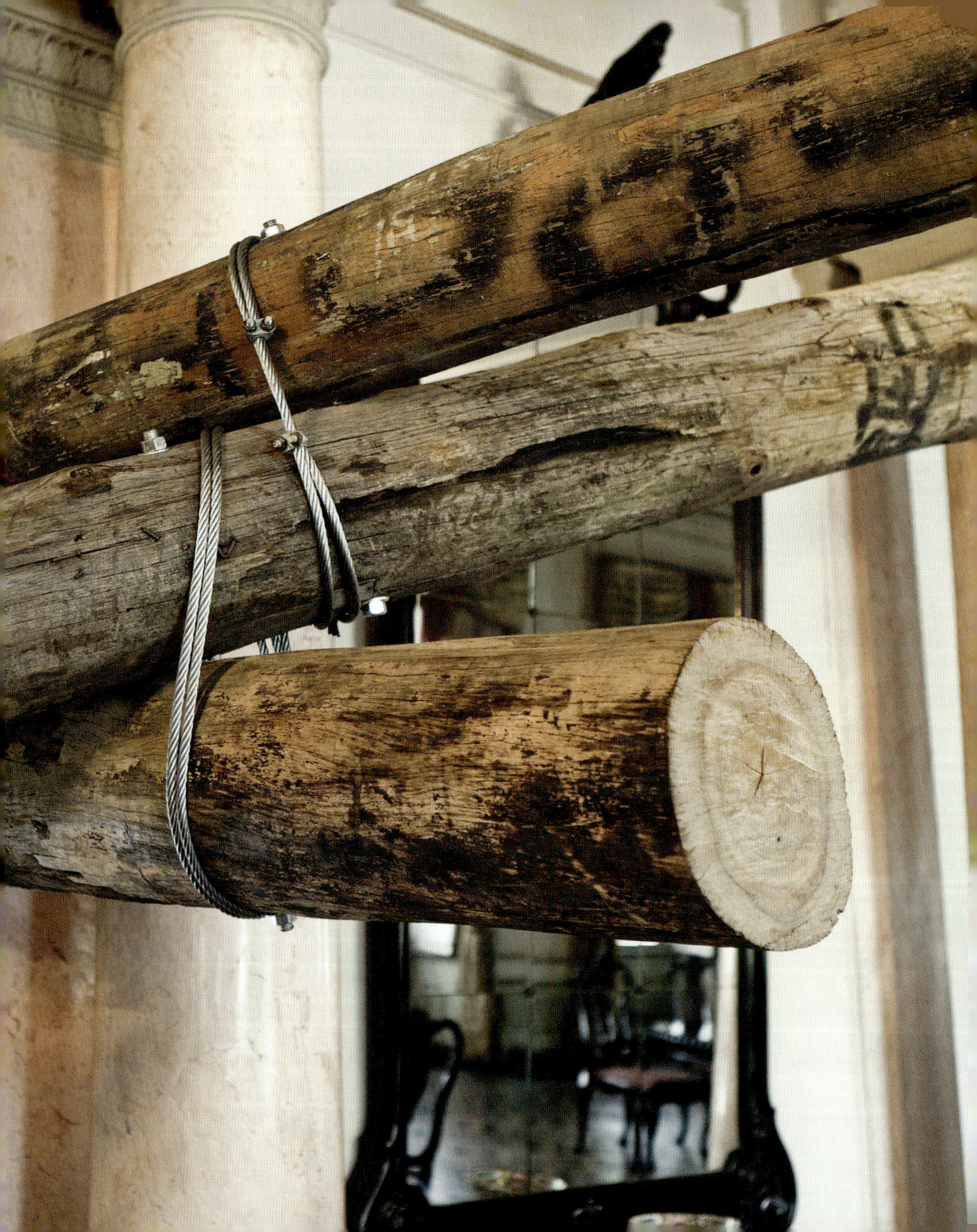

ROTEIRO PARA VISITAÇÃO

PALÁCIO DA ACLAMAÇÃO, SALVADOR, 2010
PROGRAMA OCUPAS, CURADORIA DE DANIEL RANGEL
13,5M DE ALTURA, 69M X 18M, MADEIRA E AÇO
[redacted] O PALÁCIO SEMPRE ABERTO. POSTES USADOS,
PONTALETES, AROEIRA ATRAVESSANDO PORTAS
E JANELAS DO HALL, DAS SALAS DE BANQUETE, DE
ALMOÇO, DO SALÃO NOBRE E DAS VARANDAS
DA ANTIGA RESIDÊNCIA DO GOVERNADOR DA BAHIA

Roadmap for Visitation

Palácio da Aclamação, Salvador, 2010

Programa Ocupas, curated by Daniel Rangel
13.5m h, 69m x 18m, wood, steel
The Palace is always open. Used telephone poles,
posts and an Aroeira (pepper tree) cross
through the doors and windows of the hallway, the Banquet
Room, the Lunch Room, the Ceremonial Hall and the
balconies of the former residence of the governer of Bahia

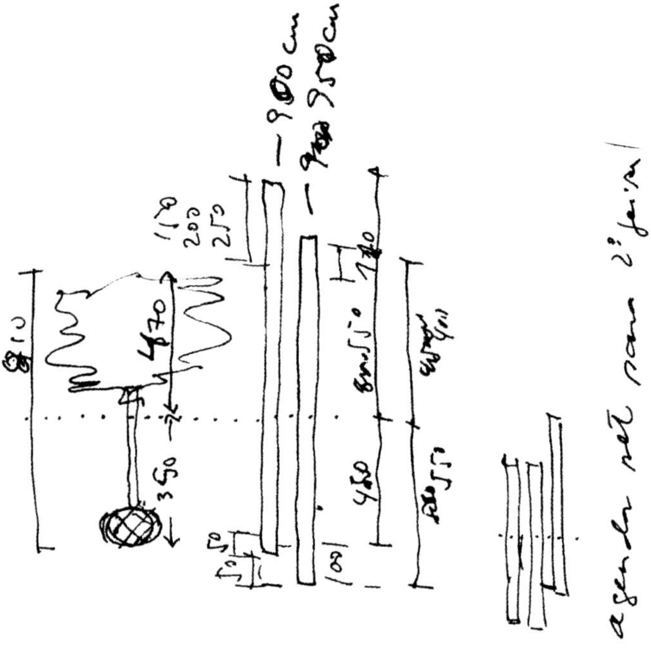
900 cm
470
350

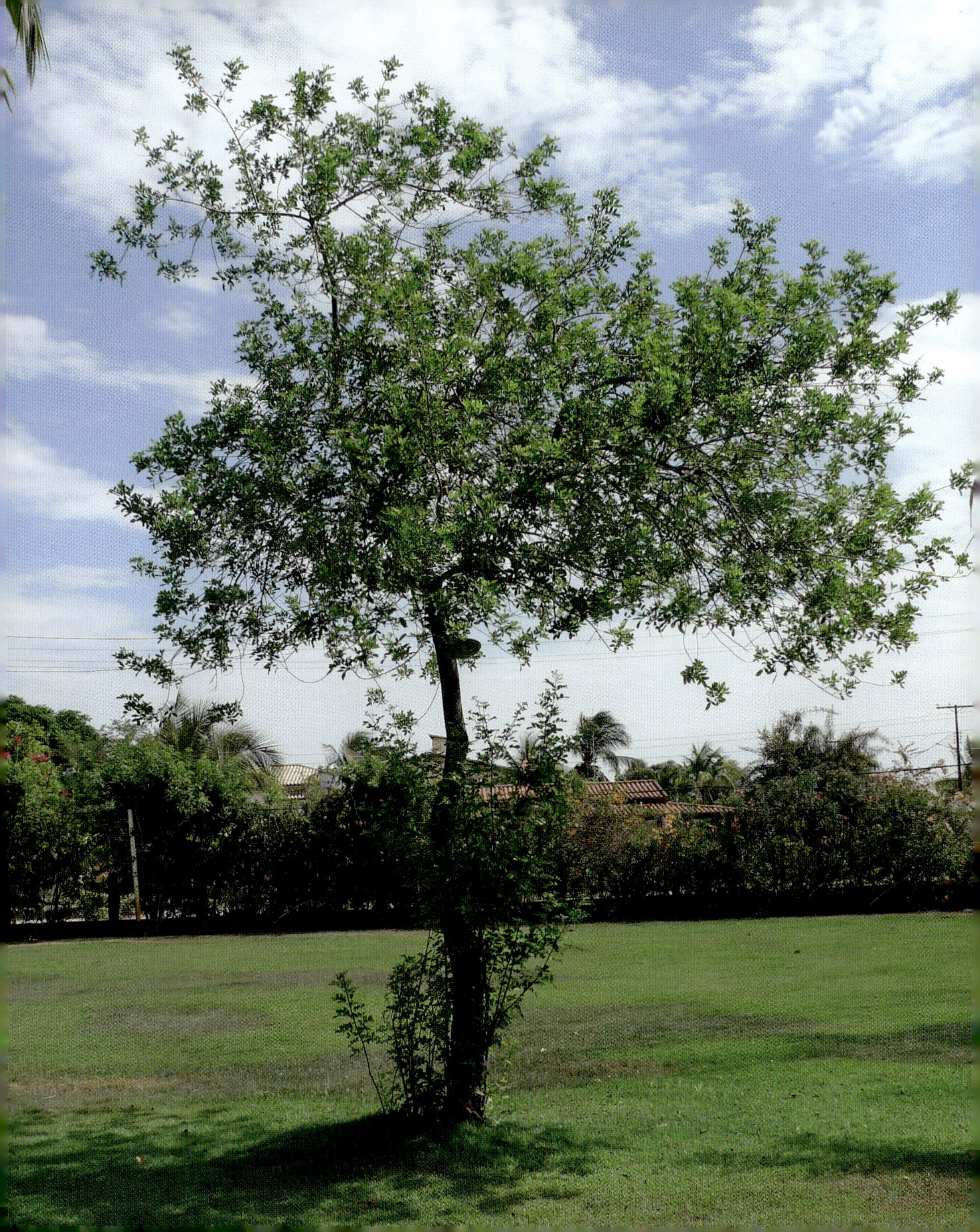

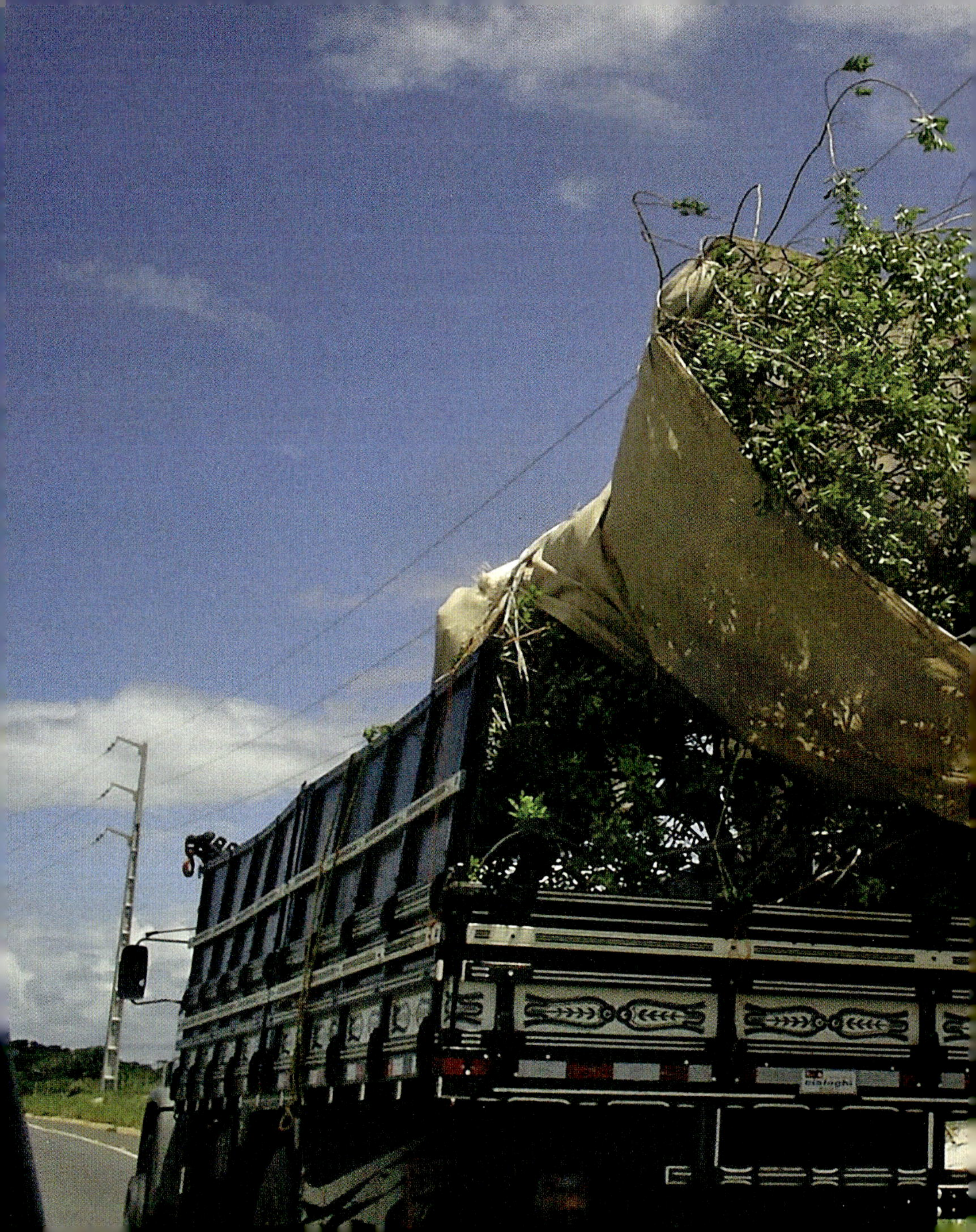

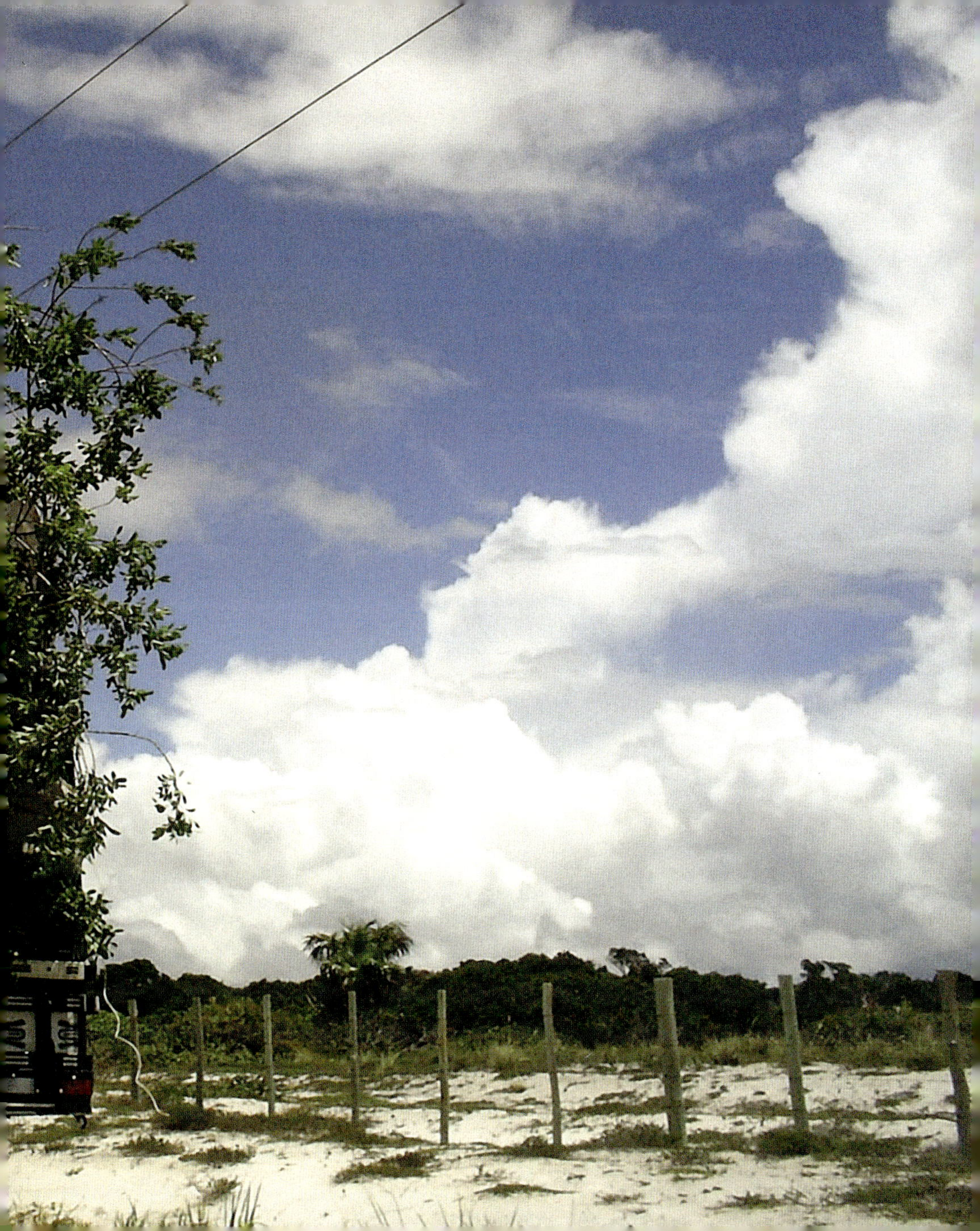

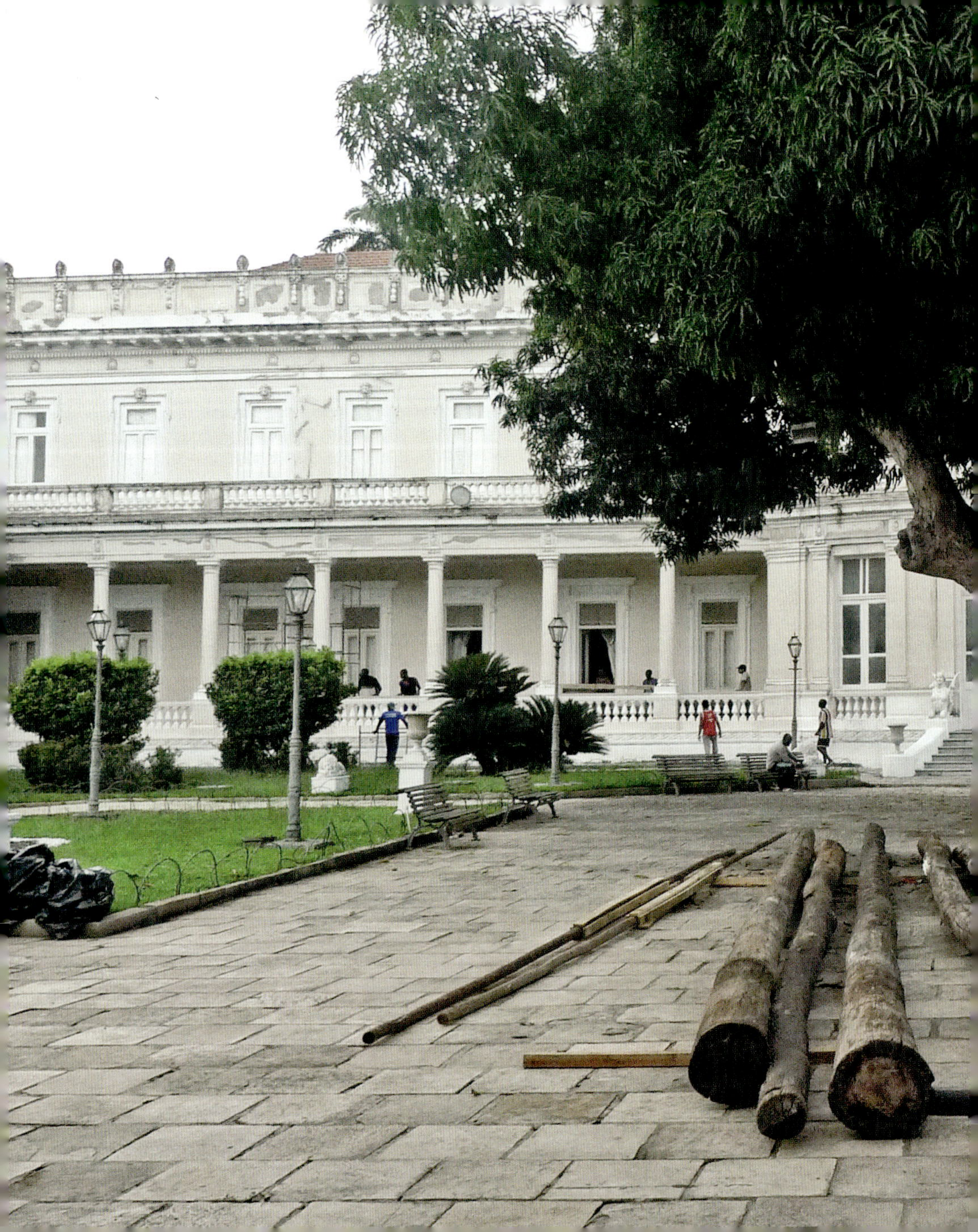

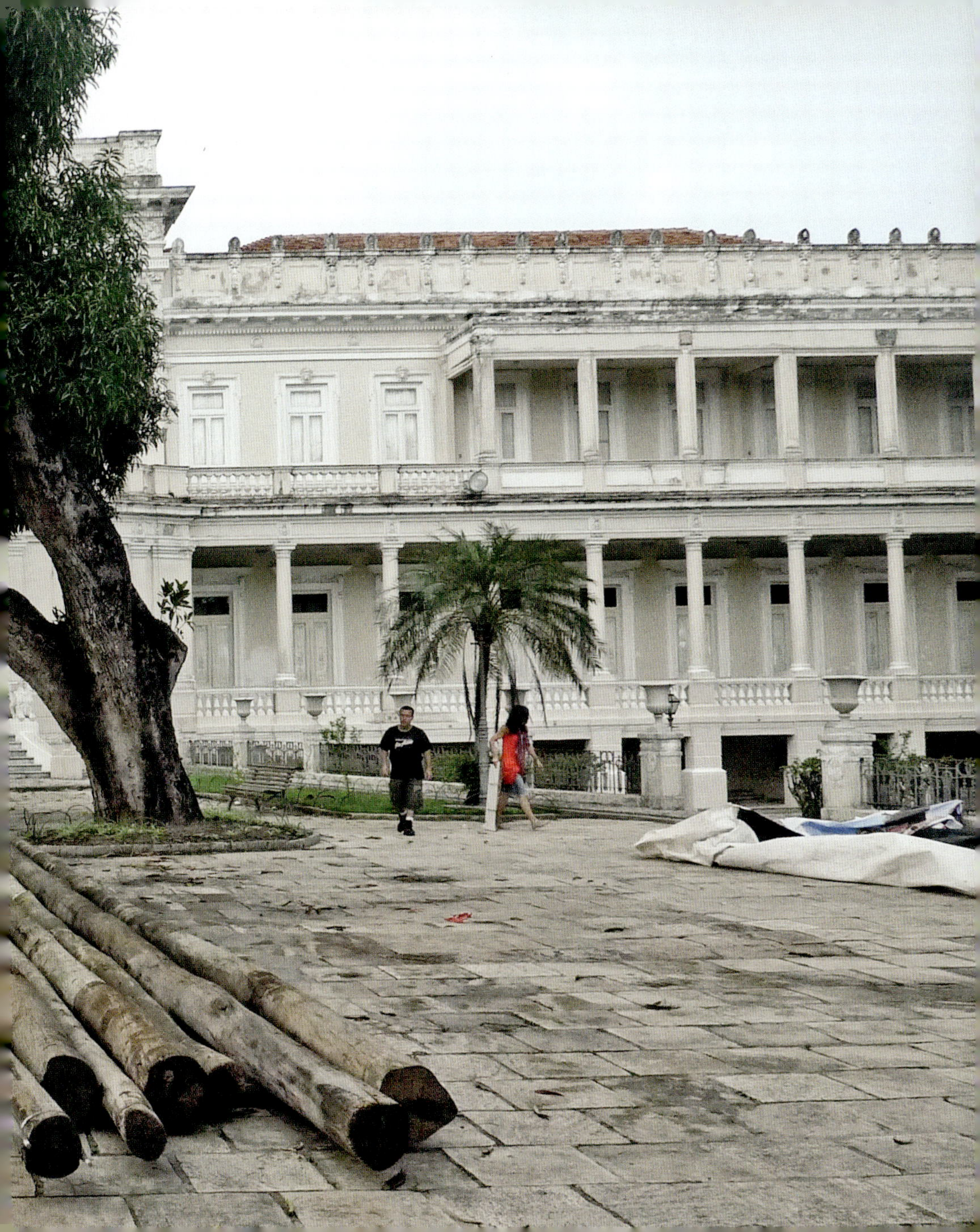

HALL DE ENTRADA

ÁRVORE, MADEIRA, TERRA, JUTA, AÇO
13,5M DE ALTURA, 17M X 10,7M
AROEIRA DE 9M, VIVA, COM TORRÃO
EMBRULHADO EM JUTA
2 POSTES DE EUCALIPTO COM 11M, DE PONTA-
CABEÇA, PINTADOS COM CAL
CABOS DE AÇO
APÓS SEIS MESES A ÁRVORE FOI REPLANTADA
EM FRENTE AO PALÁCIO

Entrance Hall

Tree, wood, soil, jute, steel
13.5m h, 17m x 10.7m
A living Aroeira of 9m, with a clod of soil wrapped in jute
Two 11m poles made from Eucalyptus,
upside-down painted with whitewash
Steel cables
After six months the tree was replanted in front of the Palace

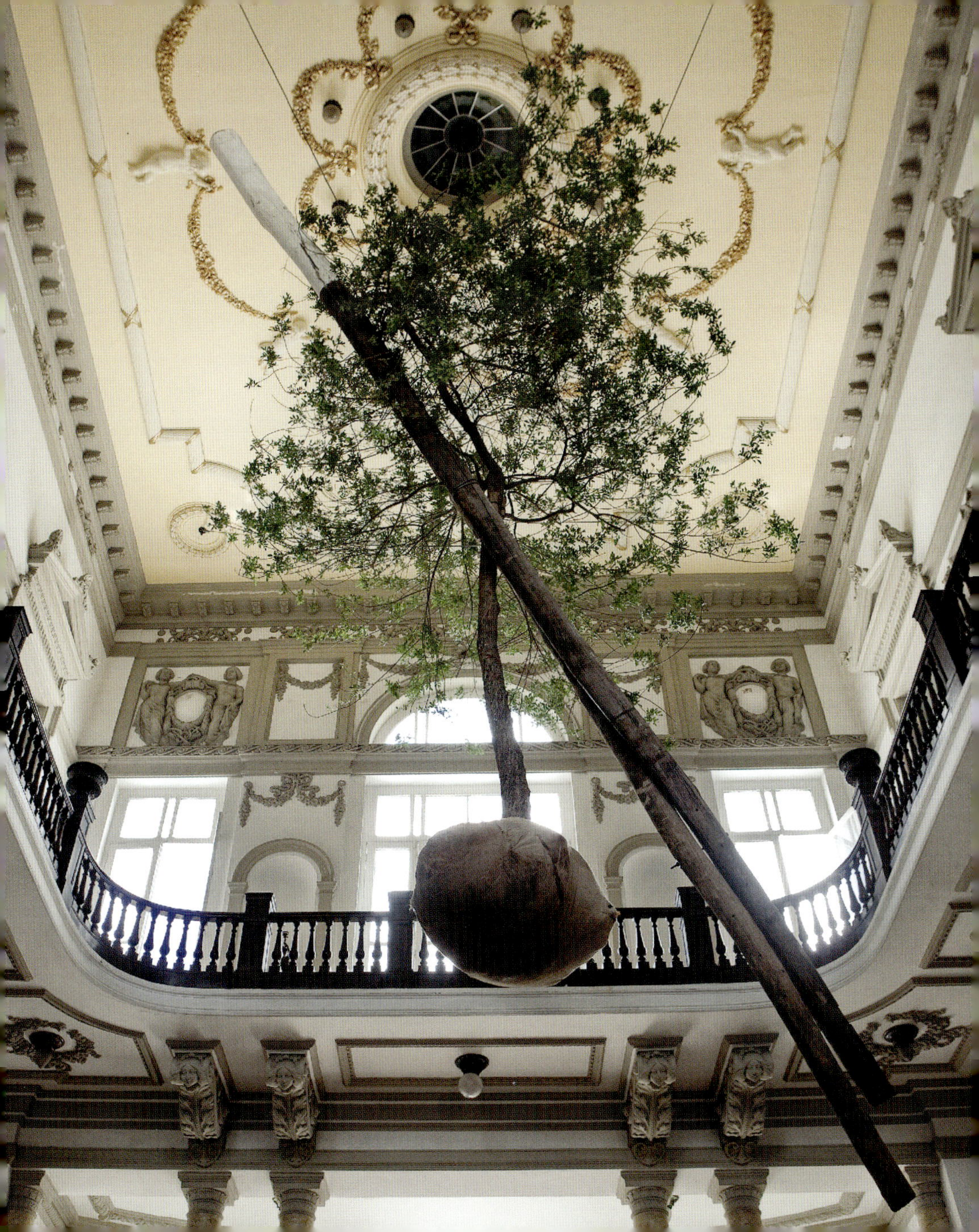

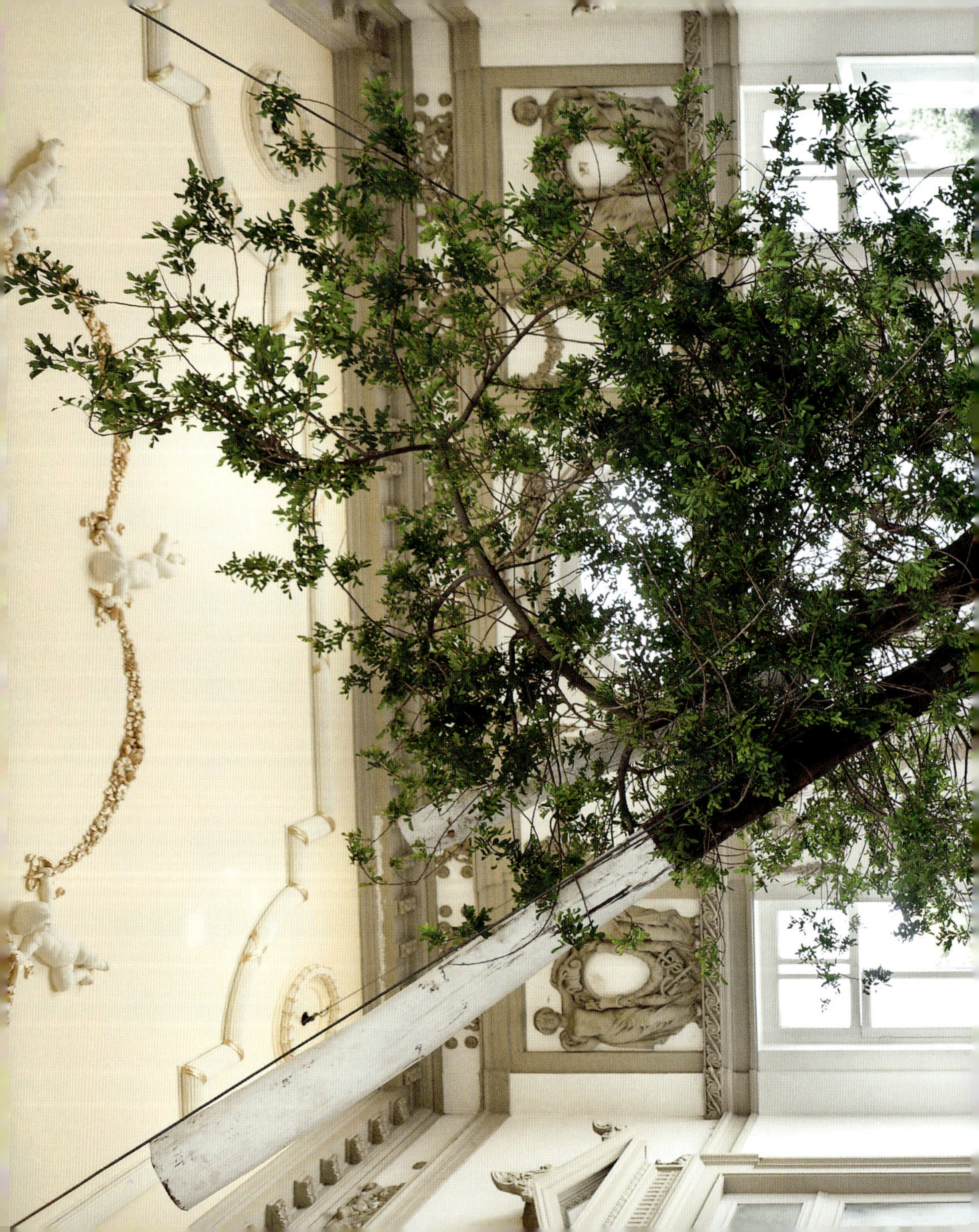

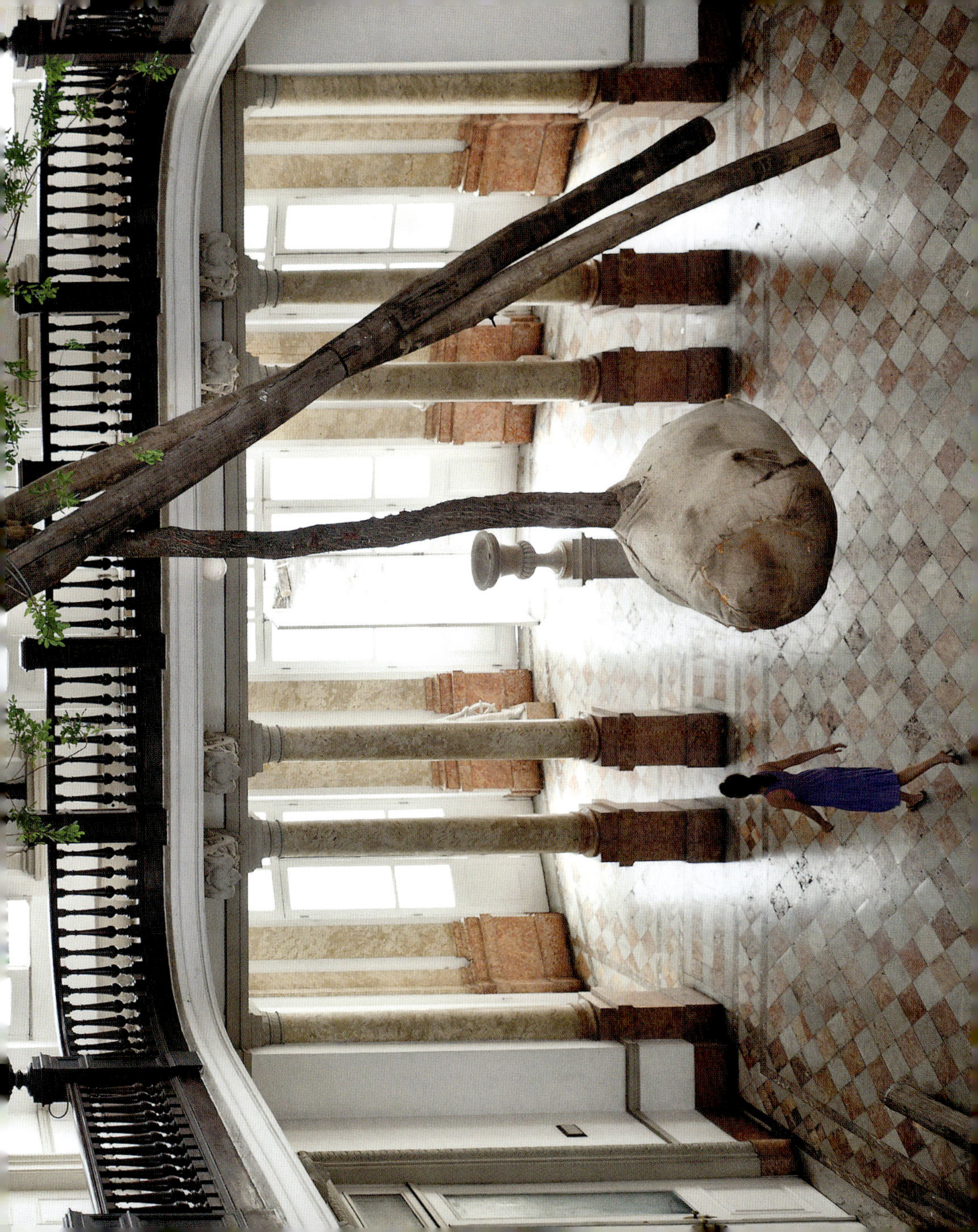

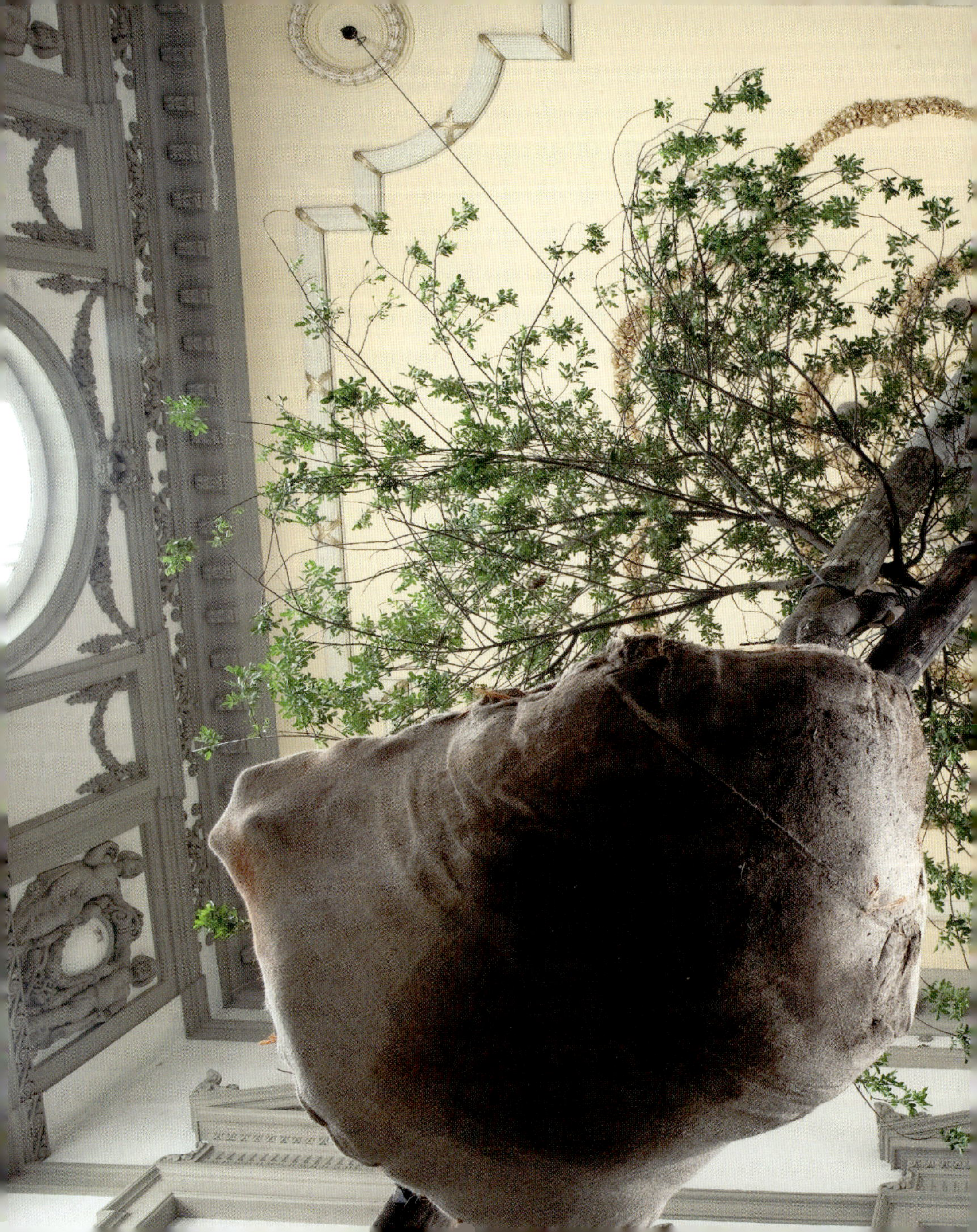

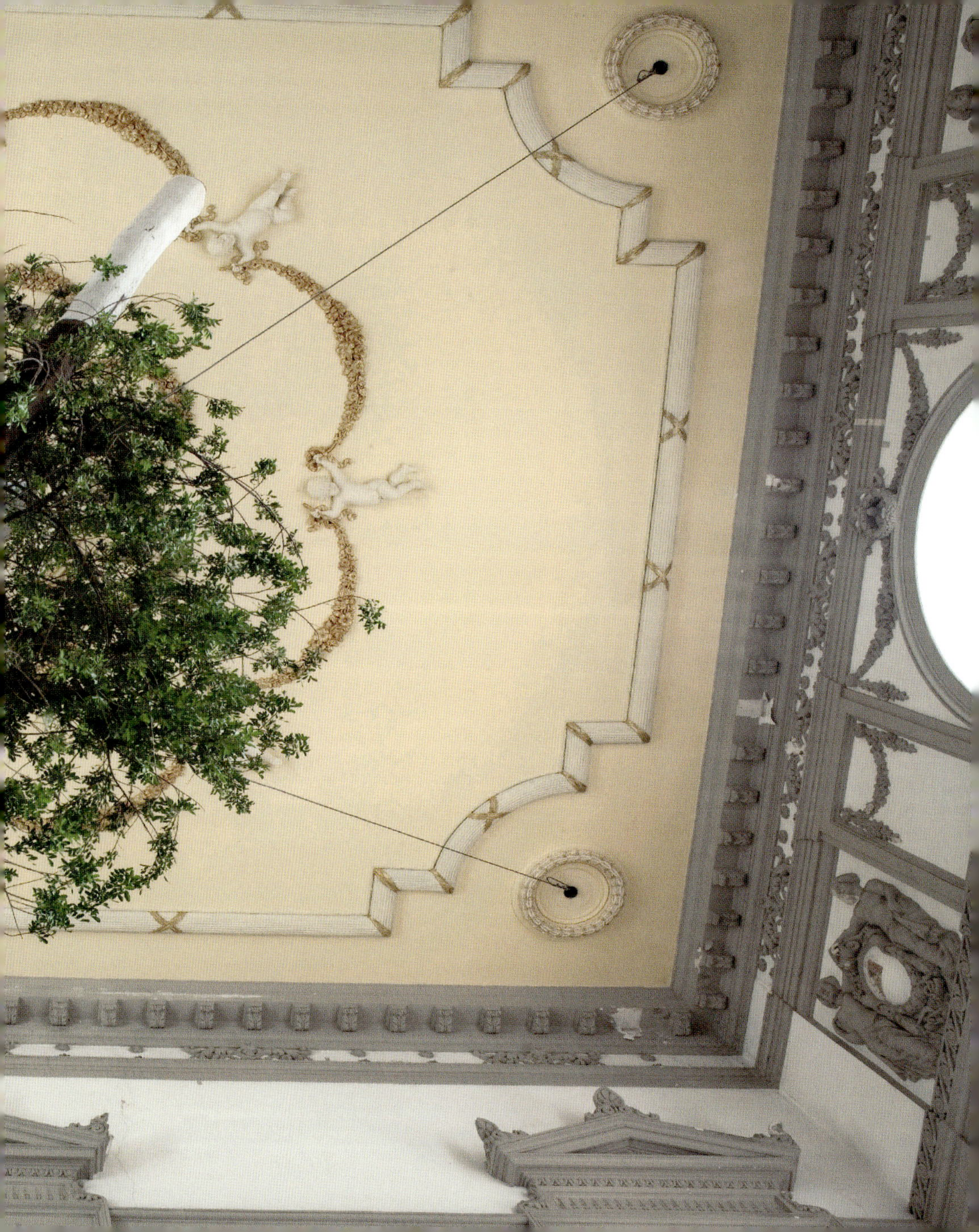

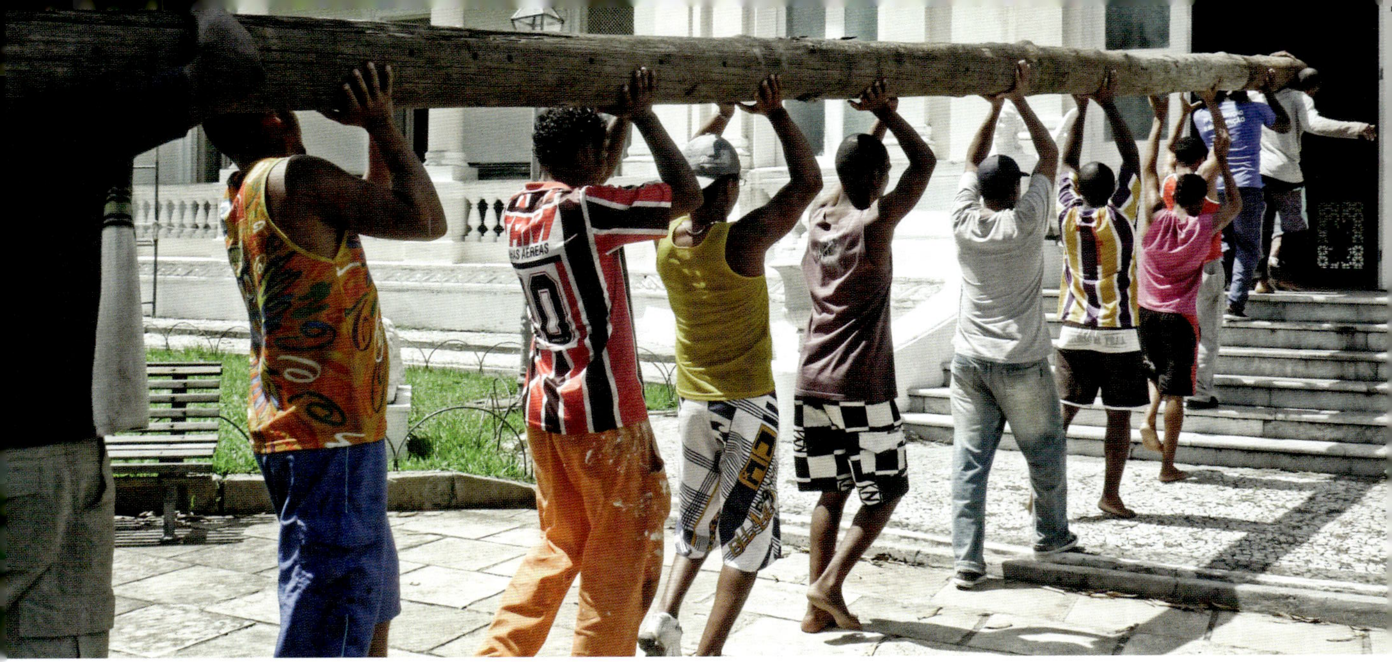

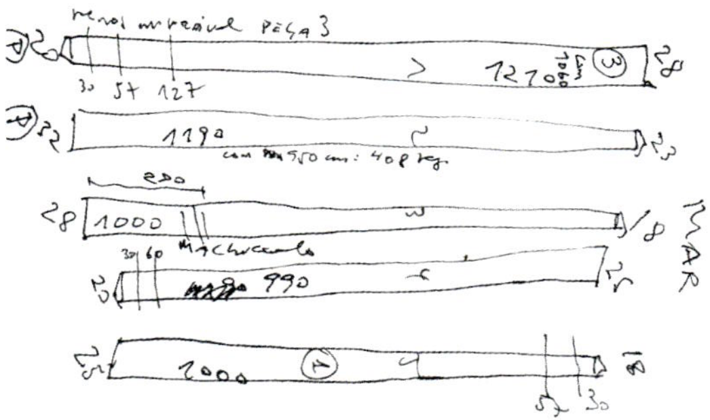
MAR

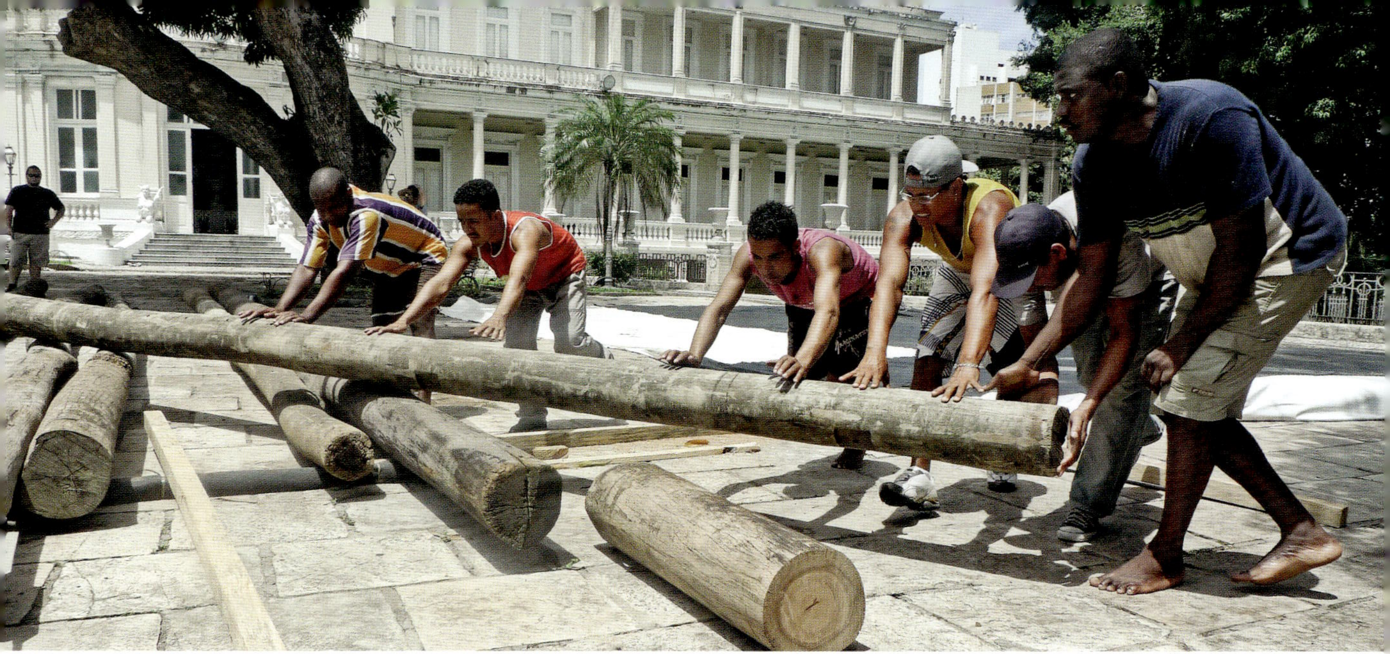

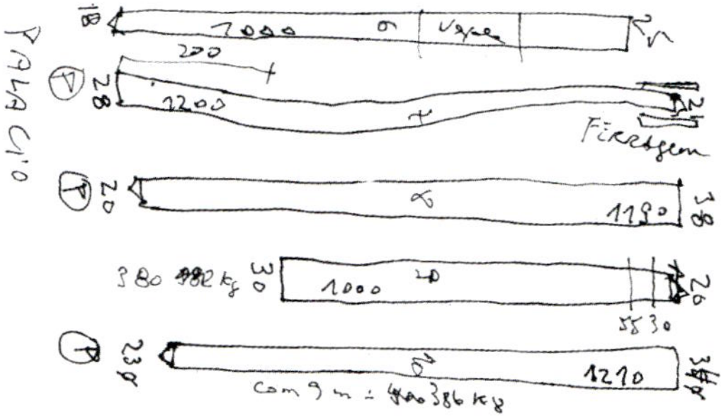
18
1000
200
28
1200
Firragem
20
1180
38
380 kg
30
1000
23ø
1210
com 9 m = 386 kg
PALACIO

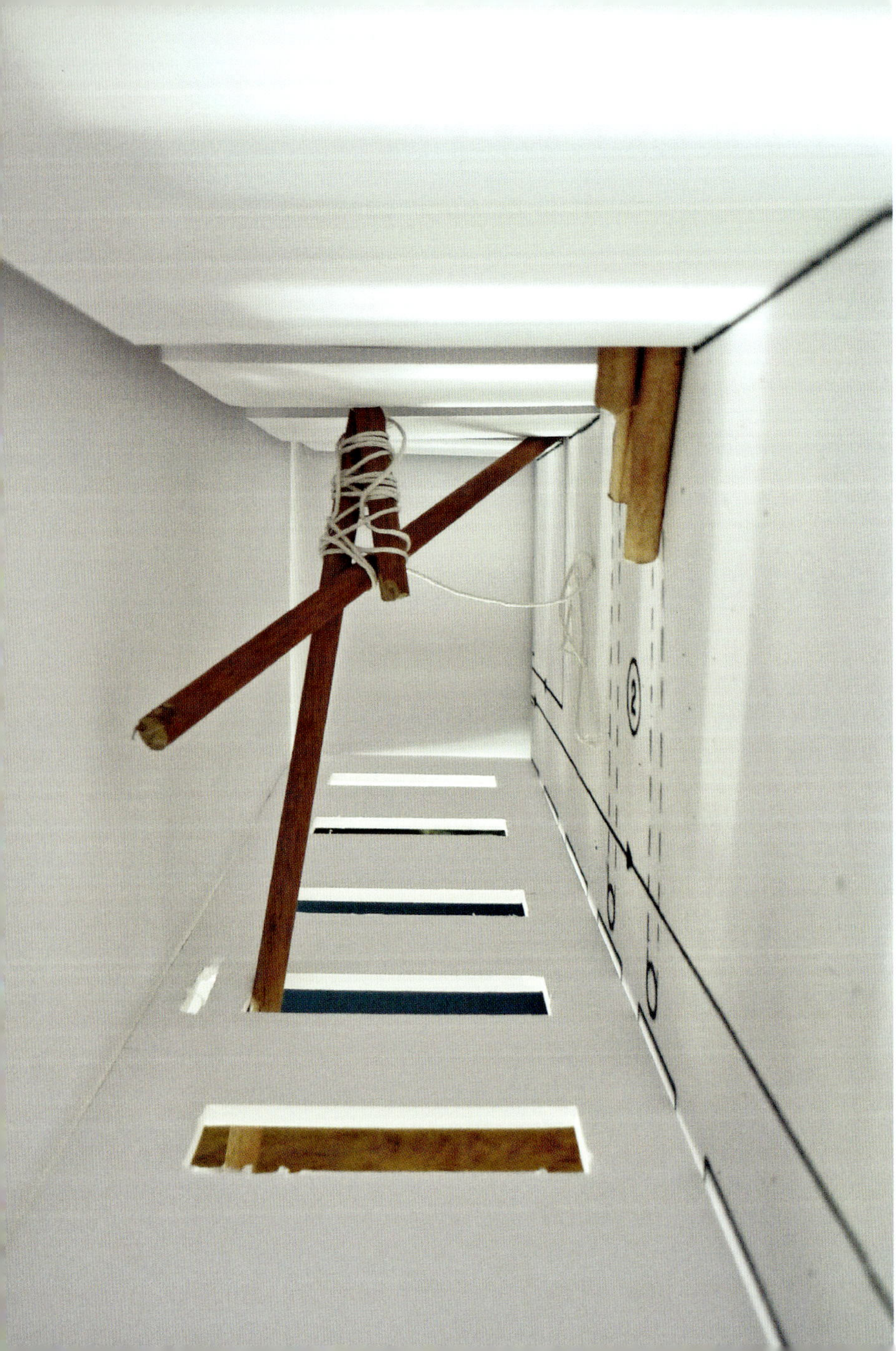
2

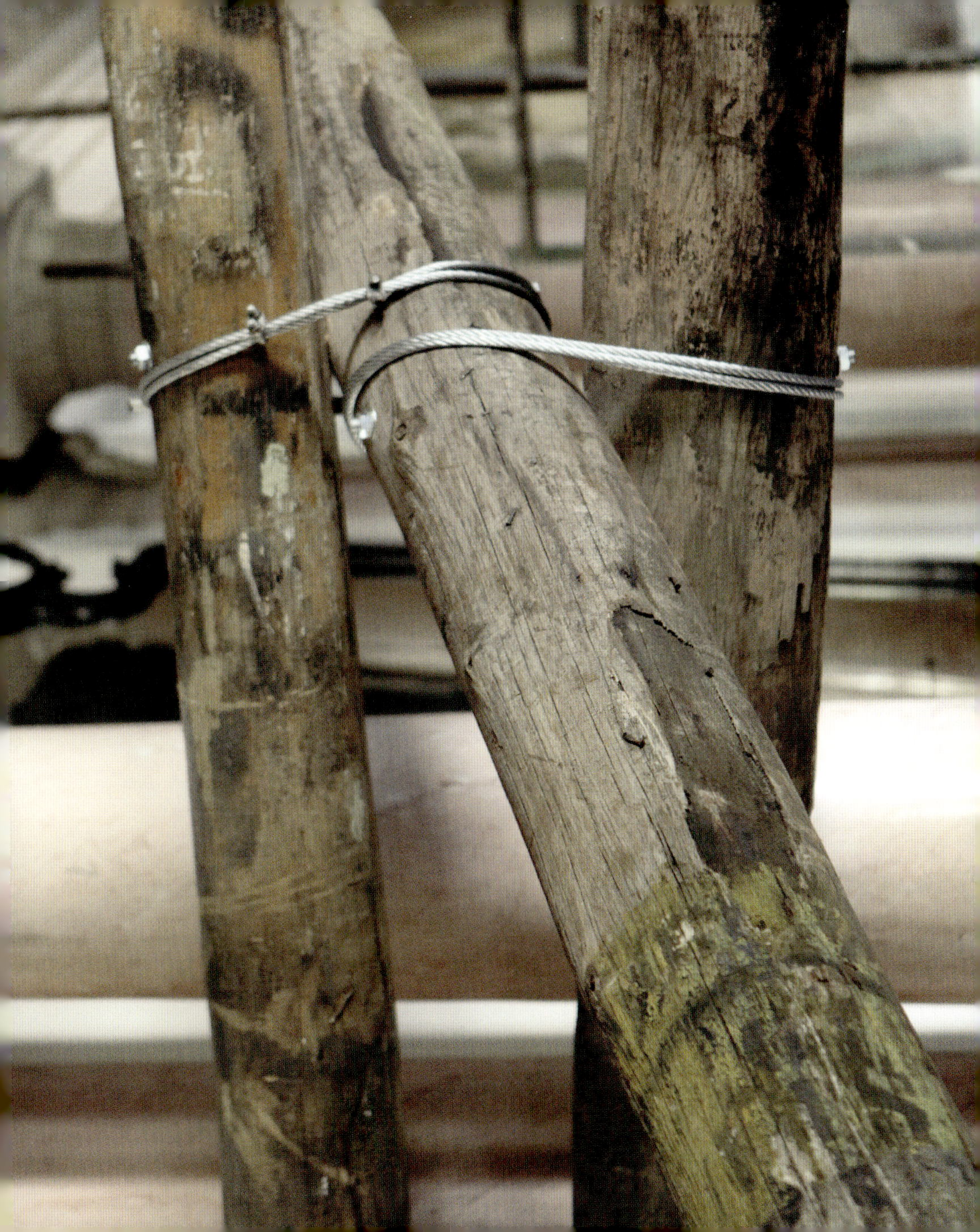

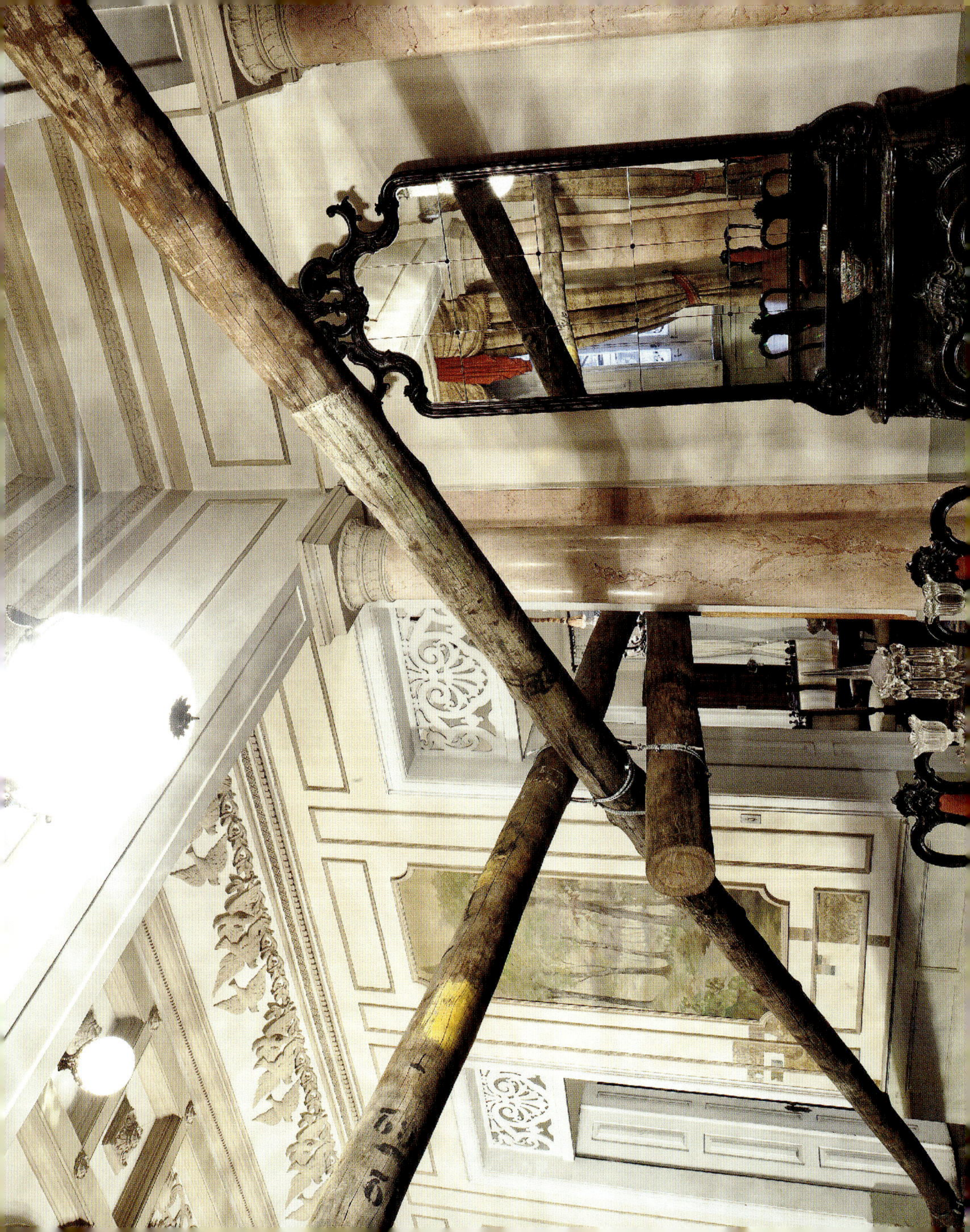

SALAS DE BANQUETE E ALMOÇO

MADEIRA E AÇO
4,8 M DE ALTURA, 24M x 18M
3 POSTES DE EUCALIPTO ENTRE 10 E 12M,
1.200Kg. CABOS DE AÇO. OS POSTES
ATRAVESSAM O PALÁCIO, SAEM PARA A
RUA E PARA O PÁTIO. A PEÇA FOI [redacted]
ERGUIDA NUMA TALHA. DEPOIS DE
SOLTA, DESCEU ATÉ PARAR NOS BATENTES.
ARMADILHA

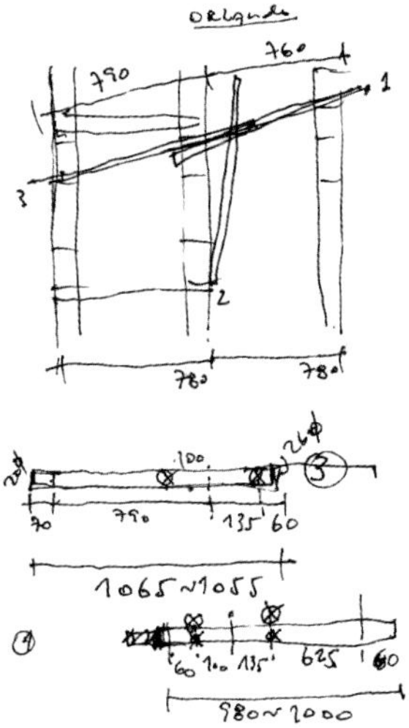

Banquet and Lunch Room

Wood and steel
4.8m h, 24m x 18m
1,200kg steel cables. The telephone poles
cross the Palace, out onto the street and the patio.
The piece was erected using a pulley. It was then realeased
and lowered until it stopped at the casements. A snare.

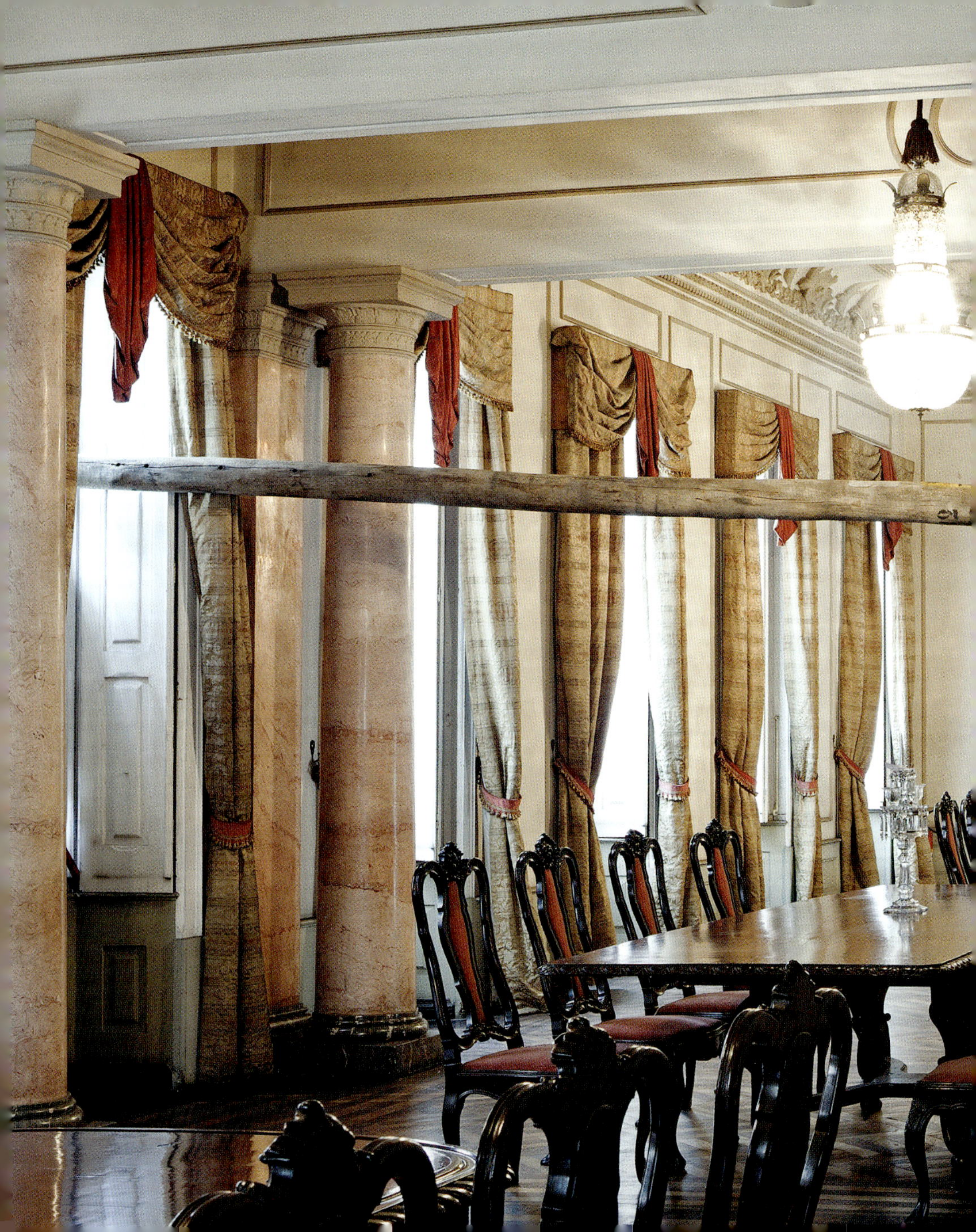

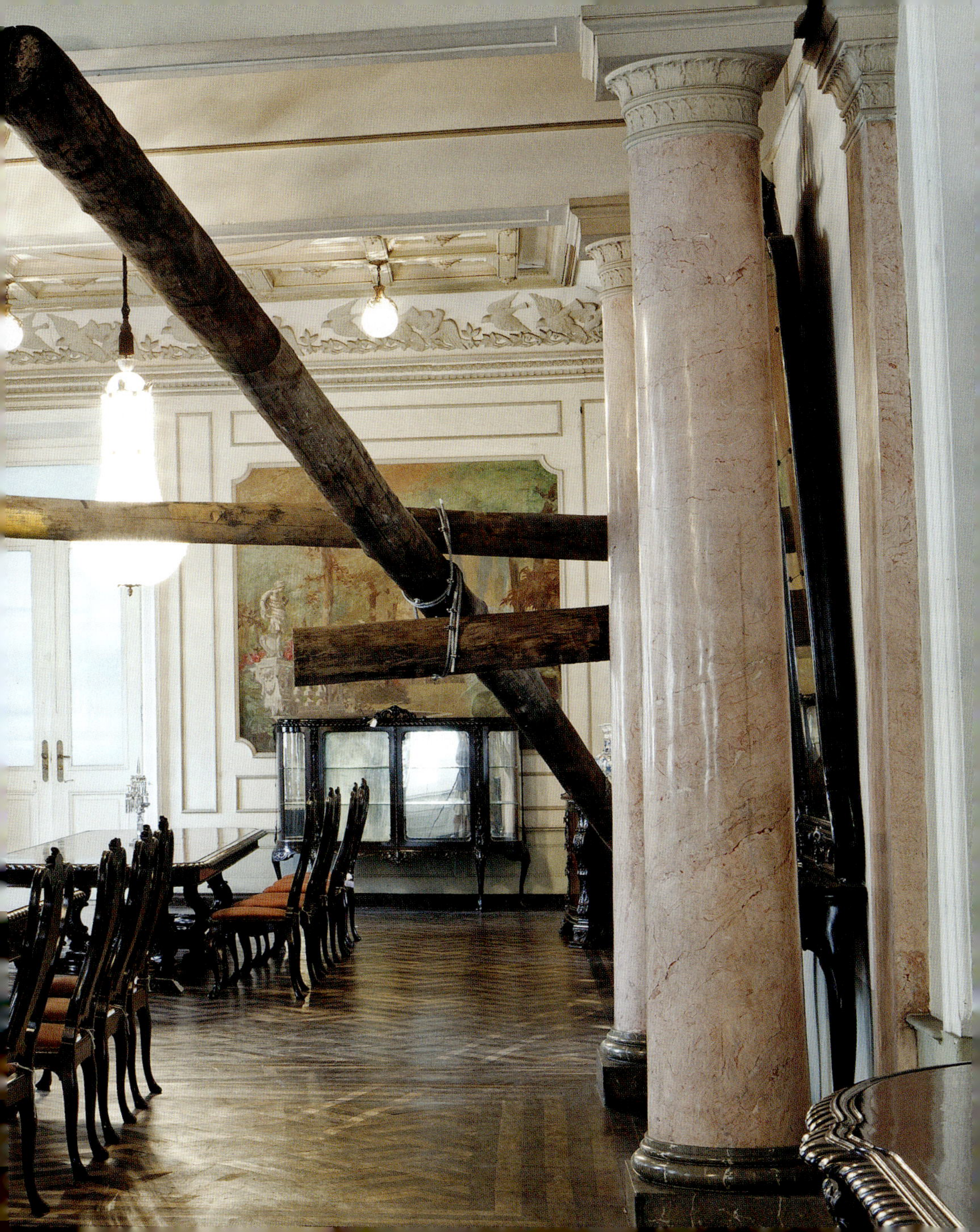

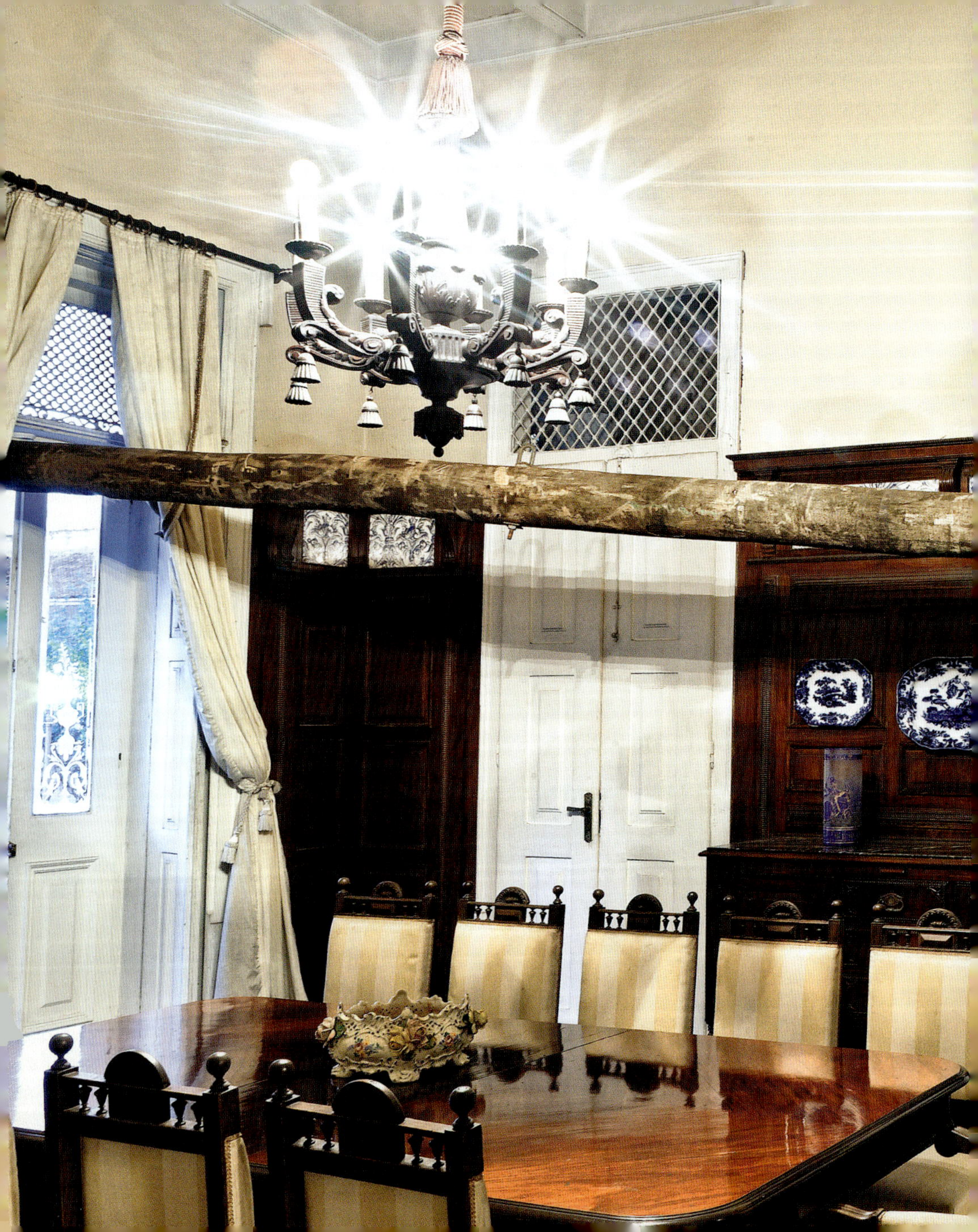

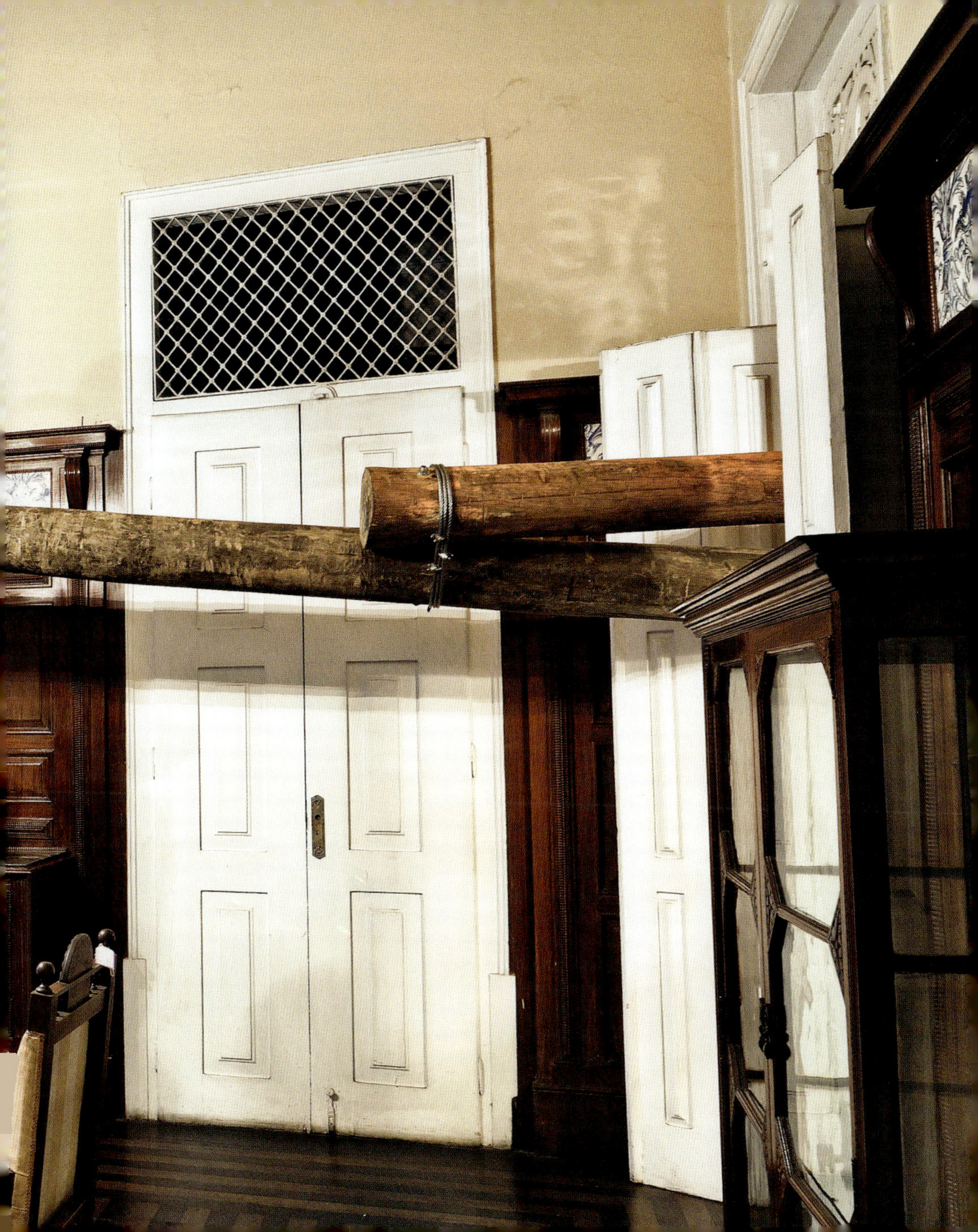

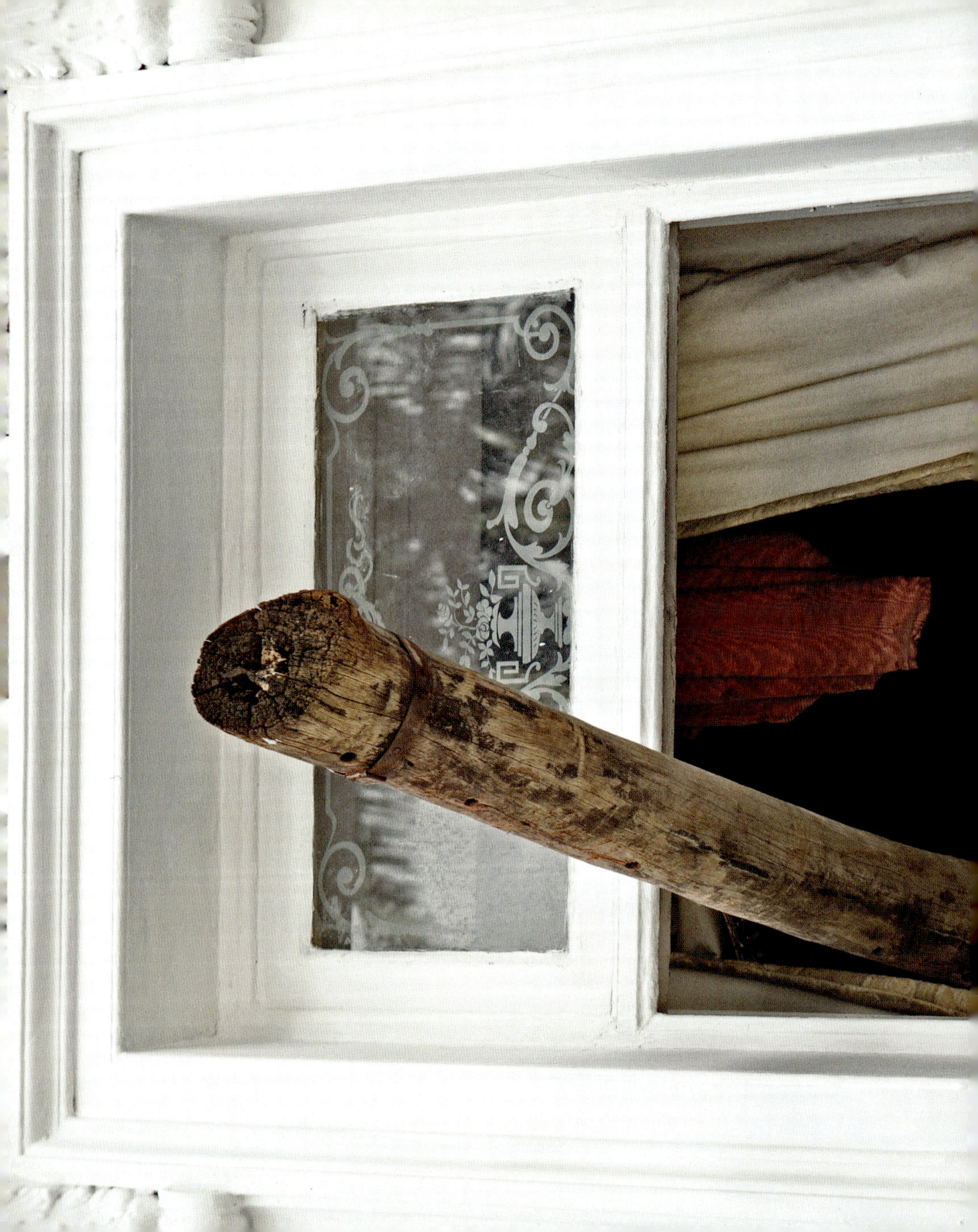

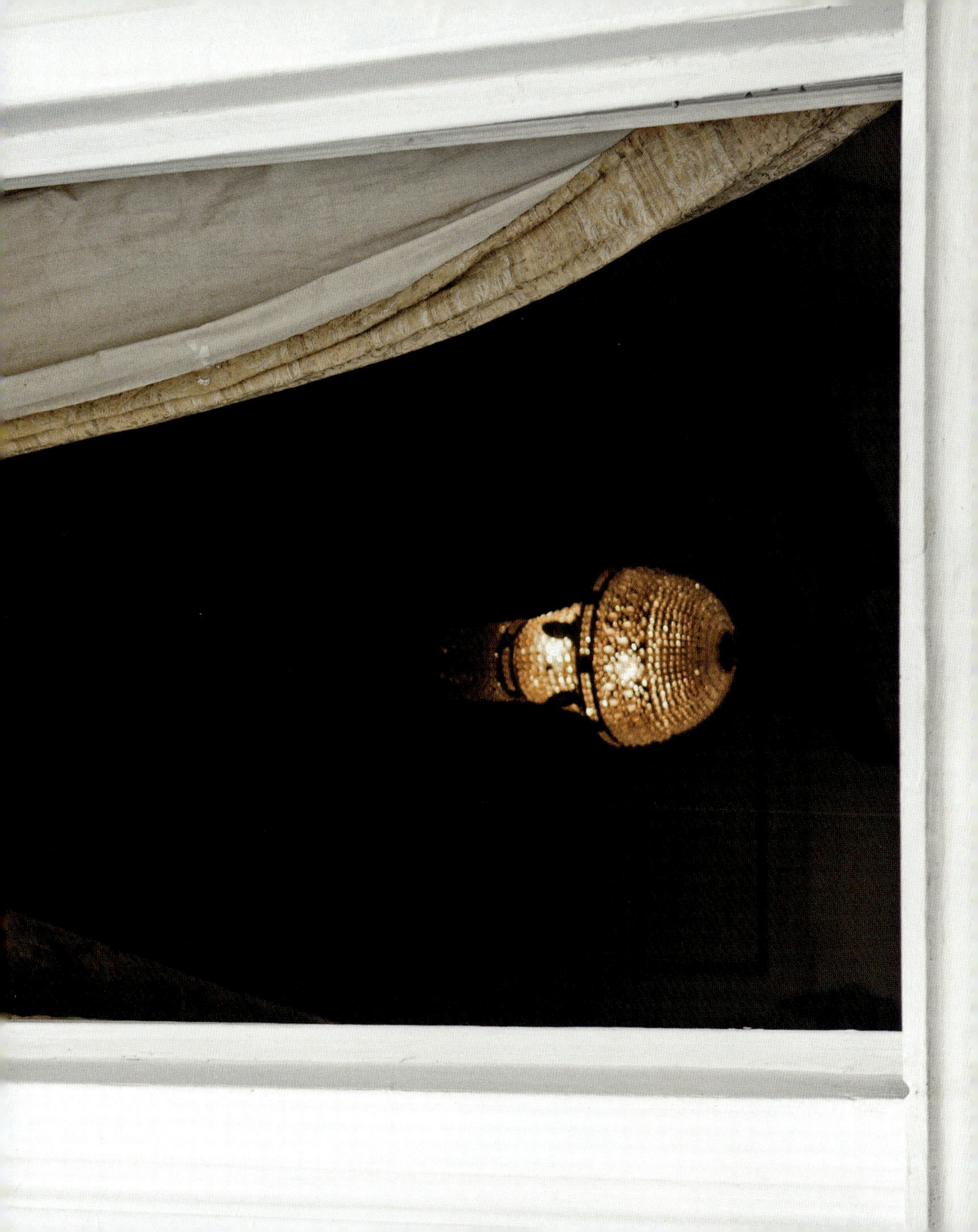

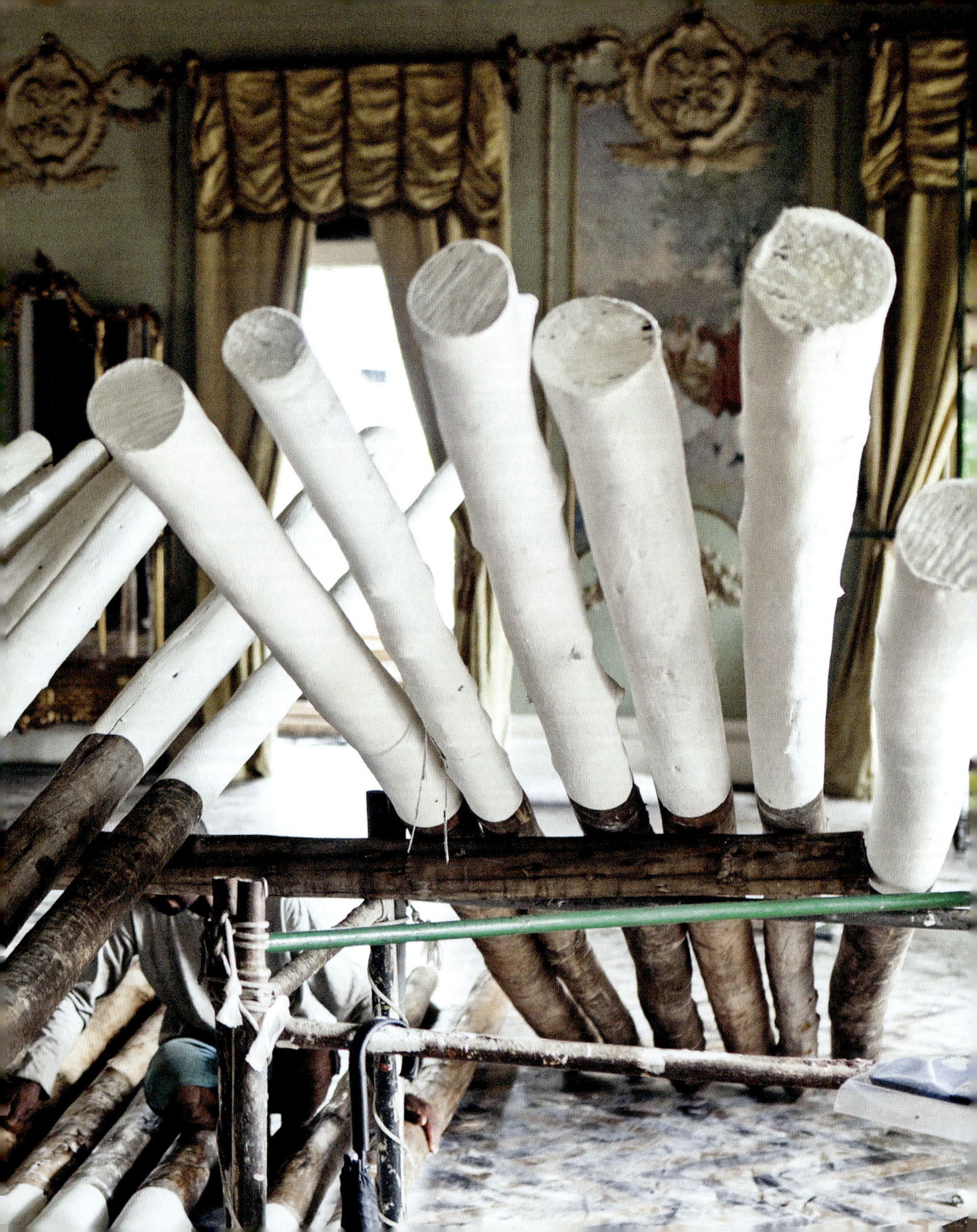

SALÃO NOBRE E VARANDAS

MADEIRA, AÇO, CORDAS, [redacted] CAL
4,8M DE ALTURA, 22M X 17M
240 PONTALETES DE EUCALIPTO
NOVOS, PARA CONSTRUÇÃO, PINTADOS
A CAL A PARTIR DO NÍVEL DE 3
METROS DO CHÃO [redacted]
PERFORMANCES DE ARTO LINDSAY
E ARNALDO ANTUNES

Ceremonial Hall and Balcony
Wood, steel, rope, whitewash
4.8m h, 22m x 17m
240 new Eucalyptus posts, for construction,
painted with whitewash three meters above floor level
Performances by Arto Lindsay
and Arnaldo Antunes

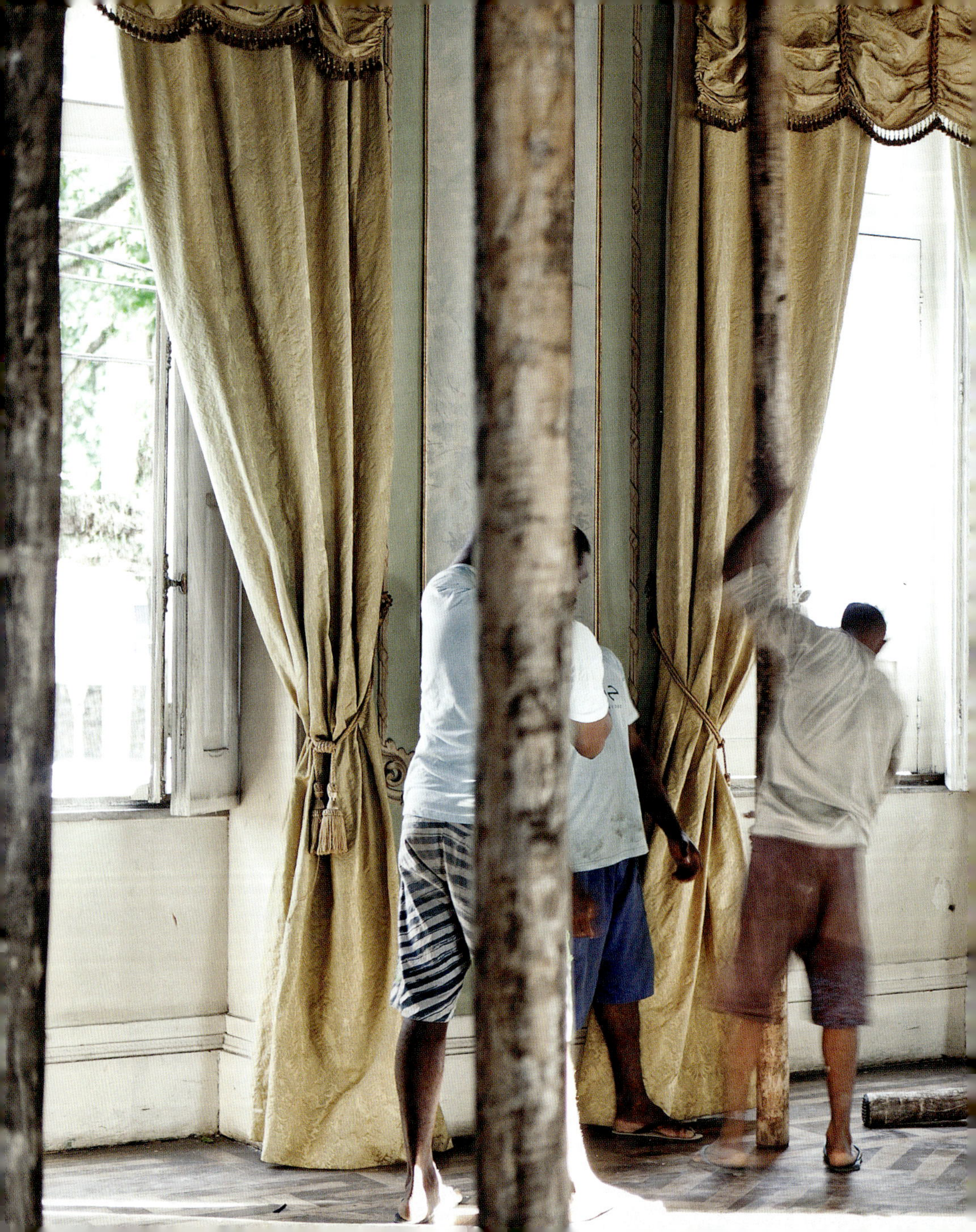

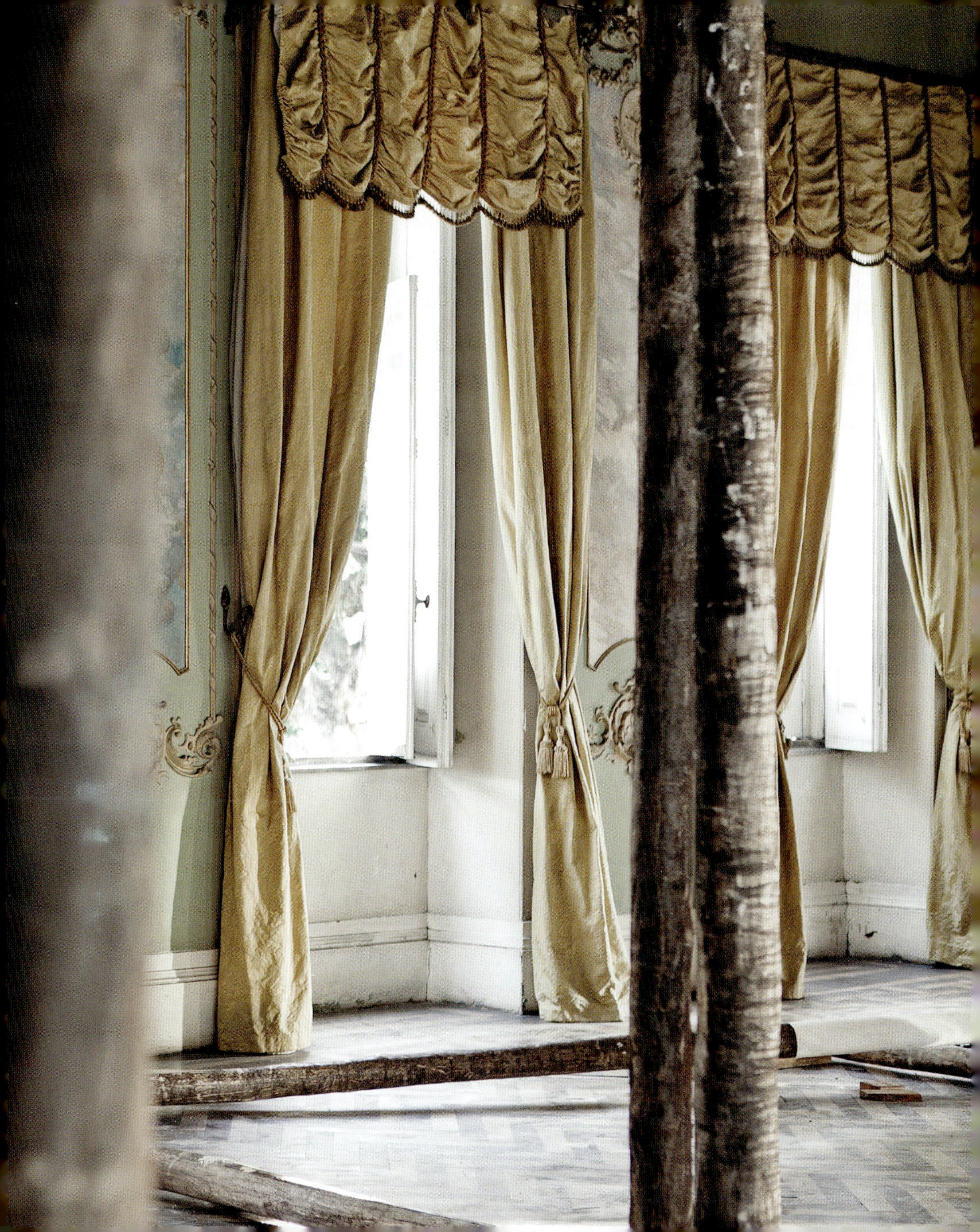

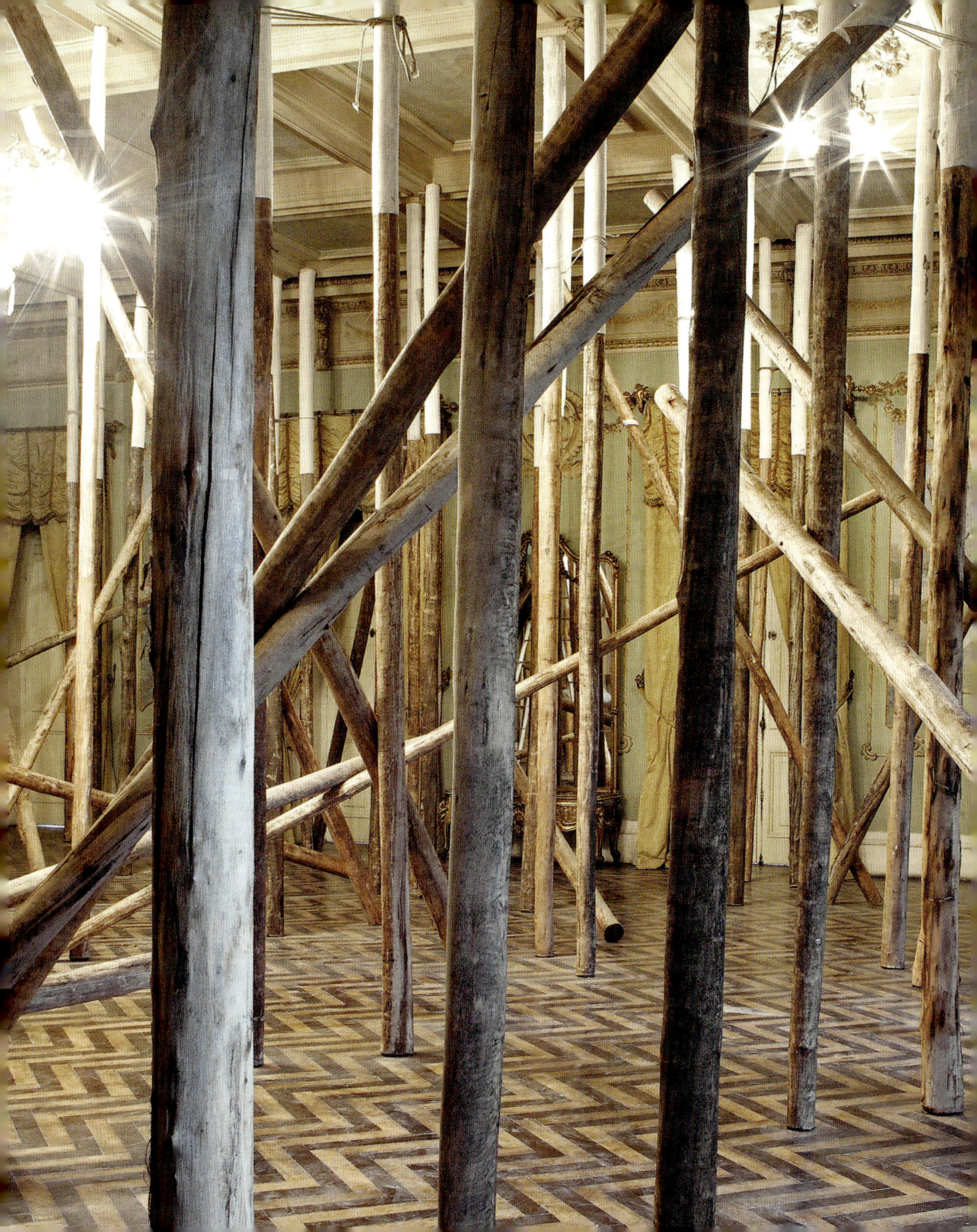

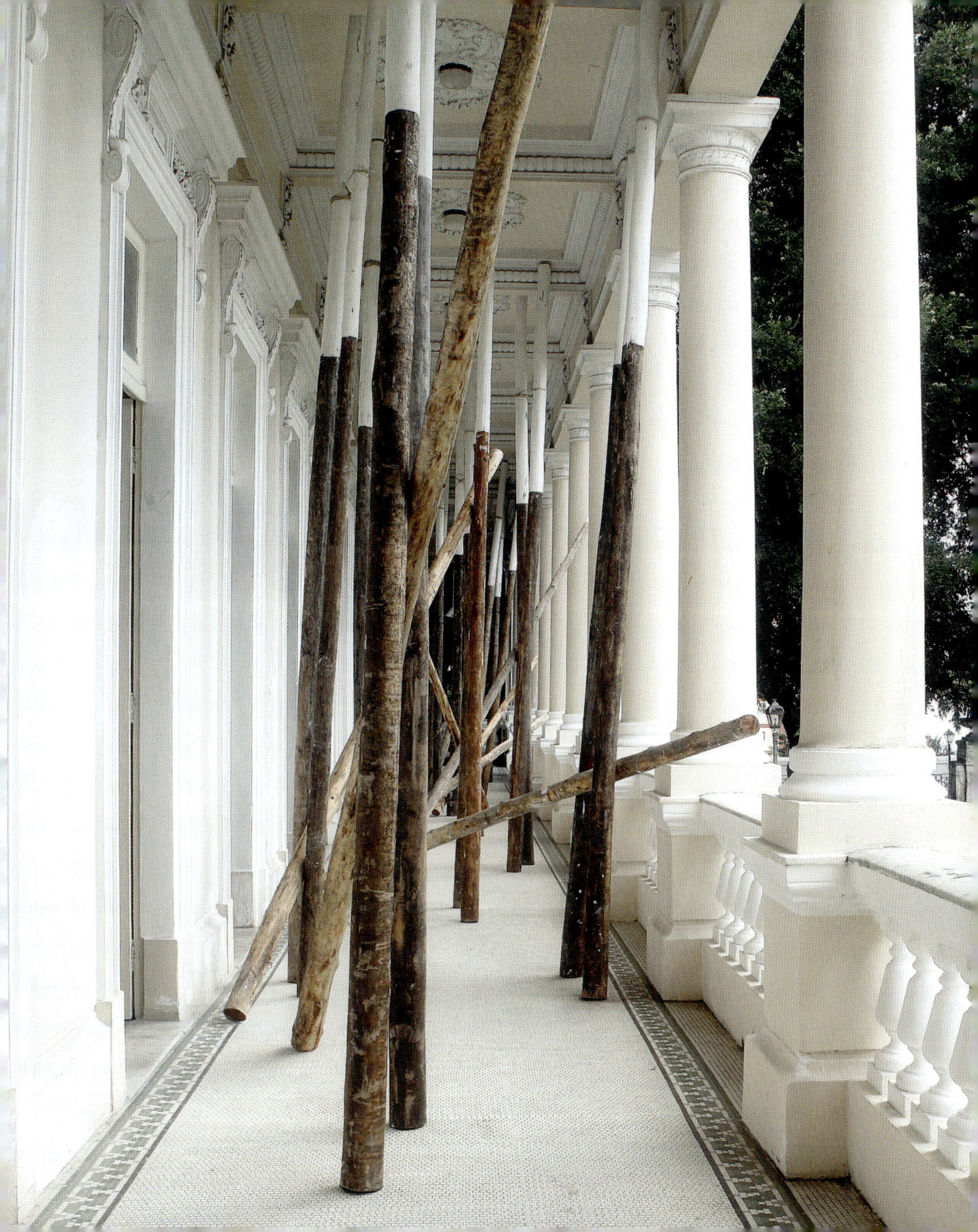

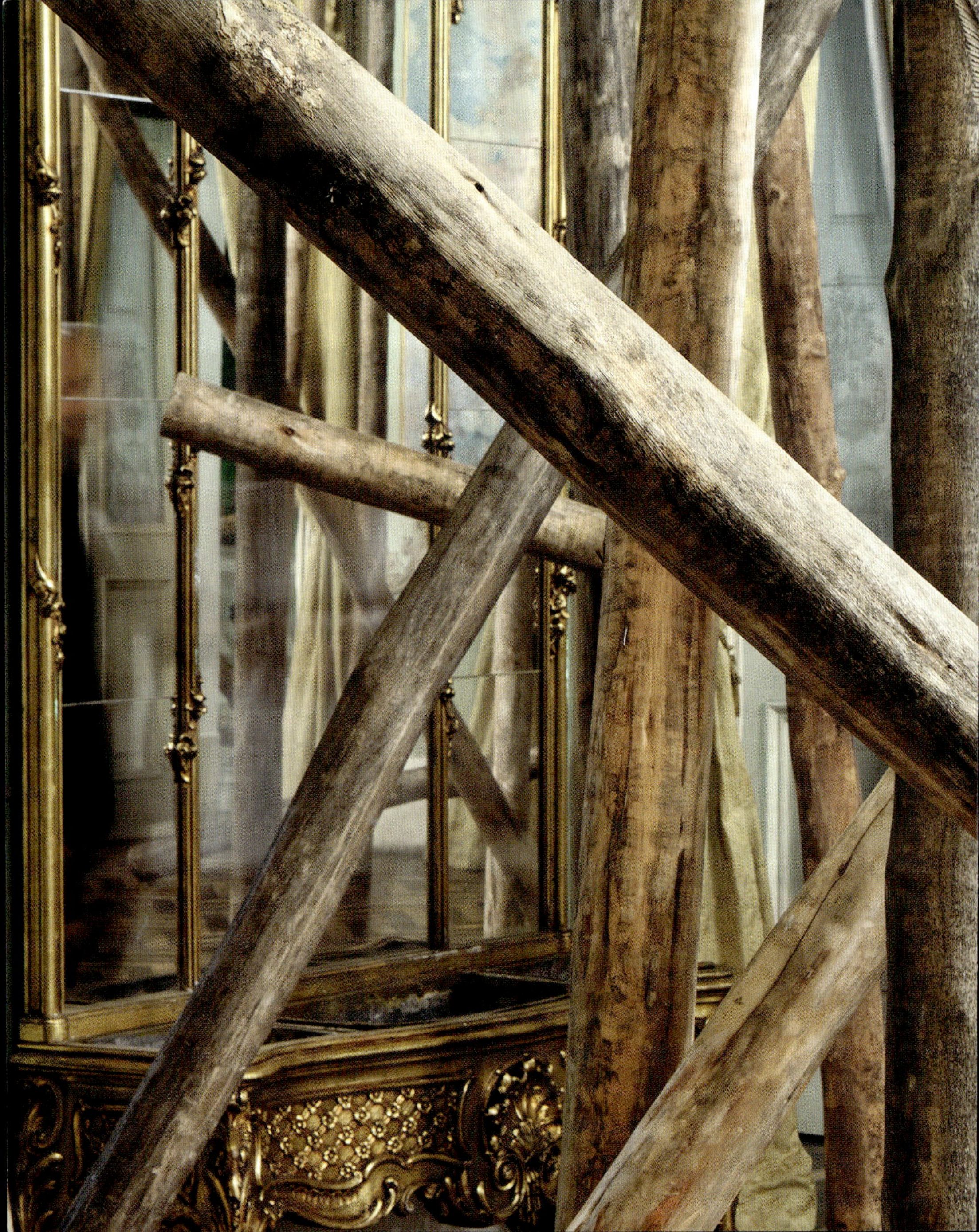

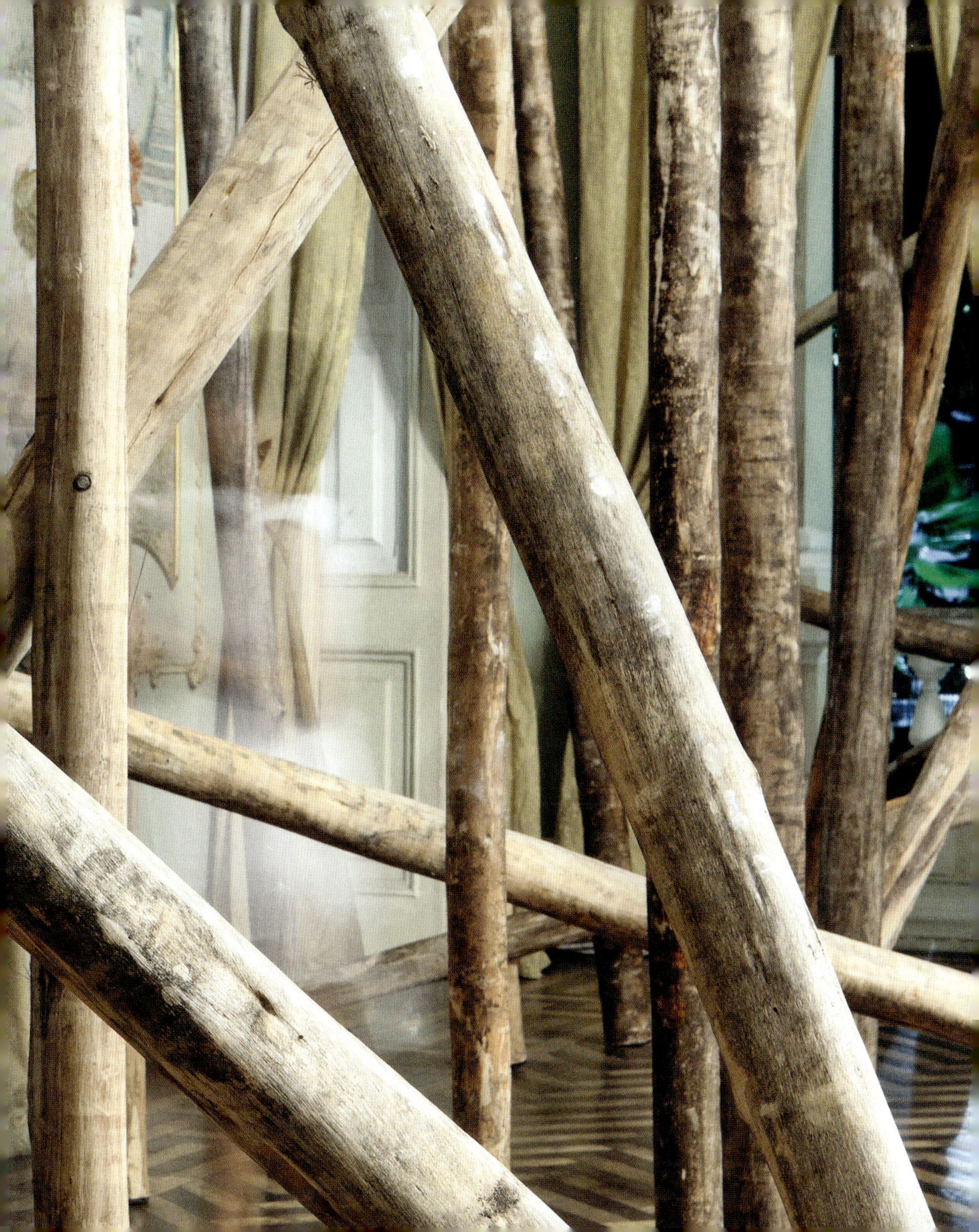

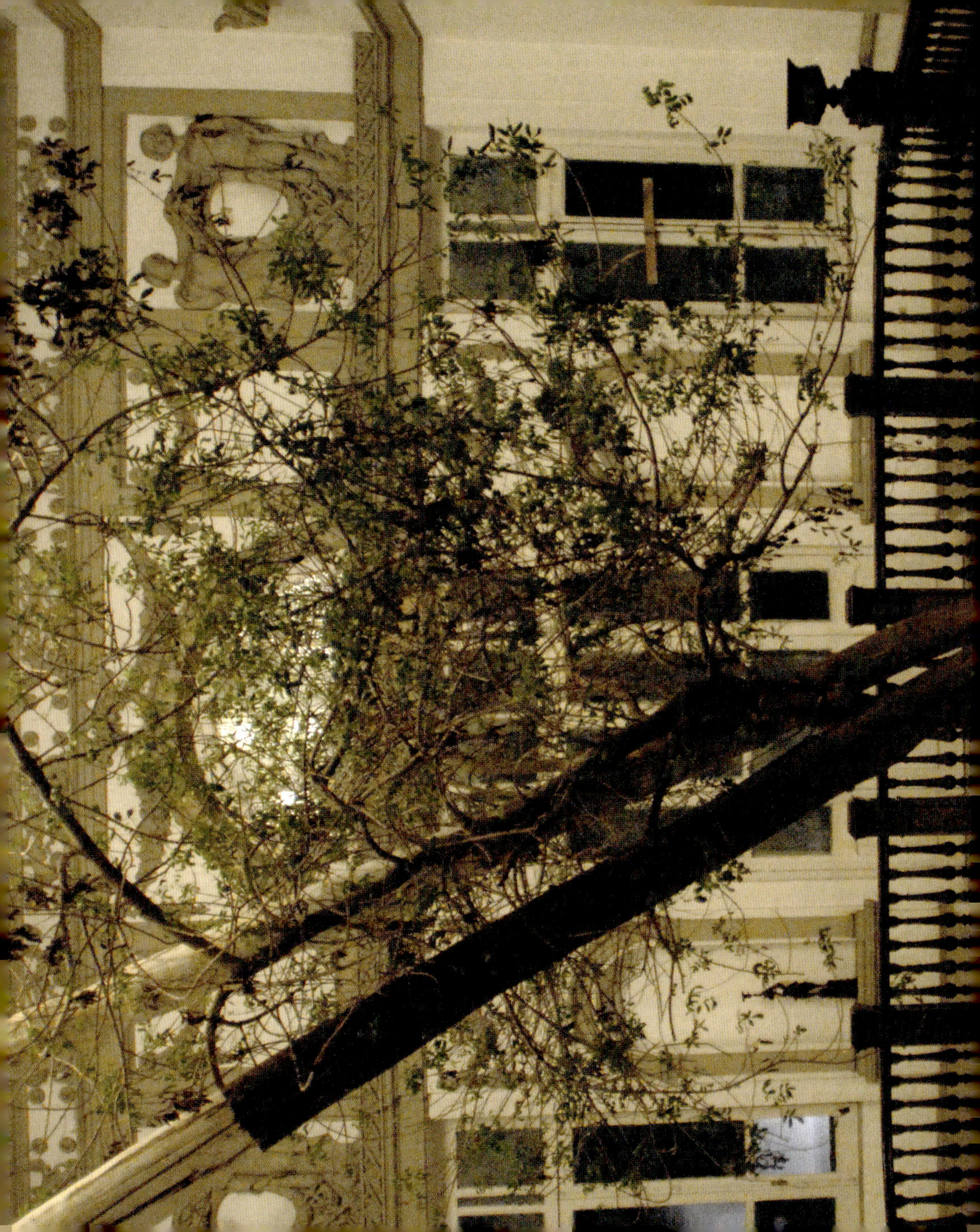

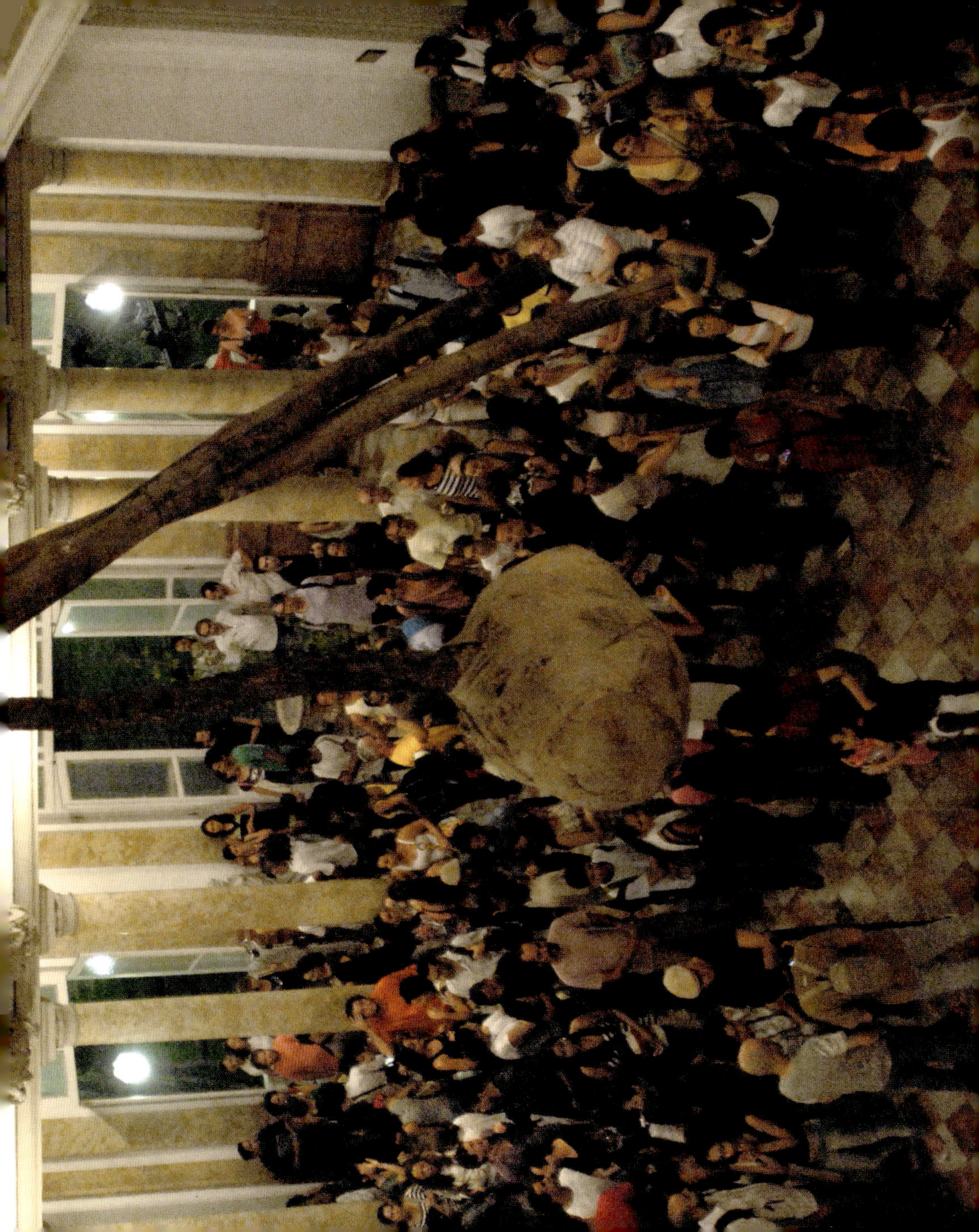

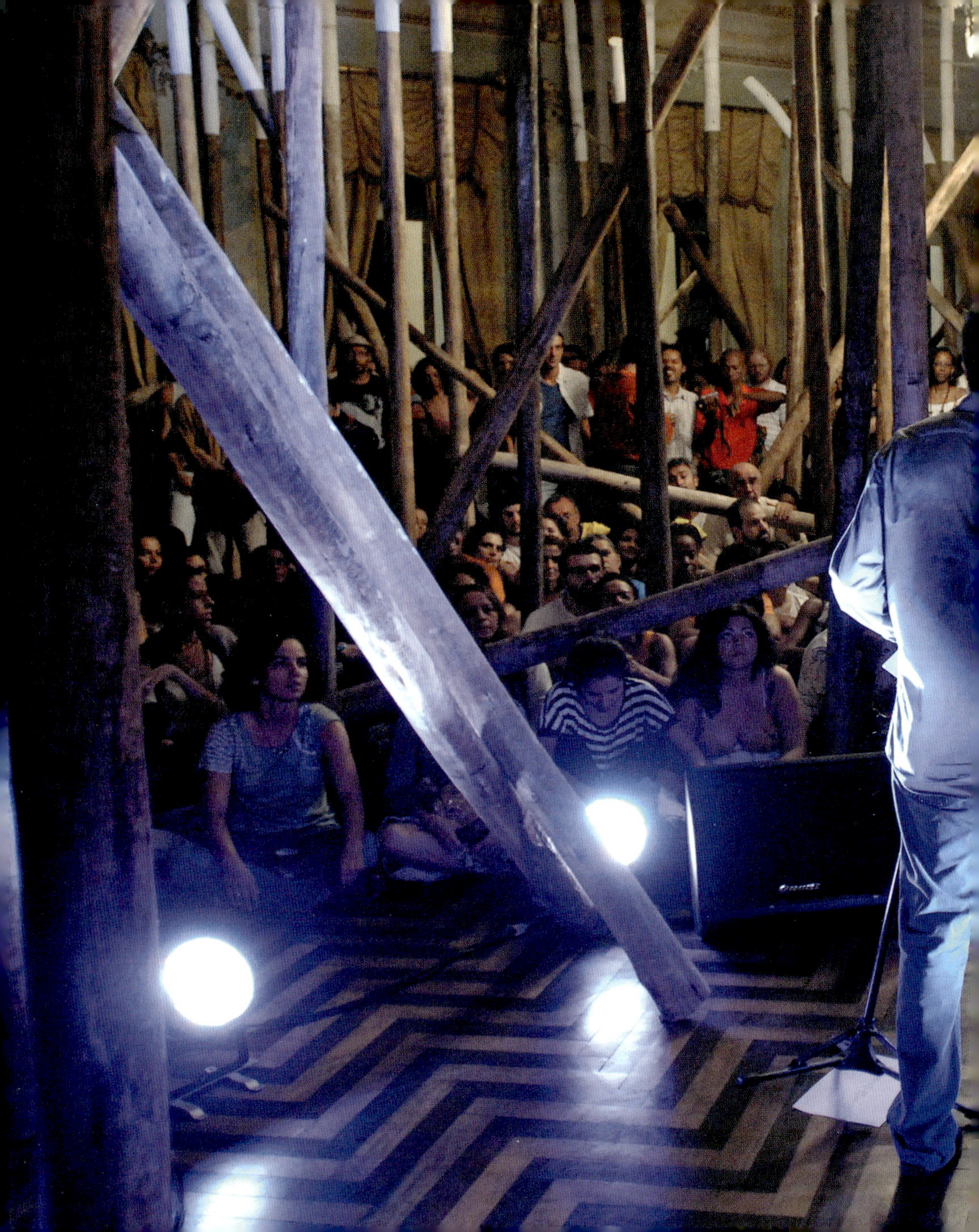

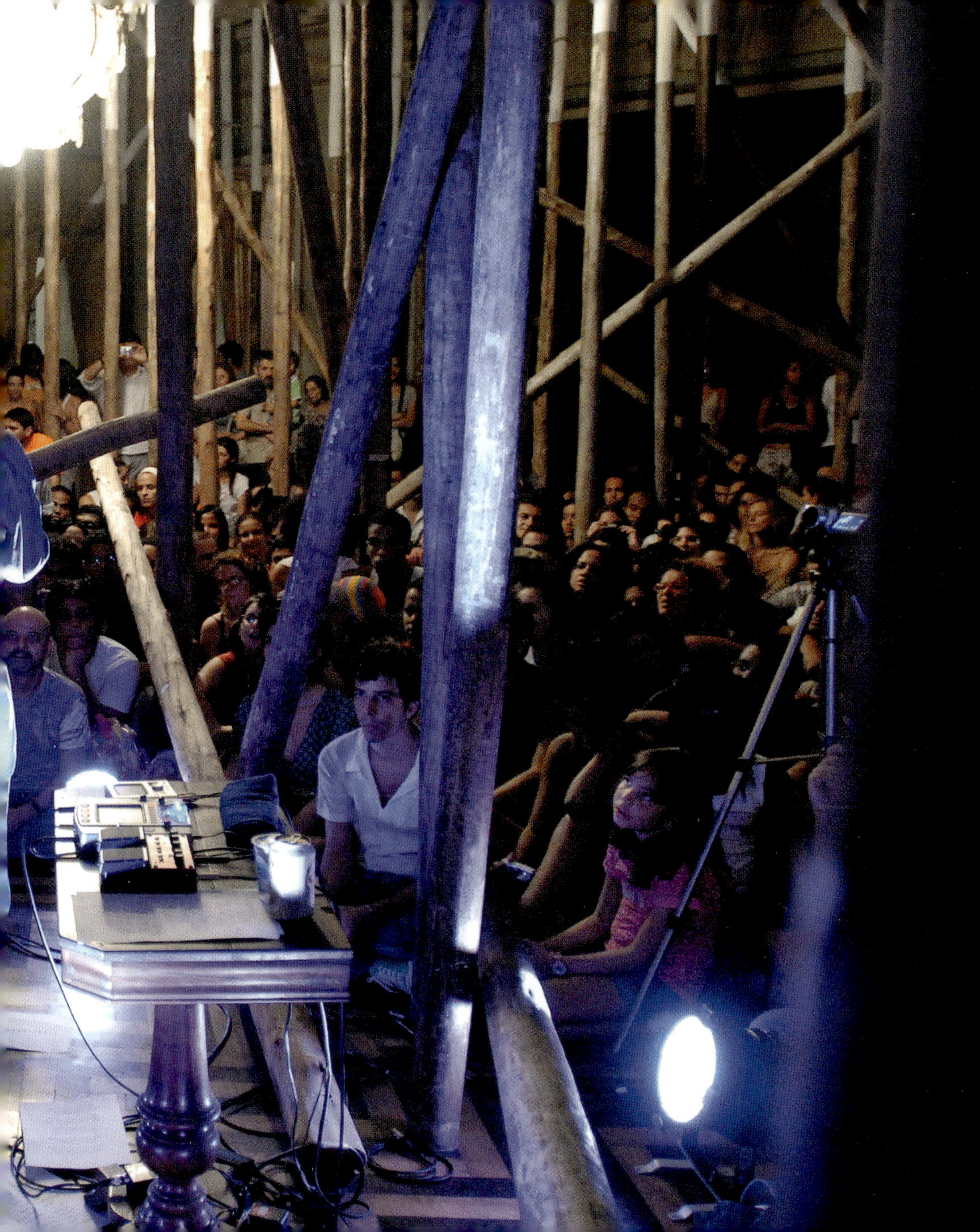

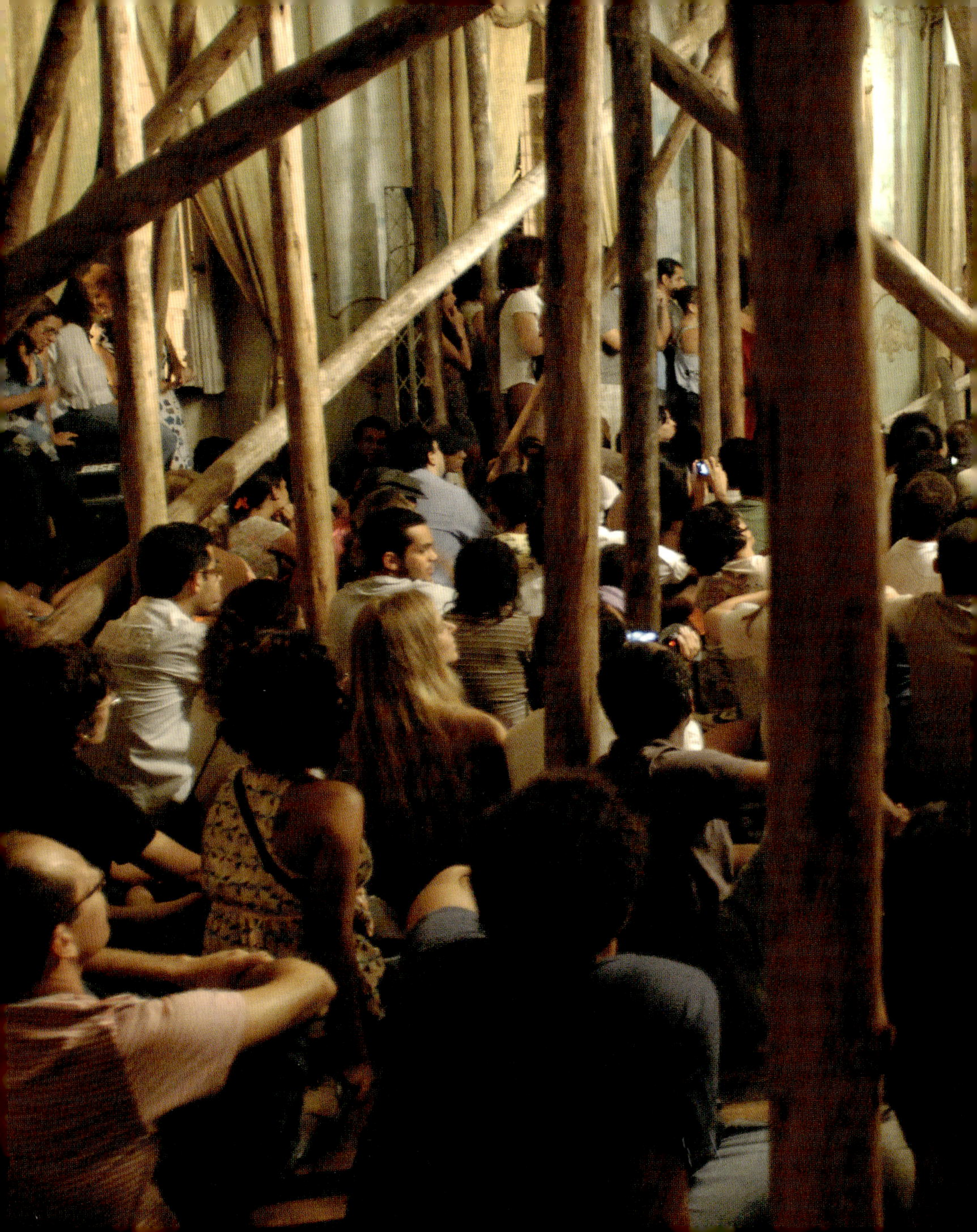

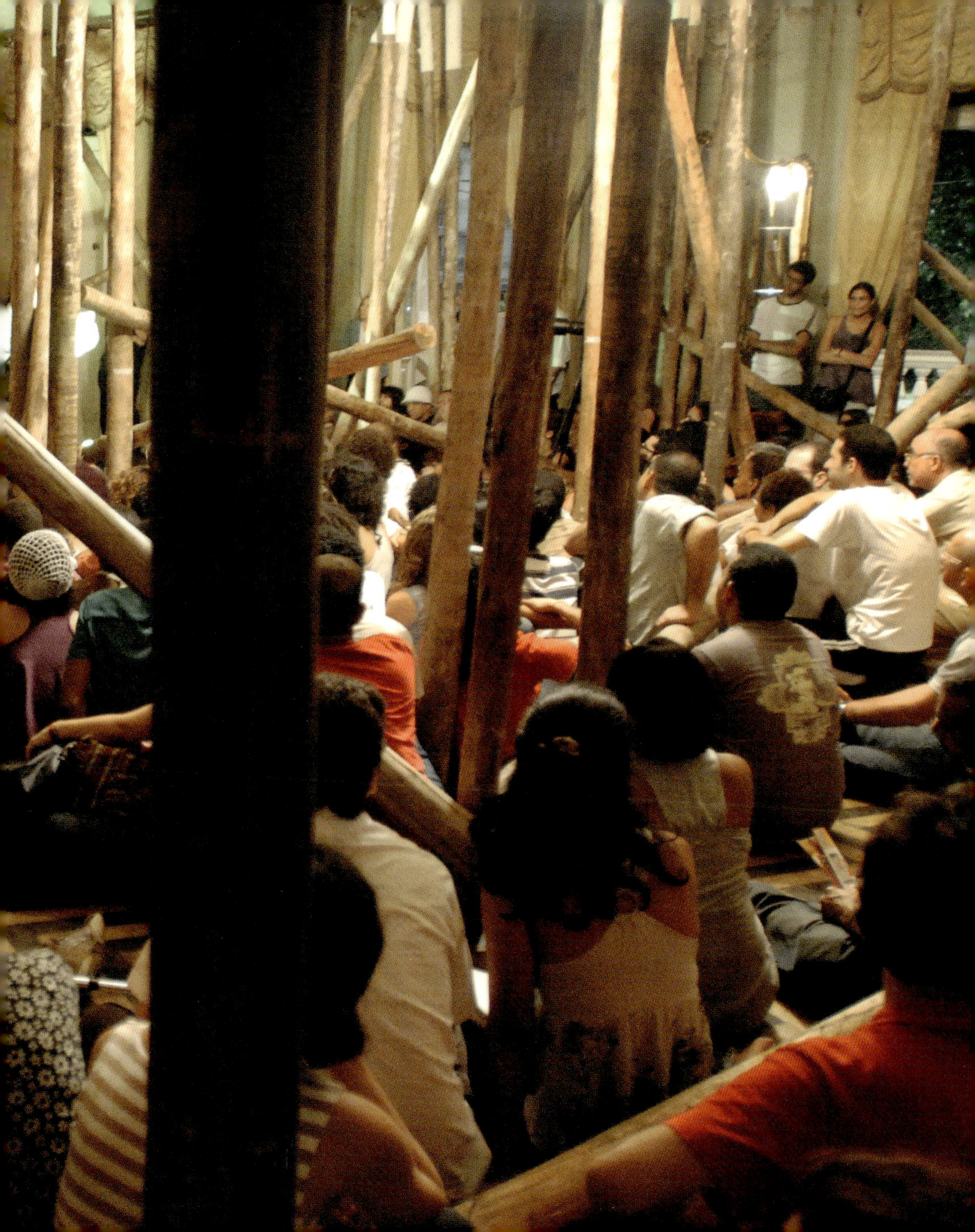

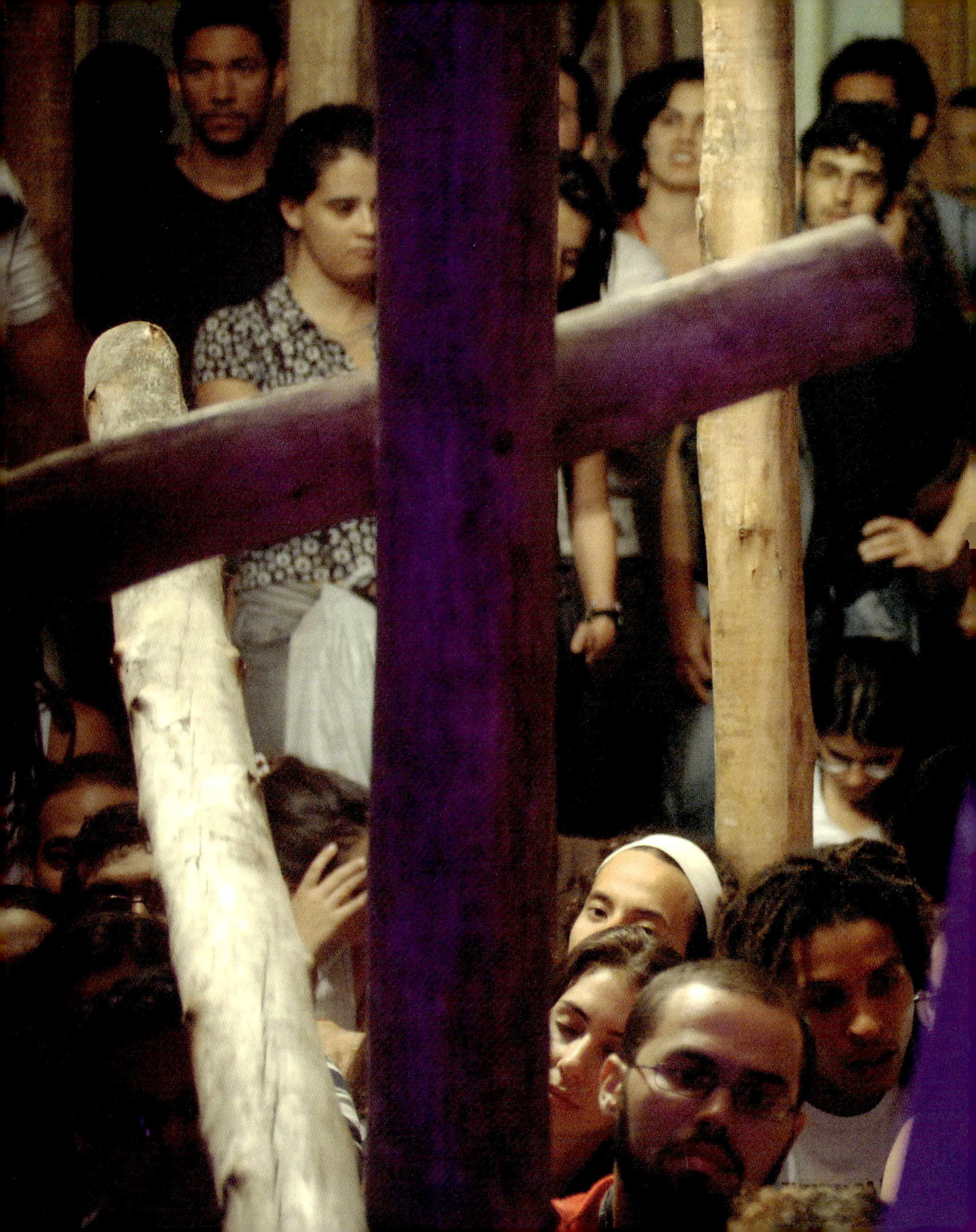

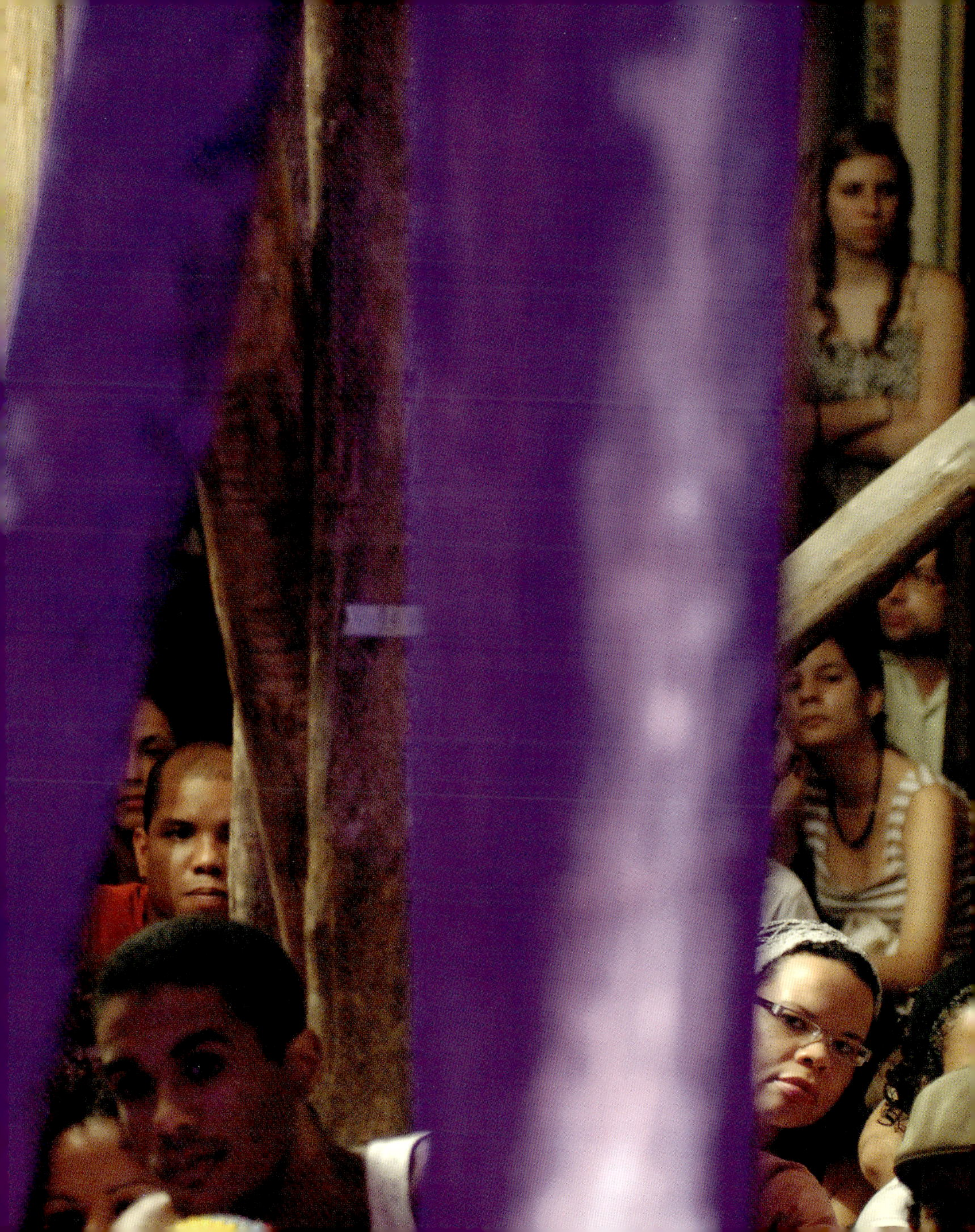

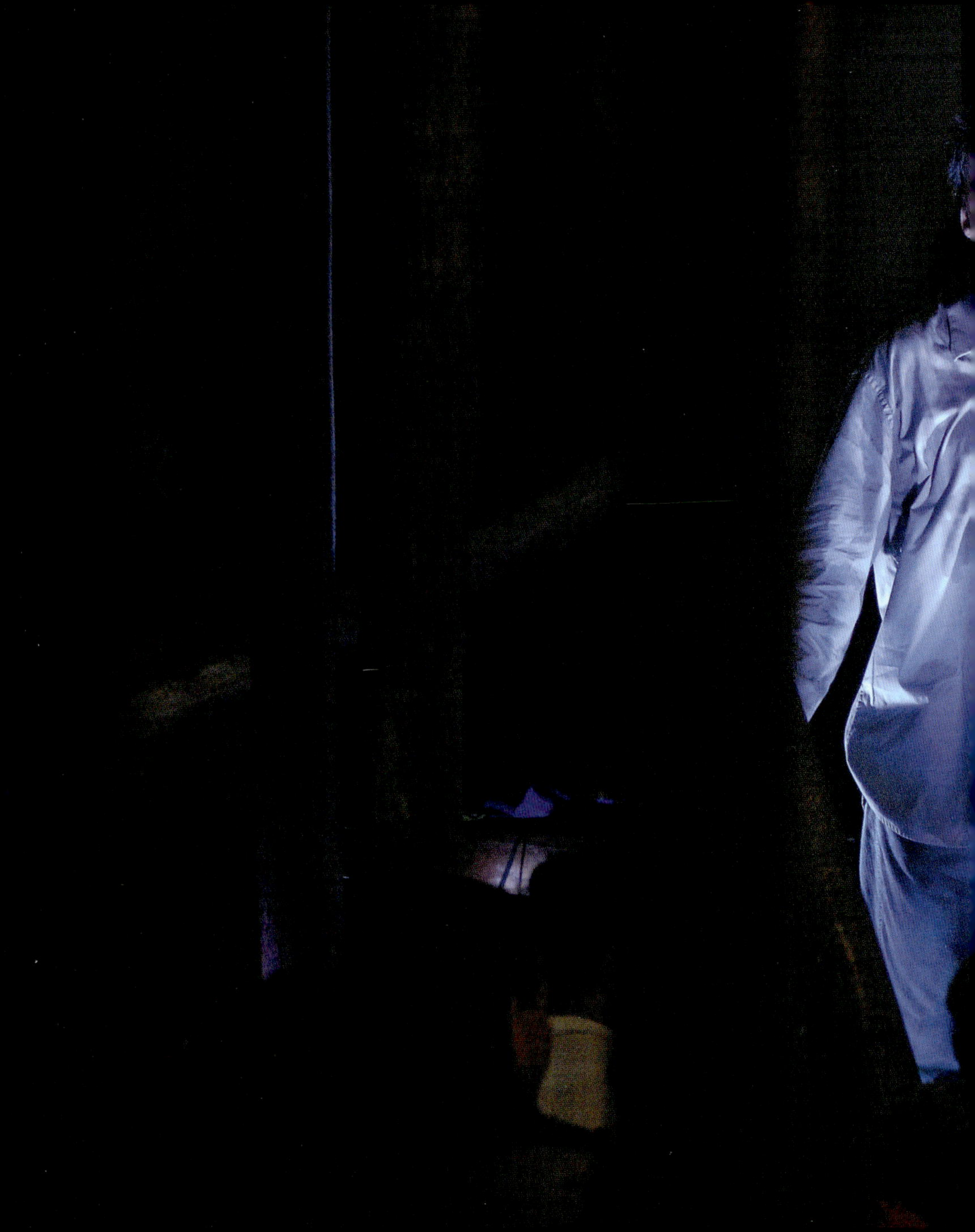

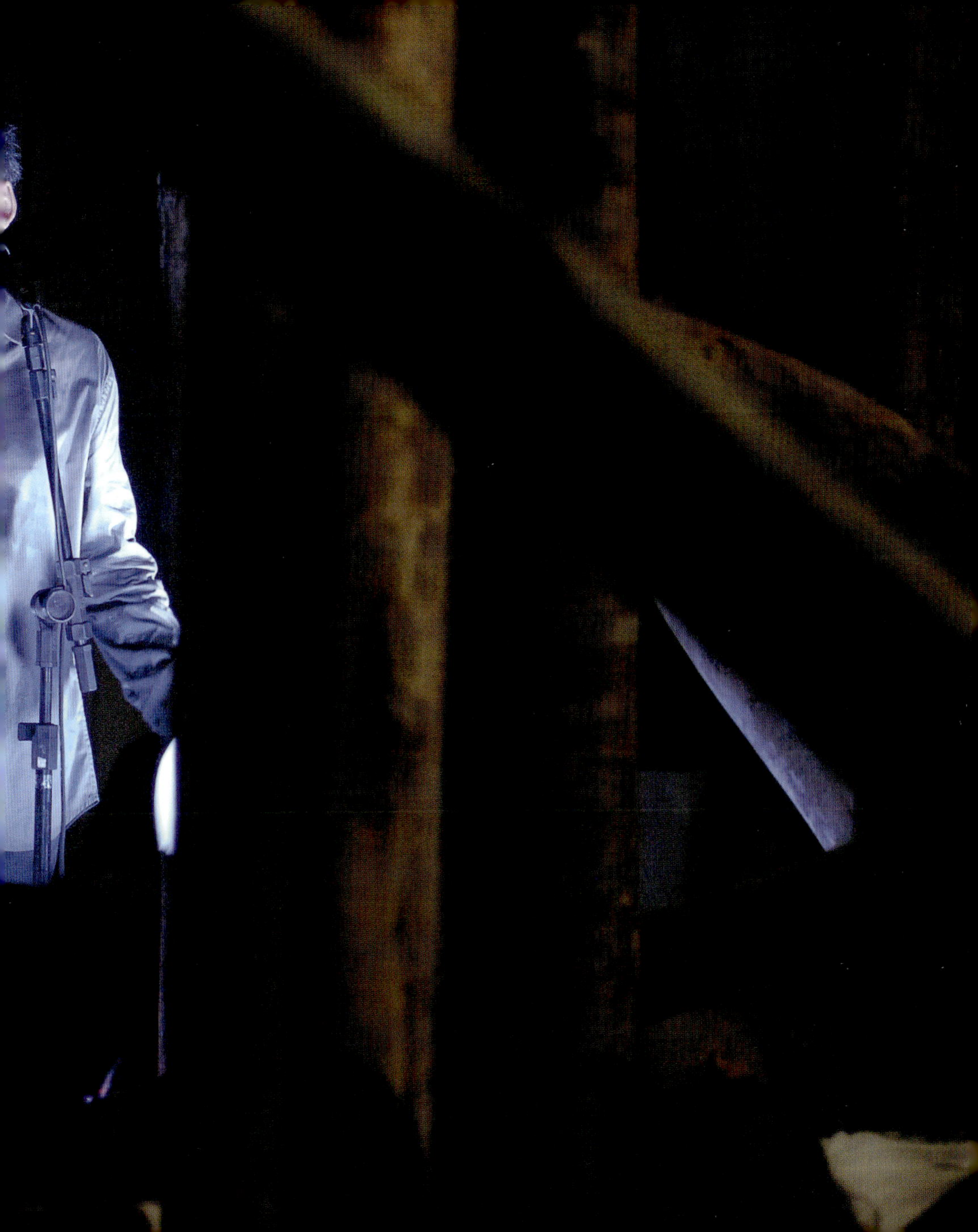

JÁ ESTAVA ASSIM QUANDO EU CHEGUEI

MUSEU DE ARTE MODERNA DO RIO DE JANEIRO, 2006
CURADORIA DE FERNANDO COCCHIARALE
GESSO, MADEIRA, FITAS DE CARGA, AÇO
6M DE ALTURA, 5X3M, 8.000 KG
AO LADO DO MAM, DO OUTRO LADO DA BAÍA, VÊ-SE
O PÃO DE AÇÚCAR. A PEÇA TENTA LEMBRAR COMO
ELE É. UM RETRATO DE MEMÓRIA. NÃO DEI UM NOME,
AFINAL ELE JÁ ESTAVA LÁ. PENDURADO, INVERTIDO,
LEMBRA UMA IMAGEM NA CÂMARA ESCURA. UMA PEÇA
ARRANCADA DA BASE. A PAISAGEM VIRA OBRA
O MUSEU VIRA PAISAGEM

It Was Like This When I Got Here

Museu de Arte Moderna do Rio de Janeiro, 2006

Curated by Fernando Cocchiarale
Plaster, wood, ratchet straps, steel
6m h, 5 x 3m, 8,000 kg
Next to MAM, on the other side of the bay, you can see the Sugarloaf.
The piece tries to remember what it's like. A portrait of memory.
I didn't name it, after all, it was already there. Hung, inverted, it reminds one of an image in a camera obscura. A piece pulled from its base.
The landscape is the work. The museum is the landscape.

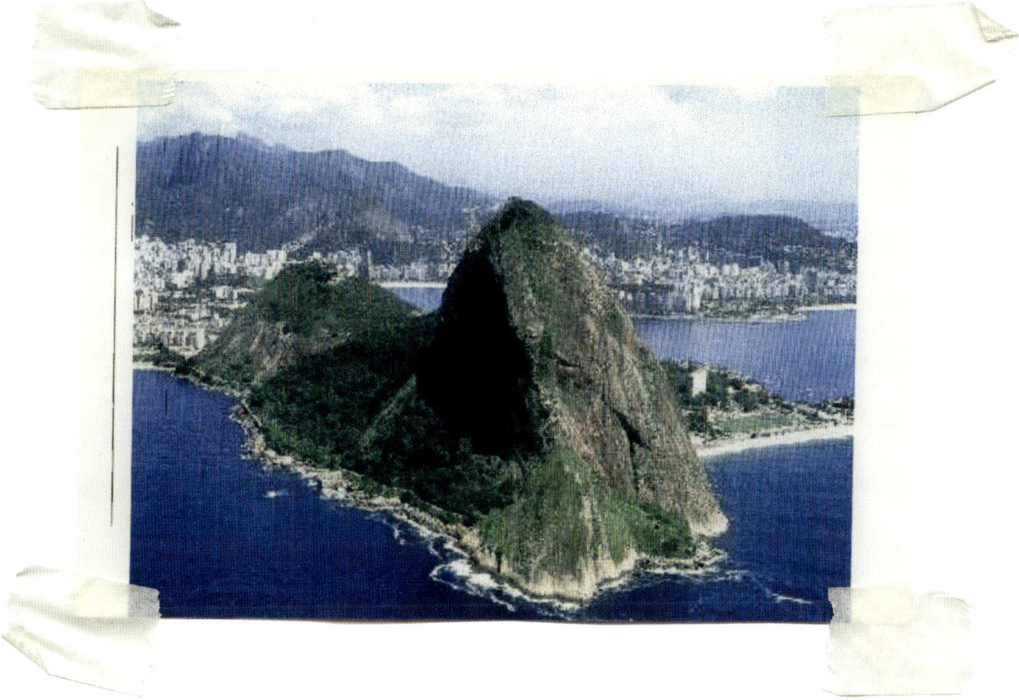

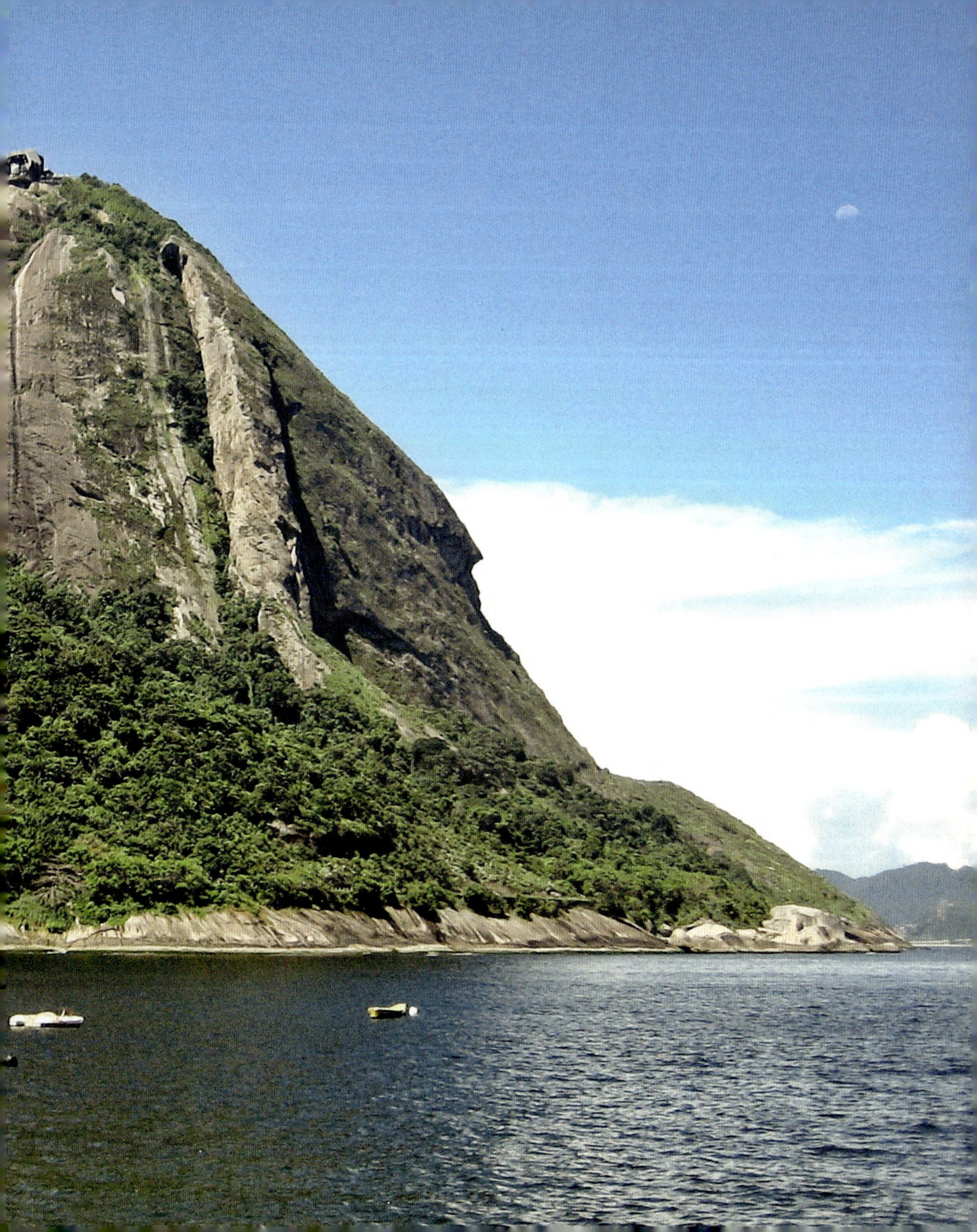

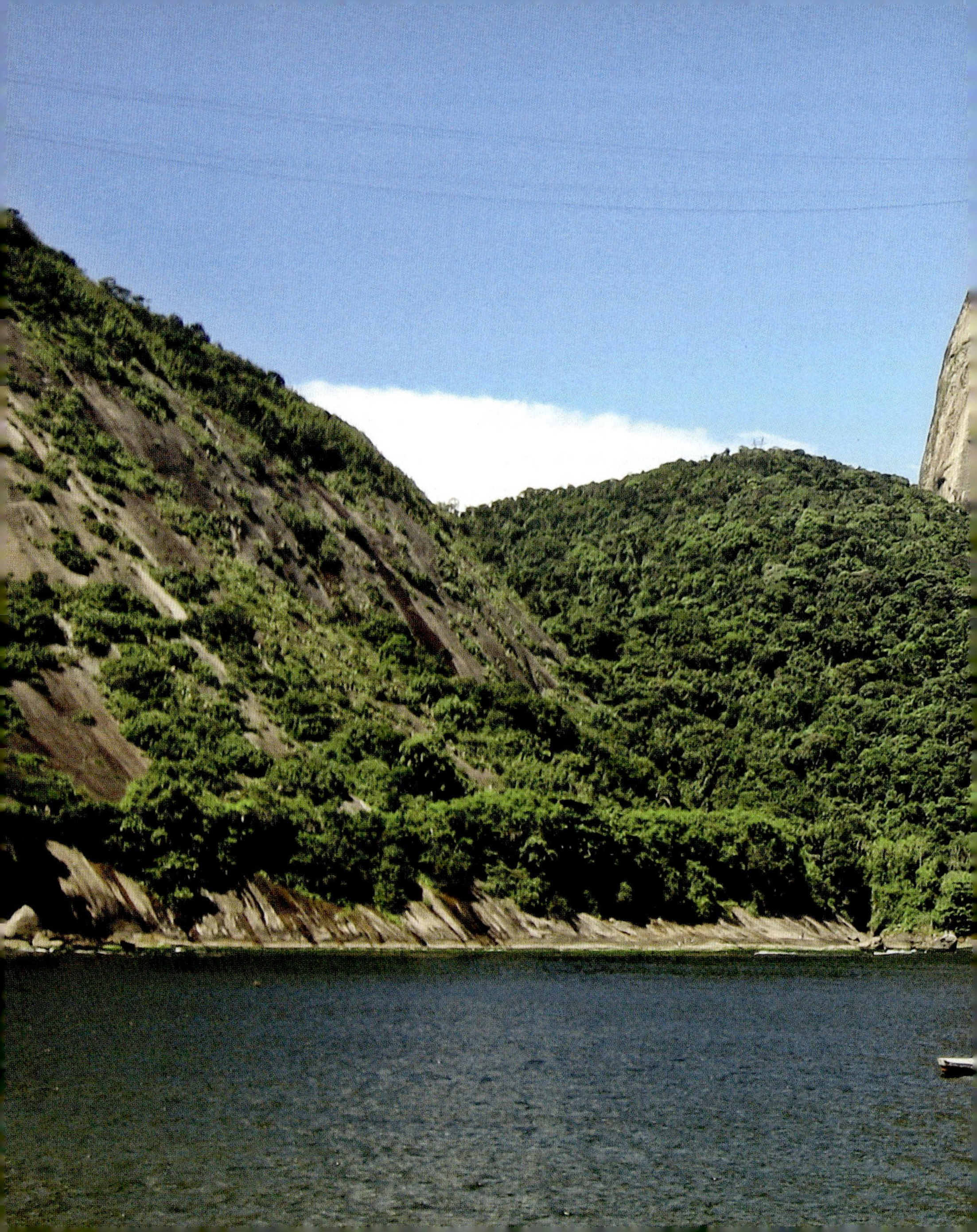

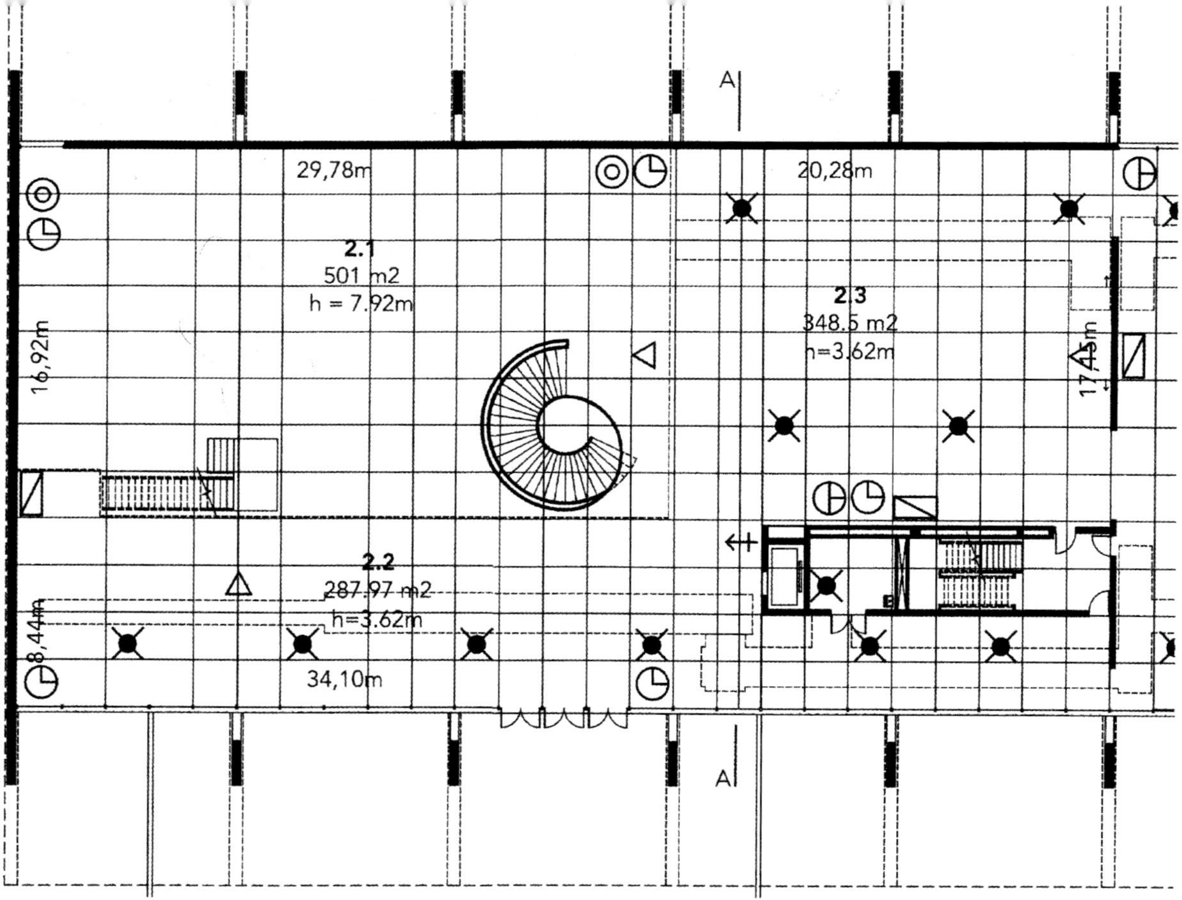

/P

360°

°

derna

Pavimento 2 - Espaços Monumental/2.2/2.3

data 10/10/2001

desenho Fernanda Barata

1/1

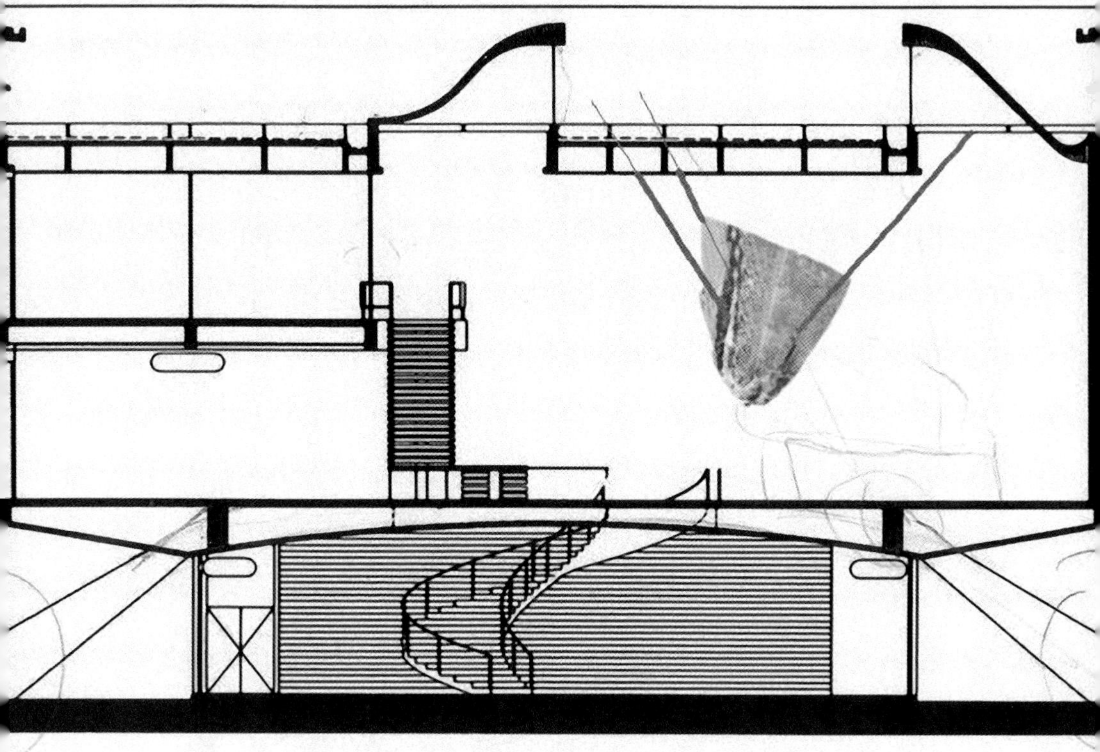

Corte A Foyer

Rio de Janeiro RJ Brasil I T +55 (21) 2240 5432 I F +55 (21) 2240 4899 I design@mamrio

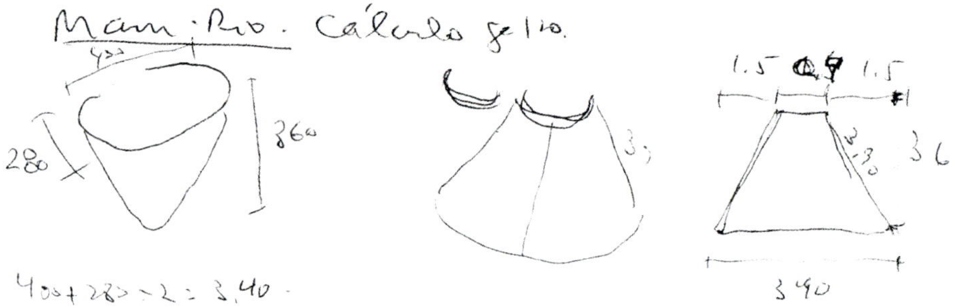
280
1.5
1.5
3.90
3 6
3.40

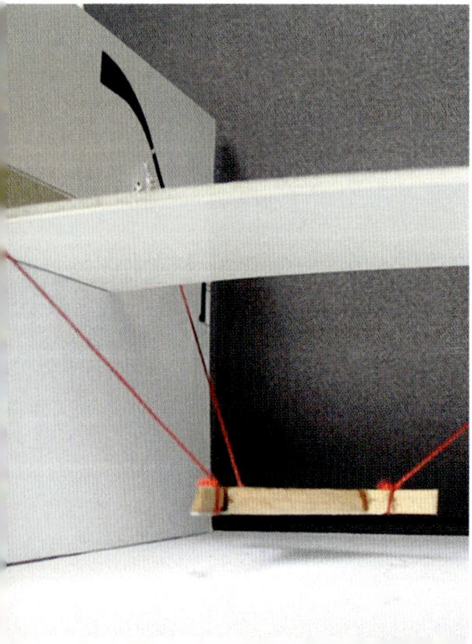

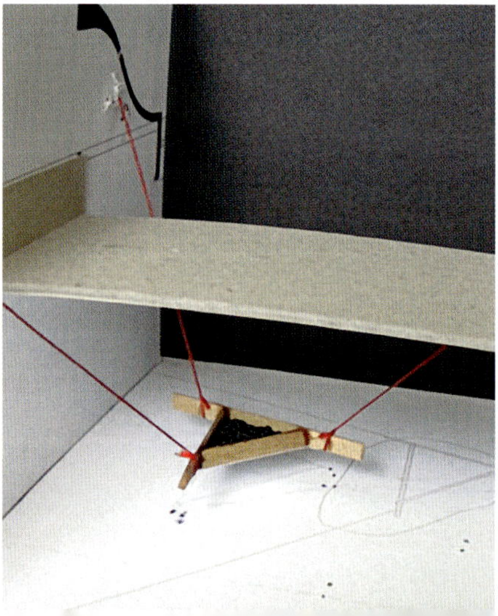

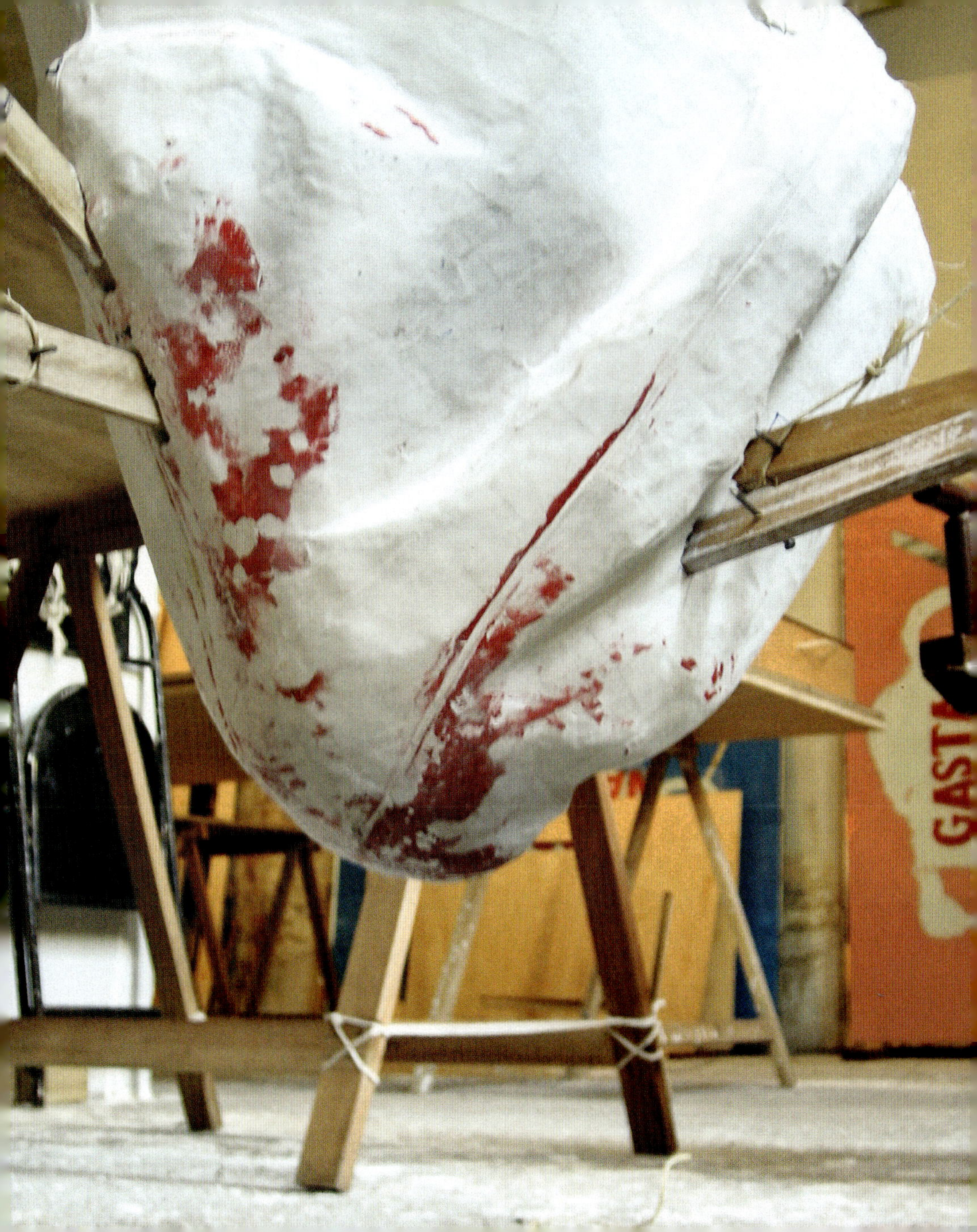

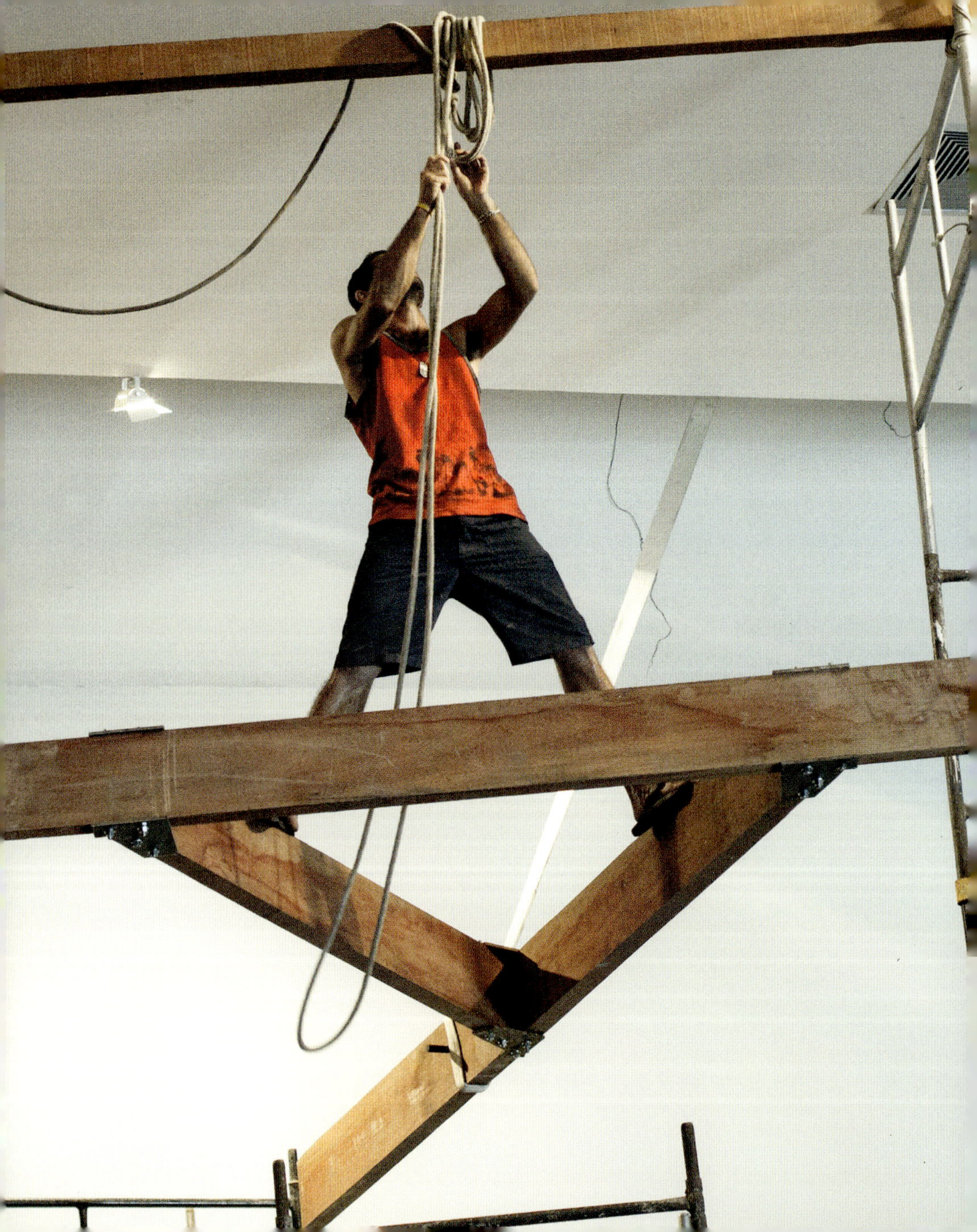

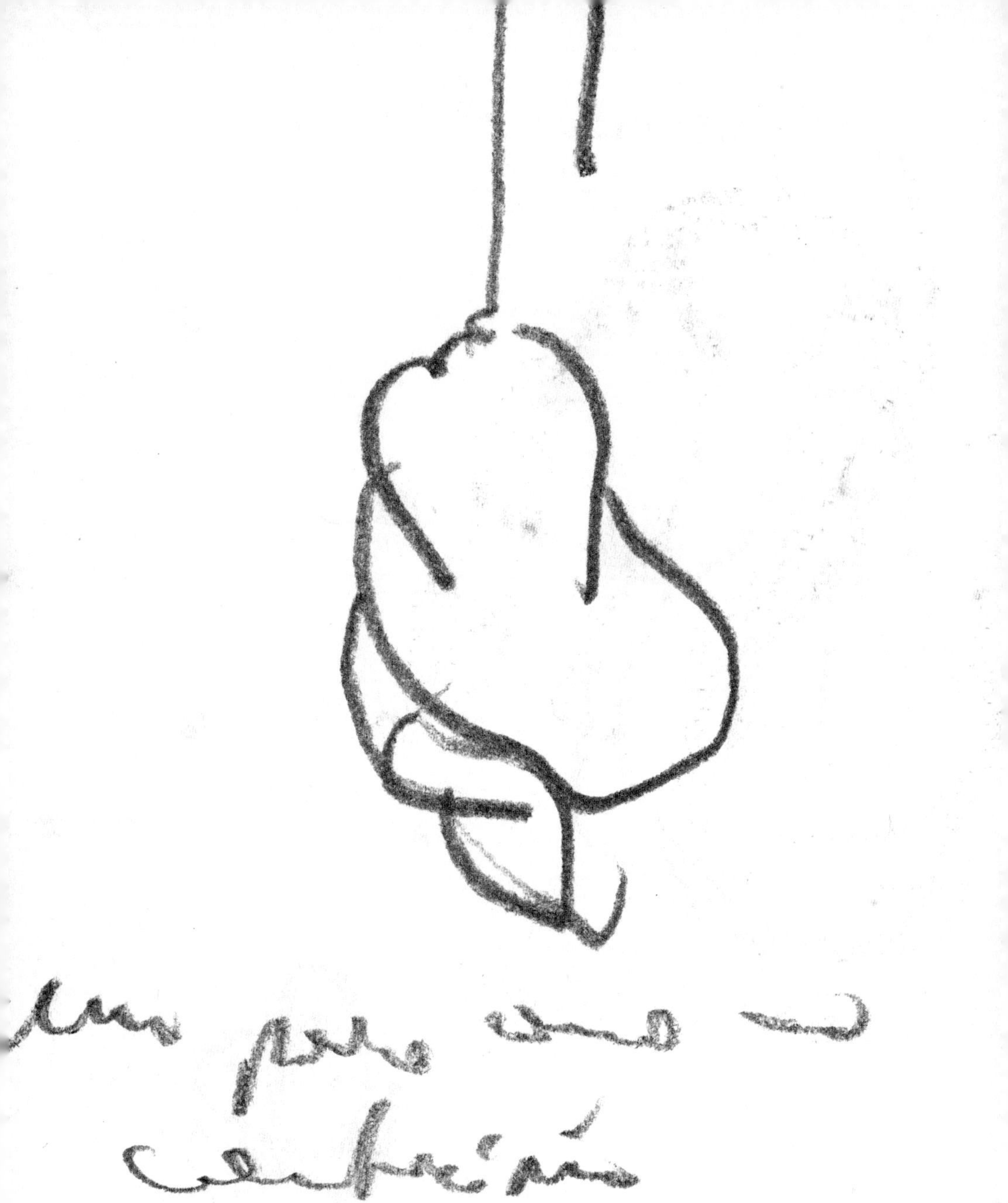

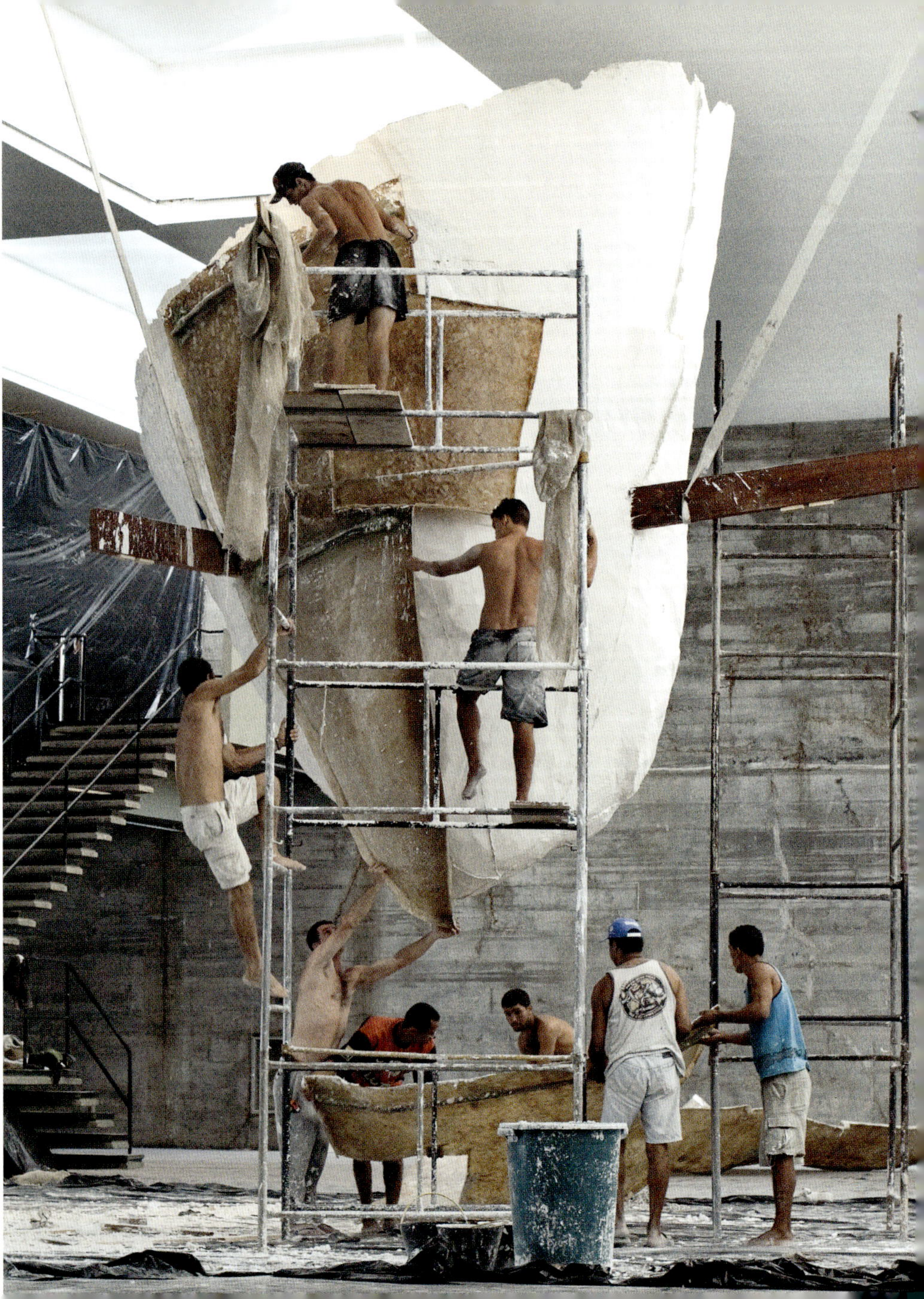

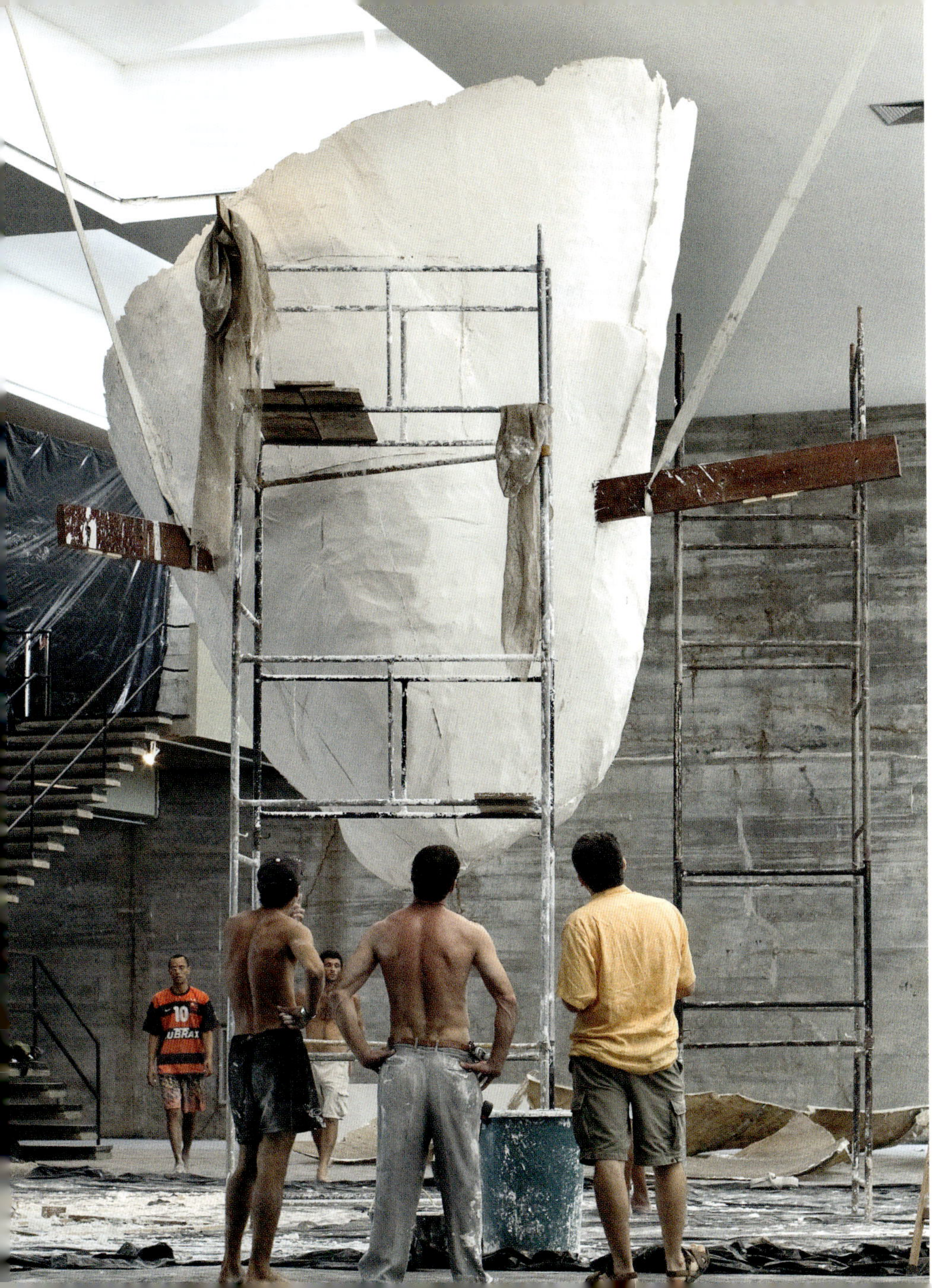
10
UBRAX

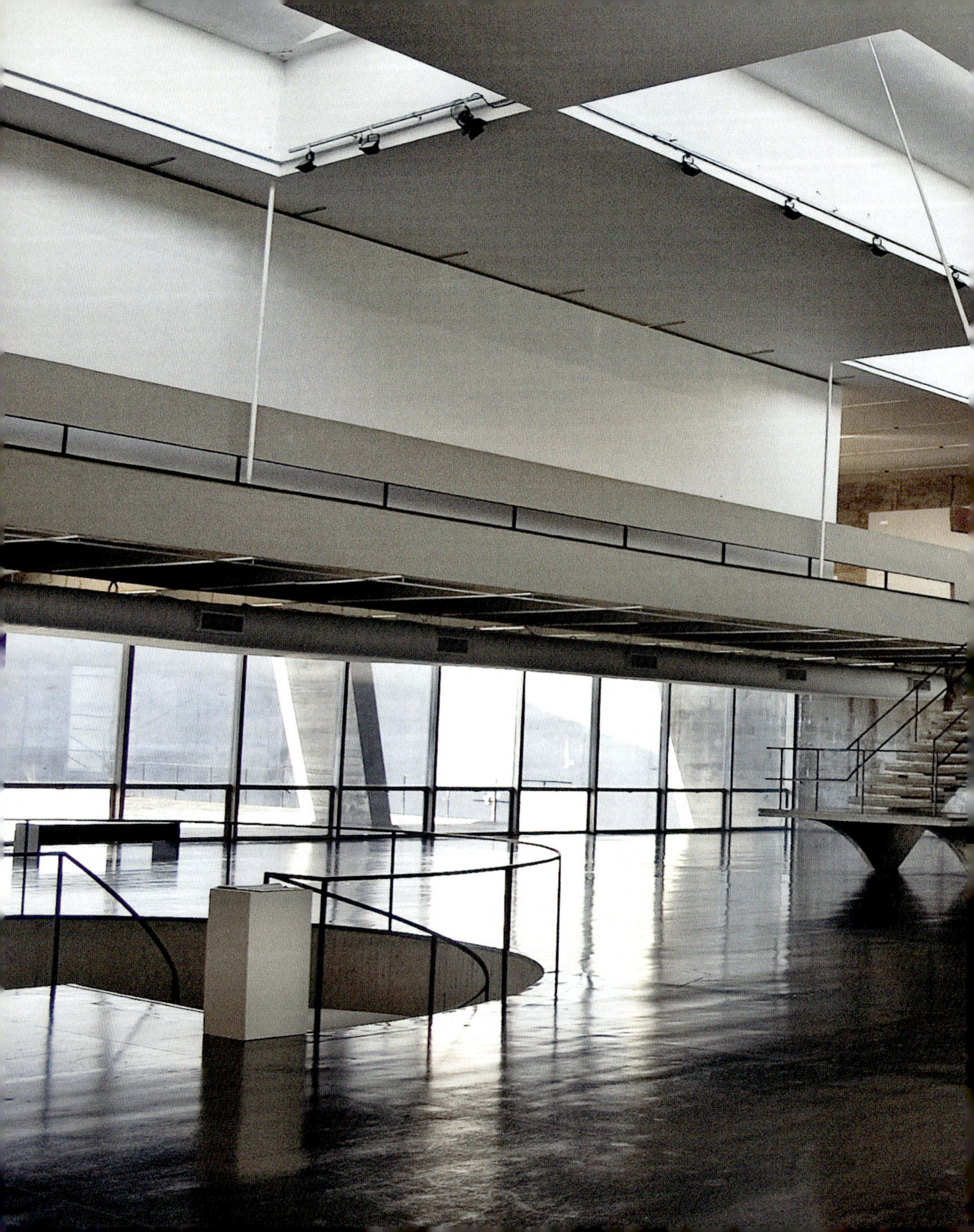

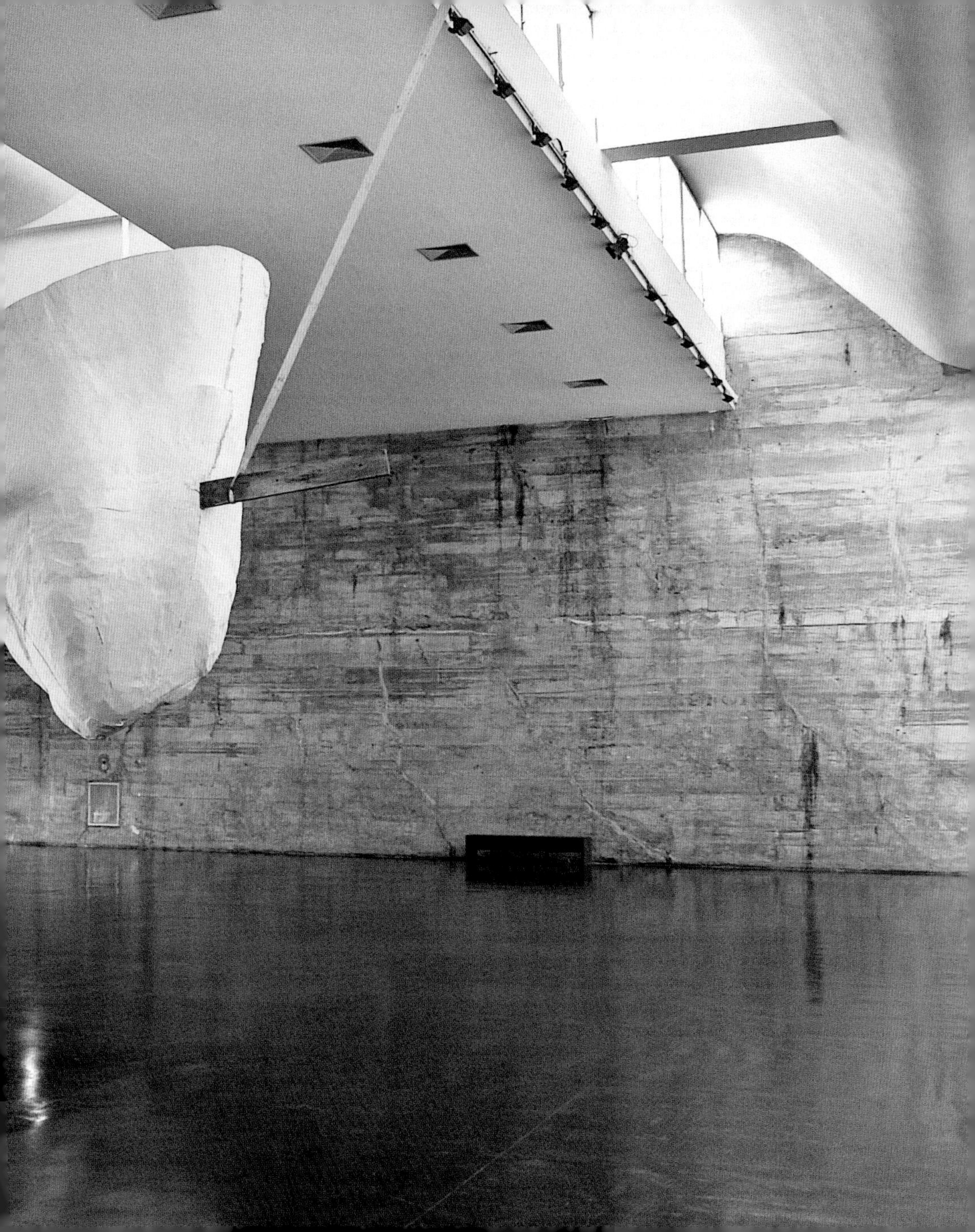

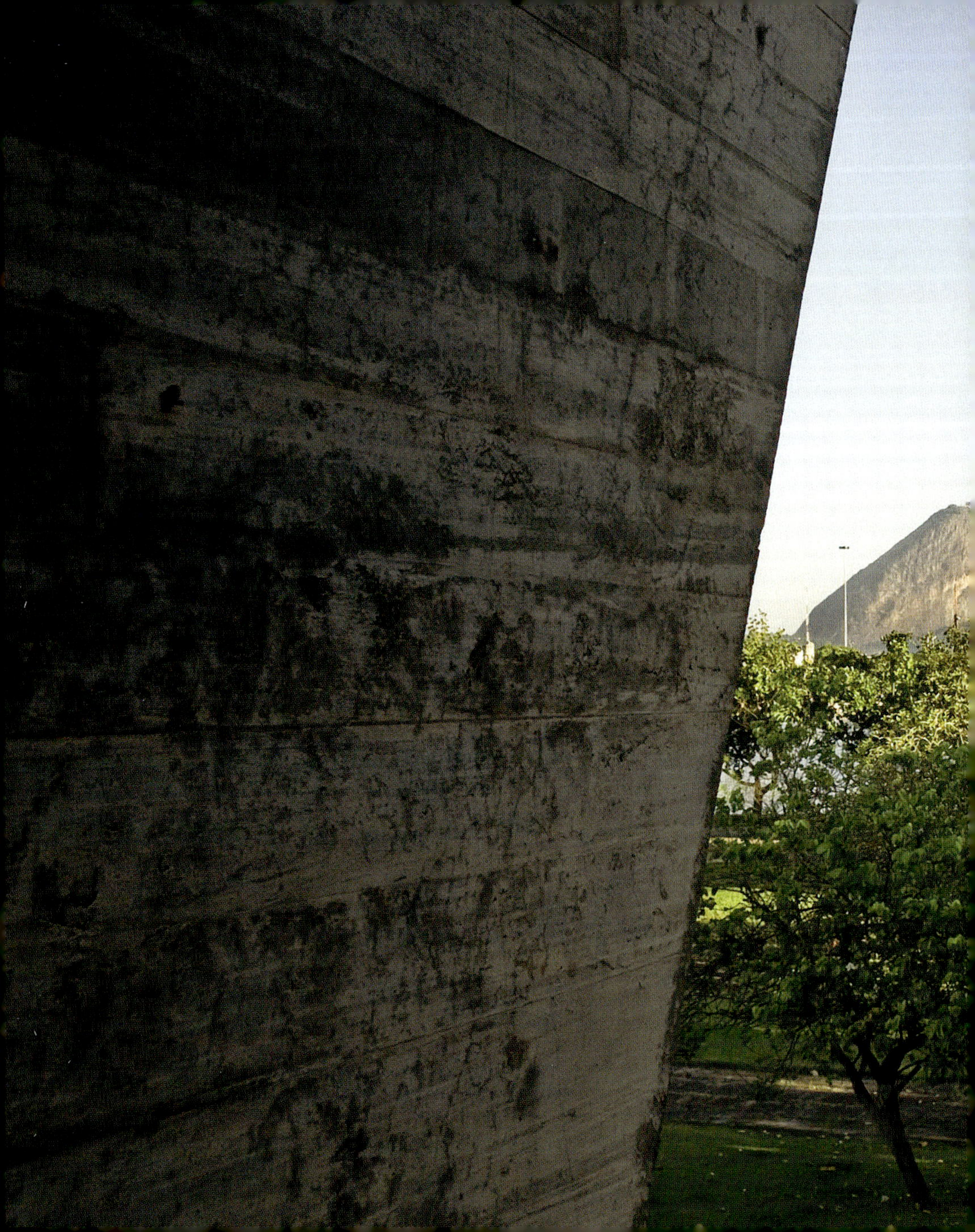

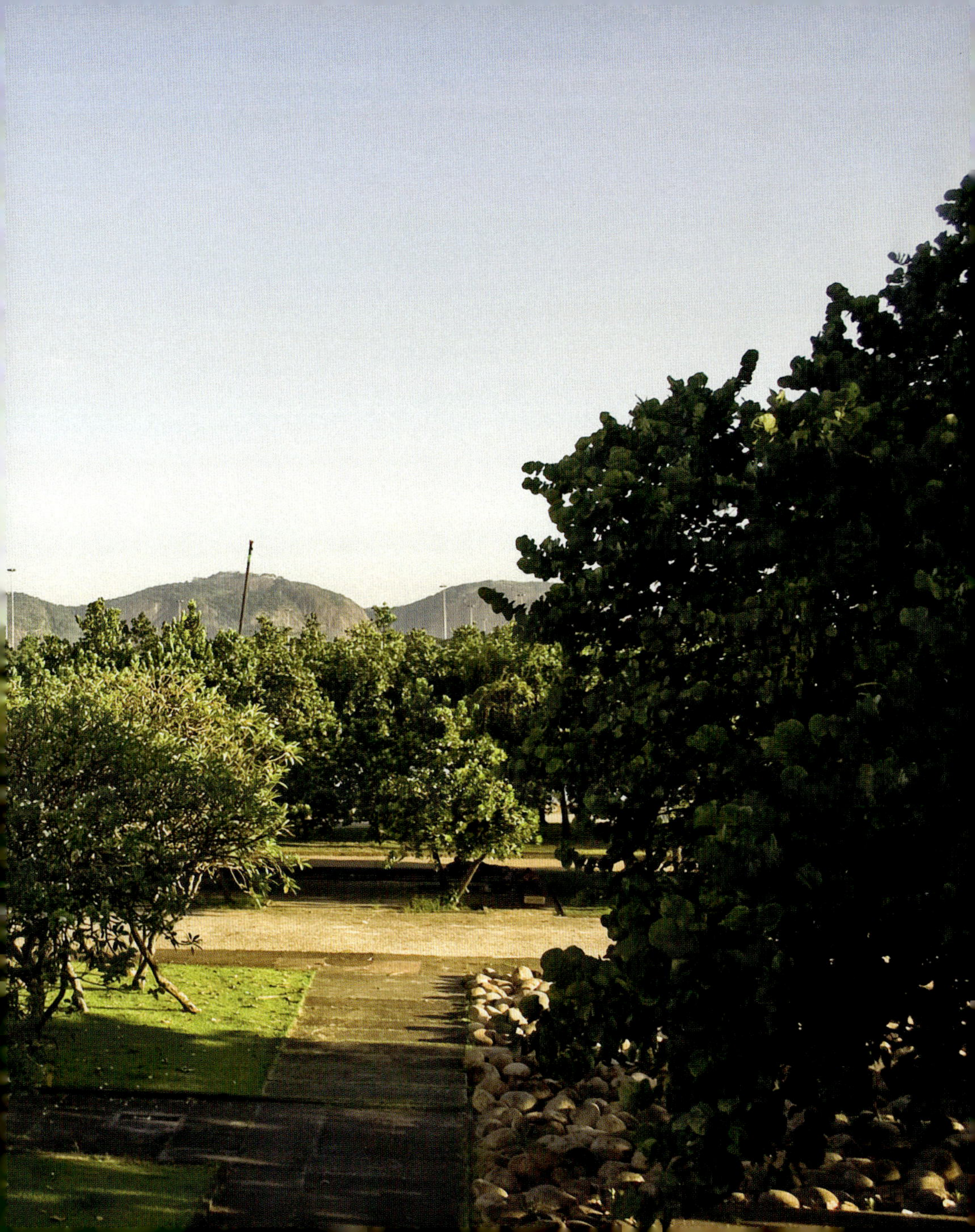

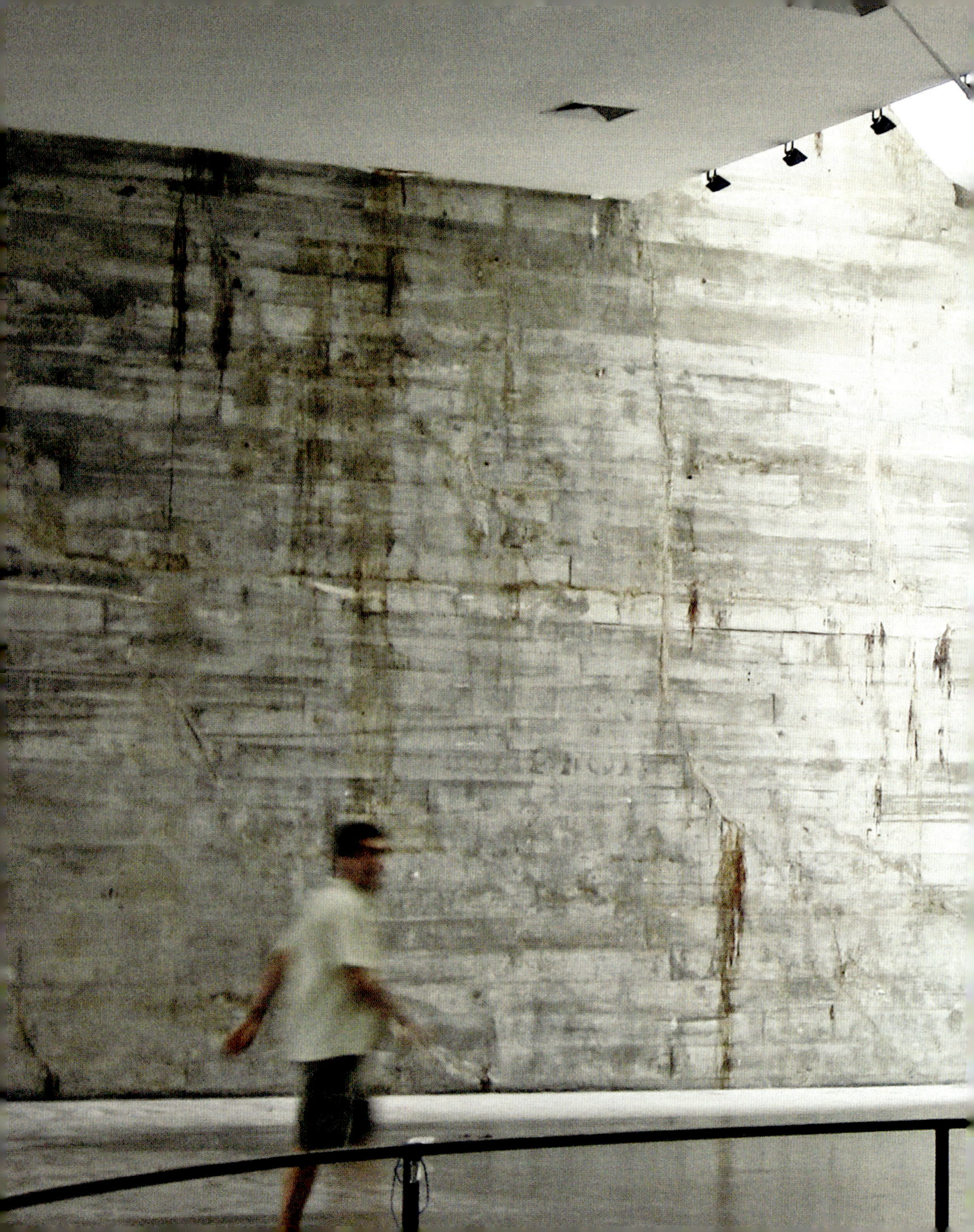

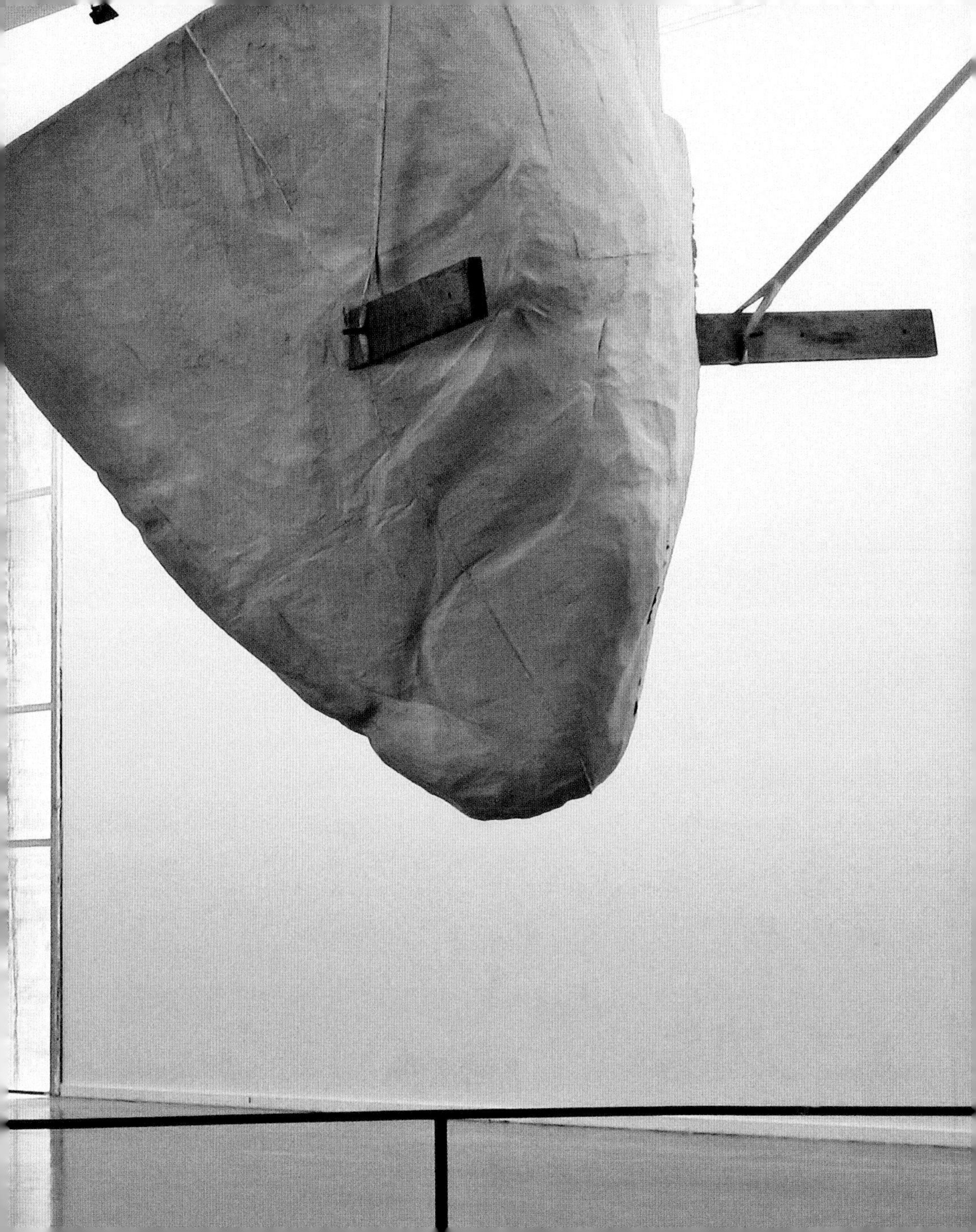

FAVOR NÃO TOCAR

CENTRO UNIVERSITÁRIO MARIA ANTONIA, SÃO PAULO, 2004
CURADORIA DE LORENZO MAMMÌ
GESSO
1,5M DE ALTURA, 5M X 3,5M, 9.000 KG
NÃO ERA POSSÍVEL APOIAR A PEÇA NO CHÃO.
RESOLVI SOLTÁ-LA DO ALTO, DEIXÁ-LA DESCER
ATÉ ENTALAR NAS COLUNAS. ELA ACHARIA A SUA POSIÇÃO.
PENSEI NUMA BARREIRA PARA QUE ELA TIVESSE
QUE SER VISTA, E NÃO TOCADA — COMO UM BICHO PRESO.

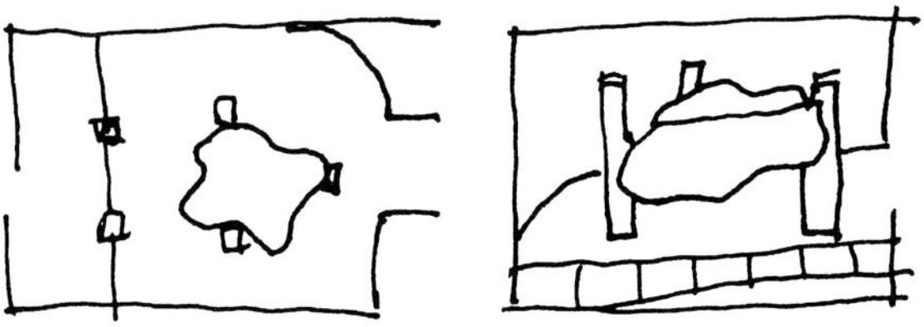

Please Do Not Touch

Centro Universitário Maria Antônia, São Paulo, 2004

Curated by Lorenzo Mammì
Plaster
1.5m h, 5m x 3.5m, 9,000 kg
It was not possible to support the piece on the floor.
I decided to drop it from the top, let it lower until it got stuck in the columns. It would find its own position. I thought of a barrier from which it had to be seen from, not touched–like a caged animal.

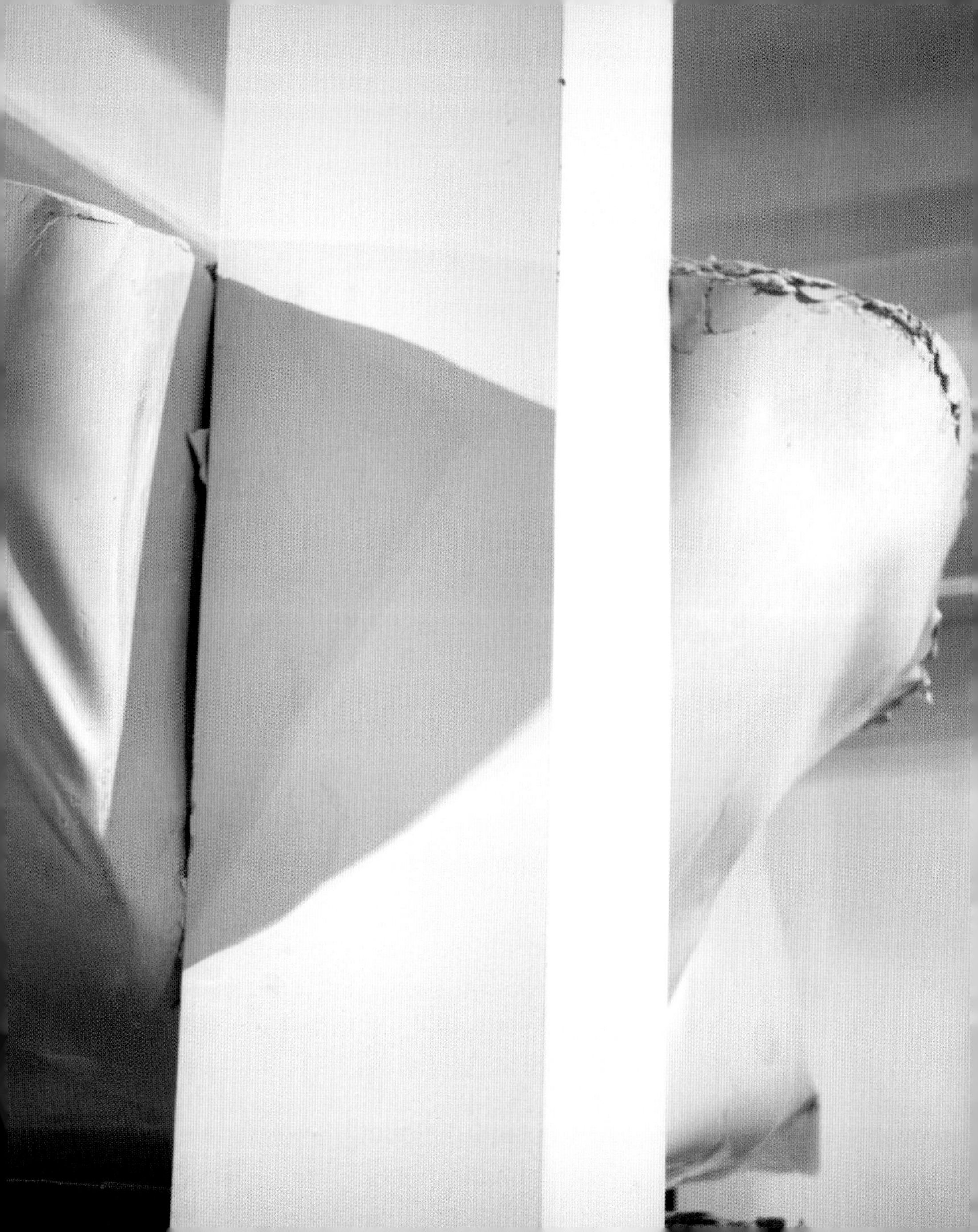

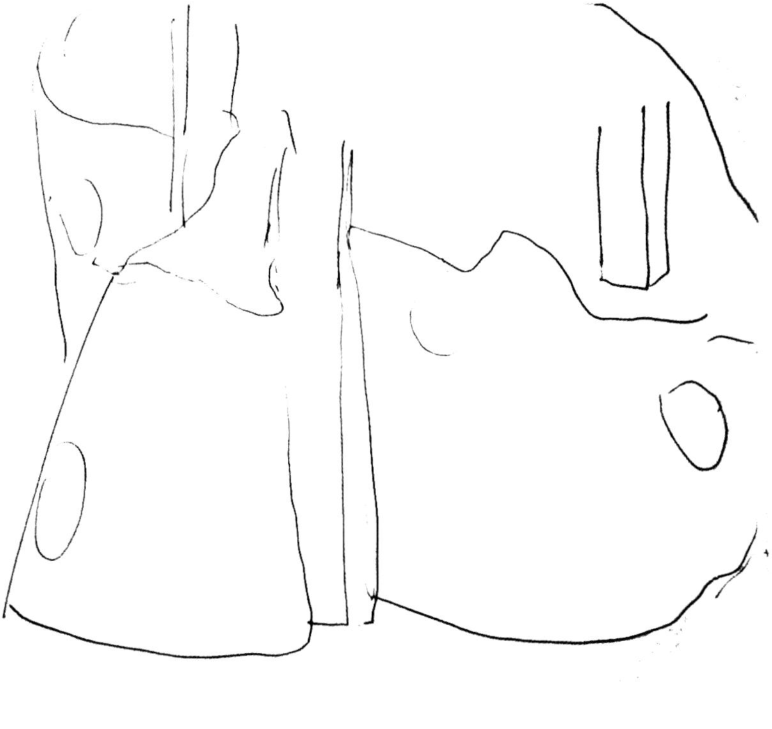

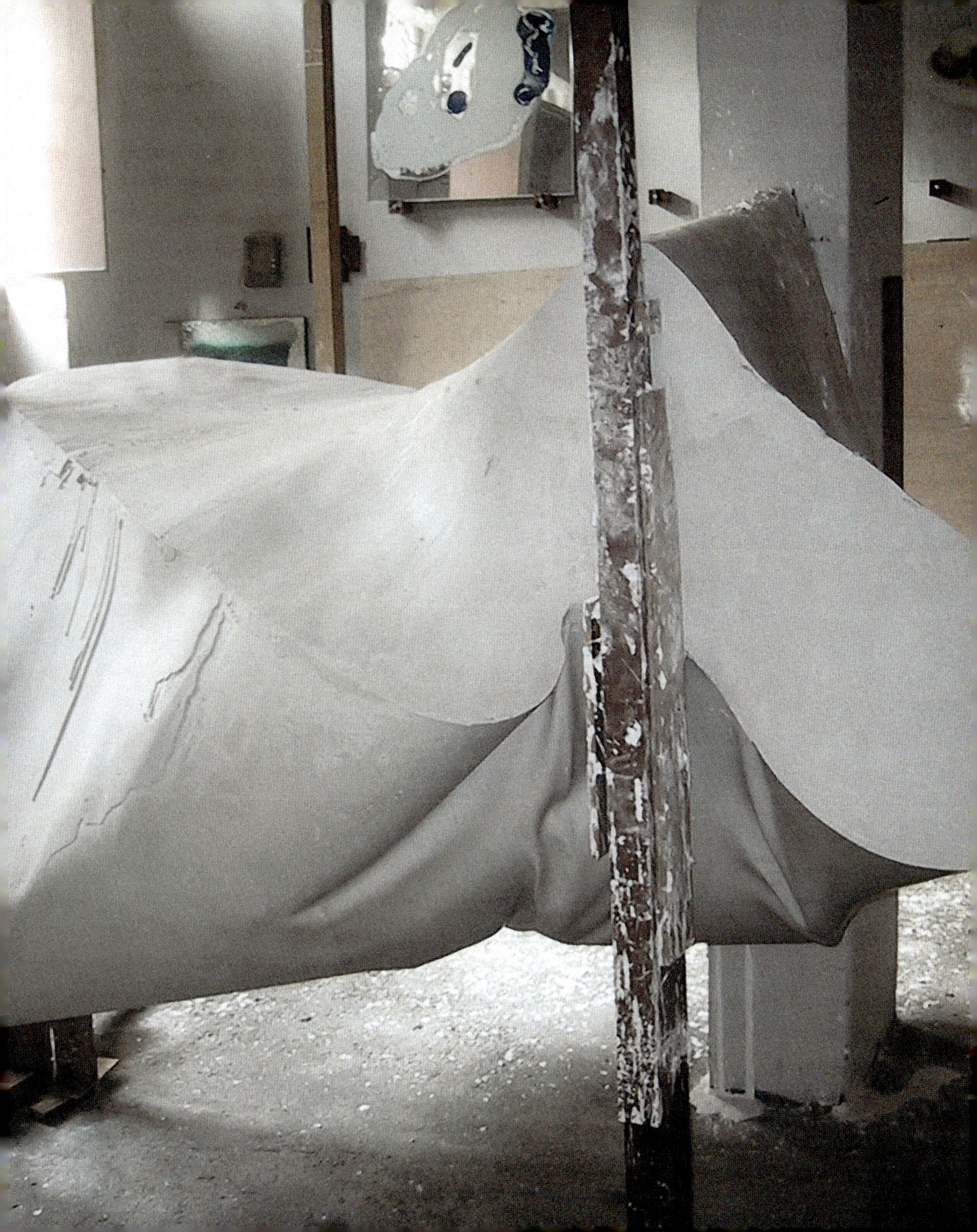

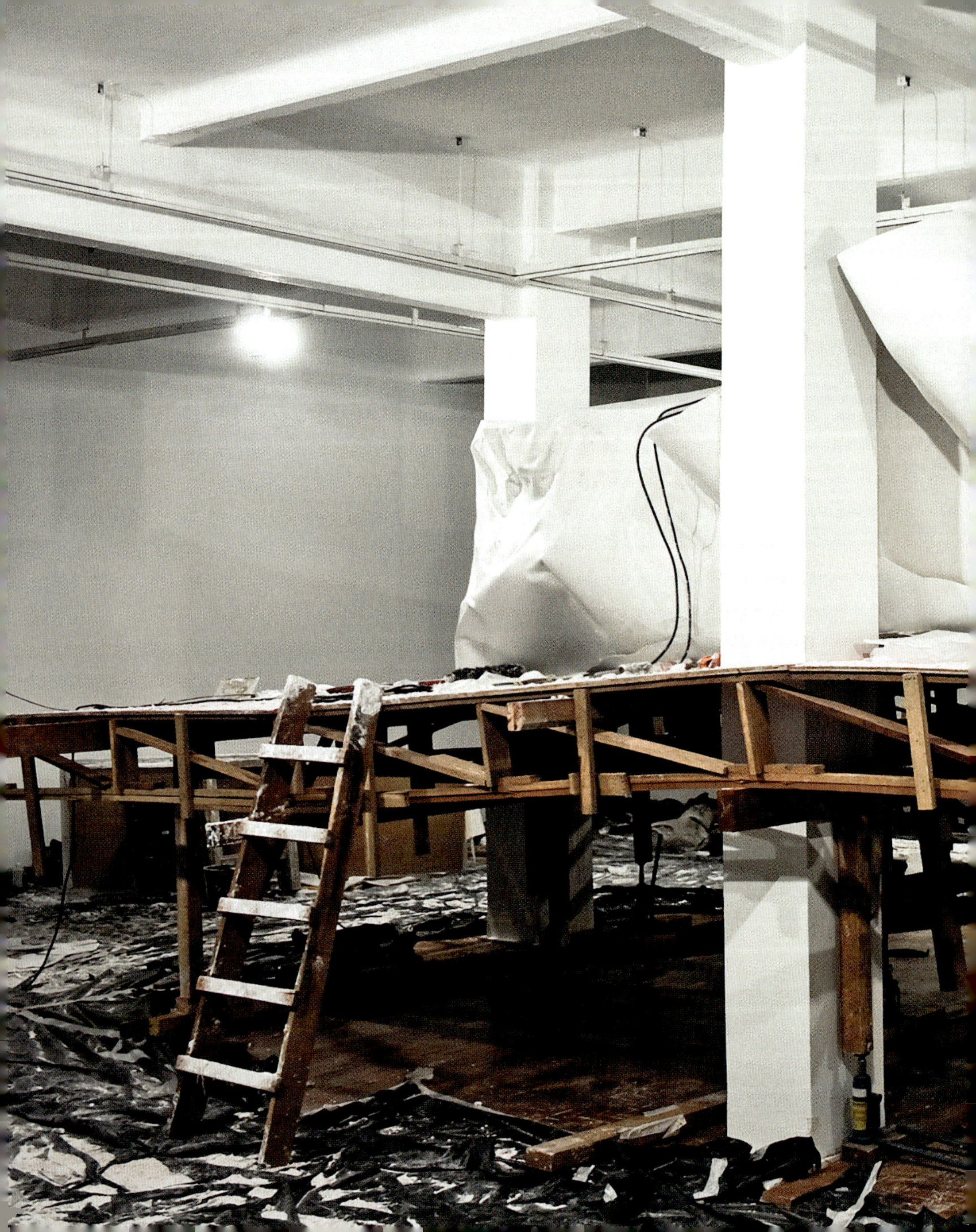

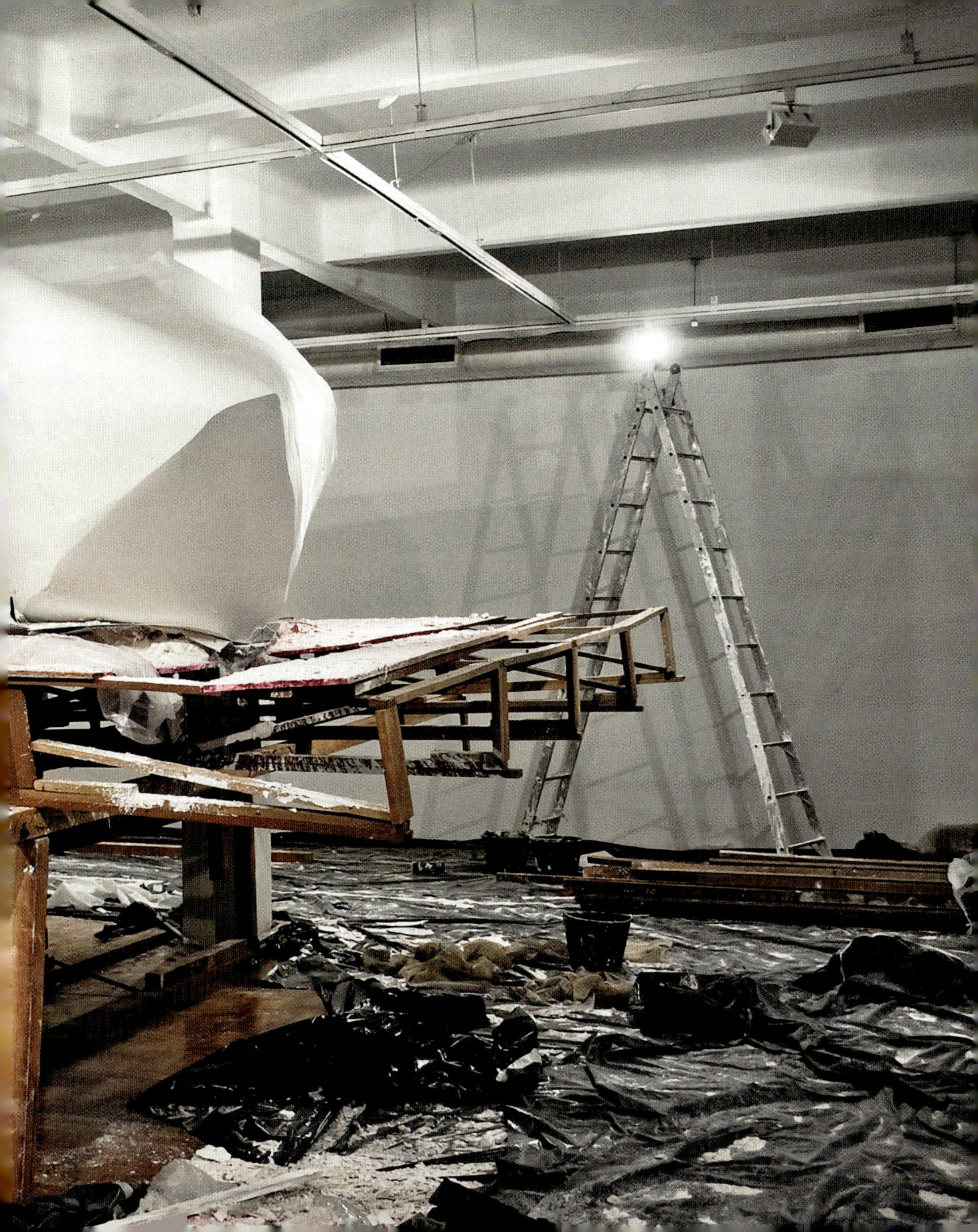

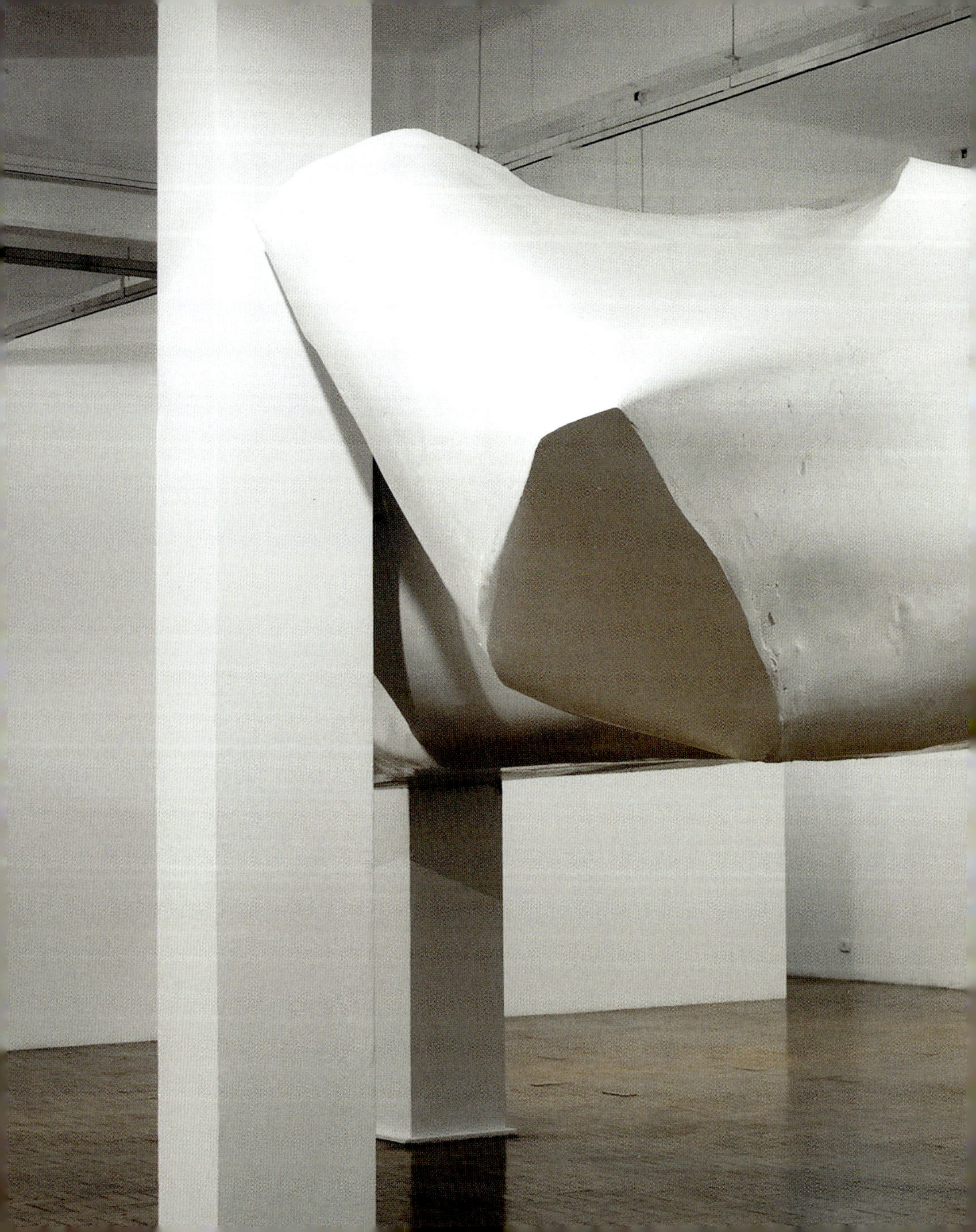

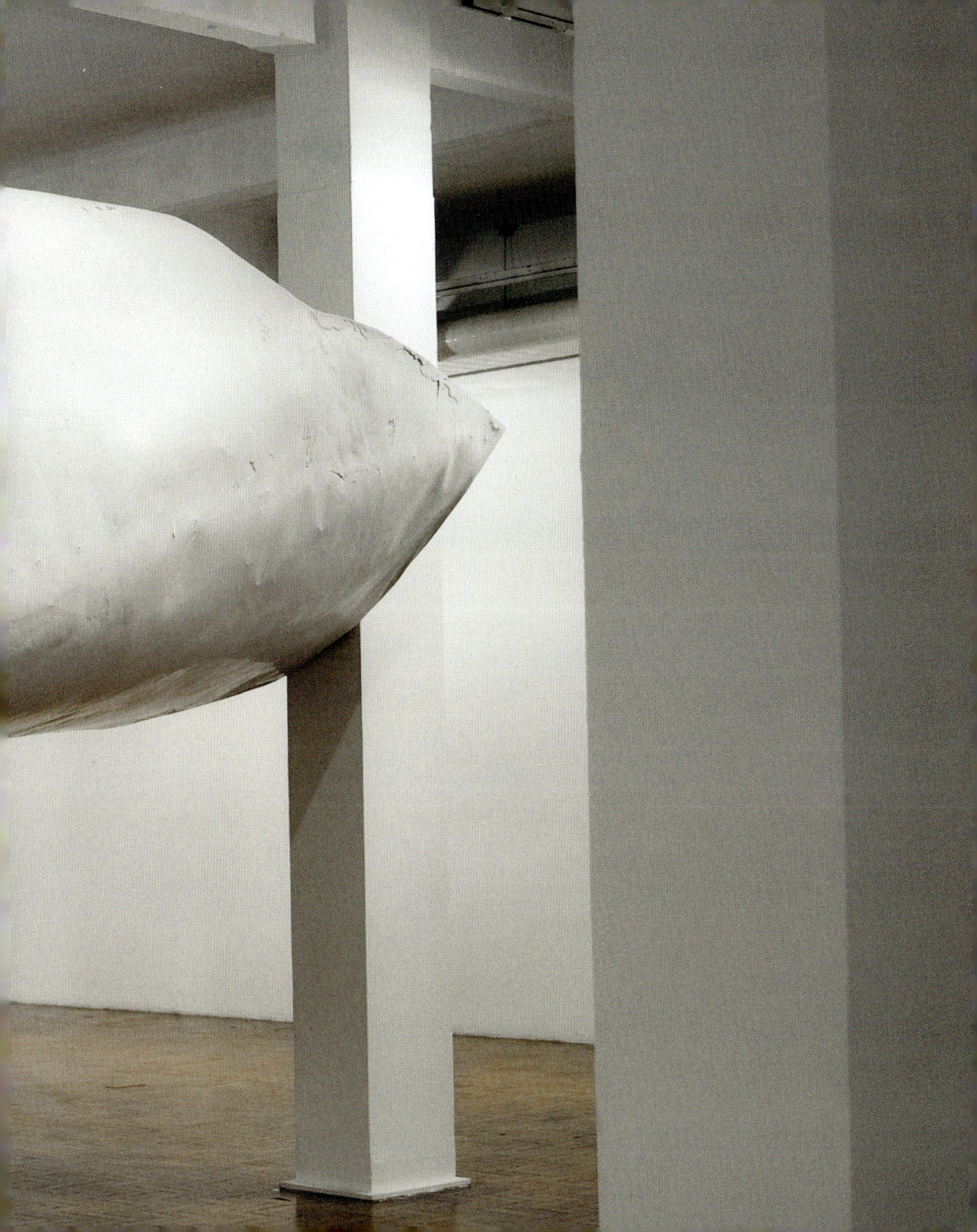

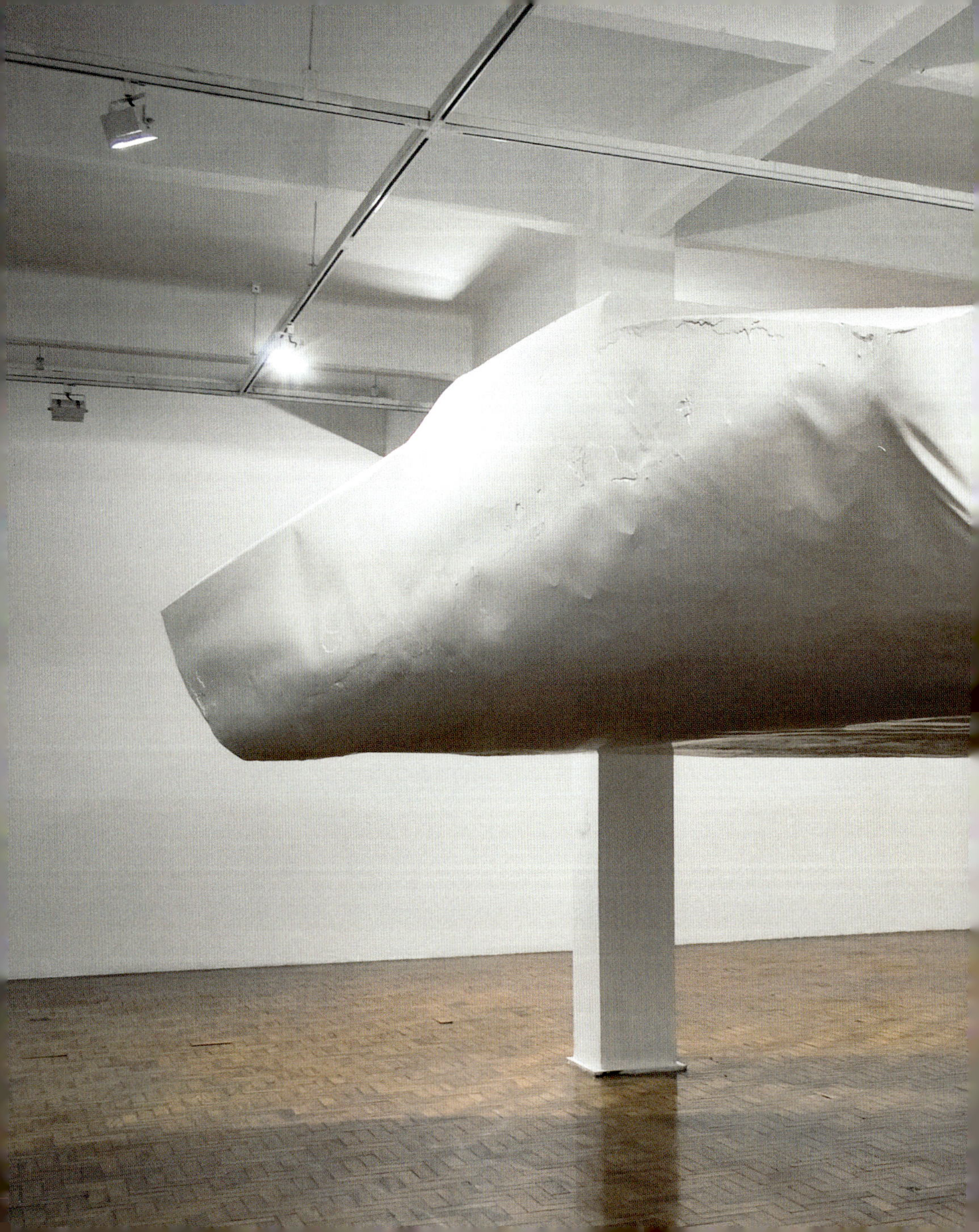

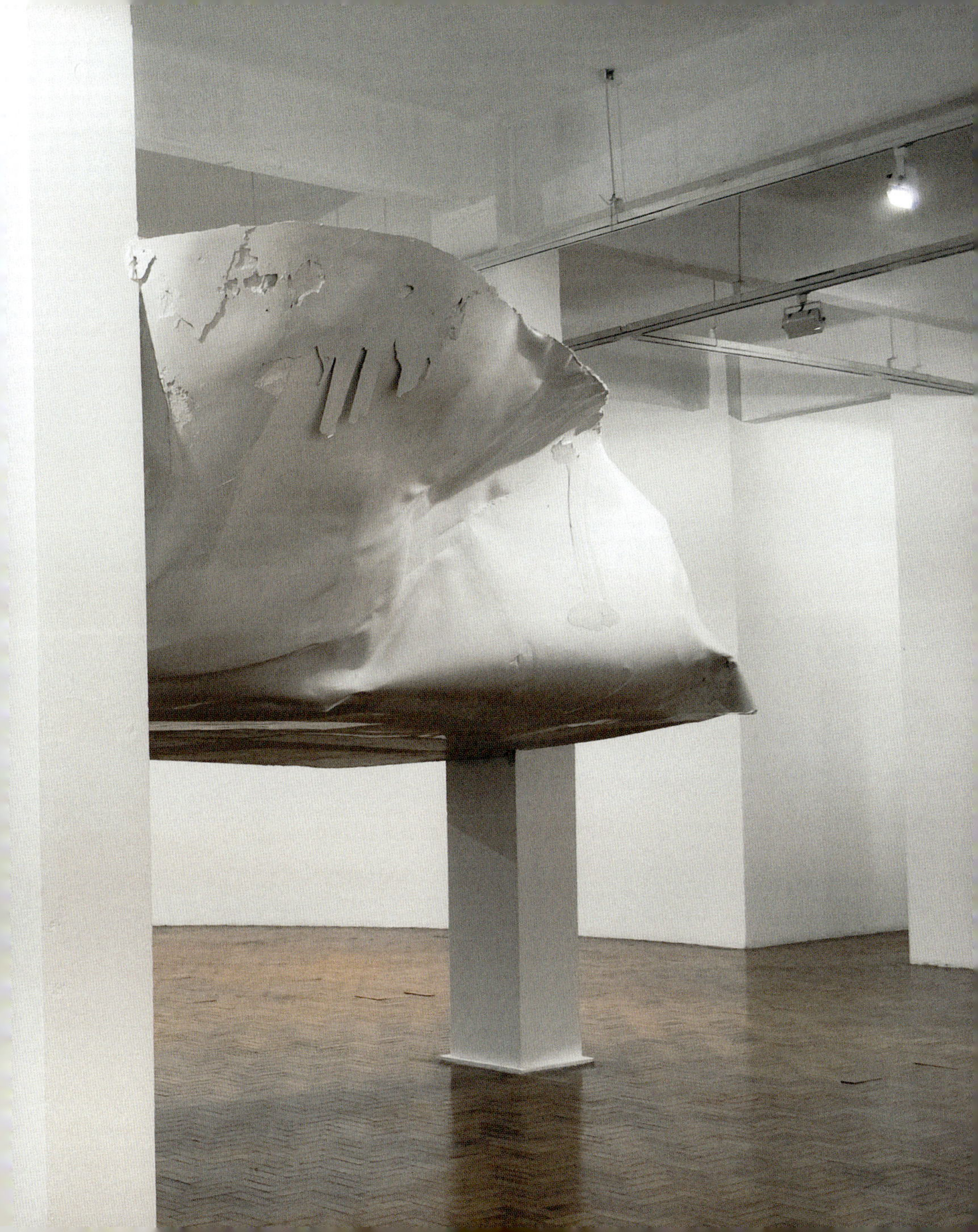

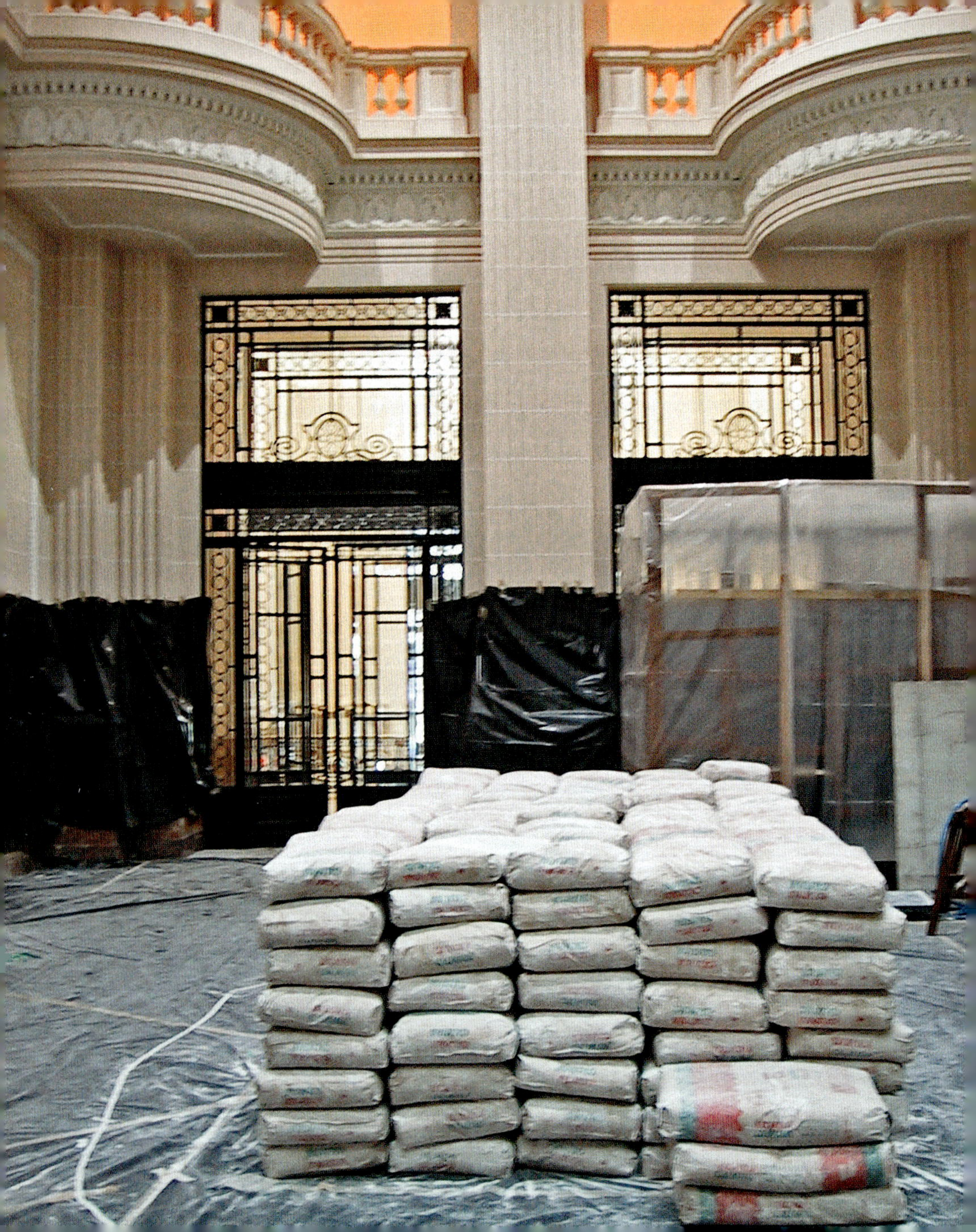

9:30	0 Sacos	88^{25}
10:00	16 Sacos	
10:15	28 Sacos	
13:50	49 Sacos	88^{25}
14:10	67 Sacos	
14:30	85 Sacos	
14:45	103 Sacos	88^{25}
15:47	154	88,25
16:30	203	88,25
17:00	231	
17:45	283 Sacos	88.25

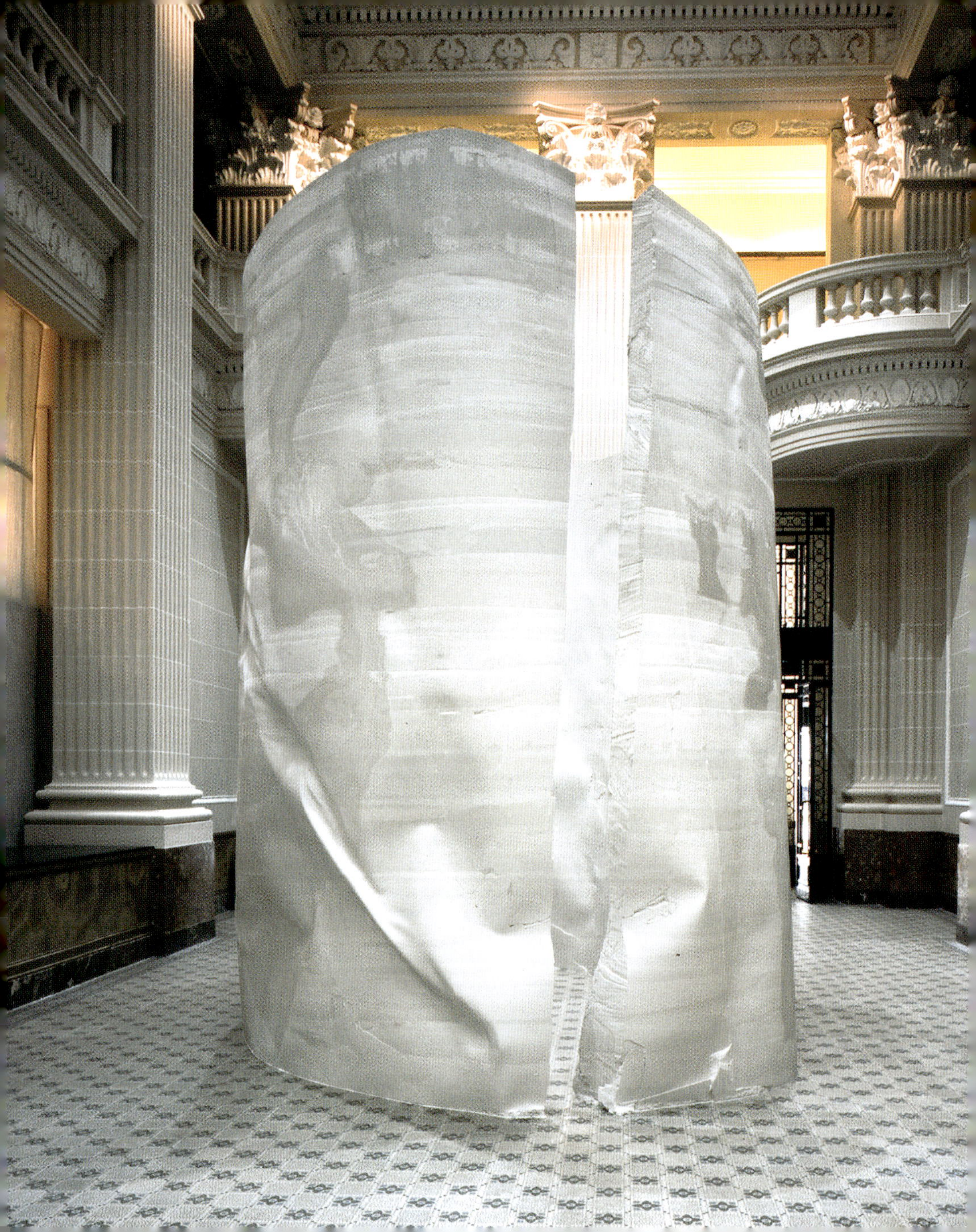

SURDA

BIENAL DO MERCOSUL, 2001
CURADORIA DE FABIO MAGALHÃES E LEONOR AMARANTE
GESSO
5M DE ALTURA, 5M X 3M, 12000 KG

Deaf

Bienal do Mercosul, 2001

Curated by Fabio Magalhães and Leonor Amarante
Plaster
5m h, 5m x 3m, 12000 kg

GIBRALTAR

CÔTE À CÔTE - ART CONTEMPORAIN DU BRÉSIL
CAPC BORDEAUX, 2001
CURADORIA DE FRANKLIN PEDROSO, NELSON AGUILAR E ÉRIC FÉLONEAU
GESSO
5,5M DE ALTURA, 5M X 3,5M, 13.000 KG.

Gibraltar
Côte à Côte–Art Contemporain du Brésil
CAPC Bordeaux, 2001

Curated by Franklin Pedroso, Nelson Aguilar and Éric Féloneau
Plaster
5.5m h, 5m x 3.5m, 13,000 kg

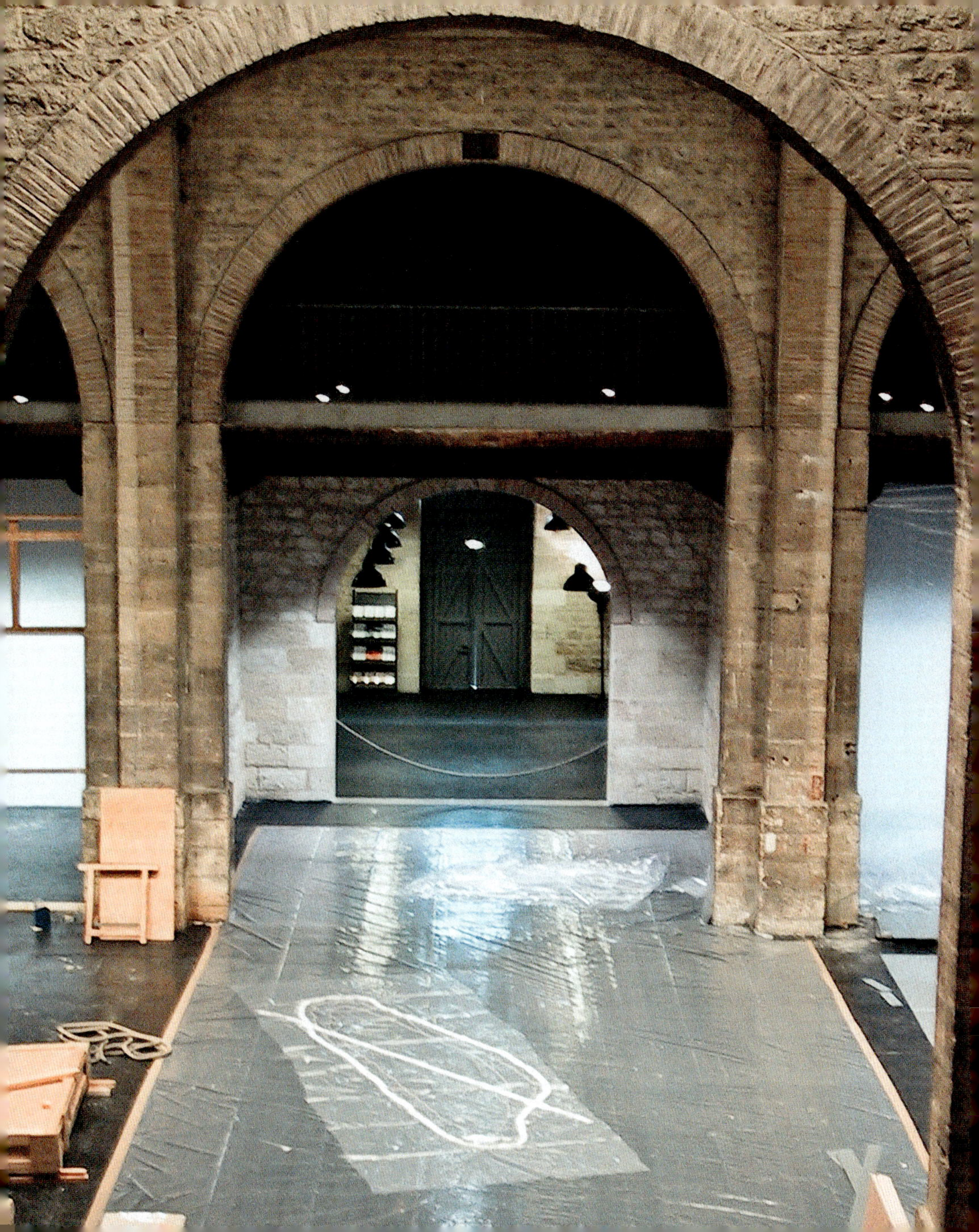

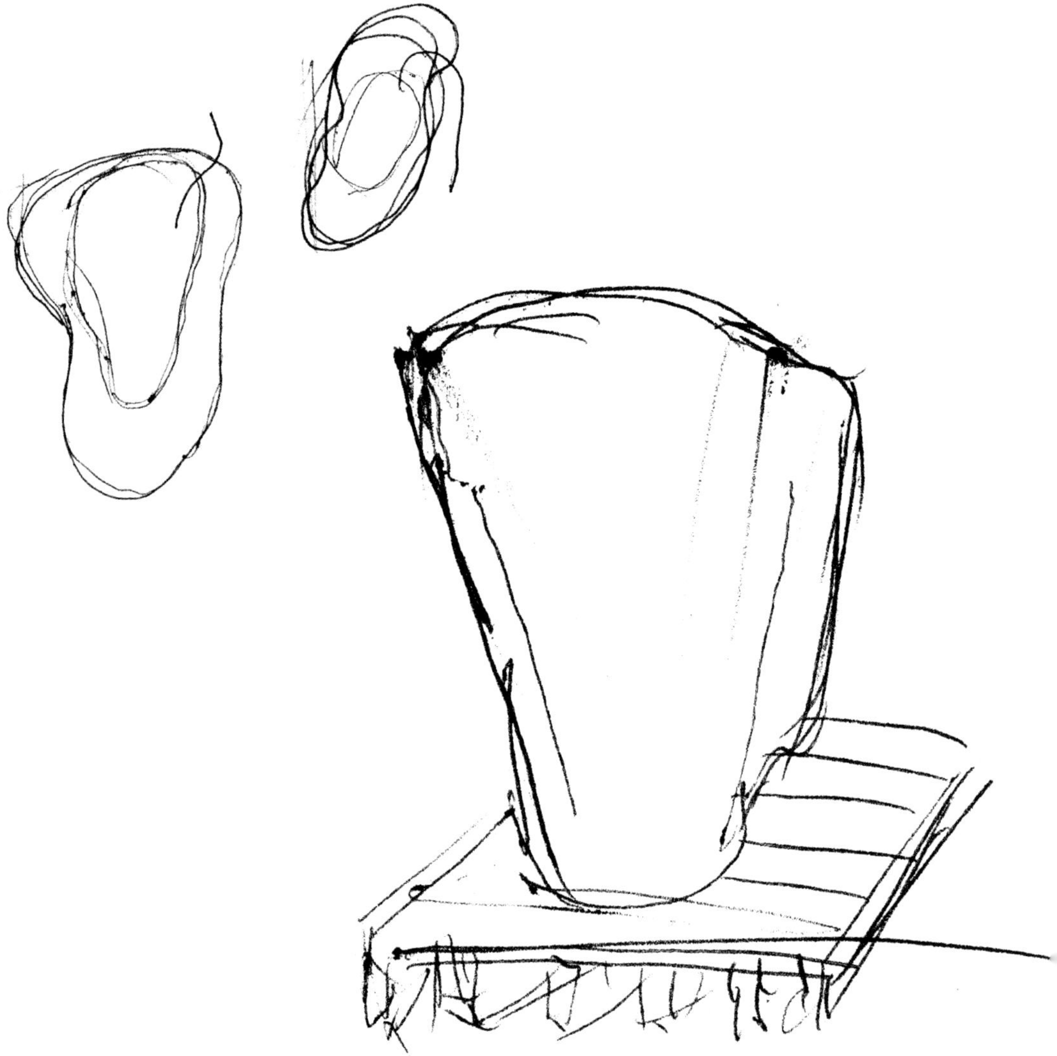

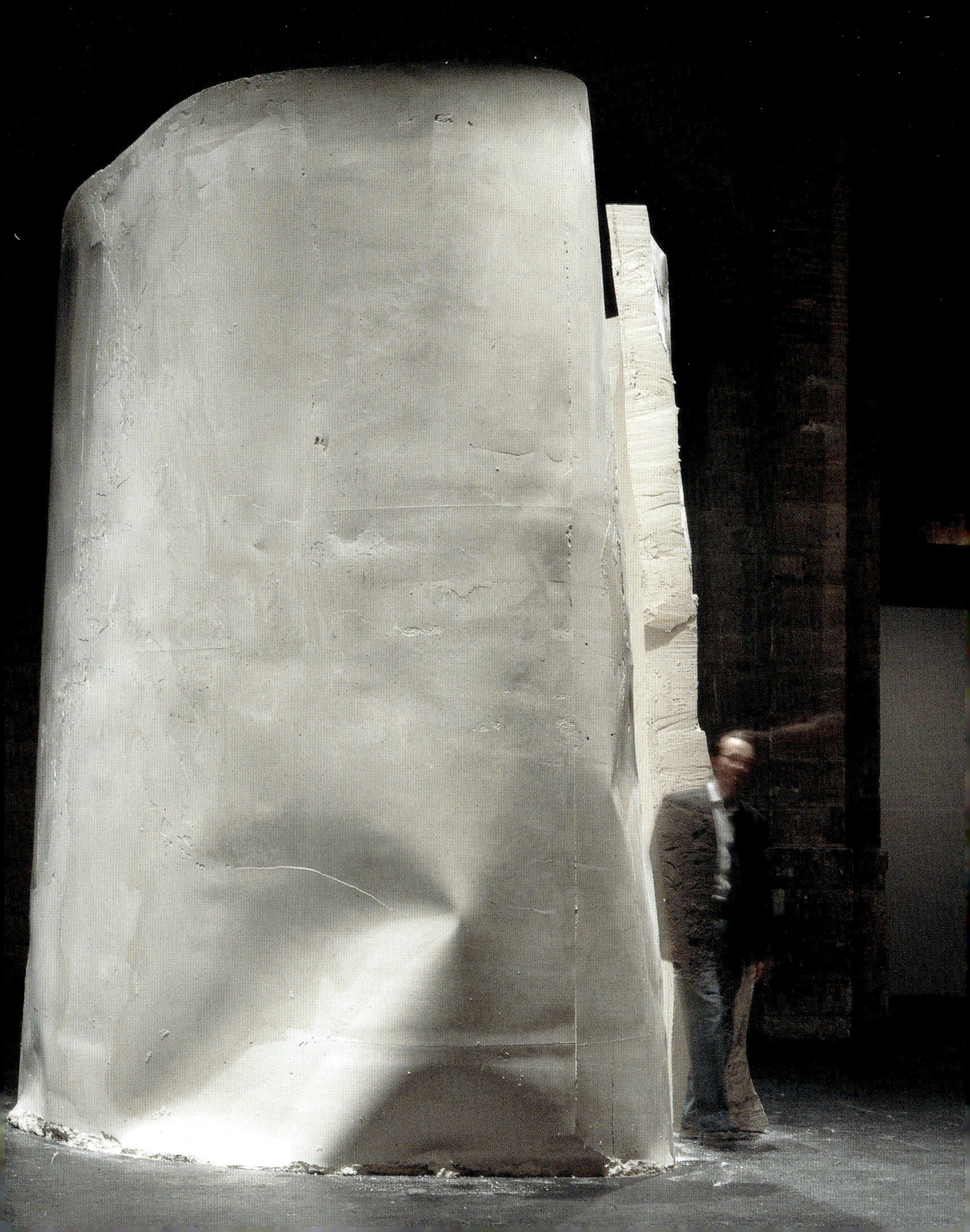

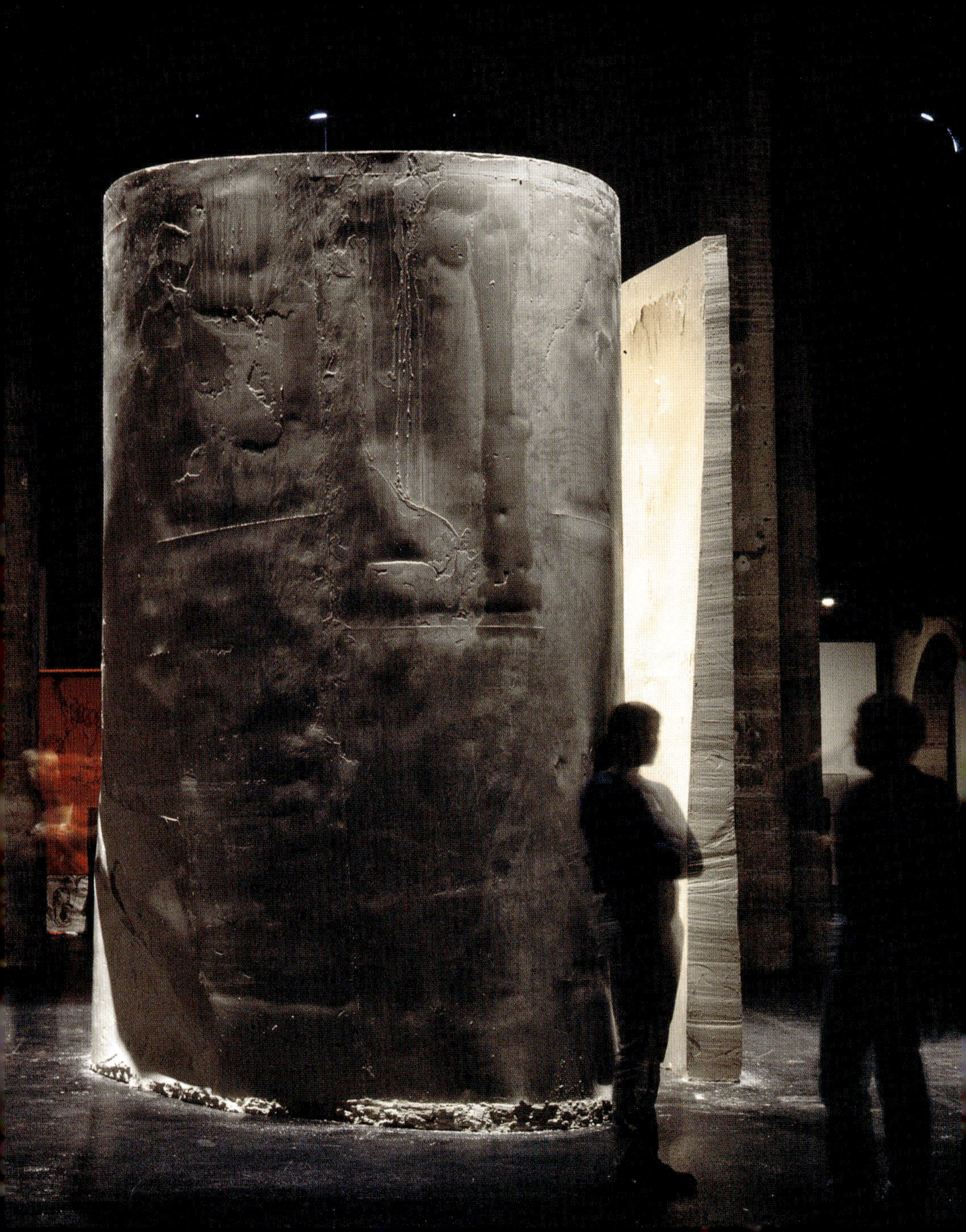

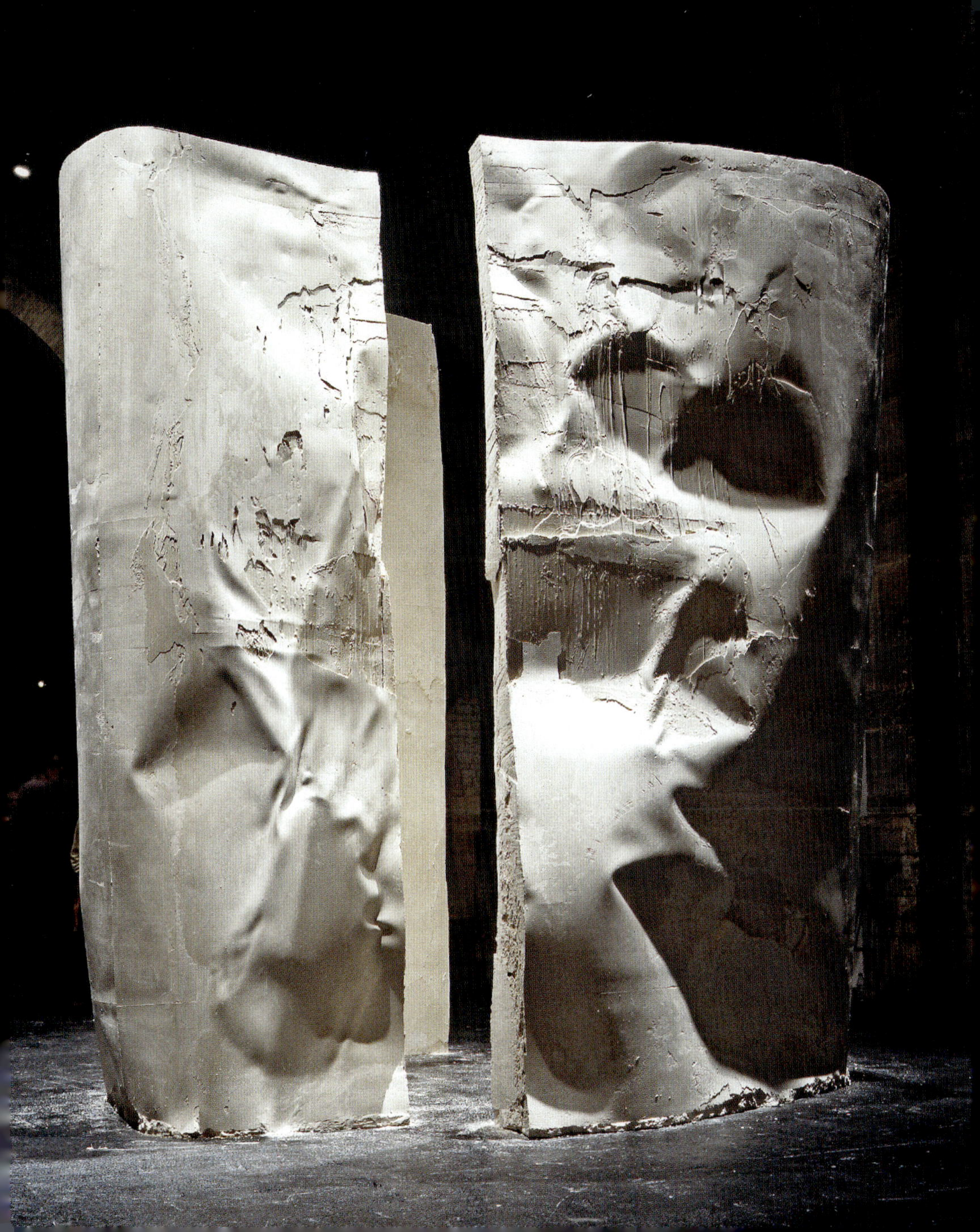

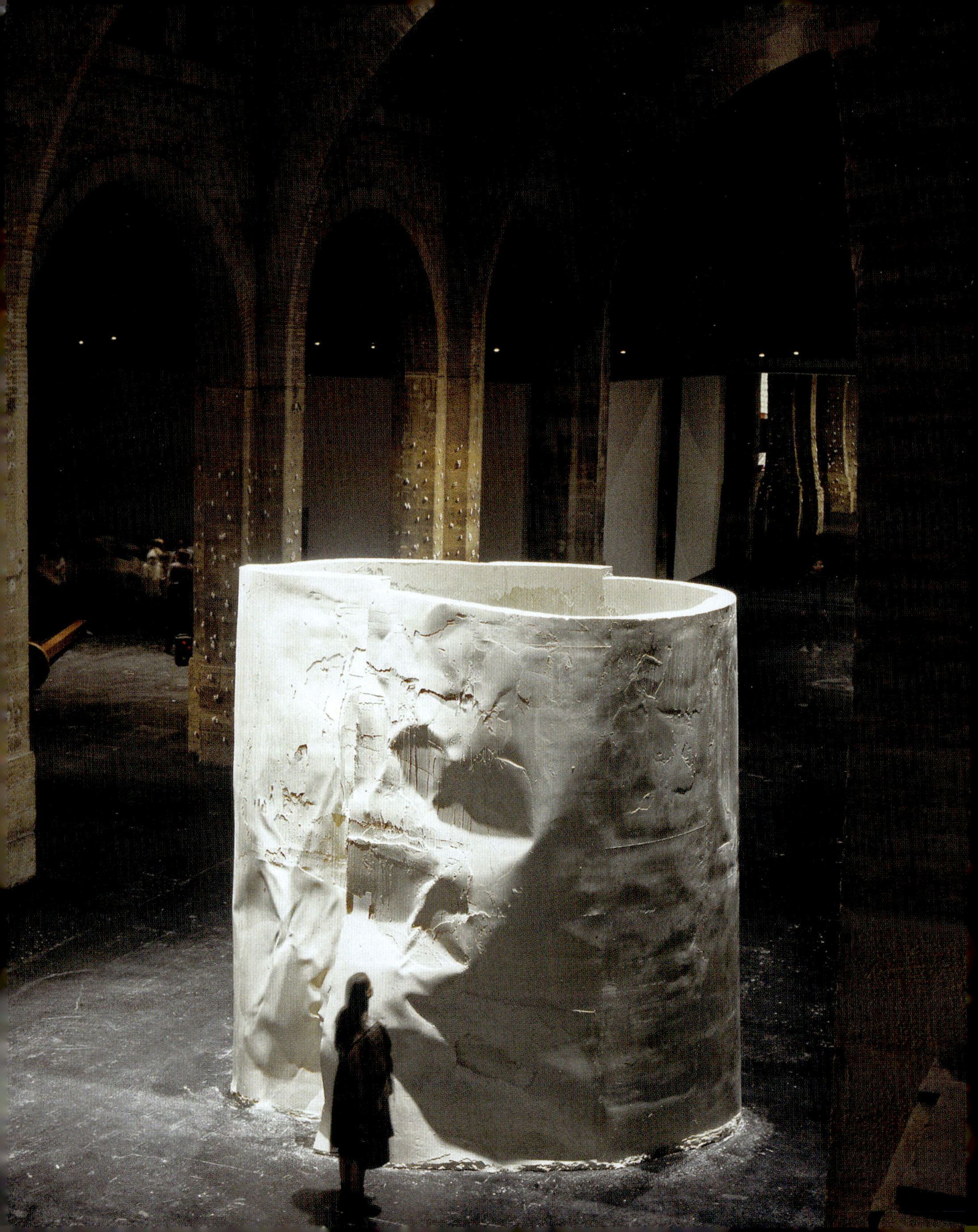

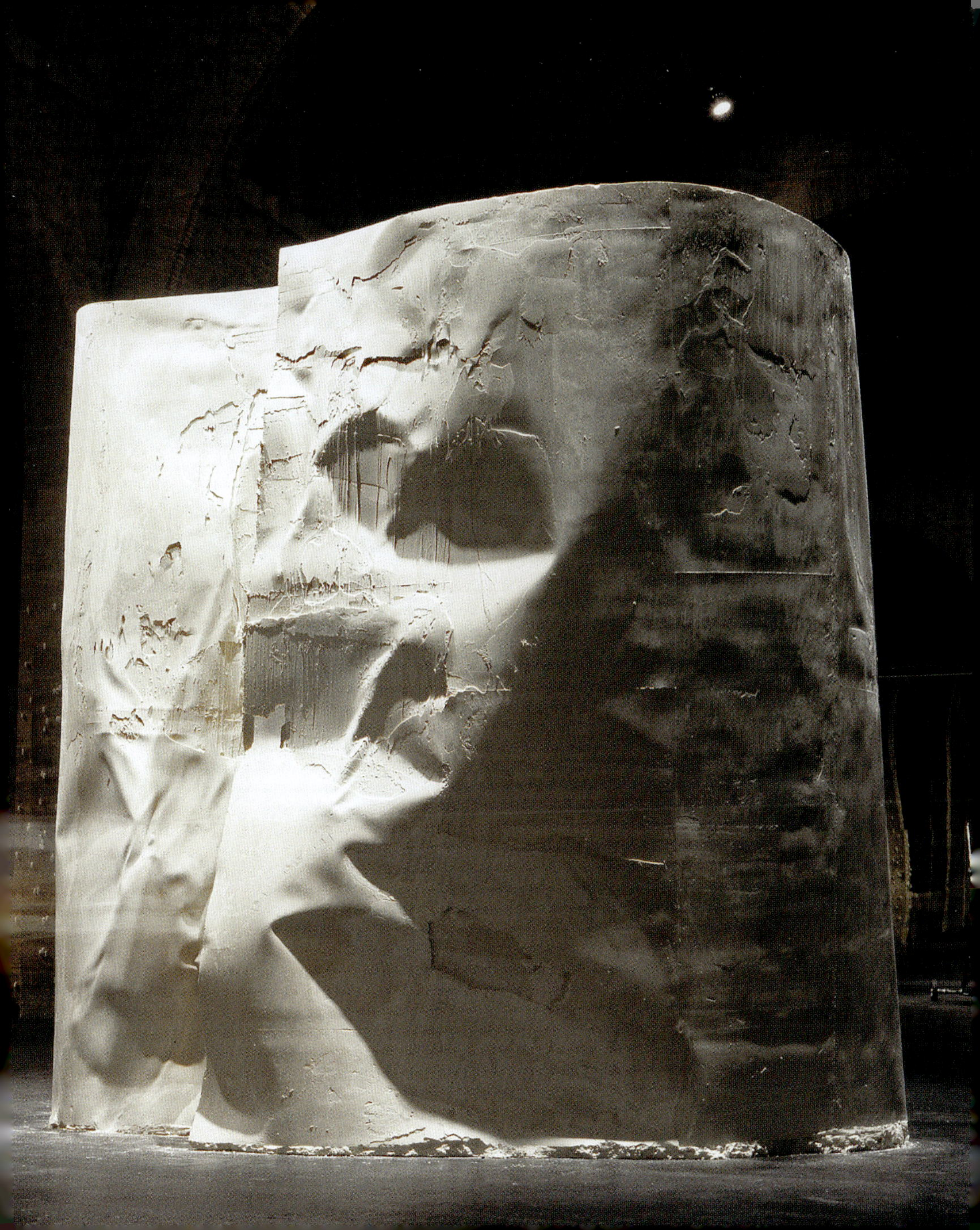

SEM FIO

ATELIER, RIO DE JANEIRO, 2009
MAQUETE E PROTÓTIPO [illegible]
TNT
4M DE ALTURA, 4M X 4M
PROJETO NÃO REALIZADO

Unthread

Artist's Studio, Rio de Janeiro, 2009

Model and prototype
TNT
4m h, 4m x 4m
Unrealized project

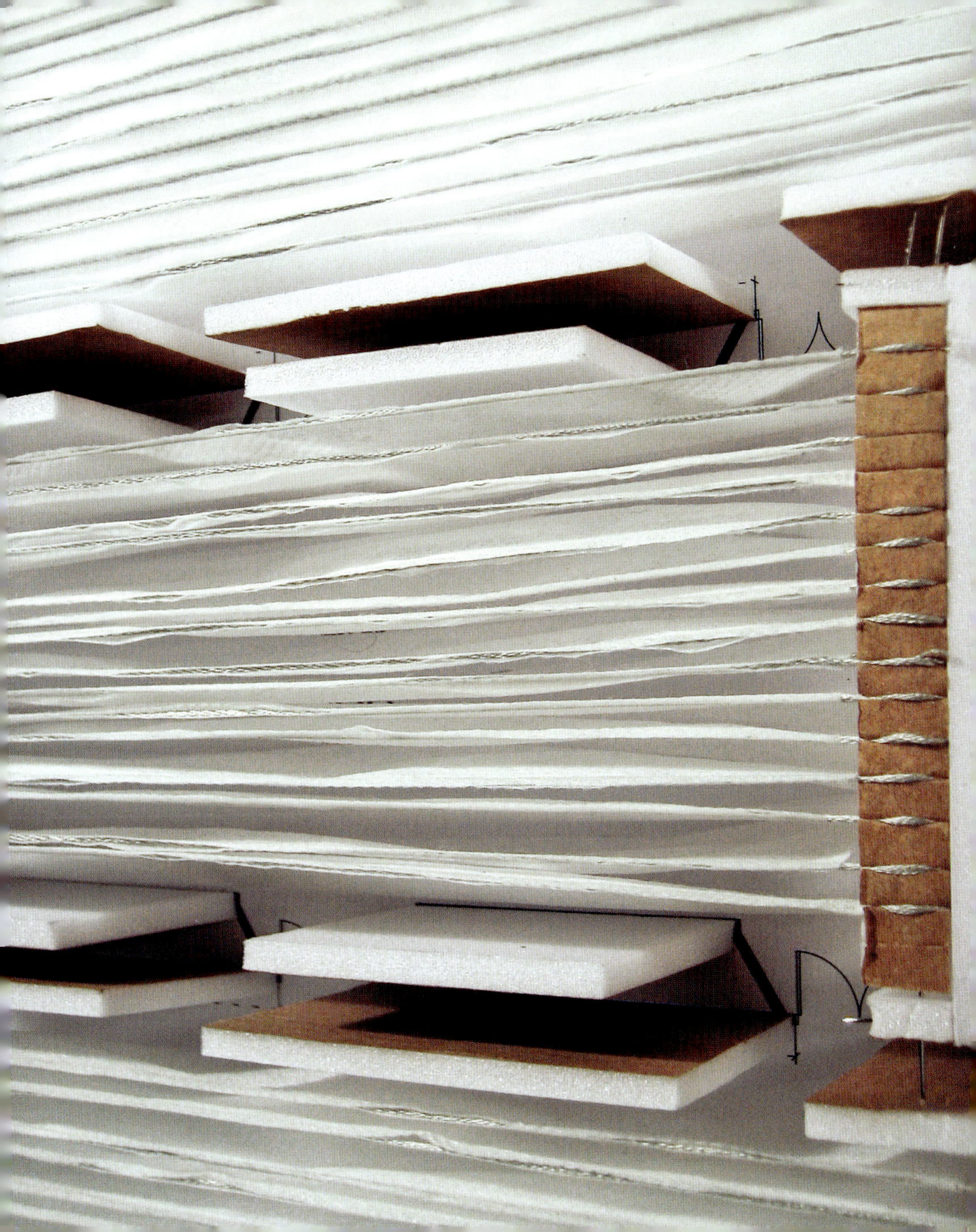

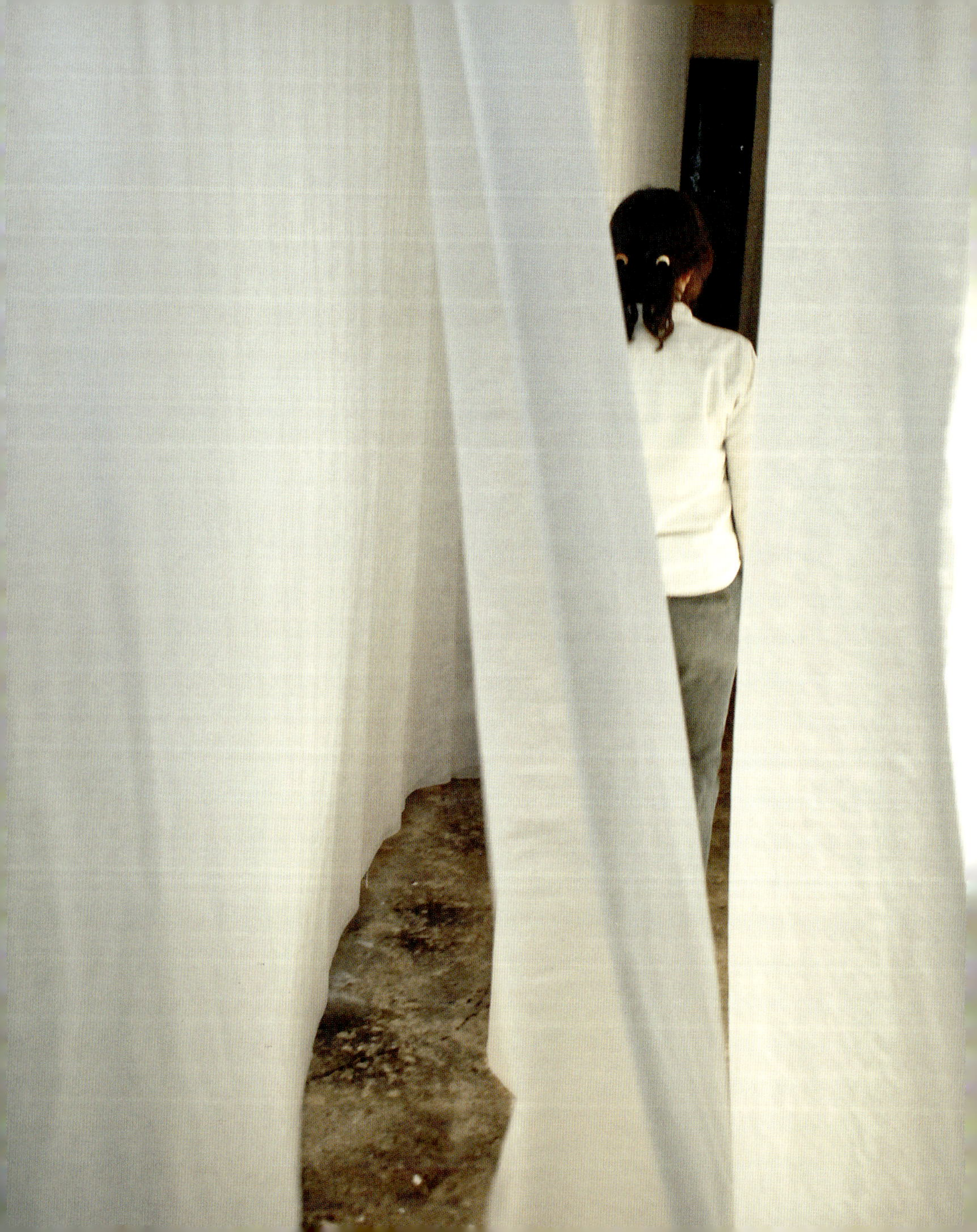

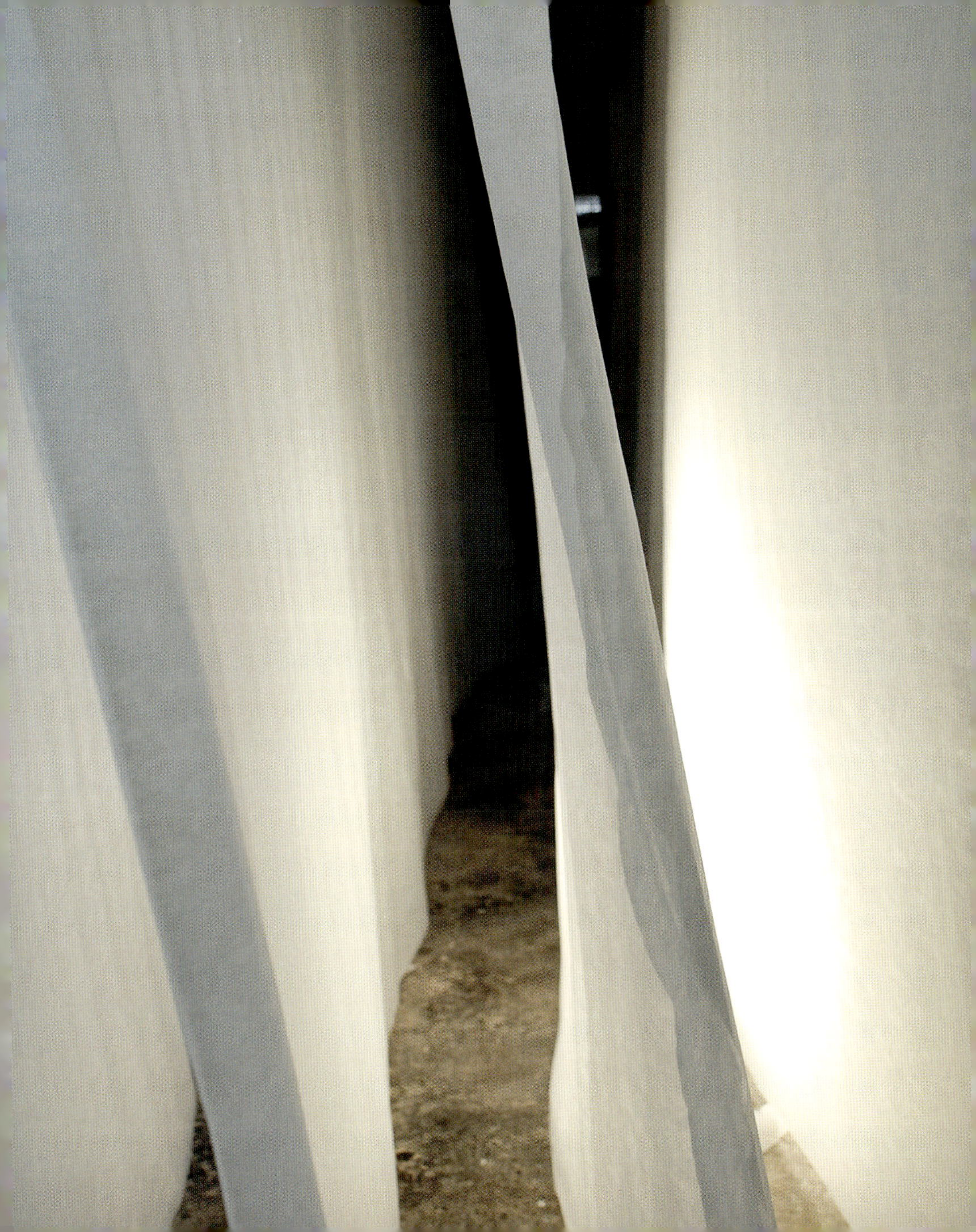

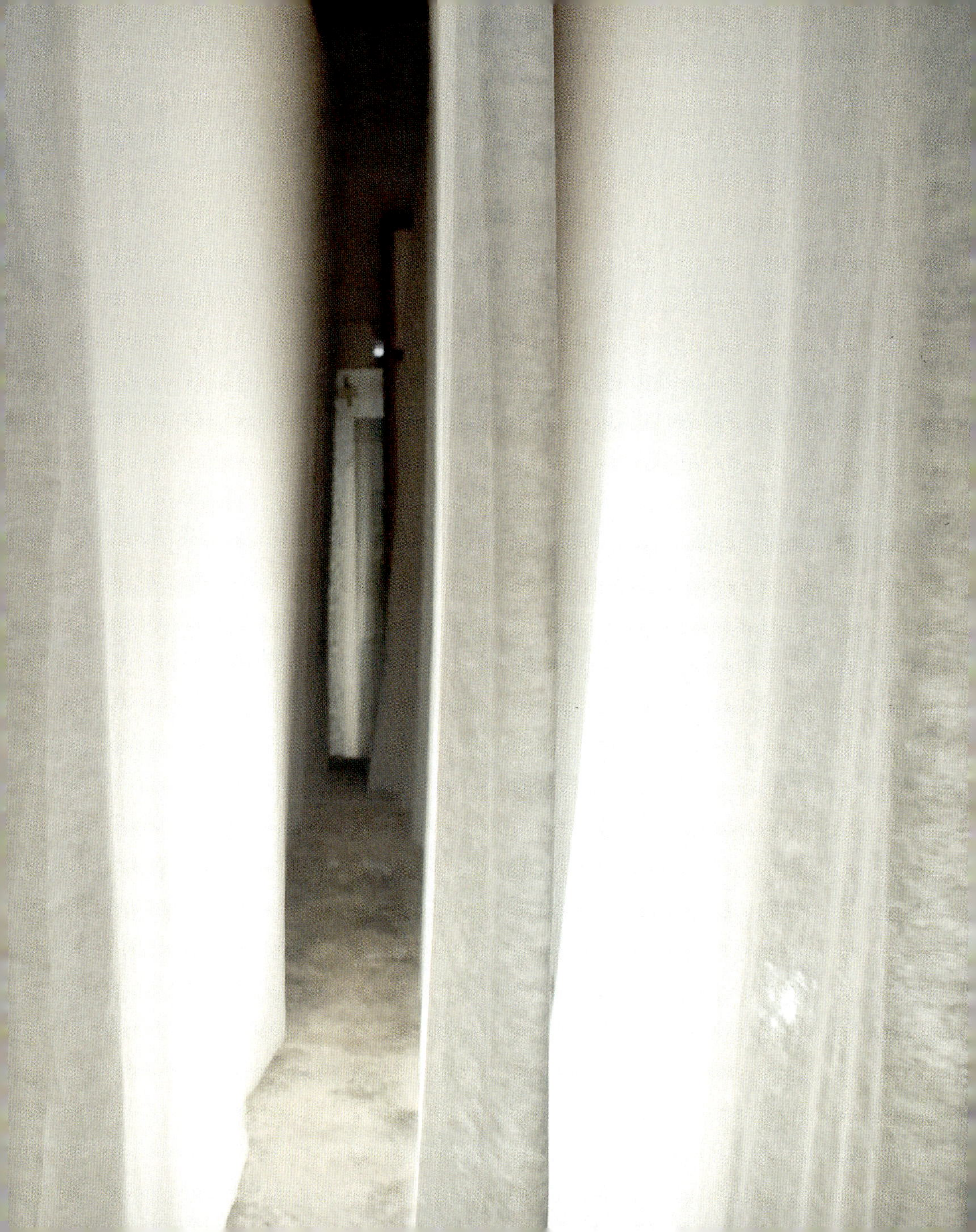

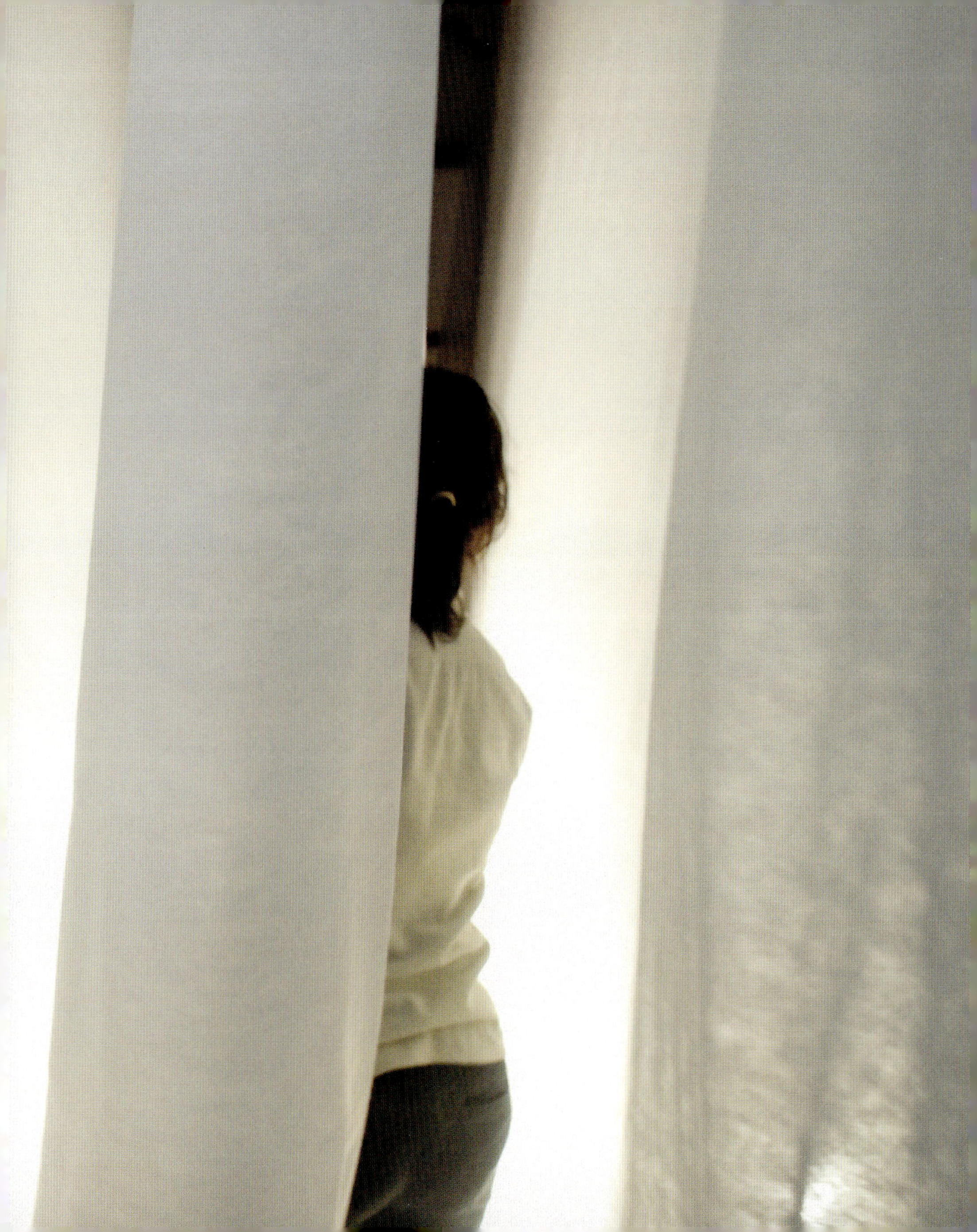

REGRA DE DOIS

FUNDAÇÃO EVA KLABIN, RIO DE JANEIRO, 2011
PROJETO RESPIRAÇÃO, CURADORIA DE MARCIO DOCTORS
204 LÂMPADAS T8, 32W, 4100°K
300 COPOS DE VIDRO (VÁRIOS TIPOS)
60 LÂMPADAS TIPO VELA 220V LIGADAS EM 110V
4 DOMBEIAS E 2 ALGODOEIROS DE PRAIA
CABOS DE AÇO, ALUMÍNIO

Rule of Two

Fundação Eva Klabin, Rio de Janeiro, 2011

Projeto Respiração, curated by Marcio Doctors
204 T8 fluorescent lights, 32w, 4,100°k
300 glasses (various kinds)
60 candle-type 220v light bulbs plugged into 110v current
4 Dombeyas and 2 Beach Hibiscus
Steel cables, aluminum

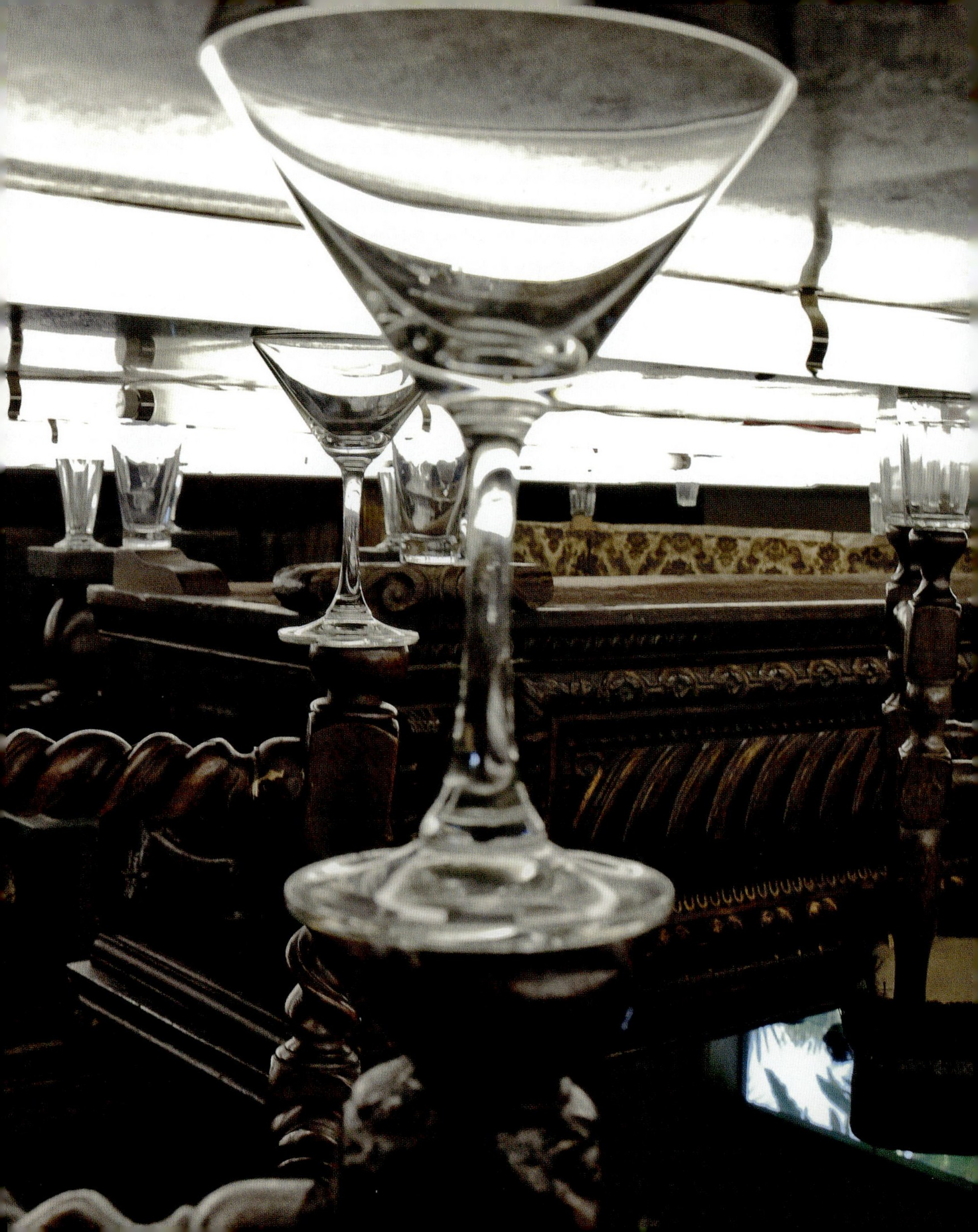

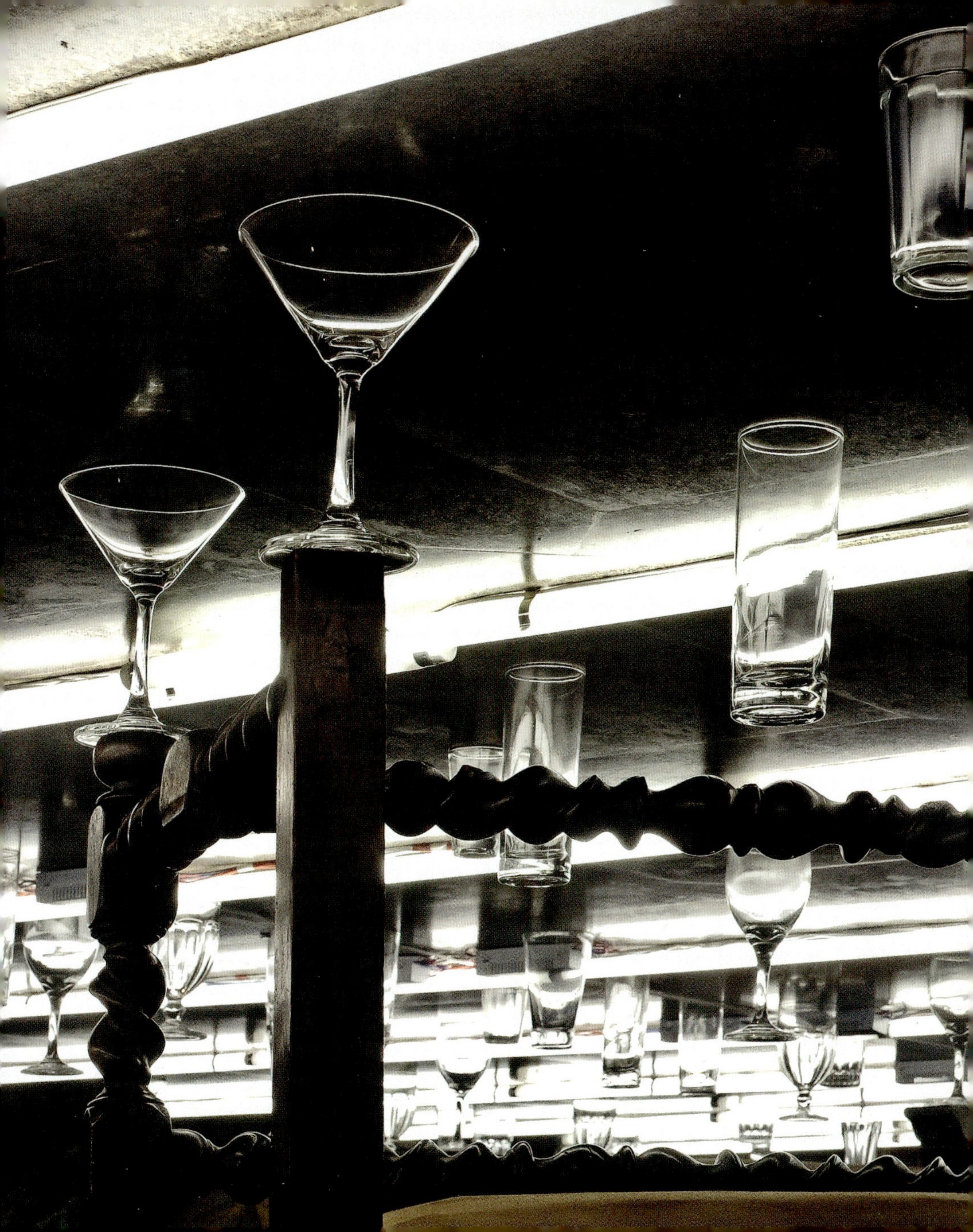

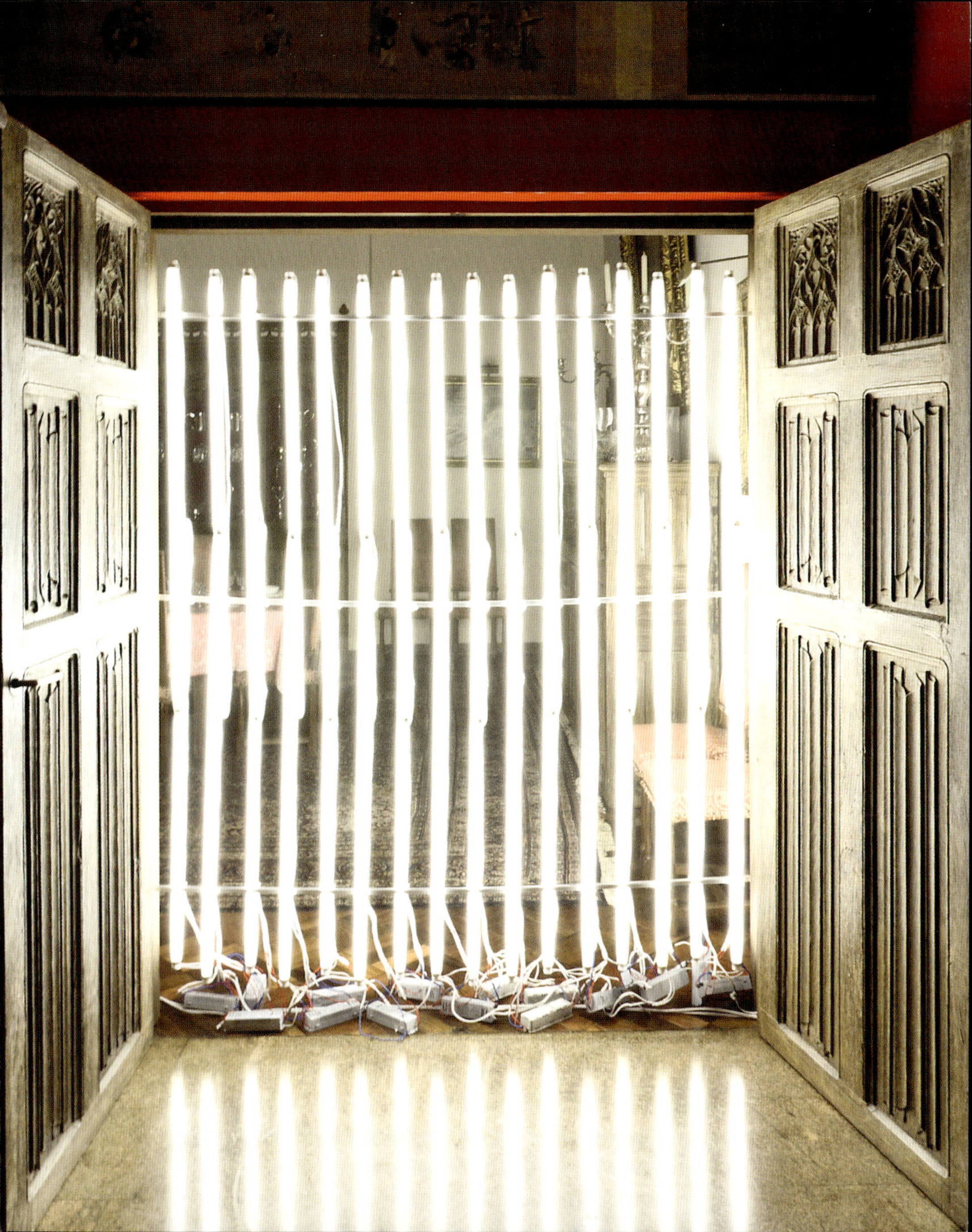

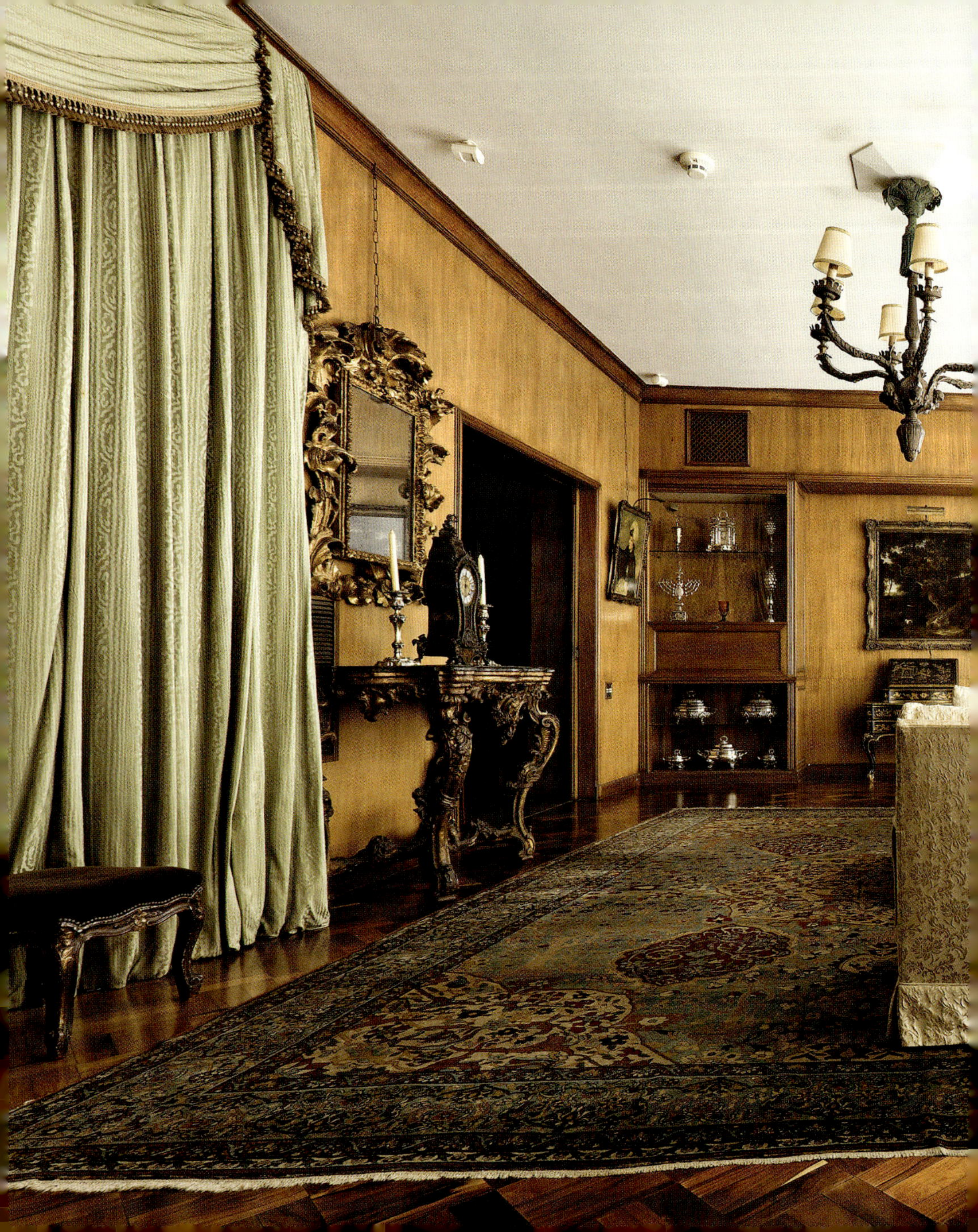

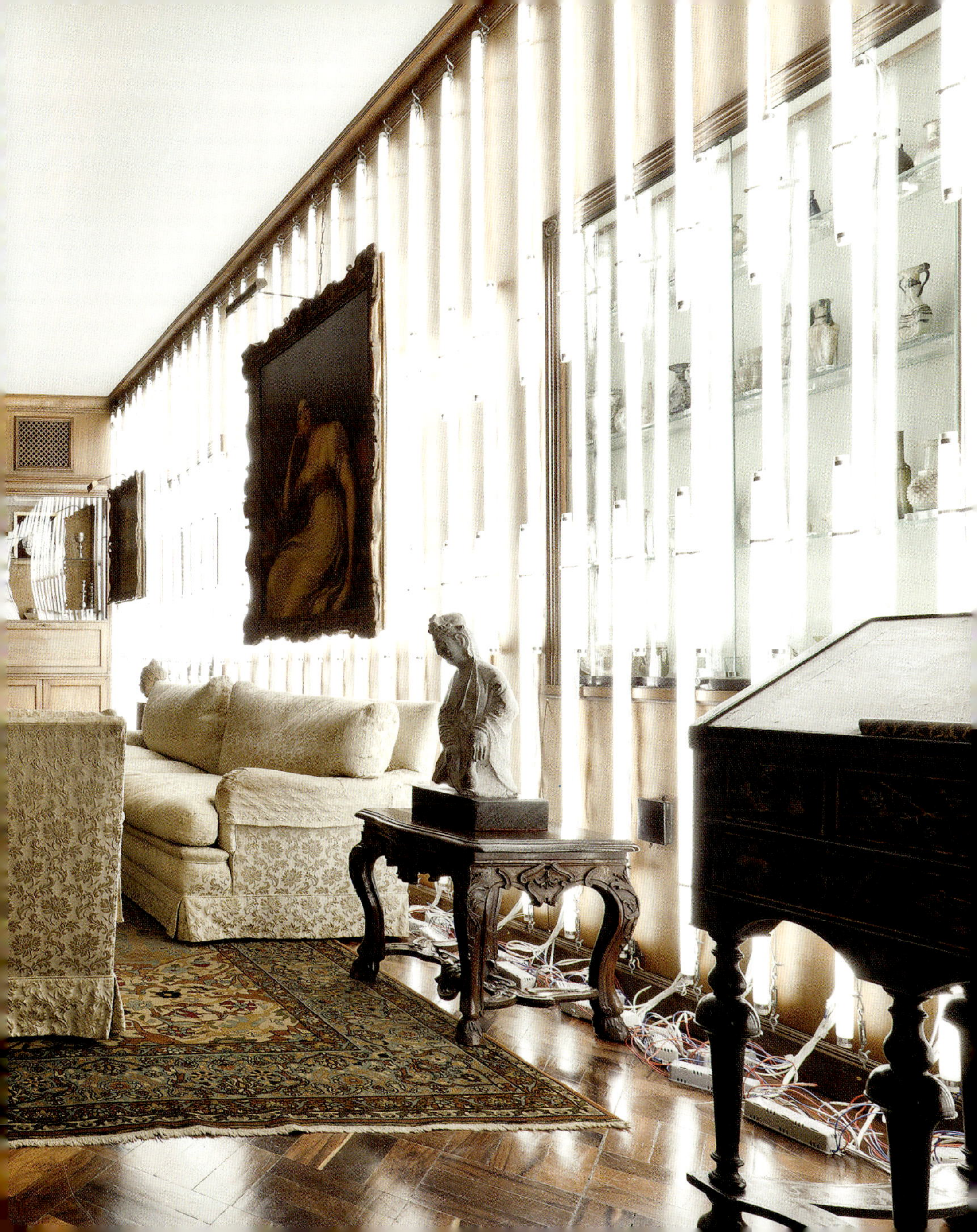

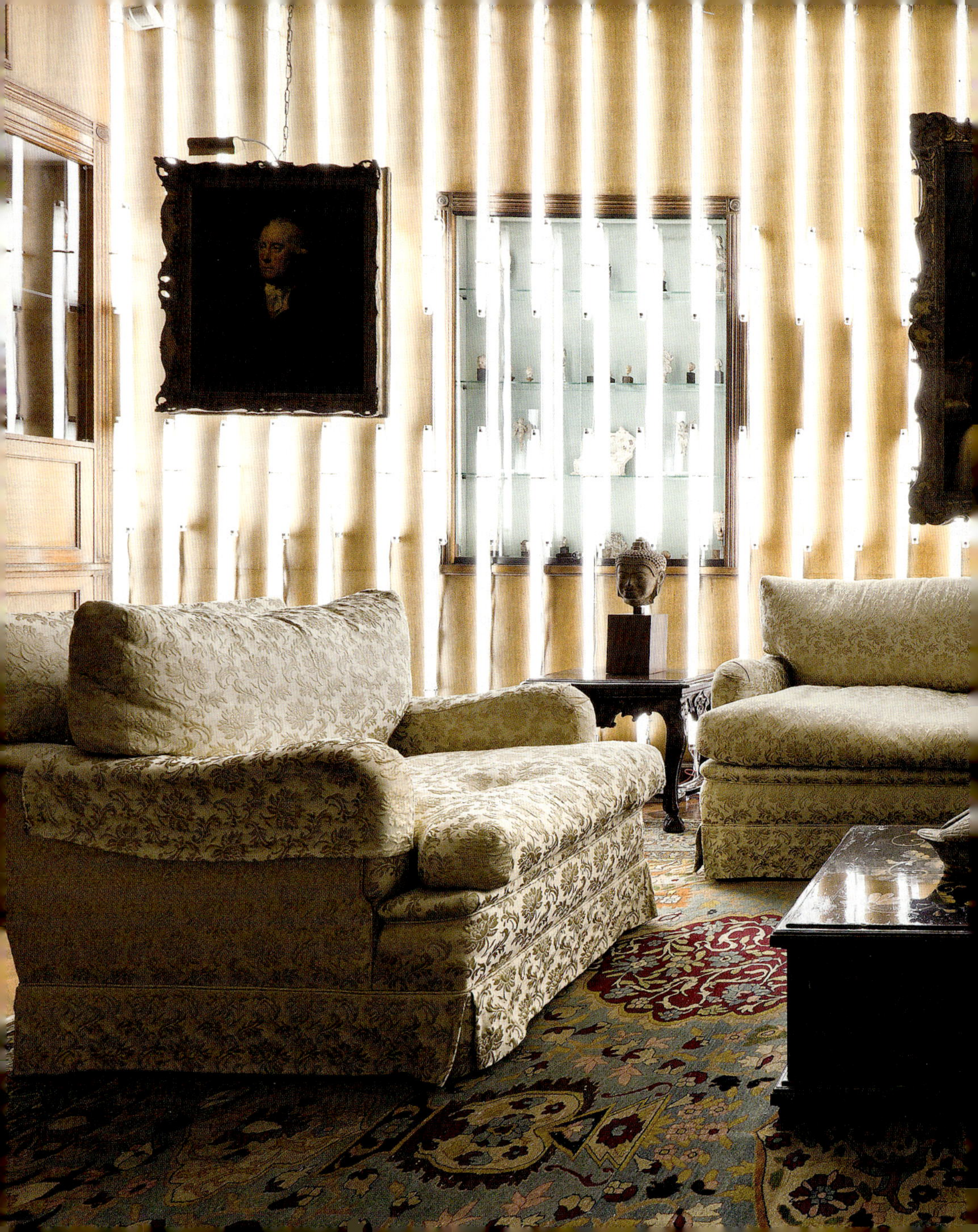

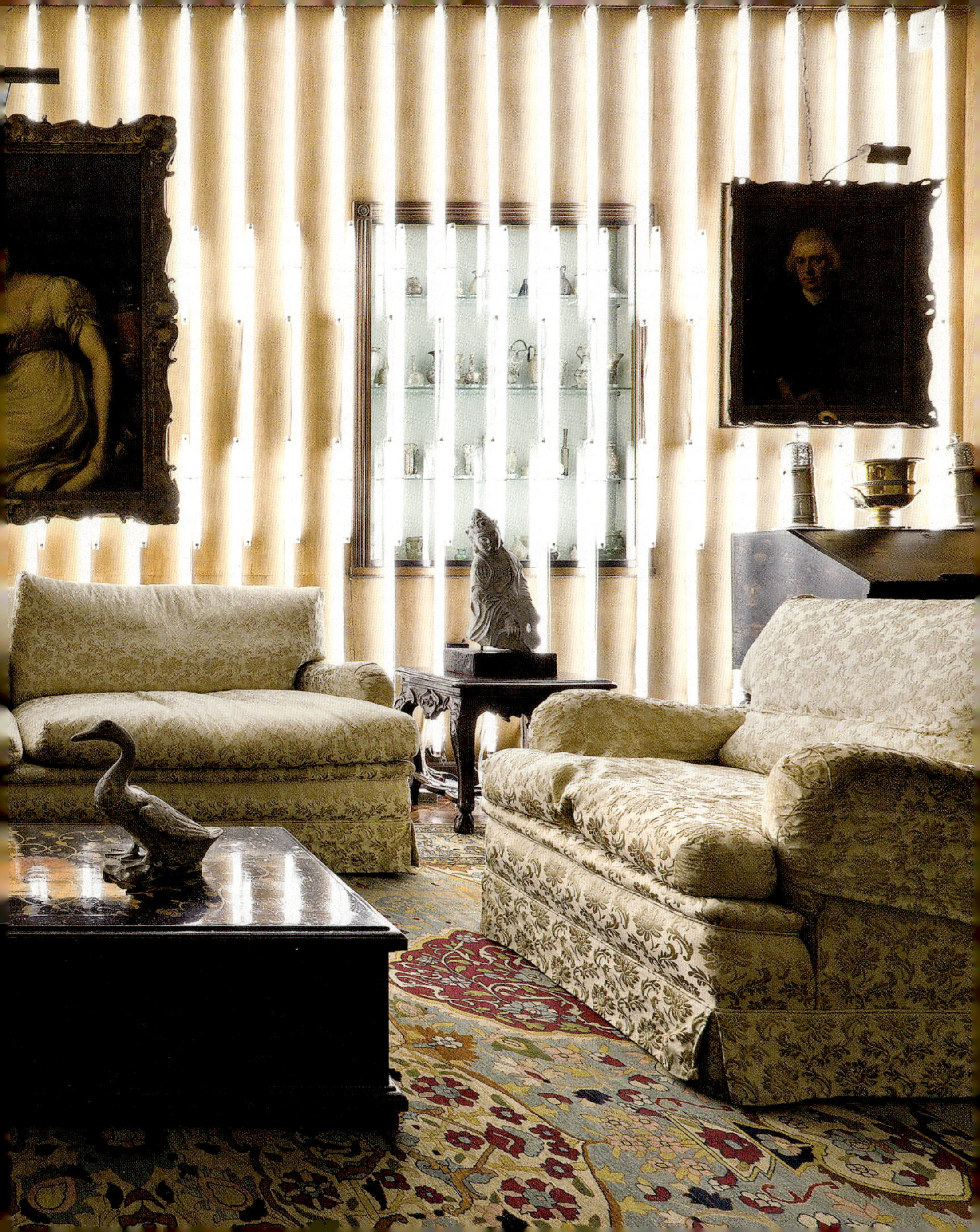

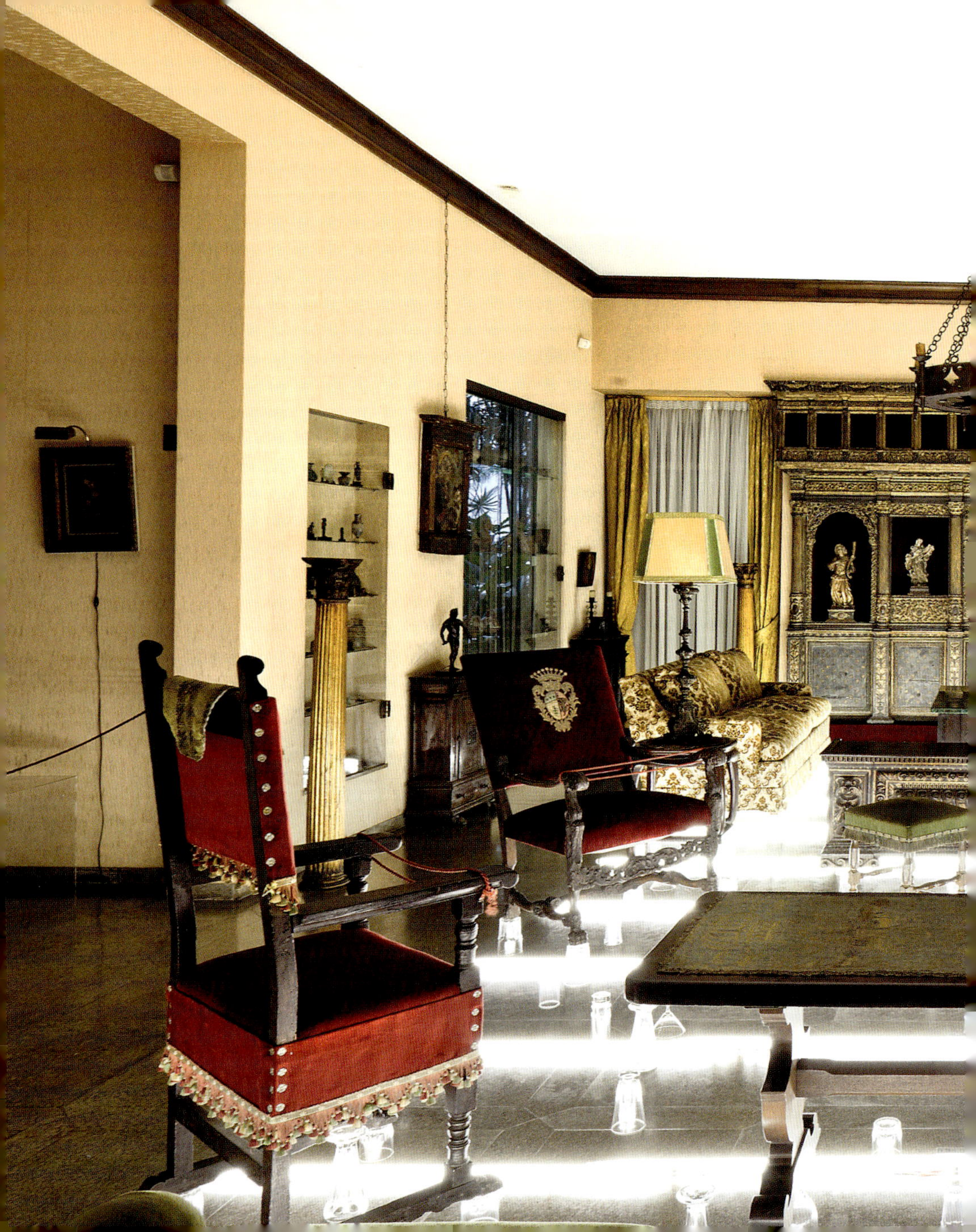

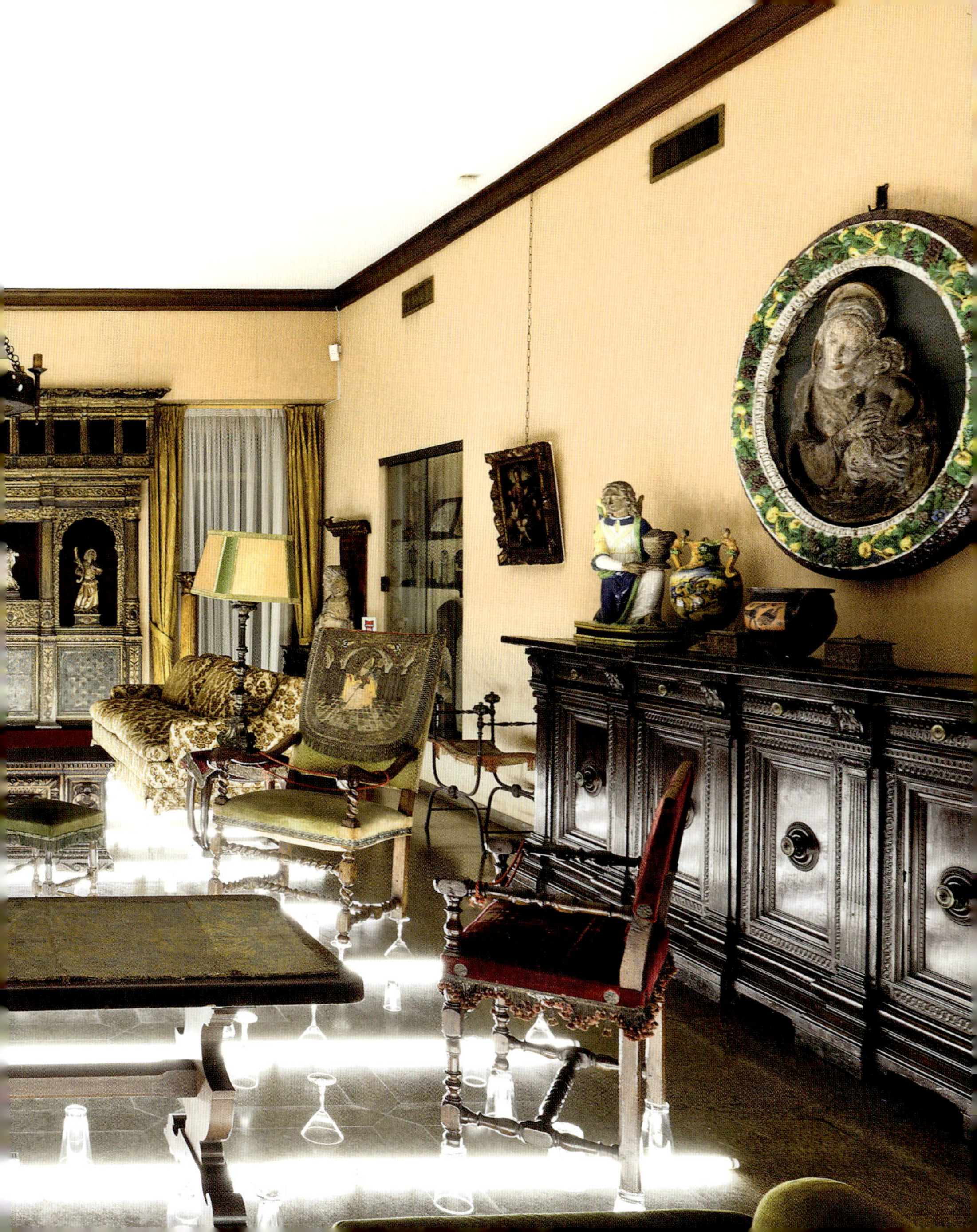

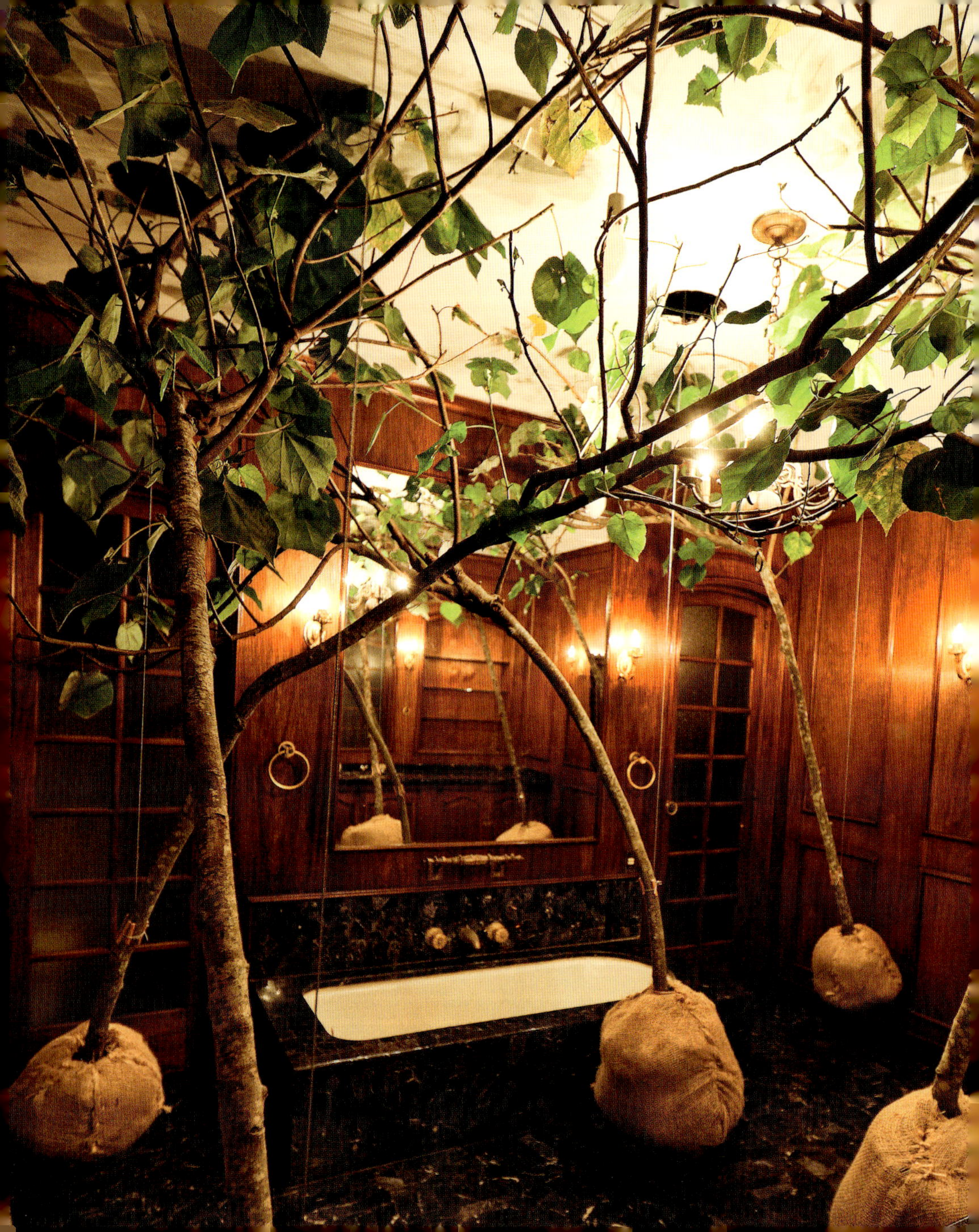

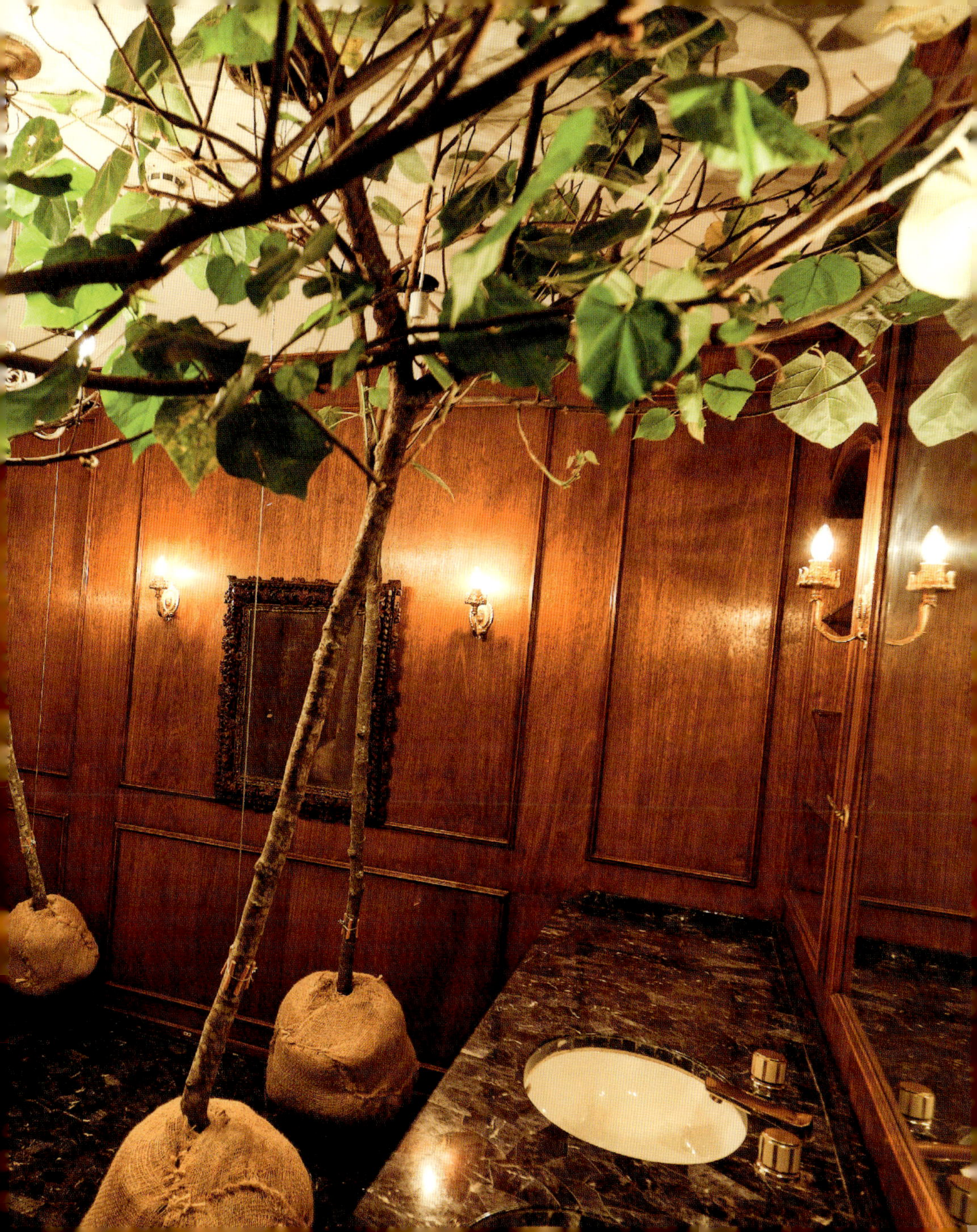

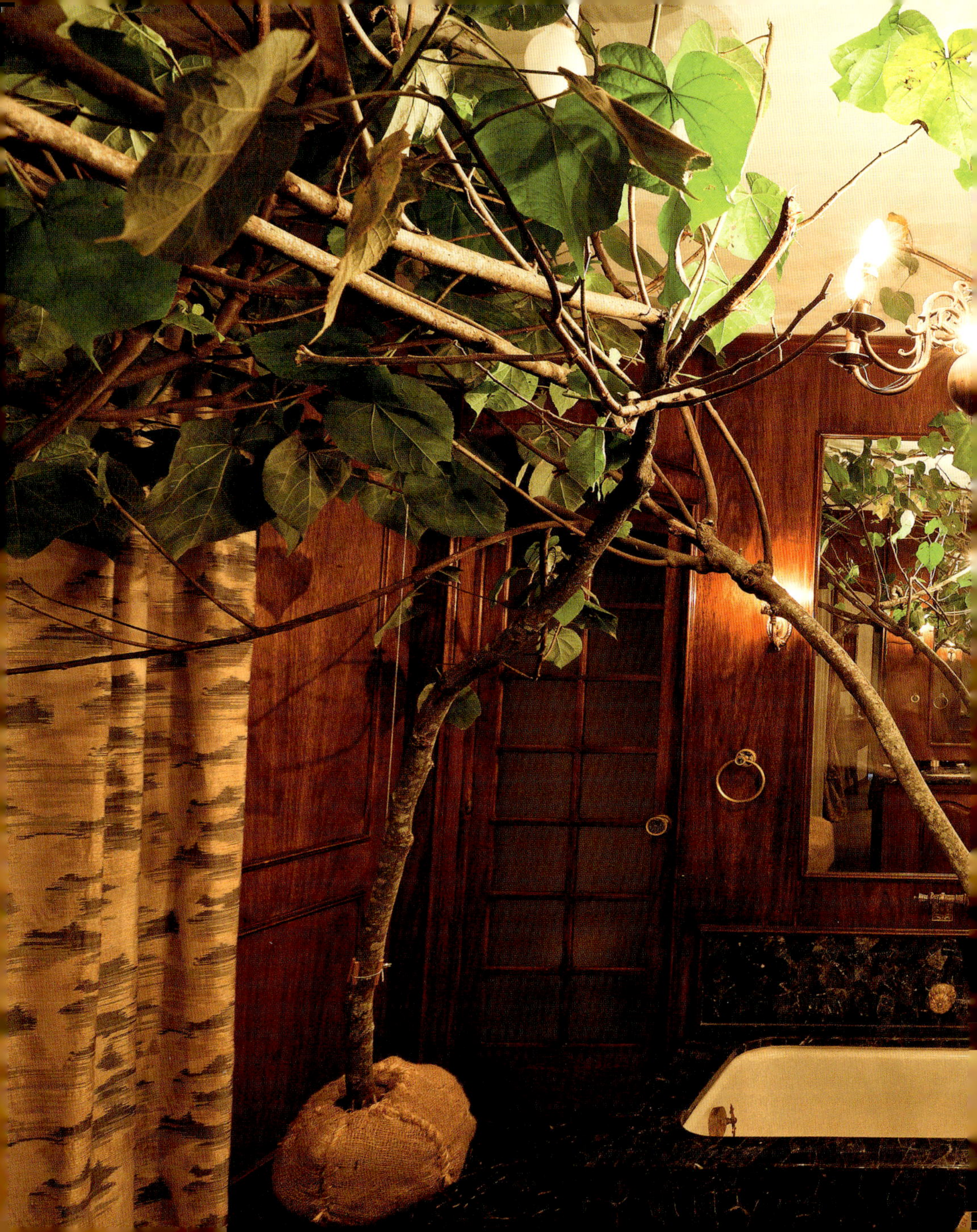

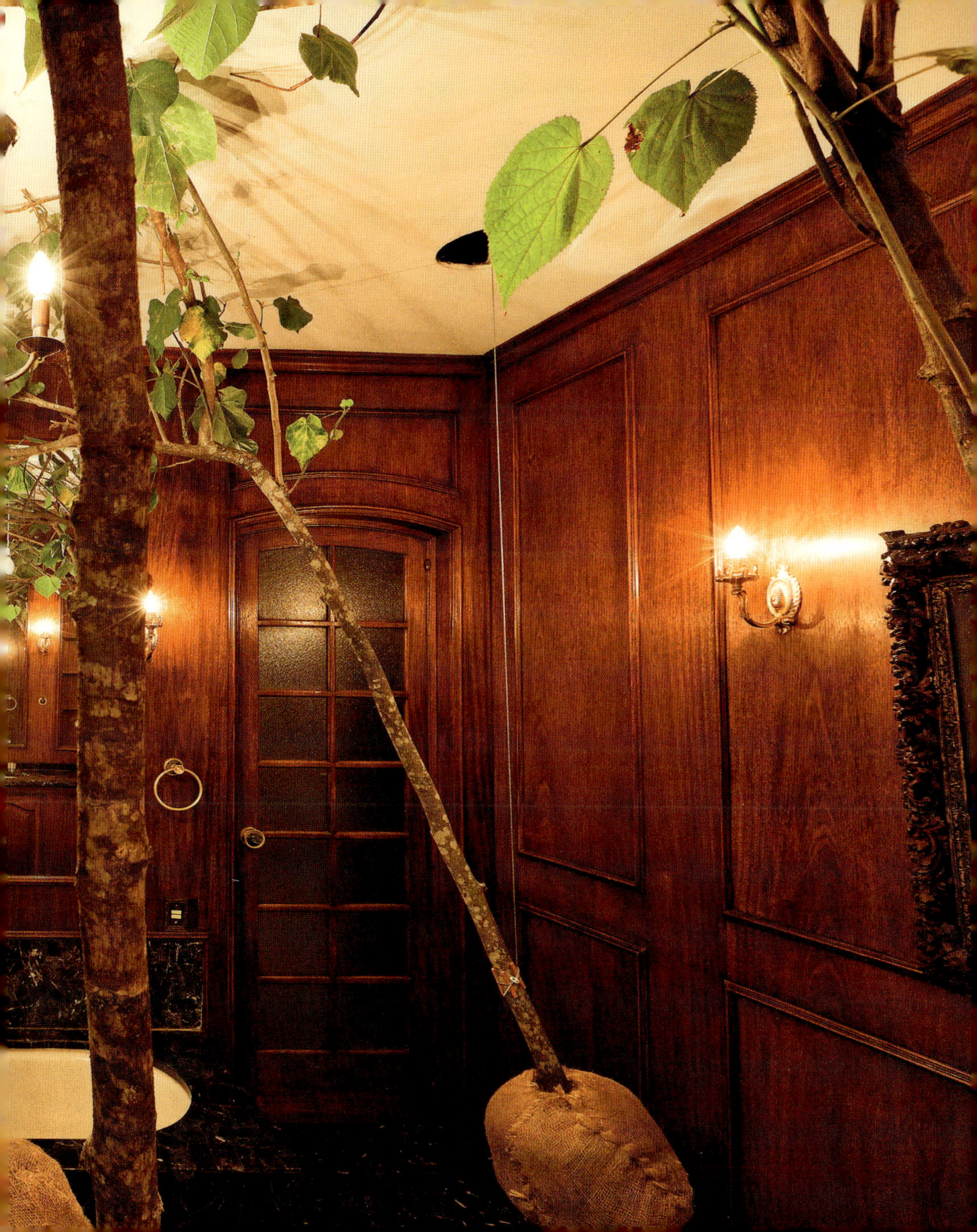

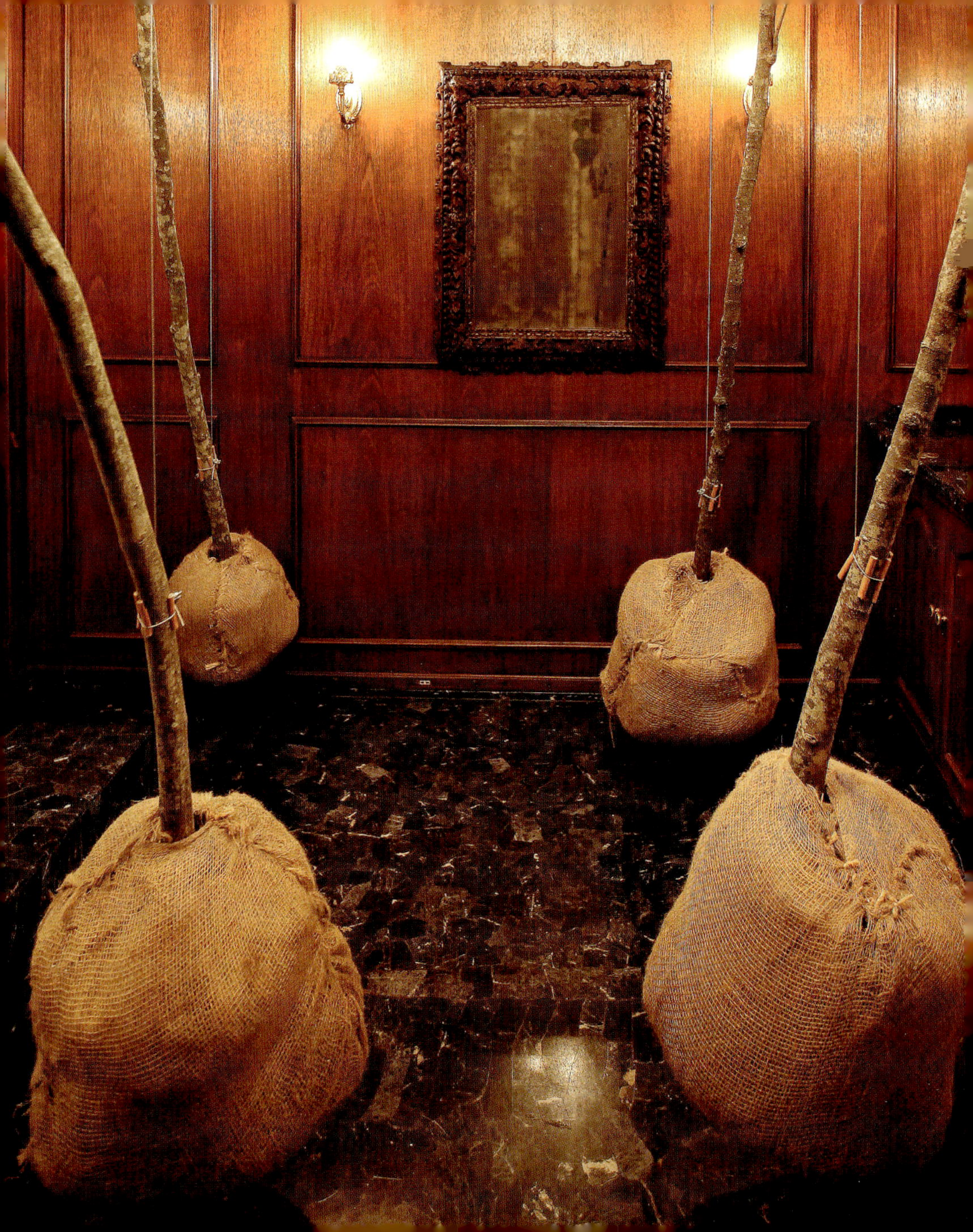

TEXTS

ARTO LINDSAY
ERASER OR BLUE AND WHITE MAKES GRAY

Apagador (*Eraser*) is a suggestion of sculpture. It does not fill the internal space with a solid gesture that impedes our entrance, but with volumes made from white sheets draped from the ceiling. These sheets of fabric flap gently in the breeze and give way with the slightest brush. They are shafts of light, or at least lit columns, empty on the inside.

The hollows of *Apagador* quickly drive us to the *horror vacuii* and to its opposite, fear of the excessively full. There is no way of knowing whether Carvalhosa erased or subtracted the internal volume of the place, if that volume simply ceased to exist as if it had never been there, or if it was torn out, leaving scars and agony. As such, we don't know if we are suffering or not. The draft in the room cannot sweep away the premonition of some misplaced weight and solidity. It makes a coffin for air. A coffin of air.

Somewhere out there in the world there must be someplace where white is the color or mourning, but that place is not here. Here the visitor hurries to fill the vacuum with all manner of spirituality.

When the incidental noises of the work cease, the sheets stop flapping in the breeze and the sound of footfalls recede, we can see that there is no silence in this place. There is always some background noise, a horizon of sound. It is the noise you get in films between a snatch of dialogue and some soundtrack. Between a rumbling sky and labored breathing, there's the voice of the film spool, the whisper of something being seen, the friction between film and projector.

We are left none the wiser as to the source and meaning of this sound until we hear the rumble of a plane flying overhead. We realize that what we are hearing is actually a recording of noise that filled that same room at some time in the past. Someone tells us that it is a recording made every night and played throughout the following day. All of a sudden, that noise sounds romantic, like the memory of a lover's moans. Yet it remains a disquieting sensation. It is as if a curtain has fallen between us and the day. This extemporal night cannot impose its darkness. Simply put, the day becomes gray and sullied with sound.

White noise contains all possible frequencies. It has no place for anything else. Its dreams and desires remain trapped within you. White noise contains all frequencies. It returns to the body what the void has stolen from it.

On erasures and their beginning—our eyes before an explosion, the instant at which the white and black fuse.

The Greeks painted their sculptures with black hair and red mouths.

We leave our plaster white.

Robert Rauschenberg erased a drawing by Willem de Kooning and presented the result as a work of his own. De Kooning was none too pleased.

In 1966 Robert Morris wrote a three-part essay entitled *Notes on Sculpture 1-3*, in which he speculated on the idea of *Gestalt* in sculpture, a sculpture whose parts are so tightly joined that perception cannot separate them and whose scale stands between the monumental and a size measured to the body.

Cy Twombly, a well-known painter, is also a sculptor.
He only works with whitewashed wood.

The Beatles' *White Album*

João's white record

Branco from the Titãs

The white teeth of a smiling Louis Armstrong

The white of Friday

The white on white of Malevich's cross or of Alberto Pitta's cloth panels

The white keys on a piano

The blanks I draw

The white women who gave themselves to me

The pale whitey

The white that is invisible to itself

White-collar white

The white man—forever in charge

The white of their eyes—fire at will

The clouds

Casper the Friendly Ghost

Let the whites work it out among themselves.

Arto Lindsay is a musician and an artist. He lives in Rio de Janeiro.

LUIS PÉREZ-ORAMAS
TO BE WHERE WE HAVE NEVER BEEN

I.

"What do you play the flute for, Olympos? Why music in solitude? There is no shepherd nor goatherd to hear it, nor is there a Nymph in his absence that would happily dance to the rhythm of your music."

So Philostratus swore to the adolescent whose beauty goes beyond the passion of the satyrs, while sleeping, and his sweat mixed with the smell of grass on which his body rested.

Why the harmony of breath that diminishes the sounds of the song, while the young Olympos, as a Narcissus facing the mirror of water, blows? Why the image turned into skin, stuck to grooved trails? Why music in abandonment, dormancy, death?

Like a premonition by Narcissus, with whom images are born in order to be extinguished immediately in their primordial instant, painting 21 of the icons of Philostratus describes a licentious and silent scene of holocaust: Olympos will be raised up, magnificent and naked, on the grasslands of desire and will majestically and indolently play his flute on the banks of a pristine lake, in order to just blow the unexpected canto of the song on the skin of the water and also see his own image shake, which others desire, and deform in the wrinkled surface that his breath moves and destroys.

A few lines before the true Narcissus, Olympos foreshadows, and has already seen the beauty of the image come undone in the folds that deform it, while its contours are shipwrecked on the draping of its liquid and exasperating density.

II.

Only the ignorant arrogance of the present has been able to sell us the idea of modernity as a scene in which, for the first time, the image dies.

Only the epidermal certainty of the present, which because of it would discover the world every time, can make us forget that the appearance of the image will always be declined upon its expiration; the emergence of art with its agony; the drive to erect the monument with the ephemeral duration of the experience that it celebrates or exorcises; the gaze of what we want to reach with the distance its image imposes upon us.

In order to name this distant object, eventually, the ancients conceived the maze of drapery, because the body is too visible, and what it breathes into desire and into life is camouflaged in its edge and sweating. What it breathes into: breath, the soul that has no form and has, maybe, every form. Then the obsessive dispersion of outer membranes that cover—let us think about fragments of Hellenistic sculpture, silent robes—canvas and drapery, clothing, vestments, linens, blankets, coats, transparent waves of silk in the wind served as an alphabet to say, with every movement, a truth, and with every gesture a revelation.

III.

Ever since I have thought about the work of Carlito Carvalhosa—white liquescences that wave by chance, painted mirrors where instead of Olympos' face we see the wave of his breath turned into a stone of colors, written word in the solitude of an invisible whip; Sugarloaf Mountain inverted in the mausoleum of the museum; an uprooted tree in the sky of the great halls of *convivium* and pageantry—I think only of shrouds that multiply their folds facing the breath of the footsteps, the noise, the solitude, the music, the immense coverings in order protect the architecture from our habitual animal customs.

What, then, is music for in abandonment; why the image in the flesh wound of the waters? Why erect the glorious adolescent with his flute? Why hide the sublime Nymph behind its cloths?

If we are only left with the image's agony, if there is no art of the monument or of the body as representation; if the image is multiplied in the vanity of its pornographic exchanges—not just in pornography, which still retains an ability of impulsive and momentary convocation, but in its sophistic aesthetic market—what do these white curtains tell us, these trees suspended from their roots, these murky mirrors?

That it is a space, any space, like a body that we inhabit; that in the severity of its durable inscription on the world is hidden the elusive multiplicity of the air that embodies it, and the hermetic numeral of its silence and echoes, that we did not hear when we saw, that only an epidermis that entirely covers can, as in those nymphs, as in that boy, herder of good goats, as in that flying Zephyr, decipher.

Why music in solitude? Why the sails with hoisted masts? To go through them, a niche of our body before it was there. To be where we have never been.

Luis Pérez-Oramas is a poet, curator and art critic. He lives in New York.

PAULO HERKENHOFF
JÁ ESTAVA ASSIM QUANDO EU CHEGUEI

On another order of reflection, *Já estava assim quando eu cheguei* (*It Was Like This When I Got Here*), by Carlito Carvalhosa, seems to allude to migration. Made by a São Paulo artist who moved to Rio, the sculpture is a decapitated Sugarloaf Mountain. Then again, it might refer to colonization: what was here before the westerners arrived was a large rock with another name. To name is to own. However, the work harks back to an even more primordial time than this when it asserts that the rock—a monumental geological accident—"was there when I got here" and had no name, only form. The artist does not establish any dichotomy between the disparate times of "arrival" and "being there before". Rather the work addresses the constitutive moment of the sentient subject. This difference between the ego and the world (that was "already" there) is consciousness itself. The affirmative title creates a point of suspension, prior to the stage of expressive intensification of its attack on the problem of artwork construction: that of keeping the unnamed in a mutating formal state. Merleau-Ponty's ontology of the visible (*it*, or that geographical mass, "was there when I got here"... *it* was already visible before my gaze) is considered from the perspective of Cézanne. If the French philosopher still dabbles in metaphysics, Carvalhosa dispenses the cultural memory of the cliff (hi symbolic history of the nation) and perhaps a Bachelardian phenomenology of the order of *La Terre et les rêveries de la volonté.* However, he knows that, essentially, he finds himself before a Merleau-Pontyan confrontation that is allusive to Cézanne: constructed humanity (th producer-subject of art: the artist) suspends its habits (such as that of considering the landscape as some thing given in painting) and reveals "the base of inhuman nature upon which painting has installed itself" If Carvalhosa's memory derives from the sensorial apparatus, its unfolding in his work has its eye on the history of art. "The landscape thinks itself in me, and I am its consciousness", wrote Cézanne. Like Mount Sainte-Victoire in Cézanne, the Sugarloaf is a mere worldly (pre-worldly) given through which Carvalhosa pits the specificity of sculpture against primordial nature (Husserl's *Erde*). Between the opacity of memory and non-knowing, Carvalhosa reveals his chiasmus: what comes from the thing (and was "already there") and what derives from himself in his work.

Paulo Herkenhoff is a curator and art critic. He lives in Rio de Janeiro.

As soon as I left, I sent Carlito a message sharing my joy from the Fradique Coutinho sidewalk. A text message, full of typos and disconnected thoughts. I think it was because of this SMS that he asked me for a talk, saying he wanted the impact without intermediation. Raw, like when I came out, still swooning, raw like: look, this is marvelous, thanks. He asked me to recount that moment, without any critical or historical constraints.

ROOMS

What I saw when I entered the two galleries were rectangular rooms made of white translucent fabric. I entered spaces with clearly defined dimensions and limits, solid spaces with right angles and corners. These rooms were not wombs, nor were they ships or airplanes, they were rooms.

SKY MOBILES

The sway of the sheets lent the rooms mobility, bringing to mind the term sky mobile. Not mobiles in the sky, but slivers of sky in motion. Standing there, inside, I watched a room glide, like you'd watch Calder's mobiles or Fred Astaire's feet. Except the mobile-room is not made of parts that balance in movement, but rather of a single piece, which is what is so intriguing about the way it composes and discomposes, and the way it is one but never whole. It is part of a whole whose size and nature cannot be divined. Maybe that's why it struck me as a mobile of—rather than in—the sky.

It is not that the draft in the gallery makes these rooms form and un-form. In fact, what forms and un-forms is the air itself.

DRAFT

The draft bellies the sheets and makes right, pleatless angles dance, which is strange, because the fabric is not a curtain and it does not hang on a window. A rectangle of sheets, with no pleats, no folds, no drift, but which allows itself to pleat, a pleated wall-skirt, a languid structure.

I walk the narrow corridor between the wall and the fabric, and the breeze created by my movements opens the way, delicately swelling the space between wall and sheet. I toy with it, moving my arm to make the sheet accompany the dance without touching my skin. I displace the air, and its existence between myself and things becomes clearer than ever before, the initial surprise becoming almost an awareness of a second skin interfacing between myself and the world. I think of the Jews crossing a parted Red Sea. I imagine the firm ground flanked by walls of water, shored only by Divine will. Here in São Paulo, the sheet withdraws before my wind, clearing my way, ushering me somewhere sheet after sheet. If I feel like it, should I stop, the air will flow back and the sheet will engulf me

SEA

Then I thought, why sky and not sea? I mean, sway is the sensation you get on boats. But I opted for sky because I didn't sway, I was still me and on firm ground, the whole time. Nothing inside drives me out of myself; these rooms make no impositions. Nothing dampens intelligence or sensation, except for the wonder and the lack of answers proper to art. If I feel cold, solitude, or if I fly in these rooms, it is I who does it; the rooms of *Faz Parte* give me these possibilities; they do not drag me out of myself.

NOTHING

Nothing is a relevant element of the room. There is nothing more I can say about that, other than that it exists and is important to them.

DUAL, SCENE AND SCENERY

When I walk down a road and see an empty space between two buildings where a house once stood, I get the feeling that I cannot recall what that house was like, because it is lost to me, no longer present even in memory. So I promise to pay more attention to the houses and buildings on the São Paulo streets I walk each day, but I know I won't do it, the sensation of death gives no respite. I will keep on losing, always.

I recall the scene from a film in which a man in a gray suit, bouquet in hand, enters an actress's dressing room and sees her silhouette behind a dressing screen, followed by part of a pale, beautiful arm as it deposits an item of underwear over the rim.

In these rooms, the sheeting obstructs our view of naked walls.

The outside space is cramped, the inside ample. When seen from the outside the sheets protect the void. When seen from the inside, they recall the drapery of a theater before curtain-call. There is a world behind them, a world of things, or perhaps a movie about to shine across some hidden screen.

Inside and outside there is draft, lightness, light and movement. The white fabric that separates inside from outside is translucent, preventing the gaze from piercing it. It is claustrophobic both within and without: outside is a narrow passage and we don't know where it leads; inside there are no windows, no contents, just an angular continuum, with no breaches or doors.

The sound reinforces this sense of duplicity, the glue that binds the void and scene of which the environment is made. It is a room, but not that room. The sound belongs to the street, not that street at that time. The street and the rooms that were there before the exhibition continue to exist. In fact, nothing here is virtual, the two sounds and rooms overlap—the existence of one interfering in our perception of the existence of the other.

It is not a question of image or representation. The fabric does not simulate a wall; it is a wall that hides another bare wall.

The walls and ceiling reconstruct the place, but from the inside out. There is no trickery or illusion, though it might seem that way. Here there is something that is not.

The *Invention of Morel*, a novel by the Argentinian Adolfo Bioy Casares (1914-1999), tells the story of a fugitive who goes into hiding on a desert island, where there's an abandoned house with a swimming pool full of putrid water and undergrowth invading the rooms. There is a woman that every afternoon walks through the flower bed, without even noticing the flowers, and sits pensively on a rock on top of the hill. There she is, every afternoon, pensive and lovely up on the hill. There is also a group of friends fooling around by the swimming pool, now filled with crystal clear water. The fugitive is afraid to show himself, but he fixes up a flower garden near the rock on the hill. Again, the woman walks over the flowers and sits on the rock. In the end, the fugitive discovers that the woman and the youths playing in the clean pool are reproductions of happy days lived in the past. One of the men has found a way to immortalize himself with his friends. Depending on the tides, a mechanism is triggered that allows times past to replay over the undergrowth and abandonment of the present.

The *Faz Parte* exhibition works a similar overlapping of existences that strike the viewer as if they were different times and even different spaces, somehow unfolding in the same place, at the same time. Even though the sound is a recording of past events, by being played back it becomes sound again, mixed over the present sound coming from the present street. In other words, the rooms and sounds both exist and are reproductions, they duplicate, modify and reinforce what we already know: the sound of the street, the space of the rooms. The walls, like white screens awaiting a movie, are the walls of a gallery with no pictures.

Beatriz Bacher is a writer. She lives in São Paulo.

IVO MESQUITA
THE SUM OF DAYS

In Christian tradition, Lent is a period of preparation for the annual celebration of Christ's resurrection at Easter. It is a time the believer must devote to prayer, penitence and charity. Among other rites and practices, church statuary is veiled during Lent in order to encourage the faithful to focus exclusively on their own thoughts and actions, standing before God without the support and mediation provided by the saints and symbols throughout the rest of the liturgical year. In other words, during Lent, iconography—representation—is erased as a test of faith. It is interesting to note that, seeing the saints all veiled, erased from the temple pedestals, one has the opportunity to be alone, face to face with their own reality, body and soul; human, without mediators.

The installation by the São Paulo artist Carlito Carvalhosa *A soma dos dias* (*The Sum of Days)* resorts to this same idea or principle, proposing to cover and erase in order to reveal or have seen. A tall and voluminous fabric construction veils and hides the architecture at the Octógono Gallery, making it disappear and, as such, interrupting the customary flow and perception of the institution's interior. The rigid geometry is countered by a labyrinth of curves and floating, diaphanous walls, susceptible to the slightest breeze and movement. Inside this other space, the gallery disappears, making way for a world of silhouettes and shadows that move to a discreet but persistent soundtrack that is somehow familiar. The asymmetric play of lamps on the walls underscores the broken parity of the original venue, creating distinct zones of light and shade and conferring a cinematic quality upon this new architecture.

The soundtrack created by Philip Glass, using several of his own compositions, underpins the time the work sets for the gallery interior. It repeats in perpetual motion an incessant, labyrinthine time, over which incidental sounds are recorded each day—conversations, footsteps, movements—captured by microphones and played back instantly through speakers. Each day a new track is laid over and incorporates that of the previous day. This accumulation, this sum of days, constitutes the experiential memory of the work's passage through the institution. It produces a happening and, simultaneously, records and stores its own presence, its history.

Ivo Mesquita is the Chief Curator at Pinacoteca do Estado de São Paulo. He lives in São Paulo.

JOÃO BANDEIRA
APART

It is always important to know the *what*. But in art the *how* tends to be even more so. But anywhere, the least you need to start with are the *where* and the *when*. The thing is, Carlito Carvalhosa's *Faz Parte*[1] is made with very little and puts all that is basic—and even what is not—under an un-decidable regime of alternacy and complementarity. The work is presently on display at the Gabinete de Arte Raquel Arnaud. For a time it was also on show at the Galeria Millan, in a form very similar to that at the Gabinete: in both cases, working with a duplication of the galleries' white cubes, in doorless, almost entirely hollow spaces outlined by thin, translucent fabric, with the aid of a cold light and occasionally crossed by a casual sort of background noise that does not seem to come from there. A sound in passing.

But the differences soon arise, referring one to the other. At Galeria Millan, the light comes from above, in three conjugated spaces, not all of which are empty: one of them contains some round plates of glass, like huge lenses, piled up on the floor. At Gabinete de Arte, the lenses are set on a table and low base, and they stand outside the space circumscribed by the drapery, which is now a single area, with two sources of light, one at the front and the other at the back of this room-within-a-room. Along the other two sides, behind the fabric, the gallery walls are clad with mirrors, one clear and the other darkened. Walking through the narrow corridor which remains between the white fabric and the bare wall of the first gallery, and the fabric and mirror-lined walls in the other, affords perceptibly different sensations, as does lifting up the drapery and slipping inside the fabric rooms of either venue. Furthermore, the sounds in one gallery are recorded in the other by an open microphone after closing hours and played back at the other on the following day in the first gallery, and vice-versa, in a sort of gap of time and space.

However, the differences are impurities of the white. Not so many as to cancel the relationship of participation between the two venues. It is as if, upon entering the place, where not much happens, all we were offered was a shoddy "this is this". Yet if there is (or there was, never mind) a near-twin of this space out there somewhere, we are also given a "this is that". Lingering awhile longer there, the experience of an embodied AND/OR may begin to flourish. And it might be many things, except peaceful. Differences arise because there is little in each part, so little that each now, each here, each this, each that is a lot—no matter in which gallery it happens to be. *Faz Parte* (*It Happens*), the mal-resigned grumble of everyday life, now comes to include *fazer a parte* (make the part), create the piece as a whole, here and now, considering the lenses and visible wires as leftovers that, after all, are also part, reminding us that there is another part there and then. This hardly seems strange in the scheduled mis-encounter that has long characterized Carlito's work. Nor does that way of life growingly immersed in the volatility of presence in which we are sometimes capable of resucitating that Cortázarian[2] feeling of not being fully there, and of making of the slightest sign an event.

* Originally published in *Folha de S. Paulo, Ilustrada*, September 13th 2008.

1 Exhibition at Gabinete de Arte Raquel Arnaud and Galeria Millan, in São Paulo, August and September 2008.

2 "I write precisely because I am only half there or not there at all. I write by default and 'dislocation', and since I write out of an interstice I always invite others to discover one of their own and to see for themselves the garden where the trees bear fruits that turn out to be precious stones". Julio Cortázar, in "On Feeling Not All There."

João Bandeira is the curadtor of Centro MariAntonia, of University of São Paulo.

The empty main hall at the Centro Universitário Maria Antonia (Ceuma) on opening night must have been quite a sight to behold, with the public all corralled behind the little white rail aligned with the first two columns. Perhaps it is something like the works by Serra that gradually close in on people, except that, here, the wall was invisible and tenuous. From the part of the hall open to the public, all you could see was a plaster block wedged in a void.

"There's none of that getting up close, slapping your beer can down on it and calling it mate!"[1]

The title of this work by Carlito Carvalhosa was supposed to be *Perna de três* (*Three-Leg Truss*), but this was changed to *Favor não tocar* (*Please Don't Touch*) during construction, when the artist decided to erect a barrier to keep back the public. Knowing this name-that-almost-was-but-wasn't allows for some initial proximity between the sculpture on show at Ceuma and a series of works the artist produced at MuBE in 1999, entitled *Duas águas* (*Two Waters*).

There would seem to be two families of titles in Carvalhosa's work: those that practically describe the physical constitution of the piece, such as *Ceras perdidas* (*Lost Waxes*) and *Espelhos graxos* (*Greased Mirrors*), and those that sit midway between technical terminology and poetic expression, between physical and metaphorical description of the work, such as *Duas águas* (*Two Waters*) and *Perna de três* (*Three-Leg Truss*), with the added coincidence of both titles including numbers.

Perna de três is a device used in construction, while *duas águas* refers to an inverted V-shaped roof that allows water to drain off on either side. The two facets of this roof-type inspired João Cabral de Melo Neto to take this as the title of a 1956 collection of published and unpublished works: one facet hermetic in nature, and the other more 'popular'; poems to read and poems to be recited.

Besides a possible relationship between the names of the works, other common denominators between *Duas águas* and the piece on show at Ceuma are the material used, the color and density disguised as levity. Might the Maria Antonia exhibition be a follow-up of the pieces exhibited at the MuBE in 1999, as if, beyond groupings by title, Carvalhosa's works also reveal a kinship of content?

This group of works is of more distant lineage to the perforated plaster sculptures shown at Galeria Raquel Arnaud in 2003, which establish greater dialogue with the glazed porcelain series of 1996/7, not so much because of the perforations, but because of a sort of "dry" finishing, unlike the "humid" finishing of *Duas águas* and *Favor não tocar*.

"The piece at the Raquel had various natures, a perforated part, a wafer-thin part, a more hybrid part, after the porcelain work. A piece you could walk around and around and it would always throw up something you hadn't noticed before. This time I figured it would be possible to see the thing with more intensity if I kept some distance from it; made the surrounding space part of the piece itself."

It is as if the distance renders the sculpture more visible, in the sense of that original experience of seeing, as opposed to the contemporary experience of "re-seeing", of which Paul Virilio speaks: "Today, we are no longer truly 'seeers' (voyants), but already 'resee-ers' (*revoyants*); the tautological repetition of the same, at work in our mode of (industrial) production, is at work equally in our mode of perception" (Paul Virírlio, *L'horizon négatif*, Paris, 1984, p. 31).

The opposite of "reseeing" is to "render the invisible visible"; the philosopher's self-ordained task. In order to combat this visual surplus that gets in the way of perception—"I was suddenly persuaded that vision gave less to see, that it was above all a process of occultation"—Virilio proposes a voluntary blindness that leads us to note the articulations between objects, not just the objects themselves, finding new and more complex forms in the intervals and interstices.

By making the surrounding space part of the work, Carvalhosa forces us to adopt a sort of involuntary blindness. In our habitual eagerness to see more and better, to see and touch at close quarters, we end up—between frustration and impotence, trapped there behind the railing—failing to see the void and to consider how the thing came to be where it is, if there might be something somewhere out of view that is holding that shapeless body up.

It is interesting that the block was lowered rather than raised into position: it was built at a tilt, above the point where it would eventually wedge. The work slid into position, and then and only then did the artist insert the steel pegs to prevent it from sliding further over the course of the exhibition, which might not actually have happened, as the ton-weight of plaster is well and truly jammed between those columns.

This suspension harks back to the "frozen moment" paintings exhibited at the Raquel Arnaud (in plaster, oil, grease and resin on mirror-glass). And also to earlier works in which the artist sandwiched wet plaster between glass. This suspension hovers somewhere between precariousness and lastingness a paradox like that underscored by Rodrigo Naves in his text on the divided nature of the work.[2]

"I like this paradox, I like the pieces to be unstable, in terms of their meaning, of the presence of the materials and their relationship with the space."

Lorenzo Mammì has some beautiful definitions for the artist's works as "in-over-your-head painting,"[3] and these can serve to clarify the current piece. This sculpture also draws us out of our depth, not out of some lack of definition between figure and background (which was what Mammì saw in the paintings from 1989), but because it sits above the line of the horizon: we don't see the topside and find ourselves on the tips of our toes, craning our necks to keep chin above water.

Another of Mammì's observations: "the truth of the work resides in some no-man's land between nothing and the anecdote."[4] *Favor não tocar* also inhabits this realm between "nothing and the anecdote" because it evokes things without imitating anything (it resembles a cloud, a plane, a ship run aground, an animal, a shark, and yet it is none of these) and also because it hides its process of construction—in line, once again, with the critic's reasoning.

"In fact, in-over-your-head sculpture would be a good name. However, I think there is a lack of definition in this piece between figure and background, and I think it transforms the scale of the room."

And, after all, is plaster a good or a bad thing?

"Plaster is an everyday material, used in everything from the cast for a broken arm to the decorative finish of a ceiling. It is a material of transition in art, nobody gives it much thought, which is why it interests me. I like the way it goes from wet to dry, the way it is so neutral it's hard to know what it is. I once went to a baroque castle in Germany, where all the pillars were of plaster made to imitate marble. It seems that in the 17th century it was more expensive and sophisticated to make mock marble in plaster than to use real marble, and that's why the pillars were all made of plaster, with the fake proving more ostentatious than the real."

1 The interventions, in quotation marks, are excerpts from an e-mail interview with Carlito Carvalhosa on July 27 and 28, 2005, concerning the exhibition at Ceuma.

2 NAVES, Rodrigo. "Óleo sobre água", in *Carlito Carvalhosa*, Lorenzo Mammì (org.). São Paulo: CosacNaify, 2000.

3 MAMMÌ, Lorenzo. Preface to the book *Carlito Carvalhosa*. São Paulo: CosacNaify, 2000.

4 Idem, ibidem.

Juliana Monachesi is a journalist and art critic. She lives in São Paulo.

We had never seen a hall of mirrors quite like this one. Mirrors that you would think defective or imperfect if you came across them somewhere, for only a manufacturing flaw could explain why the reflection we expect to stare back at us is obstructed by some caked layer or smudge that blots out our faces, some form of seepage trapped and immobilized on the inside. We see ourselves in these mirrors, but cannot quite discern what it is that has butted in, or whether it is there to be seen or to prevent us from seeing.

A mirror is not just any surface, but one that inevitably stokes our narcissistic impulses. There is no resisting the allure that draws the eye unappealably towards that surface, in which we see ourselves twofold: in the painting and in the mirror. And that intruder, which belongs to the "painting", stands between us and our reflection, and we have to dodge it in order to see ourselves. So the defect is actually an effect? The "mirror mirror on the wall" is occupied by something other, and we don't know how it got there. How did it get inside? What work is this that a viscous, greasy material can produce, having infiltrated and settled therein, unwanted, making a nuisance of itself? It has raised from horizontality to verticality, like a puddle that is flung in our faces; a floor become wall, stamping the totalizing visual violence of our day into those pools of grease, which, at least, are the material itself, without manipulation.

These paintings that put our reflections inside them are also mirrors. We are in there when we look at them and see ourselves seeing. Yet the surface is smeared with something we cannot identify. Some homeless image now squats there, where people come and go, glancing quickly before moving on but never staying. The mirror has become a viscous window display, robbed of its original use, hijacked by a gooey substance that has this tacky glittery aspect of more than dubious taste, an effect the grease exploits to create this visual intrigue.

As I see it, through what goes on in the mirrors, Carlito Carvalhosa gives continuity to the impulse toward form that is proper to painting, but which will, from now on, reside in the oscillating and the ambivalent, the upstanding and the suspect, the vulgar and the sophisticated, transferring autonomy of form to the behavior of a single ordinary material, grease. The mirror surface strives to repel the prevailing principle of total plasticity expressed in these greasy blotches and smudges, as theirs is an unpleasant blur, the antithesis of unequivocal specular clarity—such that the resulting visual experience suggests a whole array of disparate references external to the form taken in isolation.

What we can see is that the work has left behind the earlier closed organization in order to exhibit an amplified and risky external contamination. The anterior form, organic and dominated by organicity, circumscribed by the monochrome and cohesion of the single material, seems here to have circulated in unsuspected or frankly suspect environments to which the mirror is a witness. These images have wandered, experienced the excessive reflection of vernacular and nauseating displays of vulgar glitter, the dubious highlighting of cultural declassification that a lack of distinction brings into relief, depreciating everything. This empire of viscous, formless narcissism might seem superficial and specular, but it is not. The task of reconverting its own marked degradation by appellative commercial consumerism to an experience of form therefore becomes an interesting challenge. We remain at some point beyond the process Andy Warhol followed at close-quarters, now dissolved into a post-kitsch emulsion of higher glamorized pop; stages of ferocious degradation that art has accompanied. Extracting some expression of beauty from this grotesquely self-satisfied countenance requires decontamination, and that means taking the fascination this sheen irresistibly holds and consigning it to suspension in a void, reconverting the enchanting fatuity that emanates from it. This shift in Carlito's work has something of contemporary architecture to it, which likewise strives to lend plastic expression to technological saturation and articulate freely the effect of the image with the possibilities of the material, and vice-versa, as do Frank Gehry's titanium curves, for example.

It is reasonable that the mirror should come after the plaster, to which it stands as an opposite; as if one absorbed and captured the other visually; as mutually negating pairs, with one striving to occupy the space of the other. And both, simultaneously, demonstrate this dysfunctional nature of the totalization of the image that the work of Carlito Carvalhosa attempts to accentuate and reveal in the current state of things: the abundance offered to the gaze and the little that taxes the eye.

Paulo Venancio Filho is an art critic and curator. He lives in Rio de Janeiro.

Oxalá is the father of the *Orixás*, responsible for molding men out of manioc dough. Divinity of peace always dressed in white, his day is Friday. *Oxalá* is worshipped through various rituals and obligations. One of these rites takes place during the *Oxalá* Festival, when the *Orixás* and the initiates parade around the *terreiro*, place of worship in *Candombé* tradition, under a large white mantle, the *Alá de Oxalá*, giving praise and receiving the *Orixá's axé* (vital force) to the slow beat of the percussion. Those huddled beneath the *Alá de Oxalá* are taken over by a sensation of peace and serenity.

That was exactly the feeling I got upon entering the installation *Apagador* at the Museum of Modern Art in Bahia, which occupies a 16th-century building where countless slaves were trafficked after being shipped over from Africa. Each of the rooms in the Museum's Chapel was filled with enormous white fabric volumes draped from the ceiling to the floor, only inches away from the walls. To get around the work, you had to walk these narrow corridors and slip in under the sheets, immersing yourself within the large, diaphanous spaces created by these white cubes of fabric.

Inside the installation it is not only the architecture of the Chapel that is erased, but also the viewer's ill-feelings and worries, resulting in a stage of contemplation and peace similar to that evoked in the ritual of *Oxalá*. This sensation is heightened by the fact that the venue is a church, which in Salvador—thanks to Bahian syncretism—is also a place for the worship of the *Orixás*. *Epababá*!! *Exêê*!

Exu is the messenger *Orixá*, an opener of paths. Though the youngest of the *Orixás*, he has earned the right to eat first and be pleased before all others. *Exu* lives at crossroads, eats chicken and palm oil, drinks *cachaça*, and has a special fondness for money and parties. His sacred trees include the Aroeira, (pepper tree). The exhibition *Roadmap for Visitation* features three large works distributed across the first floor of Aclamação Palace. The place, formerly the Governor's residence, sits at a crossroads in downtown Salvador.

The first work was a huge Aroeira, suspended two meters off the floor in the middle of the imposing Entrance Hall. Alongside this magnificent tree was a pair of ten-meter-long posts, also suspended, transforming the set int a sort of trident, *Exu's* tool.

The visual impact and poetic

density of the piece inhabited Aclamação Palace for seven long months; seven is also *Exu's* number. At the end of the exhibition, the tree was replanted in a garden in the Palace grounds, where it still stands today. A tree, which would normally seed, grow and die in the earth, and feed from roots embedded in the earth, is here hung above the ground in a noble, almost celestial hall. This must be a work of *Exu*, the messenger who acts between Heaven and Earth!

The second piece was done in the Banquet Hall, filled by three long hardwood tables, adorned with crystal chandeliers and decorated with frescoes. Lampposts, which were once trees and later illuminated paths, form a sort of fallen cross that cuts violently through the architecture, breaching walls and windows, contrasting starkly with the nobility of the furnishings and décor.

The last of the three works was on the veranda and the Ceremonial Hall, once a venue for official balls, soirées and funerals, among other activities governed by *Exu*. Hundreds of ceiling-high beams formed a dry, leafless forest dialoguing directly with the building's grounds and gardens.

In the middle of this hall, an enormous and imposing crystal chandelier holds out against the "lances" driven into the historical and visual opulence of the space. Jabbed like a voodoo doll, exorcising the ghosts of the artist's own elitist up-bringing, putting him in touch with that which is essential in art, opening paths to the world. *Laroyê*! *Mojubá*!

The *Orixás* govern all. *Oxalá* and *Exu* are the only pair in the pantheon that everybody has. Even if we don't realize it, there are always *Orixás* along the way.

Daniel Rangel is a curator and *Arabadá* of the *terreiro Ilê Omorodé Axé Orixá N'la*.
He lives in Salvador.

BIBLIOGRAPHY
CARLITO CARVALHOSA

"OUT-DOORS", um jeito urbano de mostrar a arte. *Folha de S.Paulo*, Geral, 15 Sept. 1984, p. 19.

18ª BIENAL, da nova pintura a John Cage. *Folha de S.Paulo*, Ilustrada, 2 Oct. 1985, p. 37.

A ARTE sem limites de Carlito Carvalhosa.
A Gazeta, Caderno 2, Vitória, 5 Nov. 1987, p. 16.

A GALERIA vai às ruas. *IstoÉ*, São Paulo, 26 Sept. 1984, p. 54.

A JOVEM transvanguarda vai à Bienal. *Folha de S.Paulo*, Ilustrada, 3 Apr. 1985, p. 31.

ABRAMO, Radha. Belas Artes, um salão polêmico. *Folha de S.Paulo*, Ilustrada, 23 Mar. 1984.

ABRAMO, Radha. Os jovens e o gestual impulsivo. *Folha de S.Paulo*, Ilustrada, 17 May 1985, p. 4.

ALVES, Cauê. Reflexos na mira. *Moderno Mam*, perfil contemporâneo, Museu de Arte Moderna de São Paulo, Oct. 2010, p. 18.

AMARAL, Aracy. Uma nova pintura e o grupo da Casa 7. *Catalogue*, Casa 7 – Pintura, Museu de Arte Contemporânea da USP, São Paulo, 30 Apr. 1985 / Museu de Arte Moderna, Rio de Janeiro, 7 May 1985.

AMARANTE, Leonor. O toque brasileiro na 18ª Bienal. *O Estado de S. Paulo*, 24 Nov. 1985, p. 44.

ANDRADE, Rodrigo. O espelho da modernidade. *Valor*, Artes Visuais, São Paulo, 28 Nov. 2003, p. 18.

AQUINO, Flávio. A Bienal total. *Manchete* n. 1748, Rio de Janeiro, 19 Oct. 1985, p. 115–128.

AQUINO, Flávio. A vanguarda na Bienal. *Fatos* n. 31, Rio de Janeiro, 21 Oct. 1985, p. 37-45.

AQUINO, Flávio. A vigorosa arte jovem do grupo 5 da casa 7. *Fatos* n. 9, Rio de Janeiro, 20 May 1985, p. 48-49.

ARAÚJO, Artur. Individuais simultâneas. *Última Hora*, UH Revista, Rio de Janeiro, 6 Sept. 1989, p. 6.

ARAÚJO, Olívio Tavares de. Brilho reconquistado. *IstoÉ* n. 459, São Paulo, 9 Oct. 1985, p. 42-45.

ARAÚJO, Olívio Tavares de. Riscos que vêm com o sucesso. *IstoÉ* nº 438, São Paulo, 15 May 1985, p. 10.

ARAÚJO, Olívio Tavares de. Tradição do rigor experimental. *IstoÉ*, São Paulo, 24 Jun. 1987, p. 13.

ARAÚJO, Olívio Tavares de. *Vogue*, Visuais, São Paulo, Aug. 1989, p. 10.

ARTES PLÁSTICAS, Carlito Carvalhosa apresenta suas peças em gesso e vidro no MuBE. *Folha de S. Paulo*, Folha Acontece, São Paulo, 28 Jun. 1999, p. 1.

AS OBRAS 'duplas' de Carlito. O *Estado de S. Paulo*, Jornal da Tarde, Visuais, São Paulo, 8 Mar. 1994, p. 12.

BANDEIRA, João. Carvalhosa duplica a experiência do cubo branco das galerias. *Folha de S. Paulo*, Ilustrada, 12 Sept. 2008, p. E12.

BARREIRO, Tania. Conceito ou estética? *Jornal do Comércio*, Panorama, Porte Alegre, 17 Oct. 2001, p. 1.

BOWE, John. Peripheral Vision. *The New York Times Style Magazine*, New York, 20 Nov. 2010, p. 22.

BRAZ, Carlos Henrique. Fase iluminada. *Veja Rio*, Exposições, 27 Apr. 2011, p. 66.

BREERETE, Geneviève. De Paris à Bordeaux, des Brésiliens d'aujourd'hui. *Le Monde*, Paris, 3 Nov. 2001, p. 24.

BRESSANE, Ronaldo. Éramos 7. *Daslu Homem*, Vol.18, Trip Editora e propaganda S/A, São Paulo, Nov. 2006, p. 80-84.

BUTCHER, Isabel / Wrede, Catharina. Obra em Progresso. *O Globo*, Segundo Caderno, Rio de Janeiro, 25 Apr. 2011, p. 4.

BUTCHER, Isabel. A cidade como inspiração. *Veja Rio*, Exposições, Rio de Janeiro, 15 Feb. 2006, p. 47.

CARAVALHO, José Eduardo. Desafio aos sentidos. *A Tarde*, Artes Plásticas, Salvador, 1 Mar. 2008, p. 1.

CARLITO Carvalhosa apresenta suas contradições em gesso no Paço. *O Globo*, Segundo Caderno, Rio de Janeiro, 8 Jun. 1999, p. 10.

CARLITO Carvalhosa. *Catalogue*, Duas Águas. Museu Brasileiro da Escultura – MuBE, São Paulo, 28 Jun. / Paço Imperial, Rio de Janei 8 Jul. 1999.

CARLITO Carvalhosa. *Catalogue*, Gabinete de Arte Raquel Arnaud. São Paulo, 8 Mar. 1994.

CARLITO Carvalhosa. *Catalogue*, Gabinete de Arte Raquel Arnaud. São Paulo, 12 Nov. 1997.

CARLITO Carvalhosa. *Catalogue*, Paulo Figueiredo Galeria de Arte, São Paulo, 3 Aug. / Galeria Rodri M. F. de Andrade – Funarte, Rio d Janeiro, 1989.

CARNEIRO, Elisa Marilia. Dois artistas no mesmo espaço. *Folha de Londrina*, Folha 2, Curitiba, 19 Sept. 2001, p. 2.

CARONE, Sara. Cerâmica Brasileir construção de uma linguagem. *Catalogue*, Centro Brasileiro Britânico, São Paulo, 5 Sept. 200

CARVALHO, Bernardo. Arte reflexiva substitui infantilismo inicial. *Folha de S.Paulo*, Bienal Brasil, 24 Apr. 1994, p. 6.

CARVALHO, Bernardo. Carlito Carvalhosa faz o olhar perder o foco. *Folha de S.Paulo*, Acontece, Mar. 1994, p. 1.

CARVALHOSA expõe na Subdistrito. *Folha de S.Paulo*, Ilustrada, 18 Jun. 1987, p. 50.

CARVALHOSA vence 9º Salão Nacional. *Folha de S.Paulo*, Ilustrada, 18 Dec. 1986, p. 37.

CARVALHOSA, Carlito. Apagador *Catalogue*, Funarte, Rio de Janeir 2008, p. 2.

CARVALHOSA, Carlito. *Catalogue* Gabinete de Arte Raquel Arnaud São Paulo, Aug. 2008.

CARVALHOSA, Carlito. Istantâne Deixa ficar. *IDI 151psicanálise e escultur/ per via di levare*, vol. 34 Publicação da Sociedade Brasilei de Psicanálise de São Paulo, 201 p. 13-17.

CASA 7. *Veja*, Exposições. São Paulo, 29 Apr. 1984.

CHIARELLI, Tadeu. Carlito Carvalhc tenta resistir à morte da pintura moderna. *O Estado de S.Paulo*, Caderno 2, 8 Mar. 1994, p. 2.

CCHIARALE, Fernando. pagador. *Catalogue*, Funarte, Rio e Janeiro, 2008, p. 4.

OELHO, Marcelo. 'Arte/Cidade 3' usca utopia pós-industrial. *Folha e S.Paulo*, Ilustrada, 12 Nov. 1997, 7.

OLUCCI, Arlene. Uma polêmica (e ra) arte descartável. *Shopping ews – City News*, São Paulo, 23 ept. 1984, p. 12.

OSTA, Marcus de Lontra. Sem sistir à tradição. *IstoÉ*, São Paulo, Jan. 1987, p. 5.

OUTINHO, Wilson. O ateliê Casa 7 ão é mais aque-le. *Folha de S. aulo*, Ilustrada, 23 Oct. 1986, p. 7.

OUTINHO, Wilson. Realidade e xpressão. *Jornal do Brasil*, Artes ásticas, Rio de Janeiro, May 1985.

YPRIANO, Fabio. Carvalhosa olda megaobras em gesso. *Folha e S.Paulo*, Ilustada, São Paulo, 8 ov. 2000, p. E5.

EBÉRTOLIS, Karen. Com as mãos o gesso. *Gazeta do Povo*, Evento, uritiba, 22 Sept. 1998.

EKEUKELEIRE, Jeannette / AAGMAN, Hugo. *Art Kitchen agazine*, Number 20, Amsterdam, ar. 2000, cover and p. 7.

ESENHO e pintura, duas nguagens, duas mostras. O *tado de S. Paulo*, Exposições, 30 pr. 1985, p. 18.

OBNER, Gabriela. Carlito arvalhosa lança seu primeiro vro. *últimosegundo.ig.com.br*, vros, São Paulo, 8 Nov. 2000.

UARTE, Luisa. Uma singular visita o Palácio. *O Globo*, Segundo aderno, Rio de Janeiro, 21 Jun. 010, p. 4.

CHEVERRIA, Regina. Um pavilhão nde a arte dá pedal. *Folha de S. aulo*, Ilustrada, 27 Sept. 1985, p. 56.

RNANDES, José Carlos. periência que vingou. *Gazeta do ovo*, Caderno G, Curitiba, 18 Sept. 001, p. 1.

RREIRA, Joaquim dos Santos. Um minho pelas nuvens. *O Globo*, gundo Caderno, Gente Boa, 29 or. 2011, p. 5.

FERREIRA, Paulo Henrique. Museu de grandes novidades. *O Globo*, Rio Show, Rio de Janeiro. 17 Feb. 2006, p. 9.

FILHO, Paulo Venâncio. Espelhos Graxos. *Catalogue*, Gabinete de Arte Raquel Arnaud. São Paulo, 27 Nov. 2003.

FORMAS mutantes de Carlito Carvalhosa. *Tribuna da Imprensa*, Bis, Rio de Janeiro, 29 Mar. 1995.

FORNES, Andrea. Talentos, telas e ateliers. *Around* n. 74, São Paulo, Oct. 1985, p. 41.

FRITSCH, Ana. Bienal do Mercosul começa hoje em Porto Alegre. *Gazeta Mercantil*, Rio Grande do Sul, Porto Alegre, 15 Oct. 2001, p. 4.

FUCHS, Franco Caldas. No meio do palácio tem uma árvore. *Correio*, Vida, Salvador, 13 Apr. 2010, p. 19.

GALERIAS expõem 15 artistas. *Folha de S.Paulo*, Ilustrada, 15 Jun. 1987, p. 26.

GALVÃO, João Cândido. A vanguarda do passado na 18ª Bienal. *Veja* n. 893, São Paulo, Oct. 1985, p. 16-23.

GALVÃO, João Cândido. Carlito Carvalhosa
liberta-se da matéria. *O Estado de S. Paulo*, Caderno 2, 10 Aug. 1989, p. 2.

GALVÃO, João Cândido. Carlito Carvalhosa.
São Paulo Vip, Mar. 1994, p. 2.

GAZIRE, Nina. Carlito Carvalhosa e Philip Glass: Música das esferas. *IstoÉ*, Bate-papo, São Paulo, 18 Aug. 2010, p. 117.

GIOBBI, César. A arte nos anos 80. *Jornal da Tarde*, Caderno de Programas e Leituras, São Paulo, 10 Aug. 1985, p. 4-5.

GIOBBI, César. Destaques da semana. *Jornal da Tarde*, Caderno de Programas e Leituras, São Paulo, 20 Jun. 1987, p. 3.

GODFREY, Dominique. Métissages brésiliens. *Sud-Ouest*, Exposition, Bordeaux, 28 Oct. 2001, p. 6.

GOMES, Márion Strecker. "Sub-distrito de arte". *Folha de S.Paulo*, Ilustrada, 16 May 1985, p. 37.

GOMES, Márion Strecker. Arte jovem em coletivas. *Folha de S.Paulo*, Ilustrada, 29 Apr. 1985, p. 26.

GOMES, Márion Strecker. Casa 7, um ateliê explosivo. *Folha de S.Paulo*, Ilustrada, 30 Apr. 1985, p. 29.

GONÇALVES FILHO, Antônio. Carlito Carvalhosa abre exposição. *O Estado de S.Paulo*, Caderno 2, 12 Nov. 1997, p. 3.

GONÇALVES FILHO, Antônio. Carlito Carvalhosa volta a expor no Brasil. *Folha de S.Paulo*, Ilustrada, 4 Jun. 1997, p. 3.

GONÇALVES FILHO, Antônio. Galeria reúne elenco eclético das artes plásticas brasileiras. *Folha de S. Paulo*, Ilustrada, 22 Sept. 1988, p. 3.

GONÇALVES FILHO, Antonio. Série analisa Carvalhosa e Carmela Gross. *Valor*, Eu & Cultura, São Paulo, 8 Nov. 2000, p. D12.

GONÇALVES, Marcos Augusto. A música deu o tom no Ibirapuera. *Folha de S.Paulo*, Ilustrada, 7 Oct. 1985, p. 19.

GONÇALVES, Marcos Augusto. Está tudo pronto para o espetáculo das artes. *Folha de S.Paulo*, Ilustrada, 13 Aug. 1985, p. 37.

GONÇALVES, Marcos Augusto. Os jovens pintores chegam à Bienal. *Folha de S.Paulo*, Ilustrada, 5 Sept. 1985, p. 37.

GRUNITZKY, Claude. Natural Invasion: Carlito Carvalhosa's Roteiro para Visitação. *Trace*, 88, New York, 2010, p. 108-111.

HERKENHOFF, Paulo. Poética da Percepção; questões da fenomenologia na arte brasileira. *Catalogue*, Museu de Arte Moderna, Rio de Janeiro, 2008, p. 39.

HIRSZMAN, Maria. As pinturas espelhadas de Carlito Carvalhosa. *O Estado de S.Paulo*, Caderno 2, 27 Nov. 2003, p. D12.

HIRSZMAN, Maria. Carlito Carvalhosa e a imprecisão dos sentidos. *O Estado de S.Paulo*, Caderno 2, São Paulo, 8 Nov. 2000, p. D8.

HIRSZMAN, Maria. Três artistas contemporâneos ocupam espaço do MuBE . *O Estado de S.Paulo*, Caderno 2, 28 Jun. 1999, p. 4.

JAPIASSU, Daniel. Peças que pregam peças. *living alone*, art, São Paulo, Oct. 2008, p. 36-39.

JOVENS artistas expõem na Folha. *Folha de S.Paulo*, Ilustrada, 18 Feb. 1986, p. 31.

LAGNADO, Lisette. Carvalhosa inova com o uso da cera. *Folha de S. Paulo*, Ilustrada, 3 Jul. 1987, p. 36.

LAGNADO, Lisette. Jovens artistas brasileiros buscam 'fama e fortuna' em cidades alemãs. *Folha de S. Paulo*, Ilustrada, 3 Jun. 1991, p. 1.

LEIRNER, Sheila. A linguagem de doze artistas nos anos 70 e 80. O *Estado de S.Paulo*, Caderno 2, 4 Oct. 1988, p. 3.

LUZ, Afonso. Sólido Insólito. *Catalogue*, Favor Não Tocar. Casa Maria Antônia. São Paulo, Jun. 2005.

MACHADO, Cassiano Elek. Exposição questiona natureza do espaço. *Folha de S.Paulo*, Ilustrada, 12 Nov. 1997, p. 5.

MAMMÌ, Lorenzo. Pinturas com cera. *Catalogue*, Subdistrito Comercial de Arte, São Paulo, 17 Jun. 1987.

MAMMÌ, Lorenzo. Preface. *Carlito Carvalhosa*, São Paulo, Cosac & Naify Edições, 2000, p. 7.

MARGUTTI, Mário. Momentos mágicos entre o formal e a não-forma. *Jornal do Commercio*, Caderno de Leilões, Rio de Janeiro, 27 Mar. 1995.

MARTI, Silas. Carlito Carvalhosa enche uma galeria de luz em nova mostra. *Folha de S.Paulo*, Ilustrada, 14 Dec. 2010, p. E4.

MASSI, Fernanda Peixoto. Esconde-esconde com jogo de cera. *Folha de S.Paulo*, Revista, Mar. 1994, p. 31.

MAYRINK, Geraldo / MORAIS, Angélica. Milionário banquete para todos os gostos. *Afinal*, n. 58, São Paulo, 8 Oct. 1985, p. 36-40.

MELLO, Chris. Um em dois. O *Estado de S.Paulo*, Caderno 2, 7 Aug. 2008, p. D4.

MENDONÇA, Casimiro Xavier de. Criando em conjunto. *Veja*, n. 870, São Paulo, 8 May 1985, p. 144-145.

MESQUITA, Ivo. A soma dos dias. *Catalogue*, Pinacoteca do Estado, São Paulo, Jul. 2010.

MILLEN, Manya. Esculturas que nascem do calor e do acaso. *O Globo*, Rio Show, Rio de Janeiro, 29 Mar. 1995.

MOLINA, Camila. Um labirinto de tecidos e música. *O Estado de S. Paulo*, Caderno 2, 31 Jul. 2010, p. 14.

MOLINA, Camila. A experiência do "perder-se no branco". *O Estado de S.Paulo*, Caderno 2, 11 Aug. 2008, p. D5.

MOLINA, Camila. O palácio de Carlito. *O Estado de S.Paulo*, Caderno 2, 13 Apr. 2010, p. 1.

MOLINA, Camila. Obras grandes criadas por um time especial de artistas. *O Estado de S.Paulo*, Caderno 2, 24 Feb. 2010, p. D5.

MOLINA, Camila. Um jardim para as experimentações. *O Estado de S.Paulo*, Caderno 2, 17 Nov. 2009, p. D5.

MONACHESI, Juliana. Da "pintura que não dá pé" à escultura que afoga. Canal Contemporâneo, 29 Jul. 2005. http://www.canalcontemporaneo.art.br/arteemcirculacao/archives/000491.html

MORAES, Angelica de. Exposições assinalam fim de um preconceito. *O Estado de S.Paulo*, Caderno 2, São Paulo, 9 Jul. 1999, p. D21.

MORAIS, Angélica. Entre a pintura e a escultura. *Jornal da Tarde*, São Paulo, 4 Jun. 1992, p. 19.

MORAIS, Frederico. Grupo 'Casa 7' no MAM: a paixão pela pintura. *O Globo*, Segundo Caderno, Rio de Janeiro, 6 May 1985, p. 6.

MORAIS, Frederico. Grupo paulista no Rio: são cinco pintores da Casa 7. *O Globo*, Segundo Caderno, Rio de Janeiro, 5 May 1985, p. 8.

MORAR na pintura. Folha de S.Paulo, Folhetim n. 440, 30 Jun. 1985, p. 12.

MOSTRA traz obras feitas 'in loco'. *Folha de S.Paulo*, Acontece, 28 Jun. 1999, p. 1.

NAVES, Rodrigo. Óleo sobre água. *Carlito Carvalhosa*, São Paulo, Cosac Naify, 2000, p. 11.

NEVES, Paulo. Livro expõe grandes blocos de Carlito Carvalhosa. *Gazeta Mercantil*, Grande São Paulo, 8 Nov. 2000, p. 8.

NO túnel da pintura. *Veja*, n. 892, São Paulo, 9 Oct. 1985, p. 90-93.

NURIDSANY, Michel. Brésil <<in>> et <<out>>. *Le Figaro*, Art Contemporain, Paris, 9 Nov. 2001.

NURIDSANY, Michel. Dynamiques brésiliennes. *Le Figaro*, La Vie des Arts, Paris, 5 Jan. 1988, p. 30.

NURIDSANY, Michel. Le moment du Brésil. *Art Press*, 121, Paris, Jan. 1988, p. 14-15.

O 3o Salão Paulista será aberto hoje. *Folha de S.Paulo*, Ilustrada, 26 Jul. 1985, p. 31.

O 7º Salão Nacional divulga pré-seleção. *Folha de S.Paulo*, Ilustrada, 10 Oct. 1984, p. 37.

OBRA em progresso, Carlito Carvalhosa. *O Globo*, Segundo Caderno. Rio de Janeiro, 4 Apr. 2011, p. 4.

OLIVA, Fernando. MAM abre exposição sobre a Geração 80. *O Estado de S. Paulo*, Caderno 2, 23 Jan. 2003, p. D1.

PEDROSO, Franklin Espath. Impermanência e transitoriedade. *Catalogue*, Museu de Arte do Espírito Santo, Dec. 2004.

PINTURA gestural e algo mais. *Folha de S.Paulo*, Ilustrada, 19 Feb. 1986, p. 37.

PIRES, Francisco Quinteiro. Contrariar convicções é o trabalho do artista. *O Estado de S.Paulo*, Cultura, 17 Aug. 2008, p. D18.

PIZA, Daniel. Coletiva ilustra crise da arte. *Folha de S.Paulo*, Ilustrada, 3 Dec. 1992, p. 10.

PONZIO, Ana Francisca. Bienal o grande espetáculo. *Jornal da Tarde*, Caderno Programas e Leituras, 14 Dec. 1985, p. 6.

PONZIO, Ana Francisca. Carlito Carvalhosa mostra em SP experiência alemã. *O Estado de S. Paulo*, Caderno 2, 4 Jun. 1992, p. 2.

PRÊMIOS do Salão Nacional Funarte, Rio de Janeiro, Jan. 1987, p. 12.

RAMOS, Paula / ALBUQUERQUE, Fernanda. A mais jovem das bienais. *Aplauso*, Porto Alegre, Nov. 2001, p. 28.

RANGEL, Daniel. Ocupas com arte o palácio. *Catalogue*, Roteiro para Visitaçao, Palácio da Aclamação, Salvador, 2010.

REIS, Paulo. Artista apresenta "criaturas". *Jornal do Brasil*, Caderno B, Rio de Janeiro, 6 Apr. 1995, p. 7.

RIBEIRO, Teresa. Carlito Carvalhosa em livro e exposição. *estadao.com.br*, visuais, São Paulo, 8 Nov. 2000.

RODRIGUES, Apoenan. Com Acordes minimalistas, Philip Glass embala a arte em São Paulo. *Hola! Brasil*, São Paulo, 13 Aug. 2010.

ROELS JR., Reynaldo. Carvalhosa: o caminho da cera. *Manchete*, Leitura Dinâmica, Rio de Janeiro, 1987, p. 78.

ROELS JR., Reynaldo. Os dois da Sete. *Jornal do Brasil*, Caderno B, Rio de Janeiro, 6 Sept. 1989, p. 2.

SACCOMORI, Camila. No princípio era o pó. *Zero Hora*, Segundo Caderno, Porto Alegre, 13 Oct. 2001, p. 6-7.

SALÃO Paulista premia. *Folha de S. Paulo*, Ilustrada, 13 Jul. 1985, p. 34.

SALÃO Paulista terá 75 artistas. *Folha de S.Paulo*, 31 Oct. 1984, p. 39.

SANTEIRO, Ana Maria. *Pasquim*, O Pasquim 21, São Paulo, 12 Aug. 2003, p. 2.

SANTOS MENDES, Euclides. Philip Glass faz som para instalação intimista. *Folha de S.Paulo*, Ilustrada, 4 Aug. 2010, p. E10.

SEBASTIAO, Walter. Carvalhosa inventa os nós. *Estado de Minas*, Artes Visuais, Belo Horizonte, 9 Sept. 2004, p. 6.

SILVEIRA MELLO, Marco. Meus Olhos e o Apagador. *Catalogue*, Solar do Barão, Curitiba, Nov. 2008, p. 19-26.

SILVEIRA, Cristiane. La Galerie des Glaces ou As Sete Faces do Dr. Lao. *Catalogue*, Solar do Barão, Curitiba, Oct. 2008, p. 11.

SILVEIRA, Cristiane. Um diálogo. *Catalogue*, Solar do Barão, Curitiba, Nov. 2008, p. 33.

SOLLER, Neide Martins. A 18ª Bienal de SP já está preparada. *Folha de S.Paulo*, Ilustrada, 19 Ma 1985, p. 33.

SOLLER, Neide Martins. A transvanguarda em revista e mostra. *Folha de S.Paulo*, Ilustrad 2 Apr. 1985, p. 34.

STANISCI, Carolina. Carlito Carvalhosa expõe seus gigantes brancos. *Jornal da Tarde*, Variedades, São Paulo, 9 Nov. 2000, p. 3C.

SUBIRATS, Eduardo. A miséria da vanguarda. *Folha de S. Paulo*, Folhetim n. 460, 1 Dec. 1985, p. 6-8.

SUTIS exercícios do pensamento. *Jornal do Brasil*, Program, Rio de Janeiro, 31 Mar. 1995, p. 25.

TALENTO não tem idade, *AT2*, Vitória, 7 Nov. 1987, p. 1.

TASSINARI, Alberto. Ceras Perdida *Carlito Carvalhosa*, São Paulo, Cosac Naify, 2000, p. 9.

TASSINARI, Alberto. Ceras perdida *Catalogue*, Centro Cultural Banco do Brasil – CCBB, Rio de Janeiro, 2 Mar. 1995.

TASSINARI, Alberto. Entre o passado e o futuro. *Catalogue*, Casa 7, 18a Bienal Internacional d São Paulo, Subdistrito Comercial de Arte, São Paulo, 1985.

TINOCO, Bianca. Carlito através dc espelho. *Jornal do Brasil*, Caderno Rio de Janeiro, 18 Nov. 2005, p. 2.

VELASCO, Suzana. Mestres de obras. *O Globo*, Segundo Caderno Rio de Janeiro, 12 Feb. 2006, p. 8.

VELASCO, Suzana. A arte ilumindada de Carlito Carvalhosa. *O Globo*, Segundo Caderno, Rio de Janerio, 25 Apr. 2011, p. 10.

VELASCO, Suzana. A caminho do MoMA. *O Globo*, Segundo Caderno, Rio de Janeiro, 23 Nov. 2010, p. 1.

VELASCO, Suzana. Galerias fechar a temporada de artes viusais. *O Globo*, Segundo Caderno, Rio de Janeiro, 26 Nov. 2007, p. 2.

VELASCO, Suzana. Salvador, nova capital da arte contemporânea. *O Globo*, Segundo Caderno, Rio de Janeiro, 9 May 2010, p. 3.

EDITORS
Alexandra Garcia
Carlito Carvalhosa

EDITORIAL COORDINATION
Ana Bial
Daniela Meda
Filomena Moscatelli

GRAPHIC DESIGN
Duas Águas
Carlito Carvalhosa
Francisca Sottomayor

LAYOUT
Luiza Kramer

TRANSLATION
Portuguese/English: Anthony Doyle
For Luis Pérez-Oramas:
Spanish/Portuguese: Damian Krauss
Spanish/English: John Laudenberger

COPYEDITING
Portuguese:
Regina Stocklen
English: Charles Gute

COPYWRITING AND PRESS OFFICE
Silvia Palombi

INTERNATIONAL EDITORIAL DIRECTOR
Francesca Sorace

PROMOTION AND WEB
Monica D'Emidio

DISTRIBUTION
Anna Visaggi

ADMINISTRATION
Grazia De Giosa

WAREHOUSE AND OUTLET
Roberto Curiale

COVER
Carlito Carvalhosa
You're Right, 2009

COVER INTERIOR
Car on tree, road to Maragogi
Rock and goats, postcard, India

DRAWING AND PHOTOGRAPHY
Mari Stockler (drawing on p. 2 and photos on p. 23, 228-229, 231, 253, 258-259, 261-263, 265, 268-271), Carlito Carvalhosa (1, 7-15, 19-22, 24-29, 41, 44-55, 57-68, 70-71, 74-75, 77-86, 88-94, 96-101, 114-115, 119-123, 126-129, 132-133, 142-144, 147-153, 155-161, 165-176, 201, 203, 207, 208- 217, 219-227, 230, 232-233, 235, 241-251, 254-257, 266-267, 272-281), Nelson Kon (124-125, 131, 134-141, 201, 206, 258, 260, 262), Isabela Matheus (16-17, 30-33, 36-37), Marcio Lima (102-111), Marcos Binns (235-239), Mario Grisolli (163-164), Diego Rinaldi (204-205), Carolina Veiga (72-73) Leticia Ramos (34-35, 38-39), Gustavo Moura (118), Luigi Stavale (260).

IMAGE TREATMENT
Patricia Thompson

We apologize if, due to reasons wholly beyond our control, some of the photo sources have not been listed.

ACKNOWLEDGEMENTS
Bia and Roberto; Daniela and Felipe; Zazá and Cello; Fernanda and Dado; Luiz and Mini; Daniel and Tamara; Luis and Samuel; Guel and Carol; Arnaldo and Marcia; Nanda and Andrucha; Regina and Estevão; Nelson and Marise; Dani and Dudu; Miguel and Hugo; Carô, Gabriel and Catarina; Adriana and Pedro; Arto; Philip; Stokes; Rebecca; Margarida; Lula and Lelê; Malu and Vik, Zita, Patrik and Ligia; Fernando; Helena; Sofia, Gil and Marina; Jai Mahal; Amanda and Renata; Nilza and Nico; Thais and Gui; Fritz and Fernanda; Maria Anna and Zé Augusto; Mari, Maria and Cecília

João Rivera, Raissa Colela, Ana Bial, Francisca Sottomayor, Antonio Valladares, Angela Gomes, Angelo Marcio, Carolina Hermeto, Danny Roland, Diogo Corrêa Maia, Fernando Laszlo, Flu, Francisco Amaral, Geaninne Guimaraes, Glenn Lowry, Patty and Gustavo Cisneros, Haroldo Alves, Isabella Matheus, Denise Andrade, Ivo Mesquita, João Bandeira, Joãozito and Lanussi, José Carlos dos Santos, Juliana Monachesi, Laufer, Leo Monteiro, Leticia Ramos, Lorenzo Mammì, Agnaldo Farias, Jacopo Crivelli, Luigi Stavale, Luiza Mello, Marcelo Araujo, Marcio Doctors, Fernando Cocchiarale, Marcio Lima, Marcus Binns, Mario Grisolli, Marli Matsumoto, Mr. and Mrs. Joseph J. Safra, Paulo Borges, Paulo Herkenhoff, Paulo Venancio Filho, Paulo Zuben, Sergio Kafejian, Stephane San Juan, Suzy Muniz

ISBN 978-88-8158-815-2 (Edizioni Charta, Milano - English Edition)

ISBN 978-85-7503-899-4 (Cosac Naify, São Paulo - Portuguese Edition)

Printed in April 2011 by Bianca & Volta, Truccazzano (MI), Italy

Edizioni Charta srl
Milano (Italy)
Via della Moscova, 27 - 20121
Tel. +39-026598098 / +39-026598200
Fax +39-026598577

Charta Books Ltd.
New York149 City (USA)
Tel. +1-313-406-8468
Cell. +1 917 460 5147 (US only)

www.chartaartbooks.it

This publication was made possible due to the generous support of Galeria Nara Roesler, São Paulo.

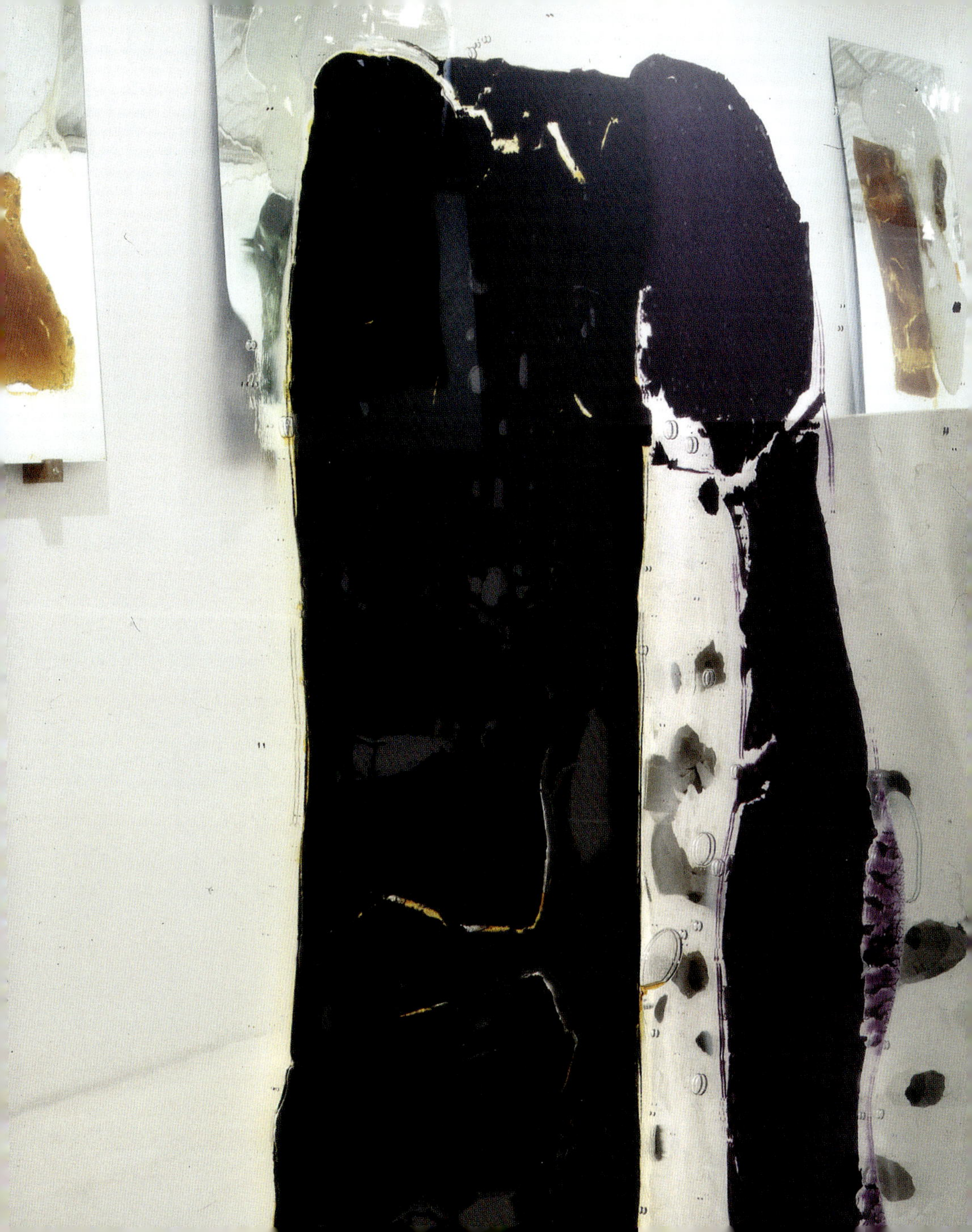

ESPELHOS GRAXOS

RIO DE JANEIRO E SÃO PAULO, 2003-2011
ESPELHOS, GESSO, GRAXA, ÓLEO, CERA E RESINA

Greased Mirrors

Rio de Janeiro and São Paulo, 2003–2011

Mirrors, plaster, grease, oil, wax and resin

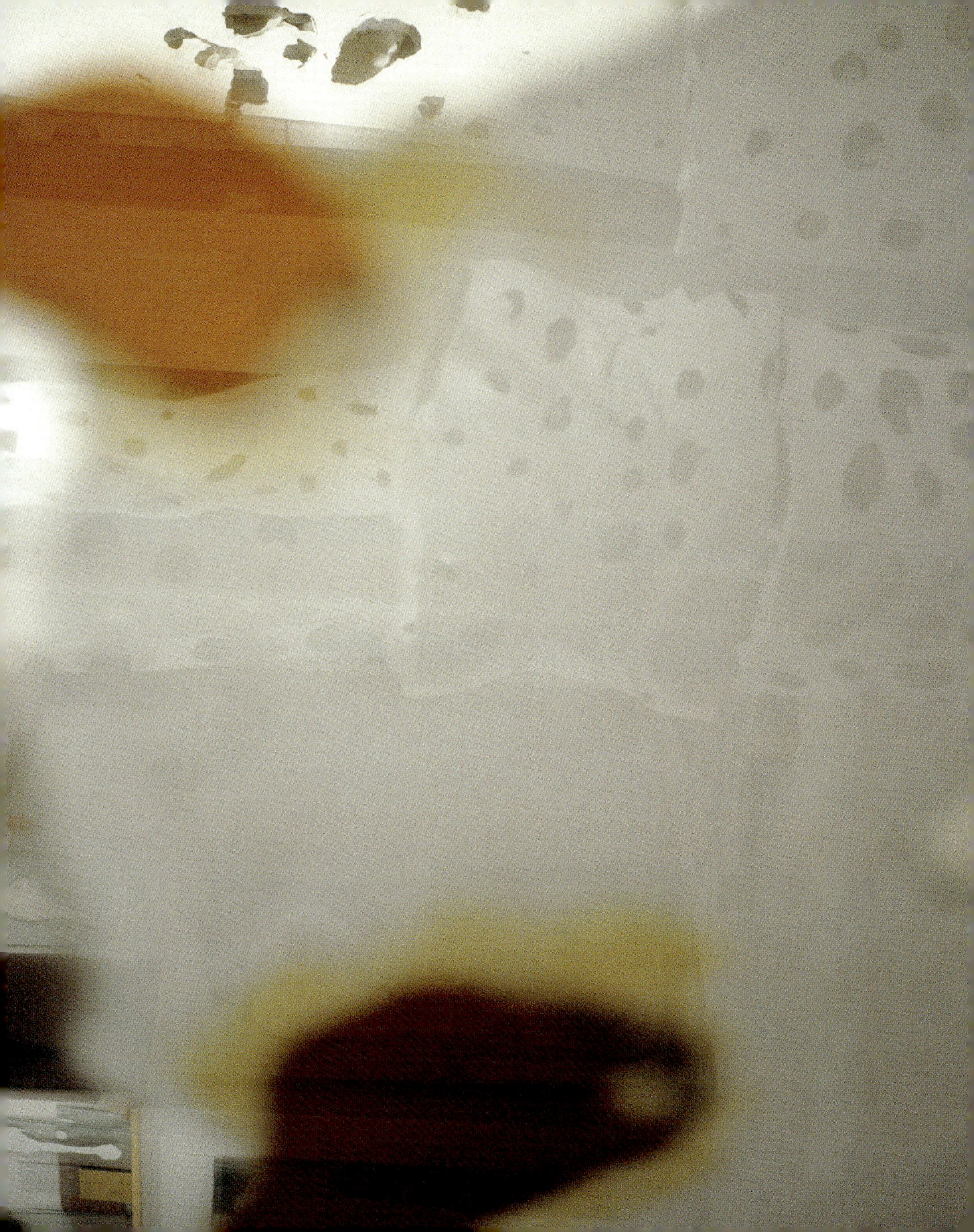

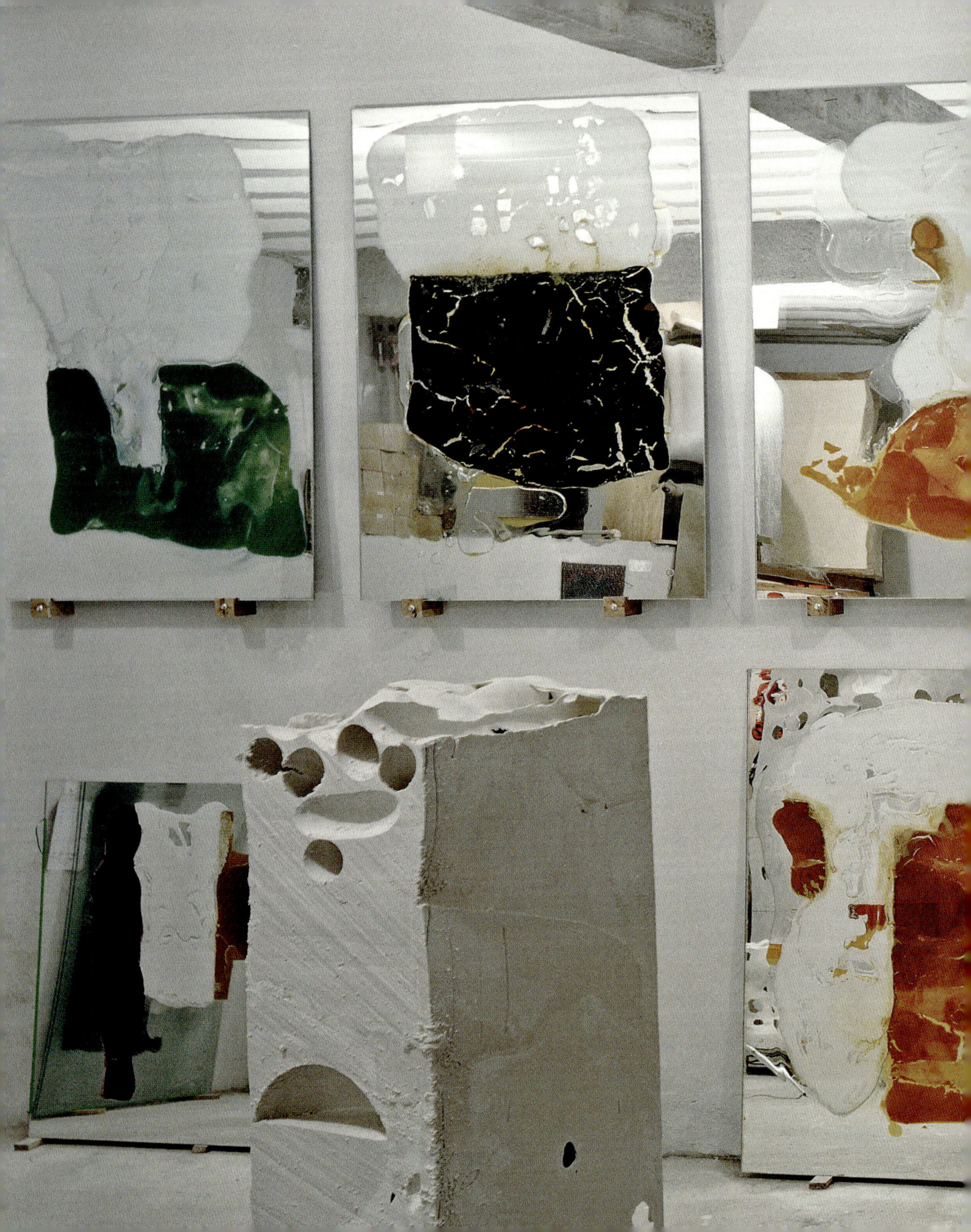

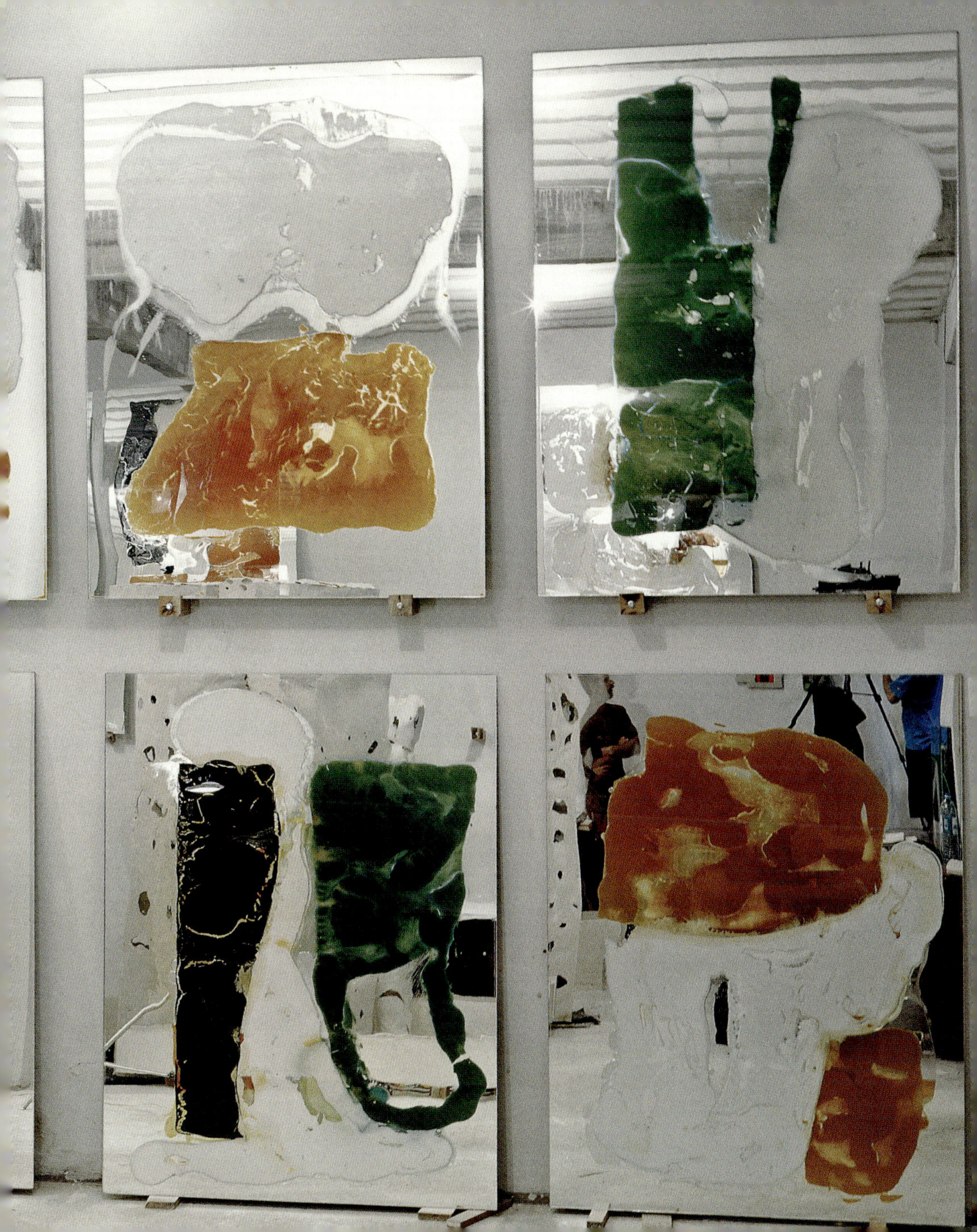

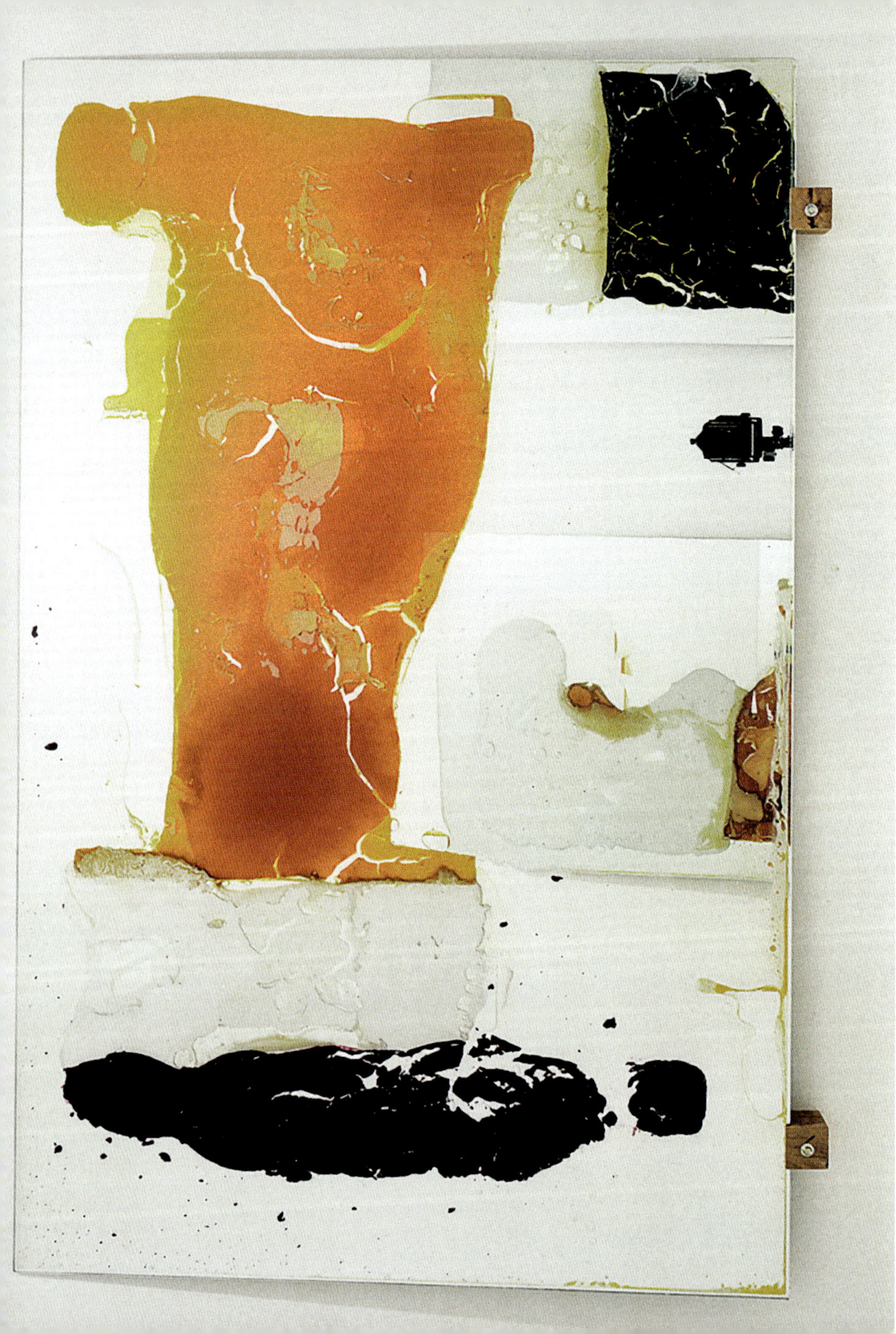

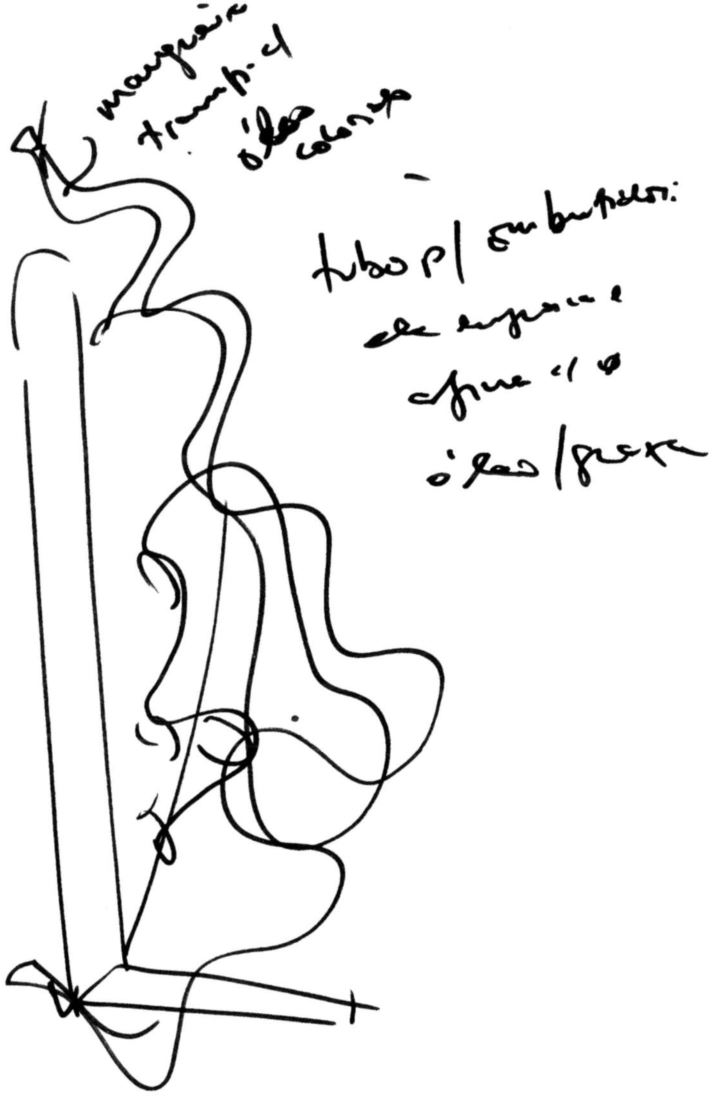

LENTES

VIDRO ÓPTICO COLADO,
50 ~ 70 CM ø

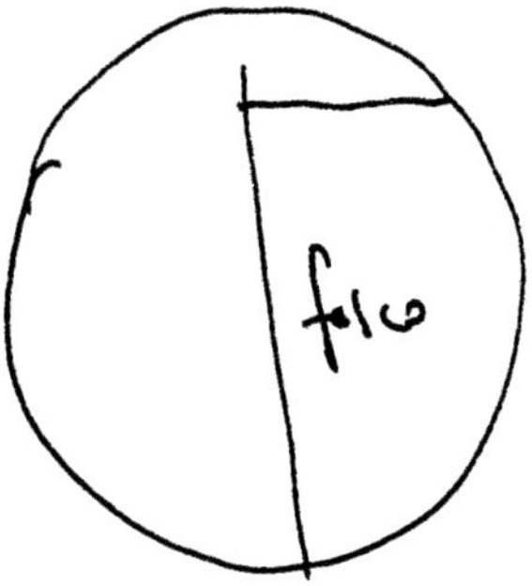

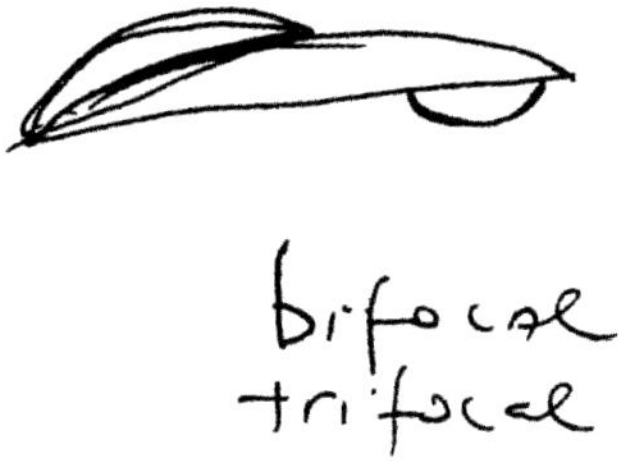

Lenses

2003–2011

Glued optical glass
50cm x 70cm ø

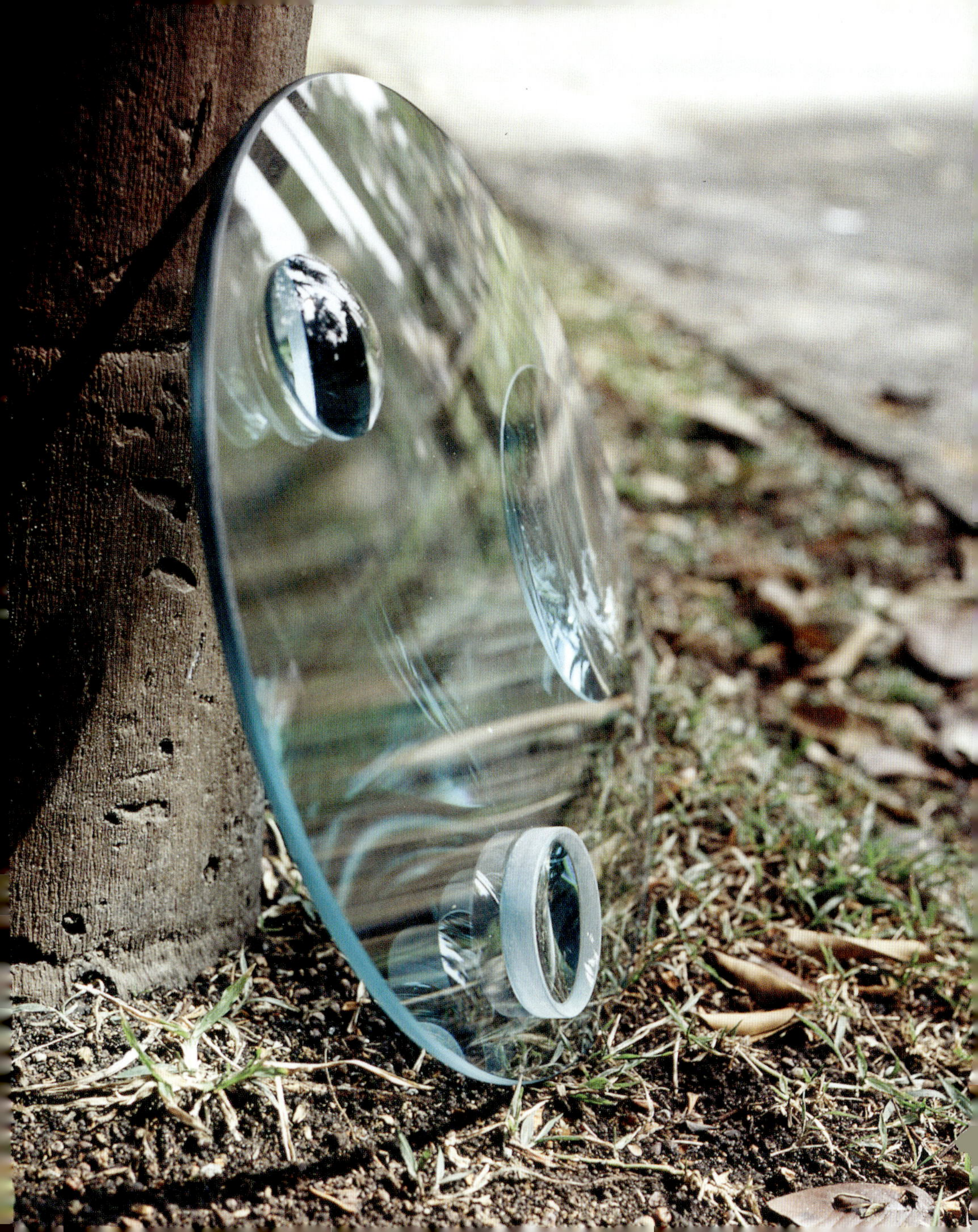

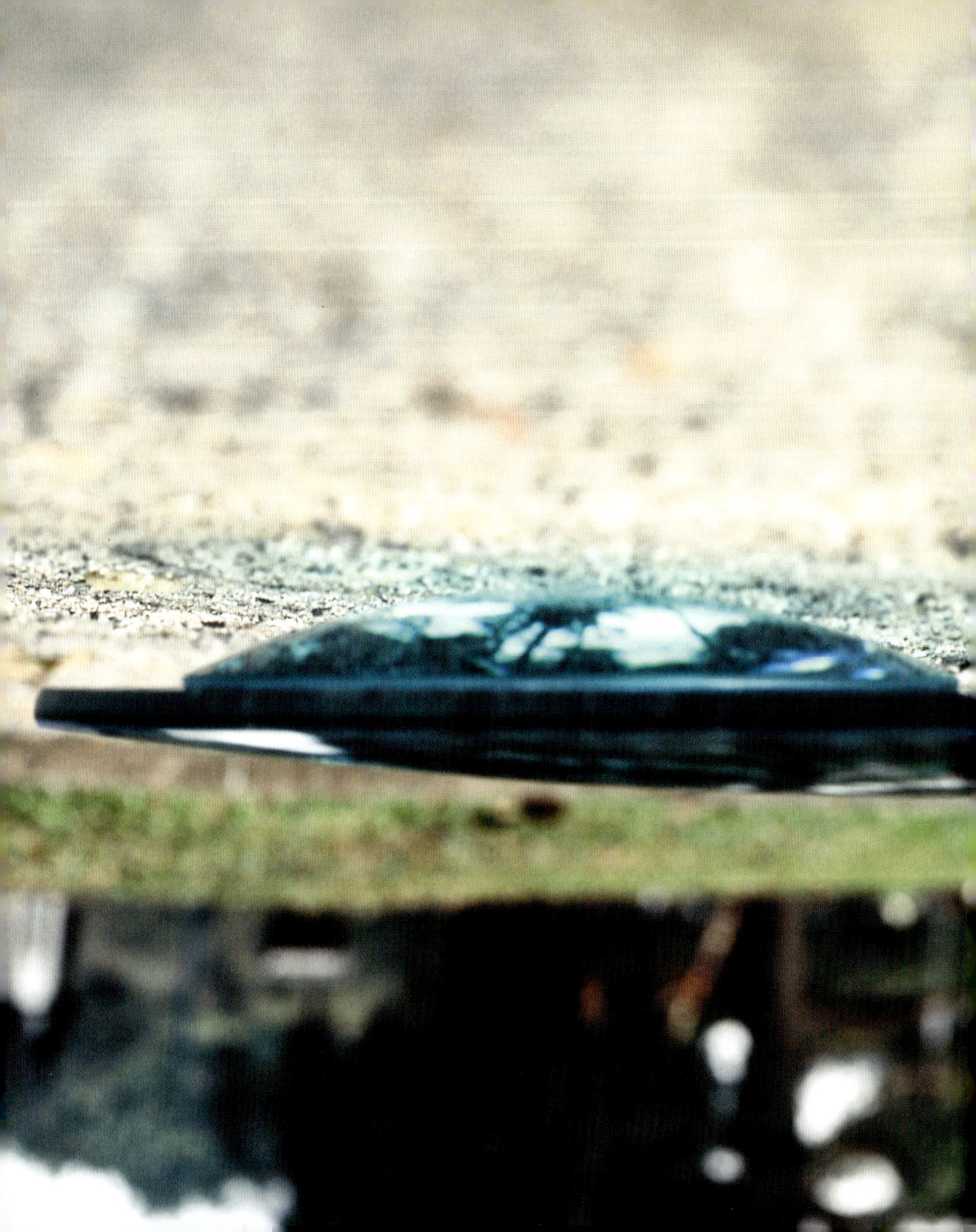

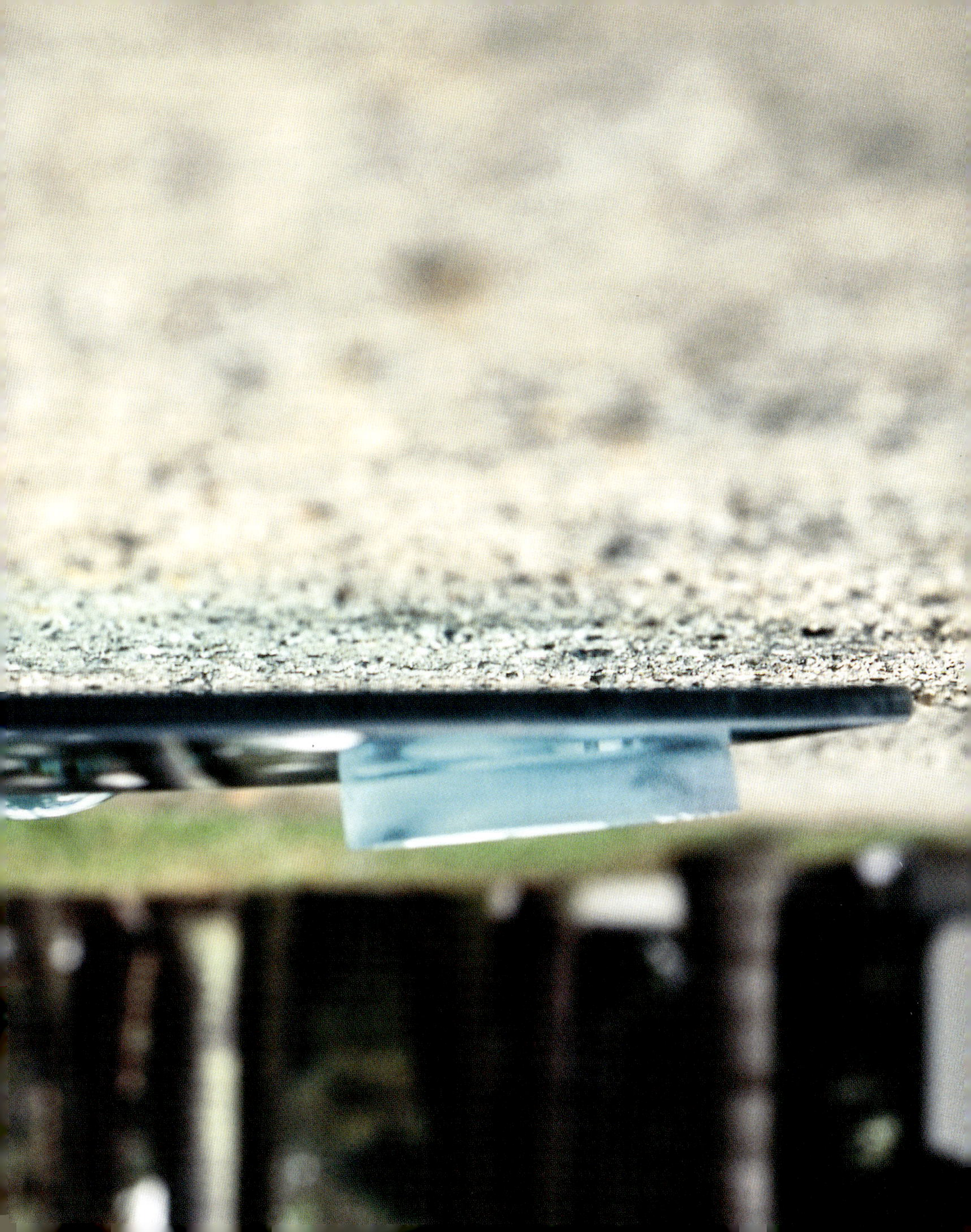

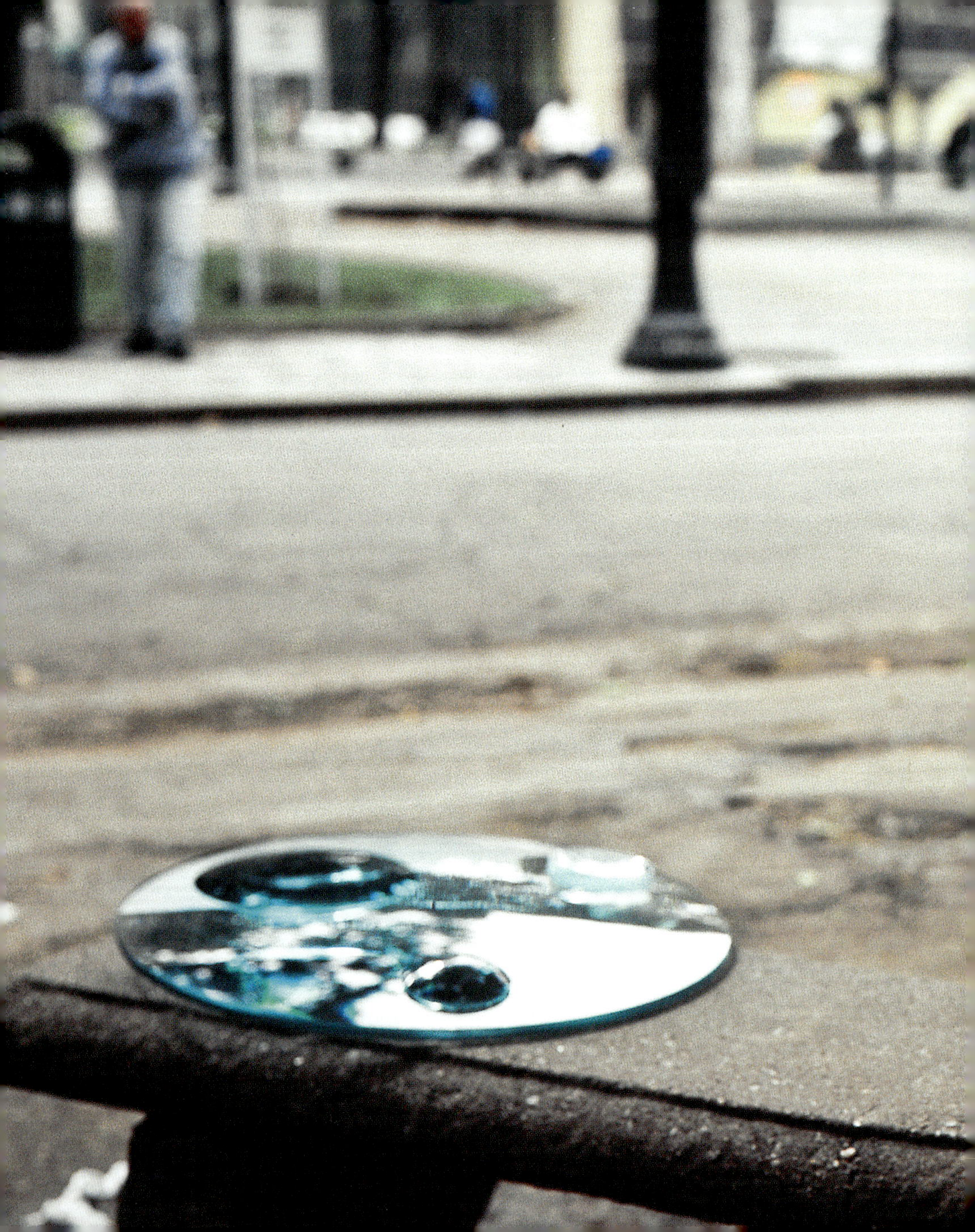

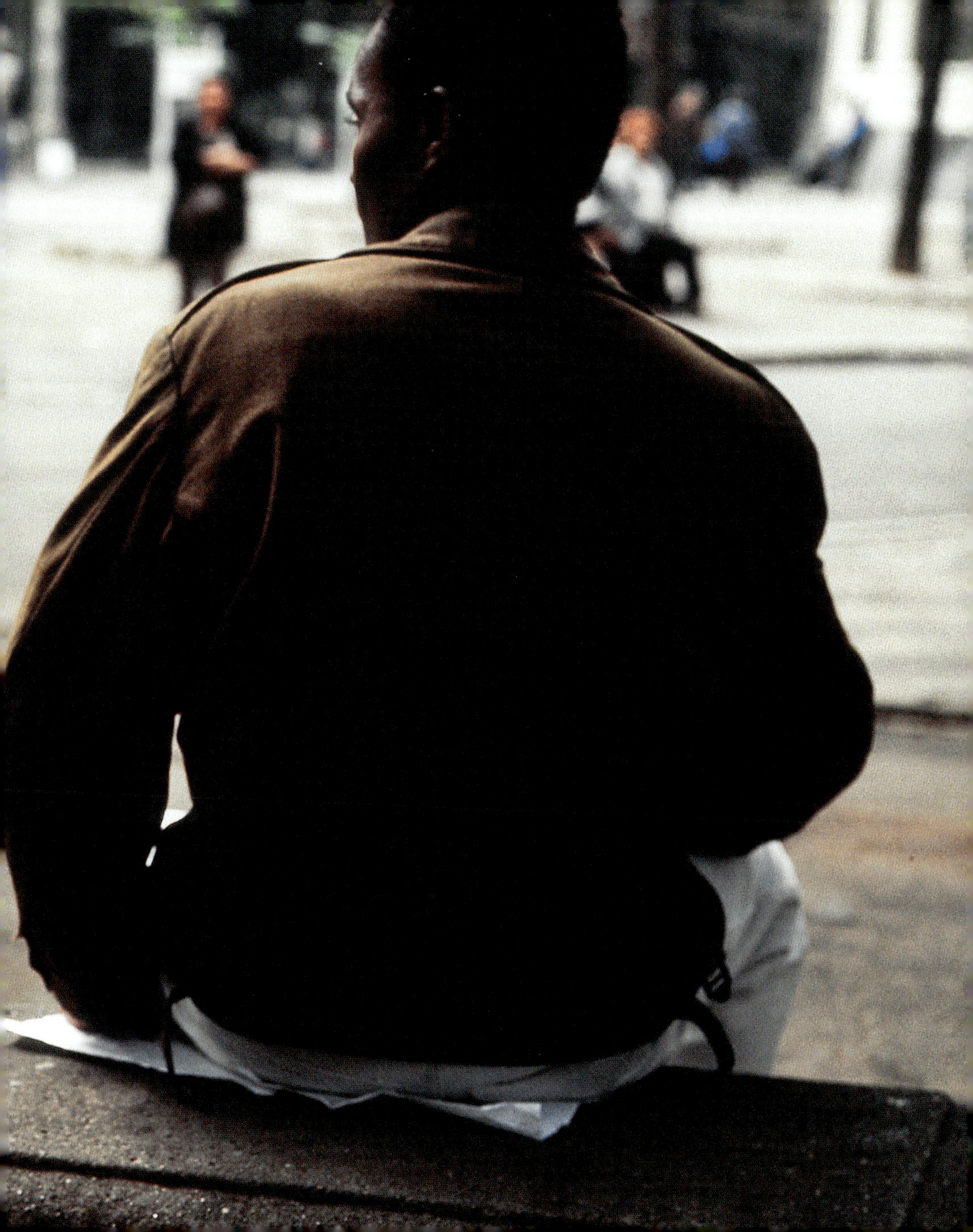

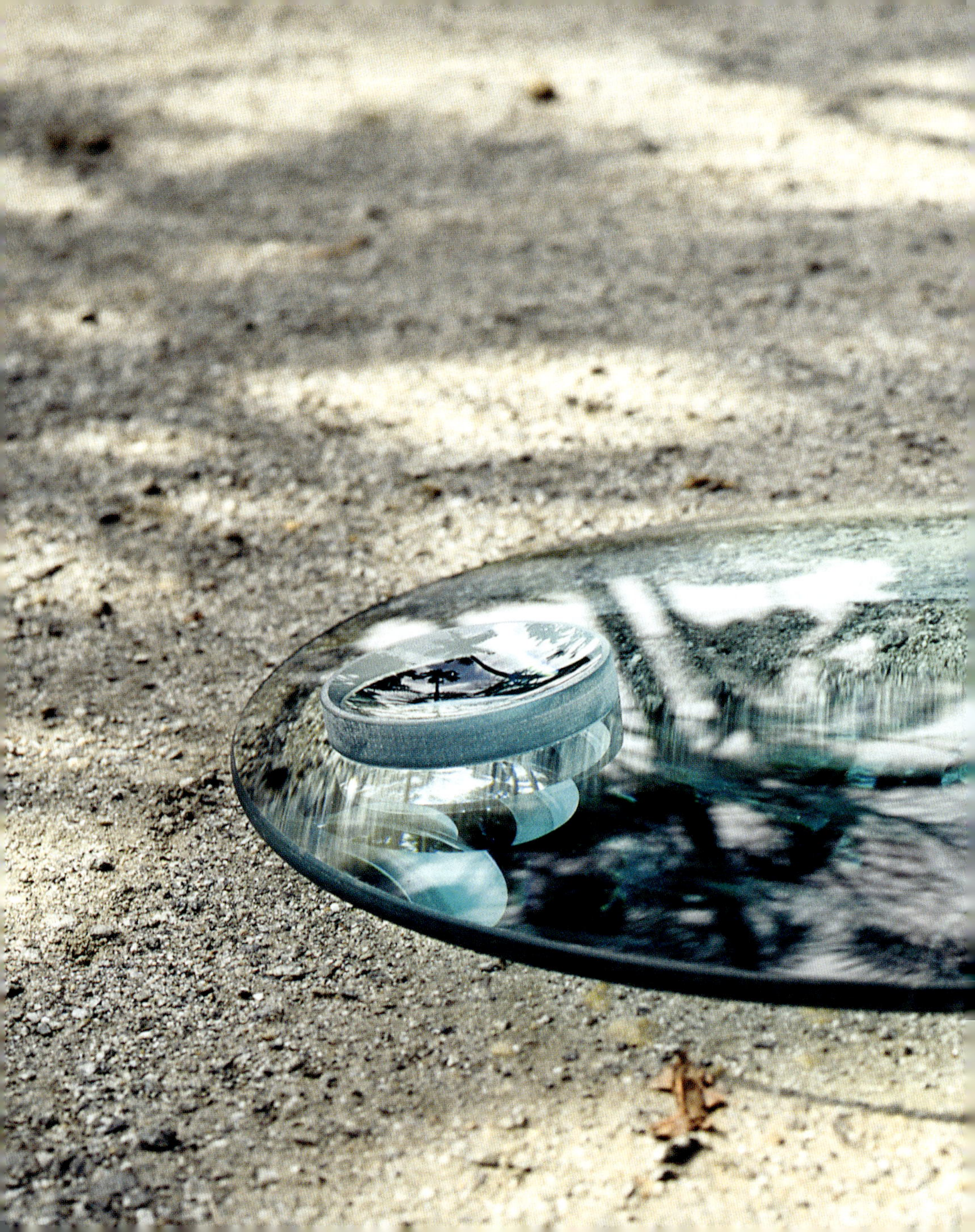

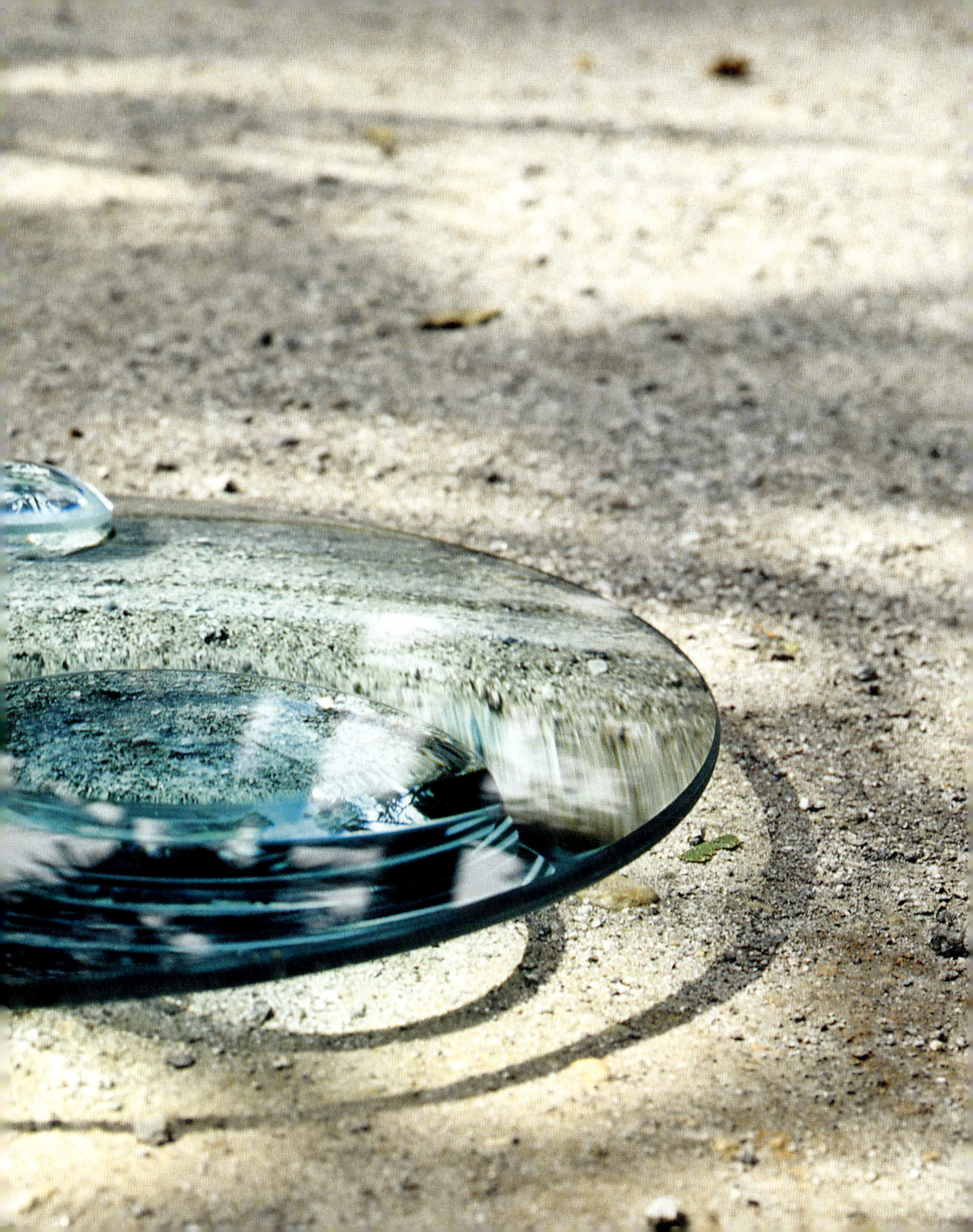

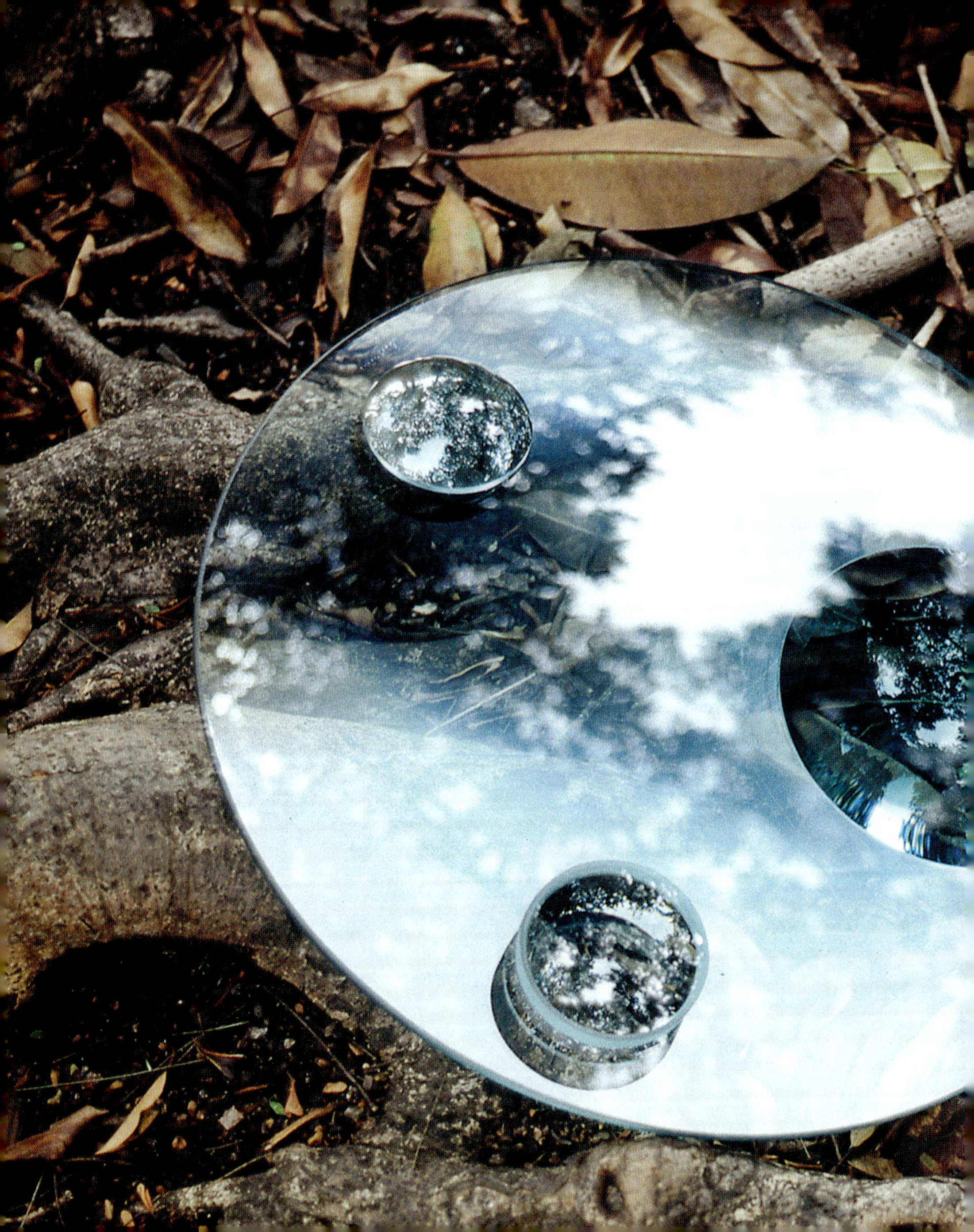

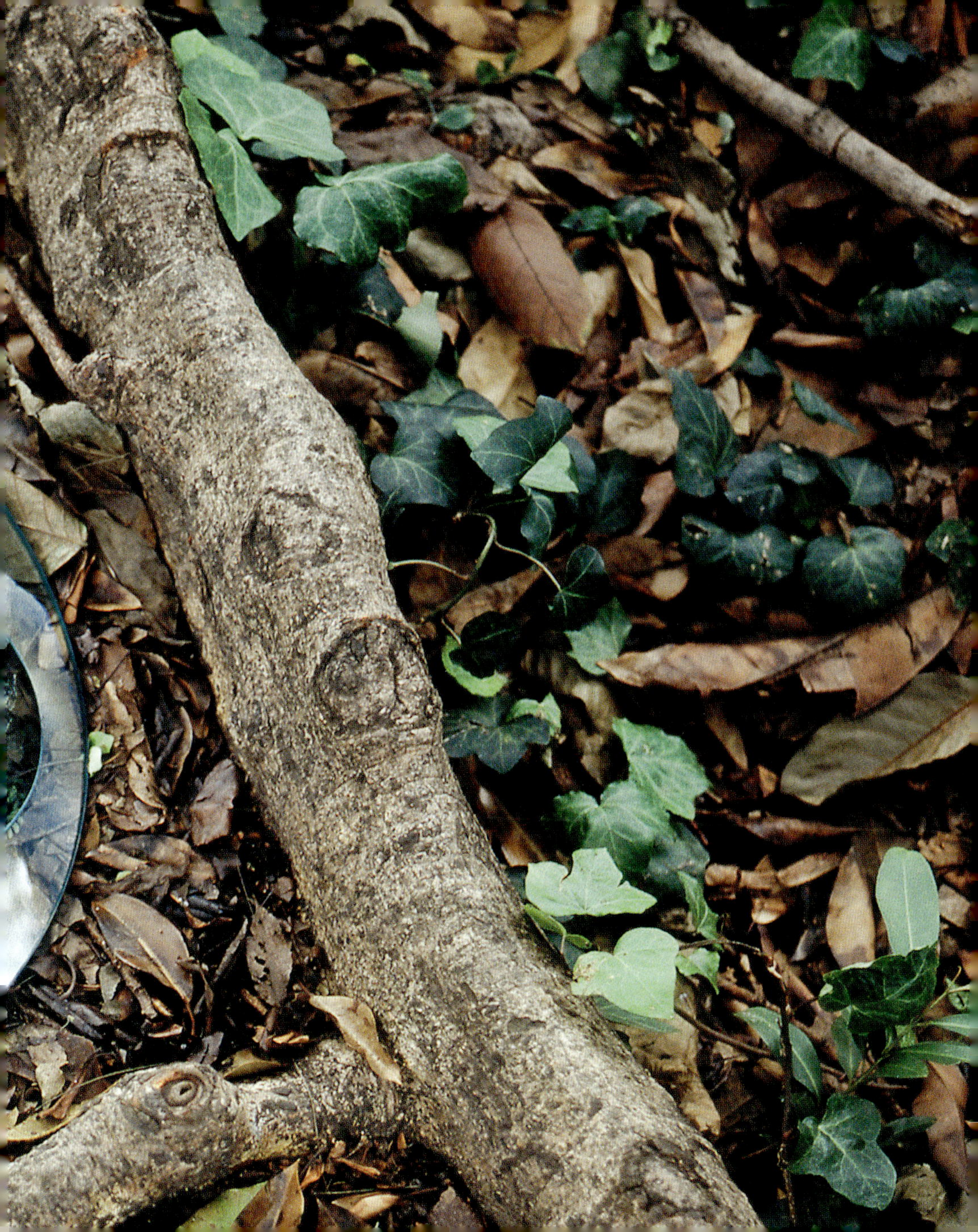

APAGADOR

MUSEU DE ARTE MODERNA DA BAHIA, 2008
EDITAL ARTE E PATRIMÔNIO
15M DE ALTURA, 10M X 12M
1.200 M^2 DE TNT 20G. EM 10 PEÇAS
OCUPANDO TODAS AS SALAS DA CAPELA
LÂMPADAS T6, 28W, 4100 °K
ALUMÍNIO, CABO DE AÇO, MICROFONE,
ALTO-FALANTE SENSORES INFRAVERMELHOS

Eraser

Museu de Arte Moderna da Bahia, 2008

Edital Arte e Patrimônio
15m h, 10m x 12m
1,200 m^2 of TNT 20g. in ten pieces
occupying all the rooms in the Chapel
T6 fluorescent lights, 28w, 4100°k
Aluminum, steel cable, microphone,
loudspeaker, infrared sensors

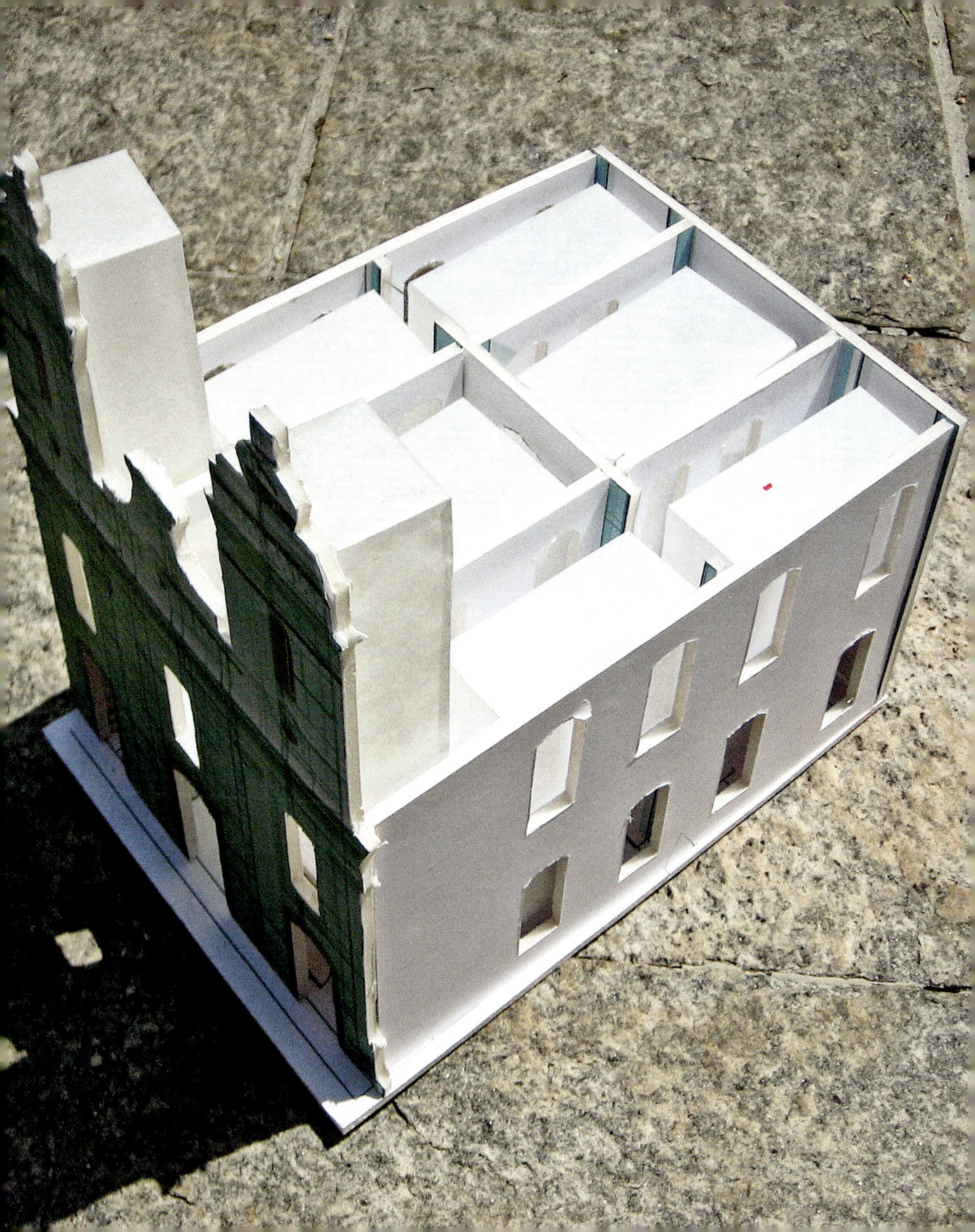

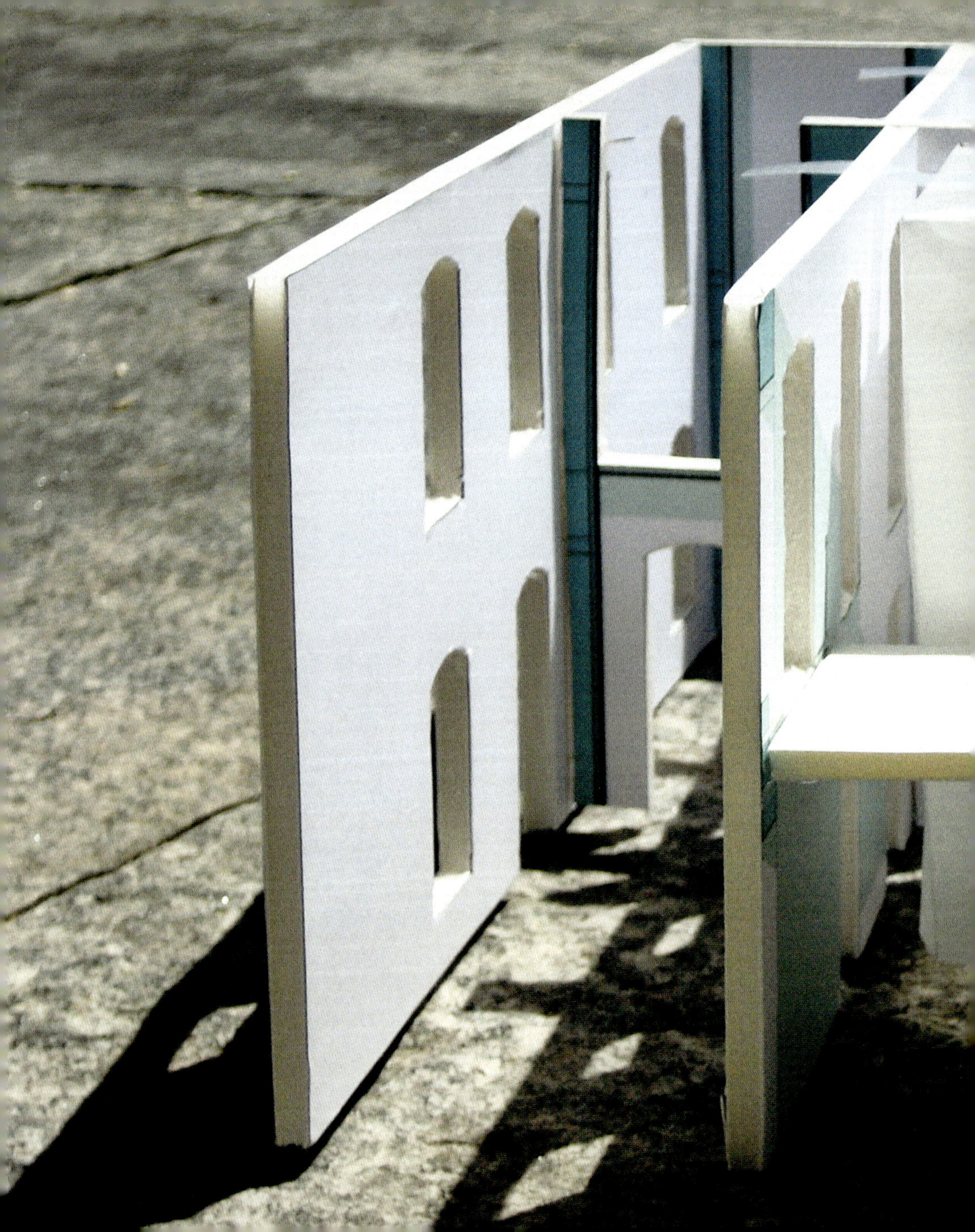

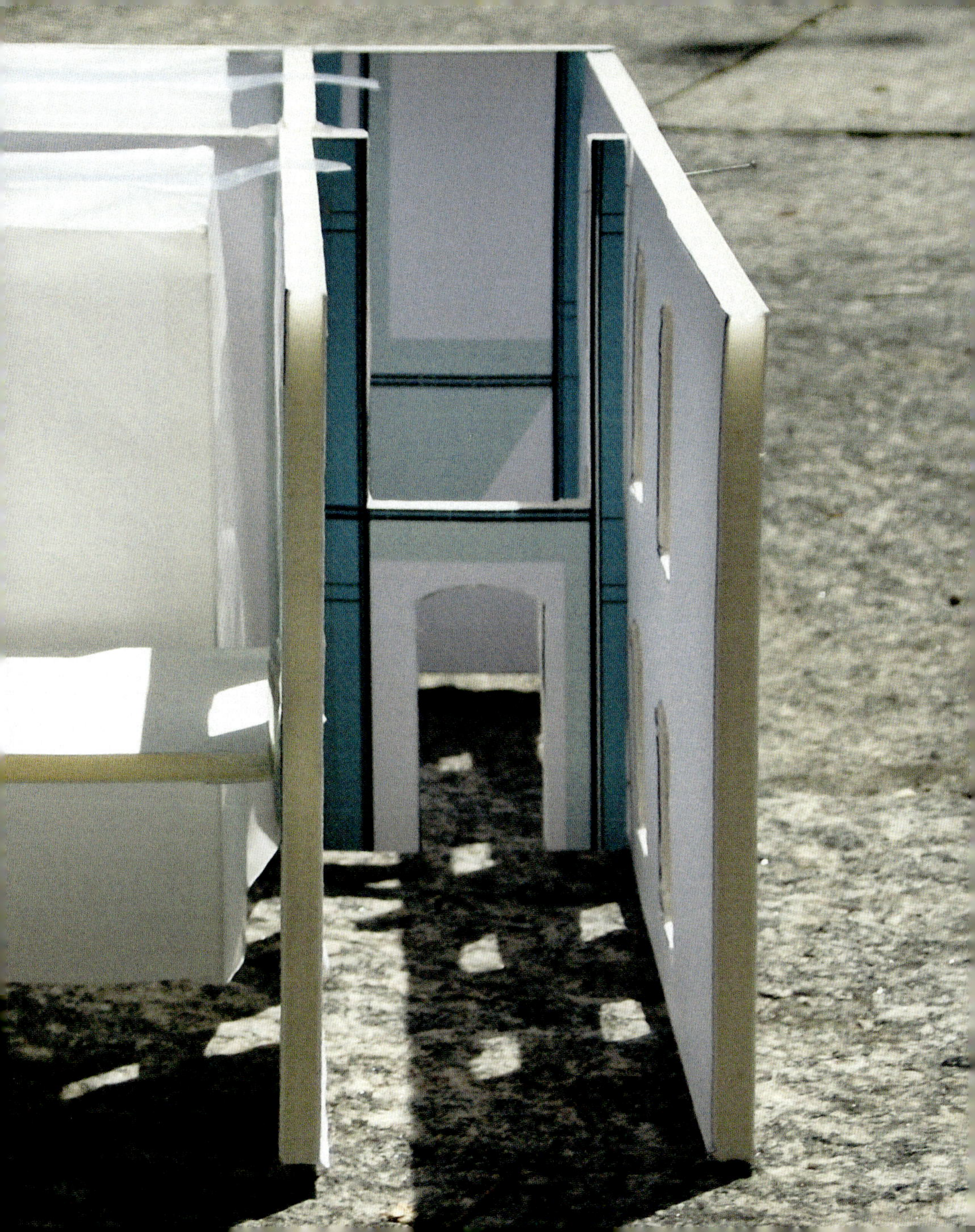

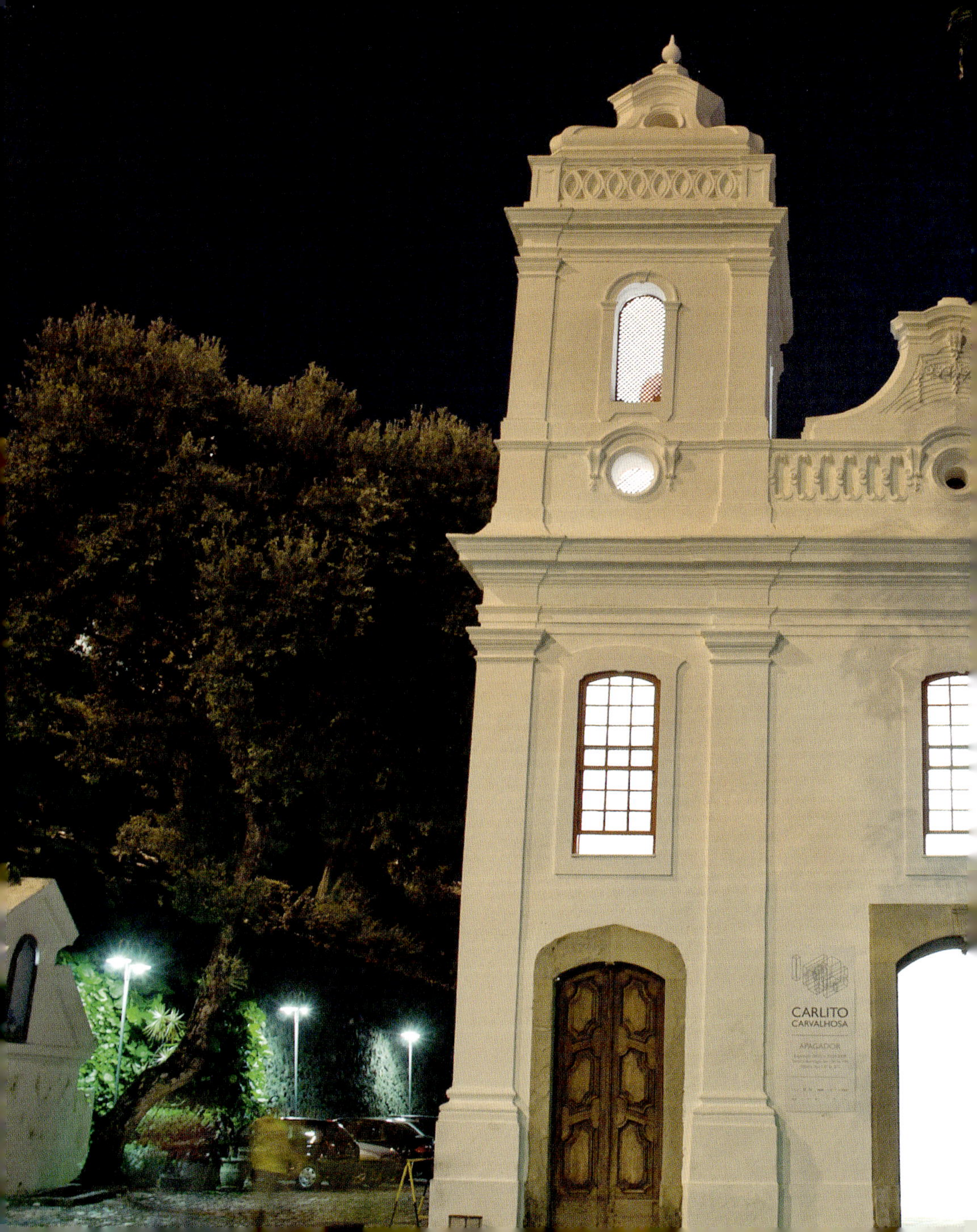
CARLITO
CARVALHOSA
APAGADOR

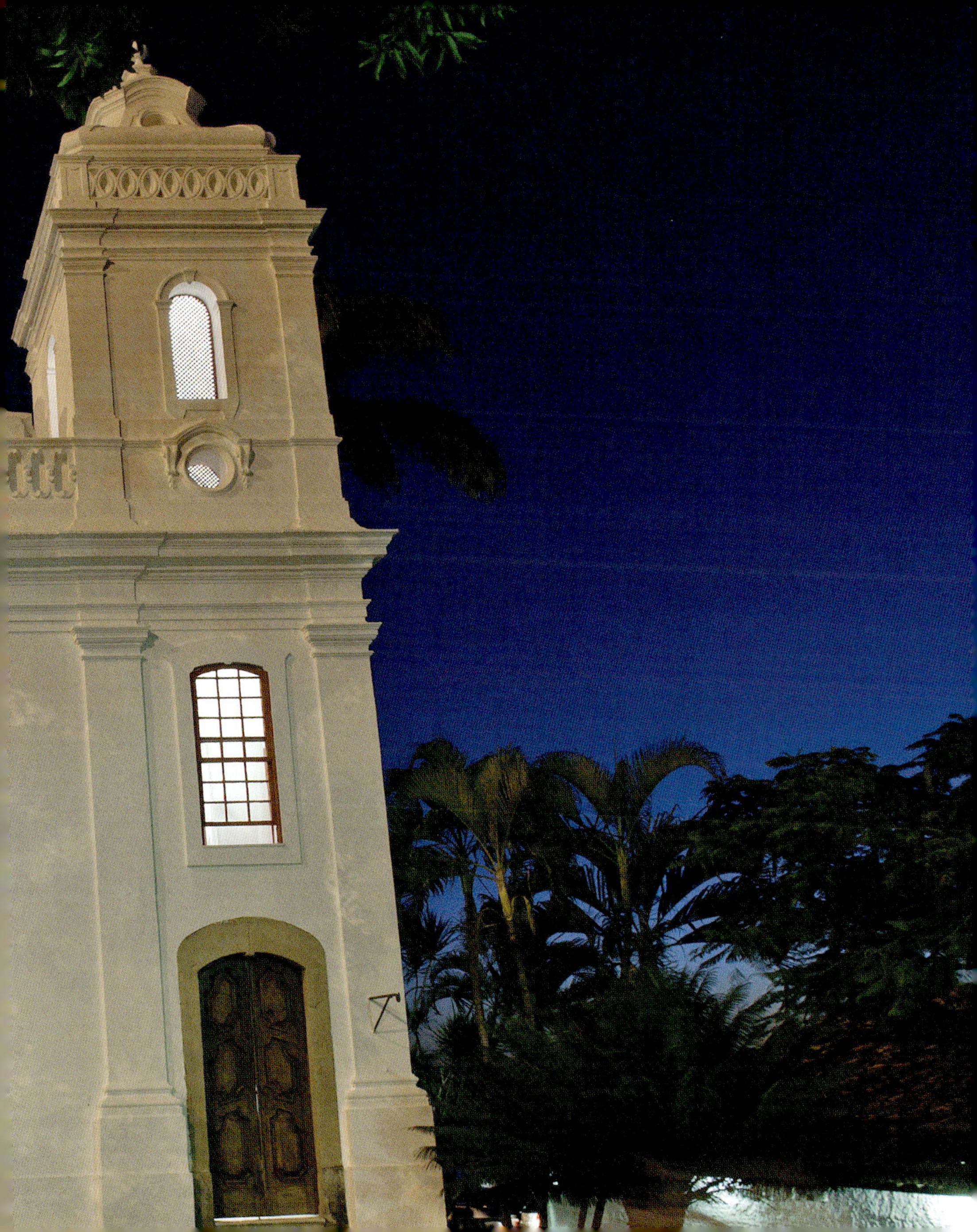

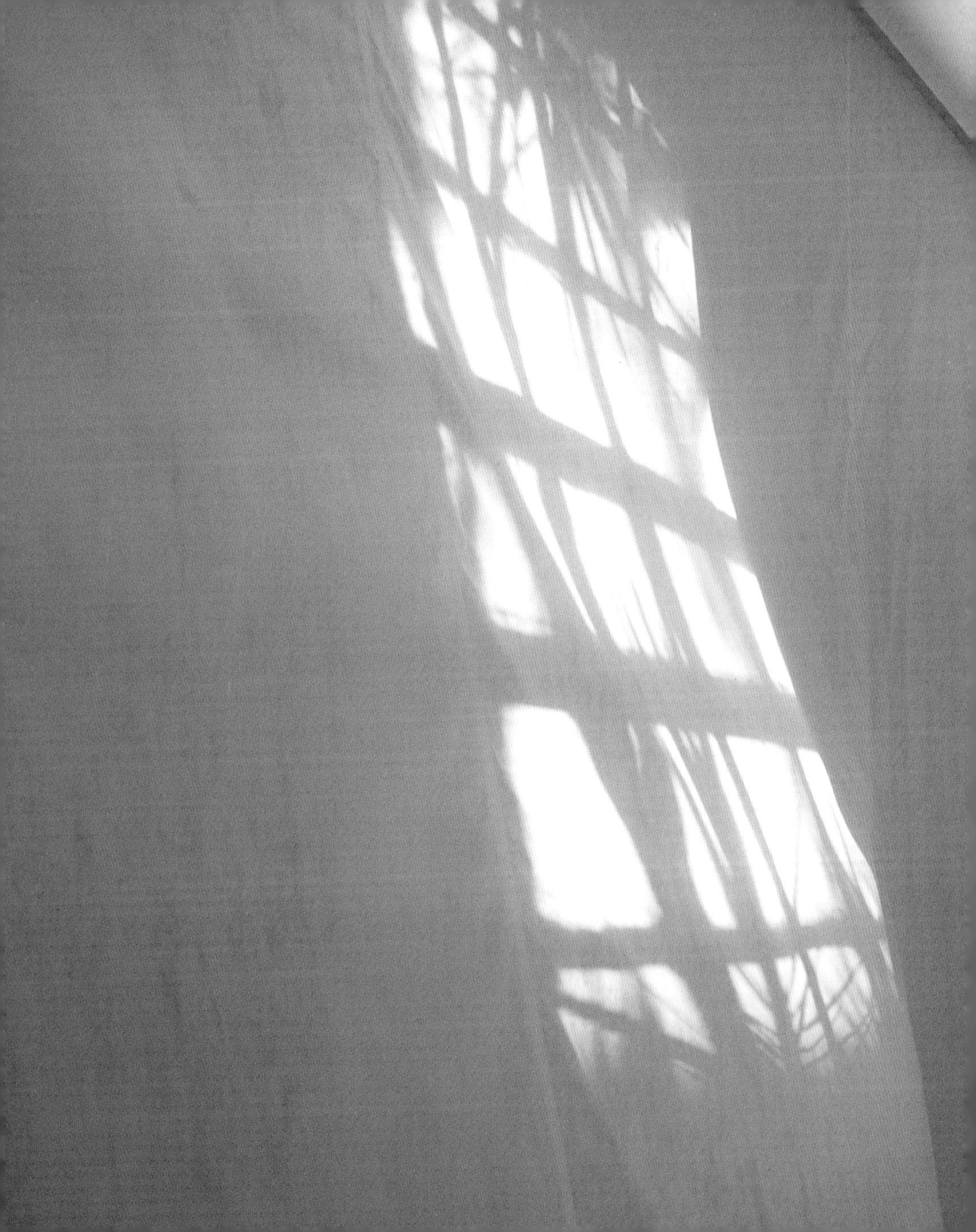

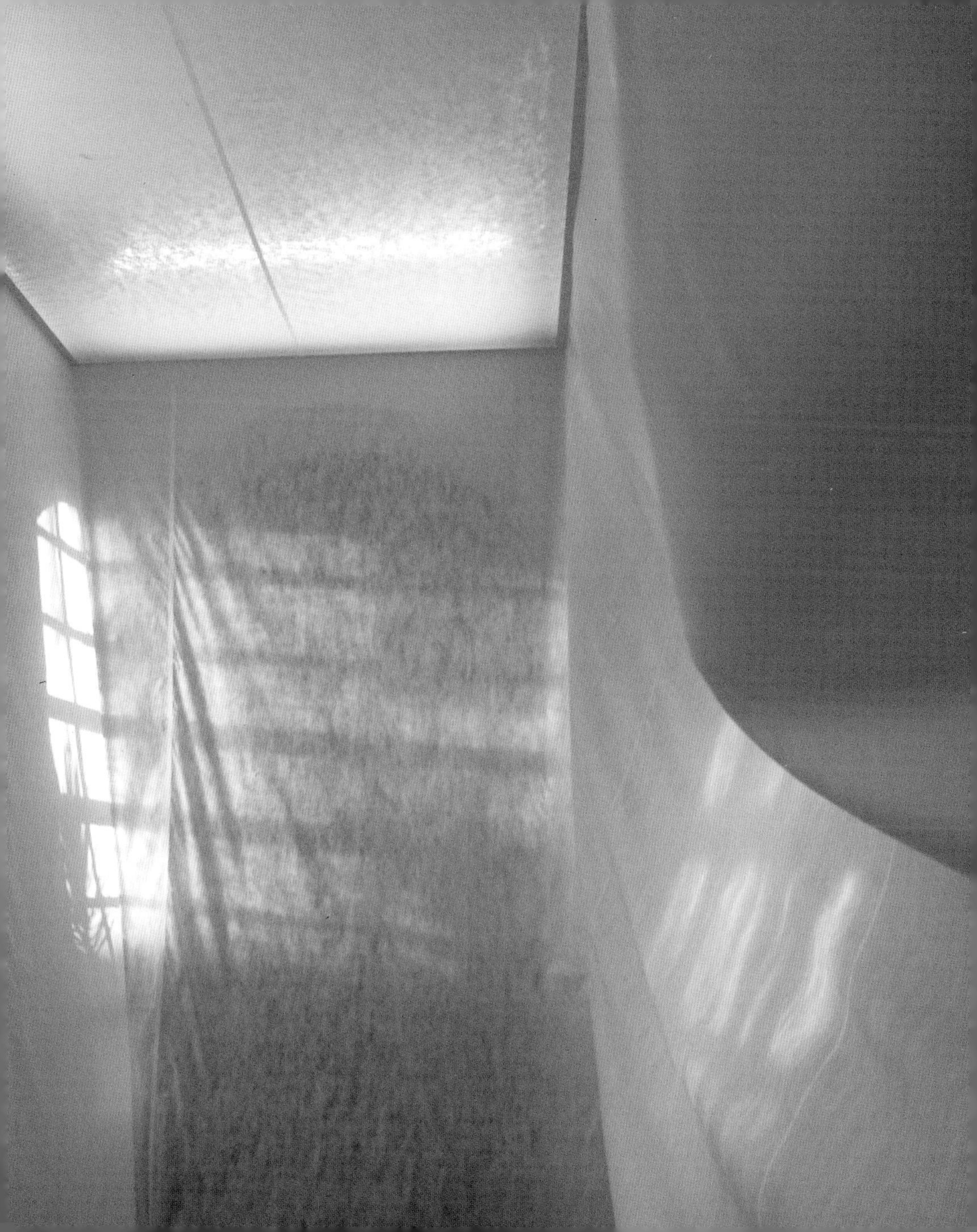

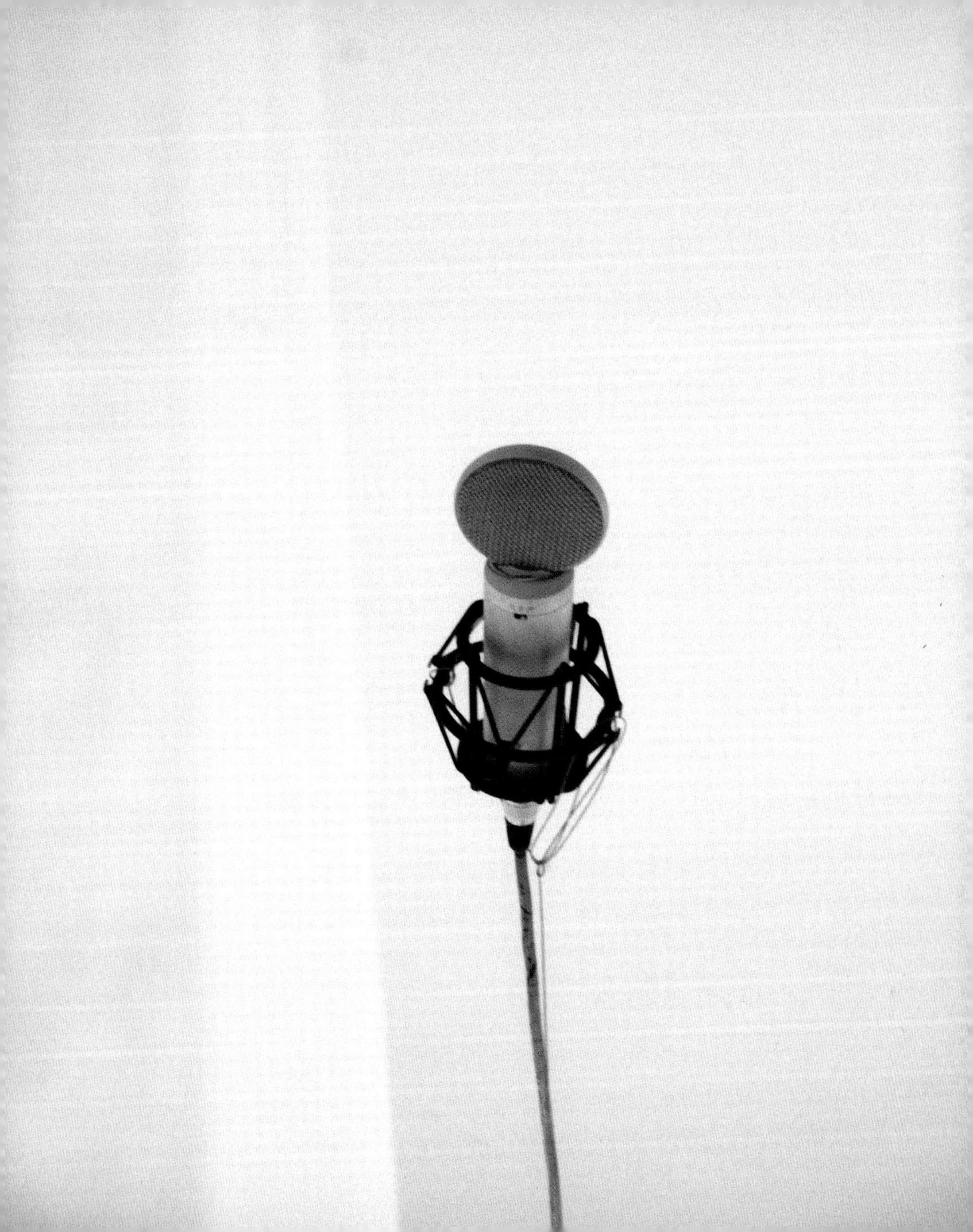

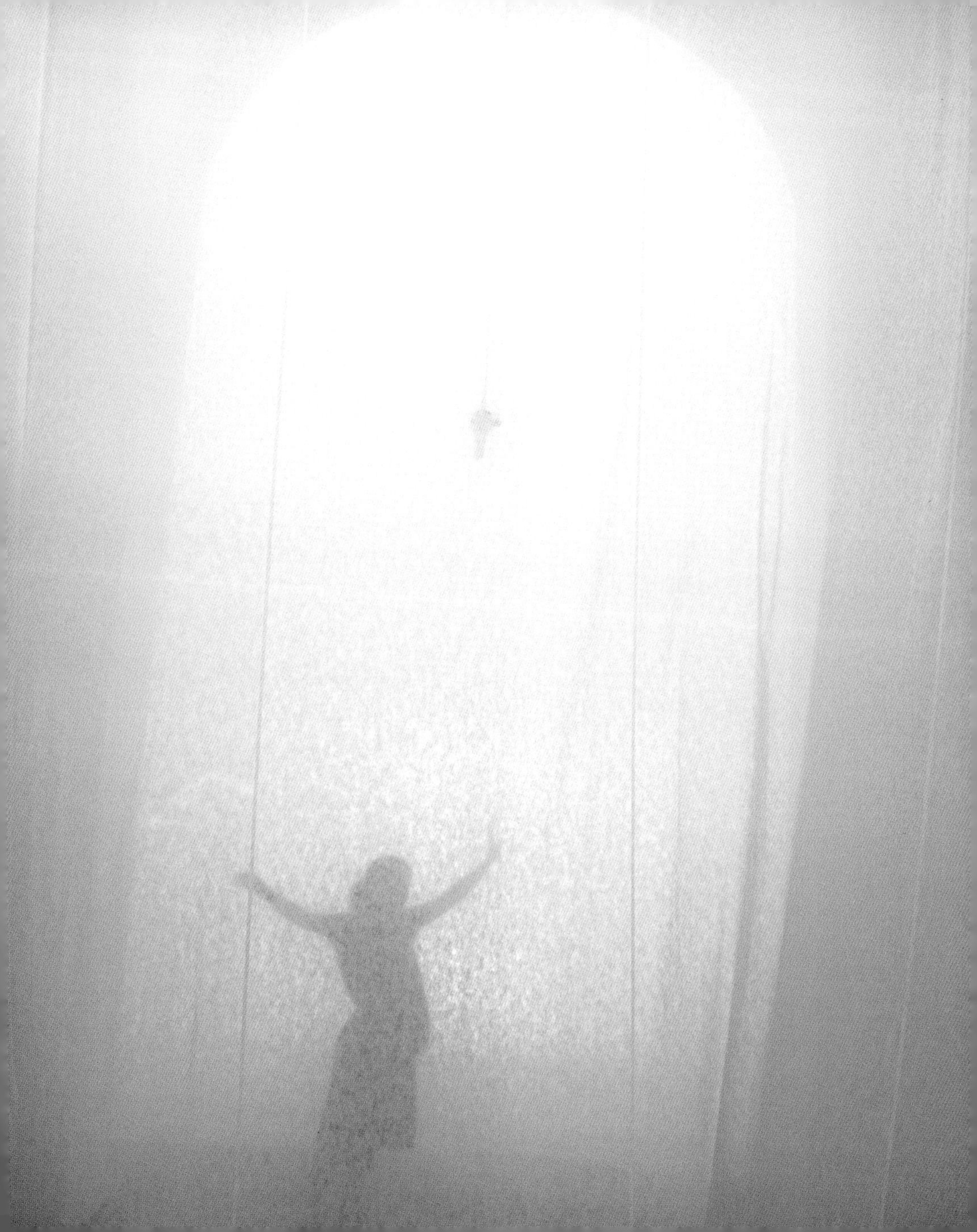

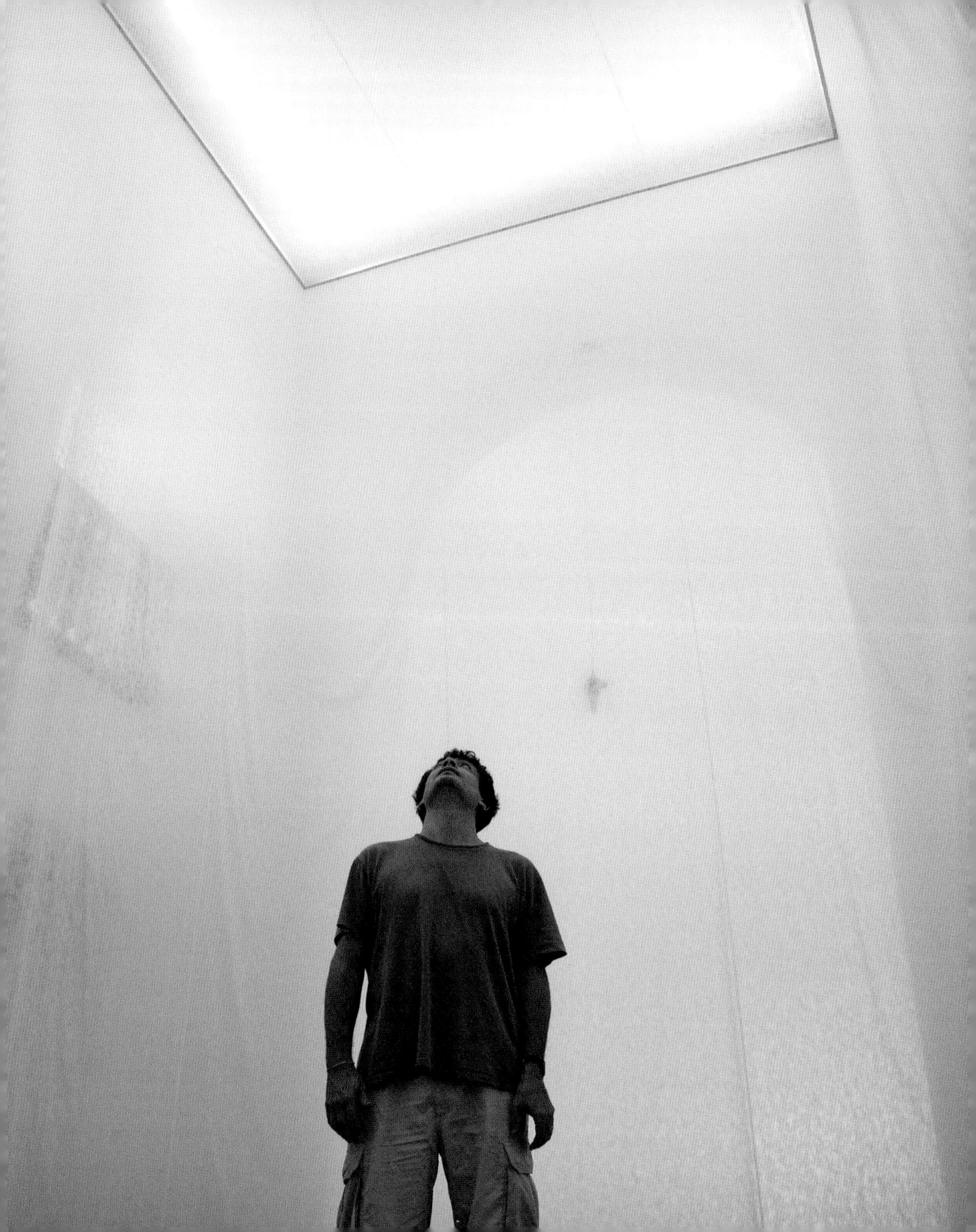

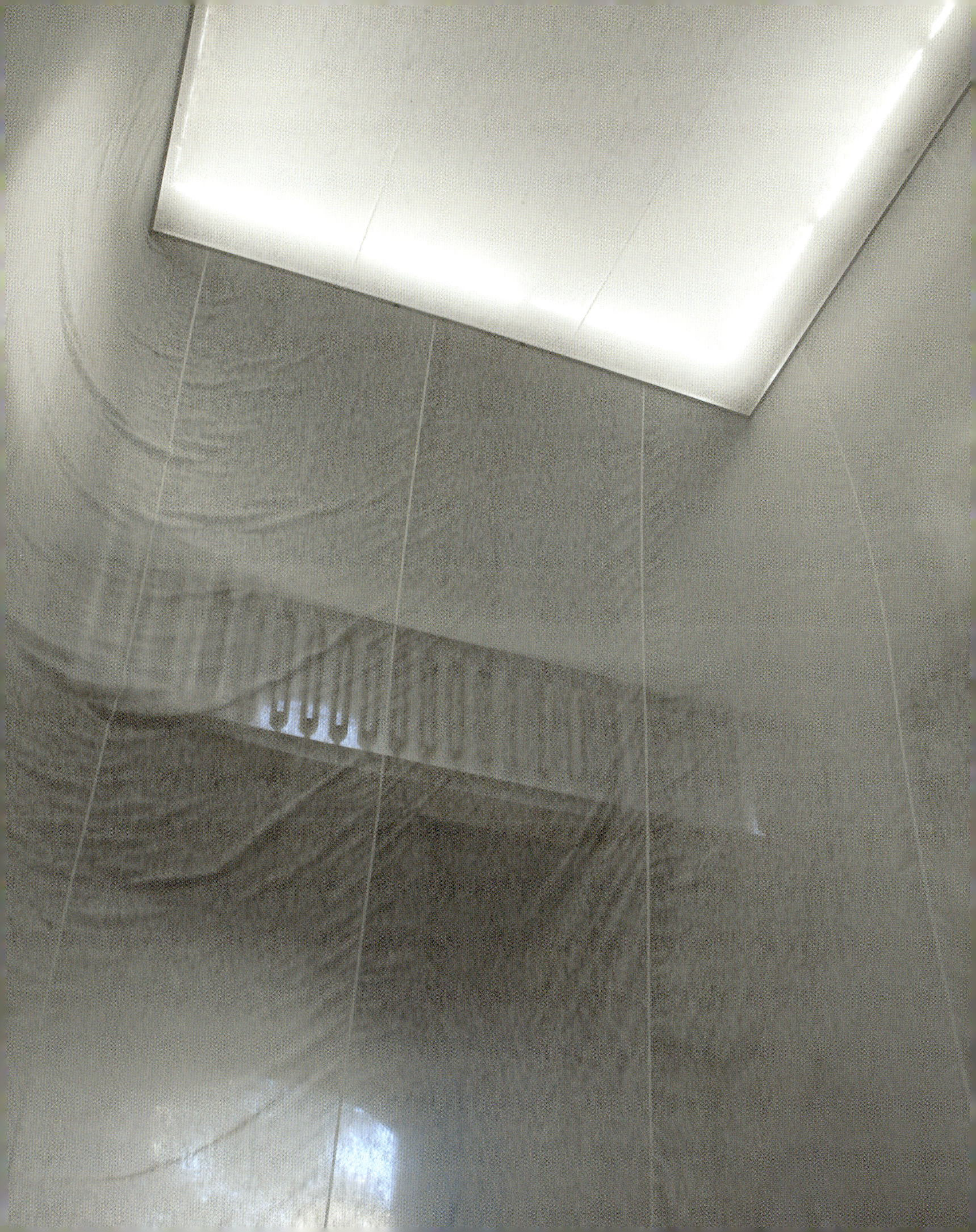

CORREDOR

MUSEU DE ARTE MODERNA DE SÃO PAULO, 2008
PROJETO PAREDE, CURADORIA DE FELIPE CHAIMOVICH
3,5M DE ALTURA, 20M X 1,8M
ÓLEO, CERA, ESPELHO, PELÍCULA ESPELHADA
LÂMPADAS T8
ESSES ESPELHOS SERIAM NATURAIS SE O CORREDOR NÃO LEVASSE AO MUSEU. POR ISSO ACREDITEI QUE CABERIAM AQUI. QUIS FAZER UM LUGAR AO MESMO TEMPO EXCESSIVO E LÍMPIDO. NOTEI QUE NÃO PINTAR O ESPELHO SERIA DESPERDIÇAR UMA CHANCE ÚNICA.

Corridor

Museu de Arte Moderna de São Paulo, 2008

Projeto Parede, curated by Felipe Chaimovich
3.5m h, 20m x 1.8m
Oil, wax, mirrors, reflective film T8 lamps
These mirrors would be natural if the corridor didn't lead to the Museum. That is why I thought they would fit here. I wanted to make a space at once excessive and limpid. I realized that not painting the mirrors would be a waste.

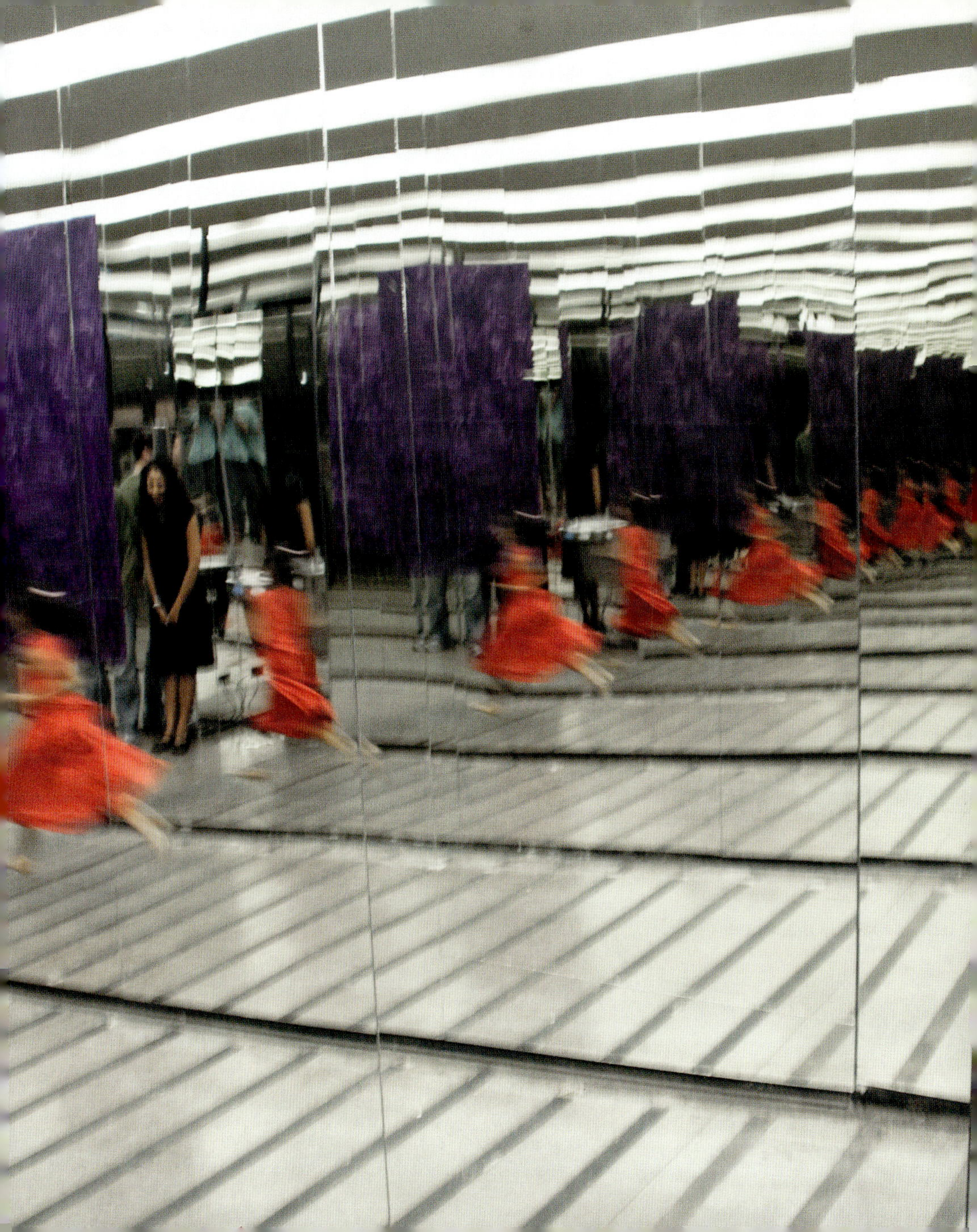

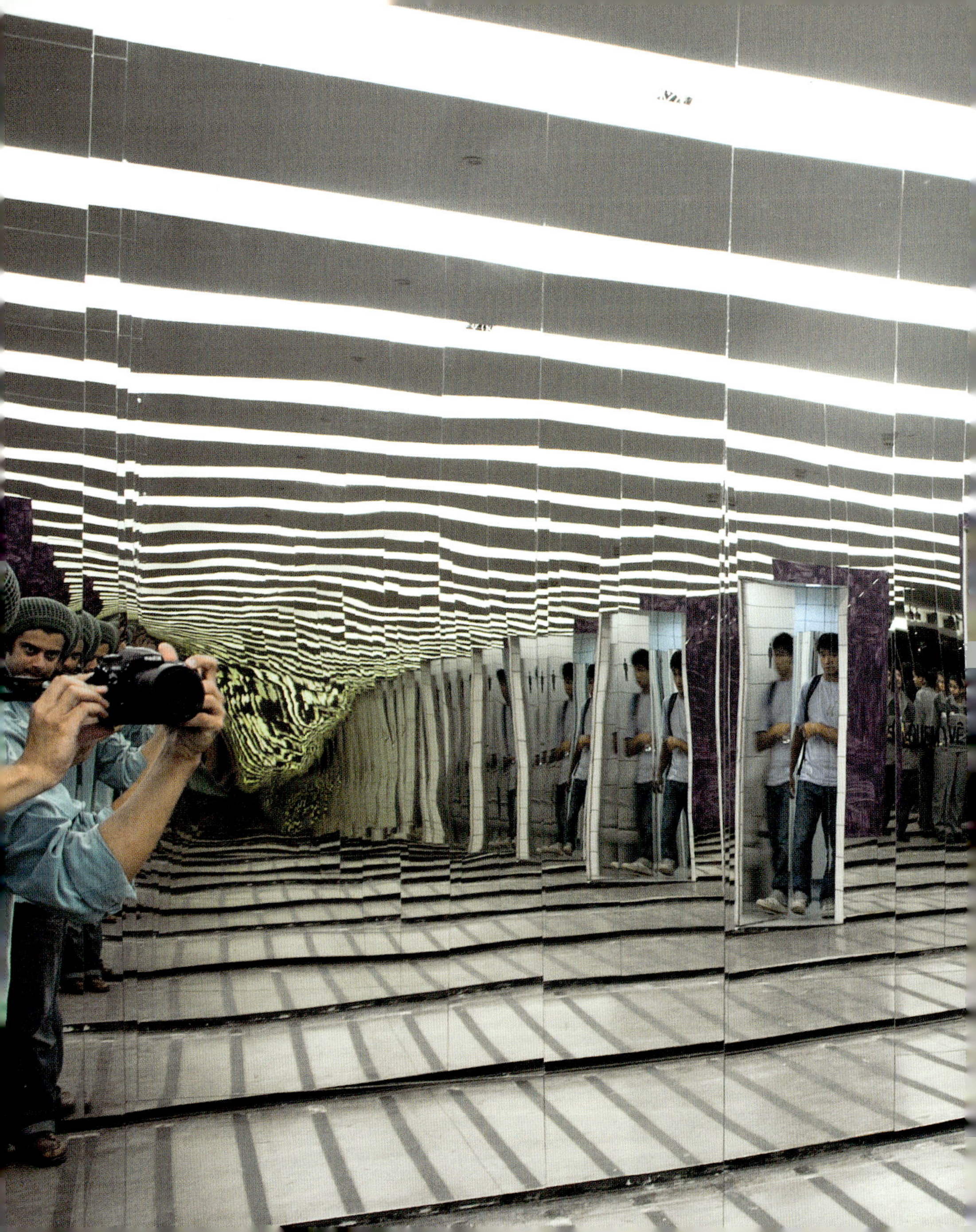

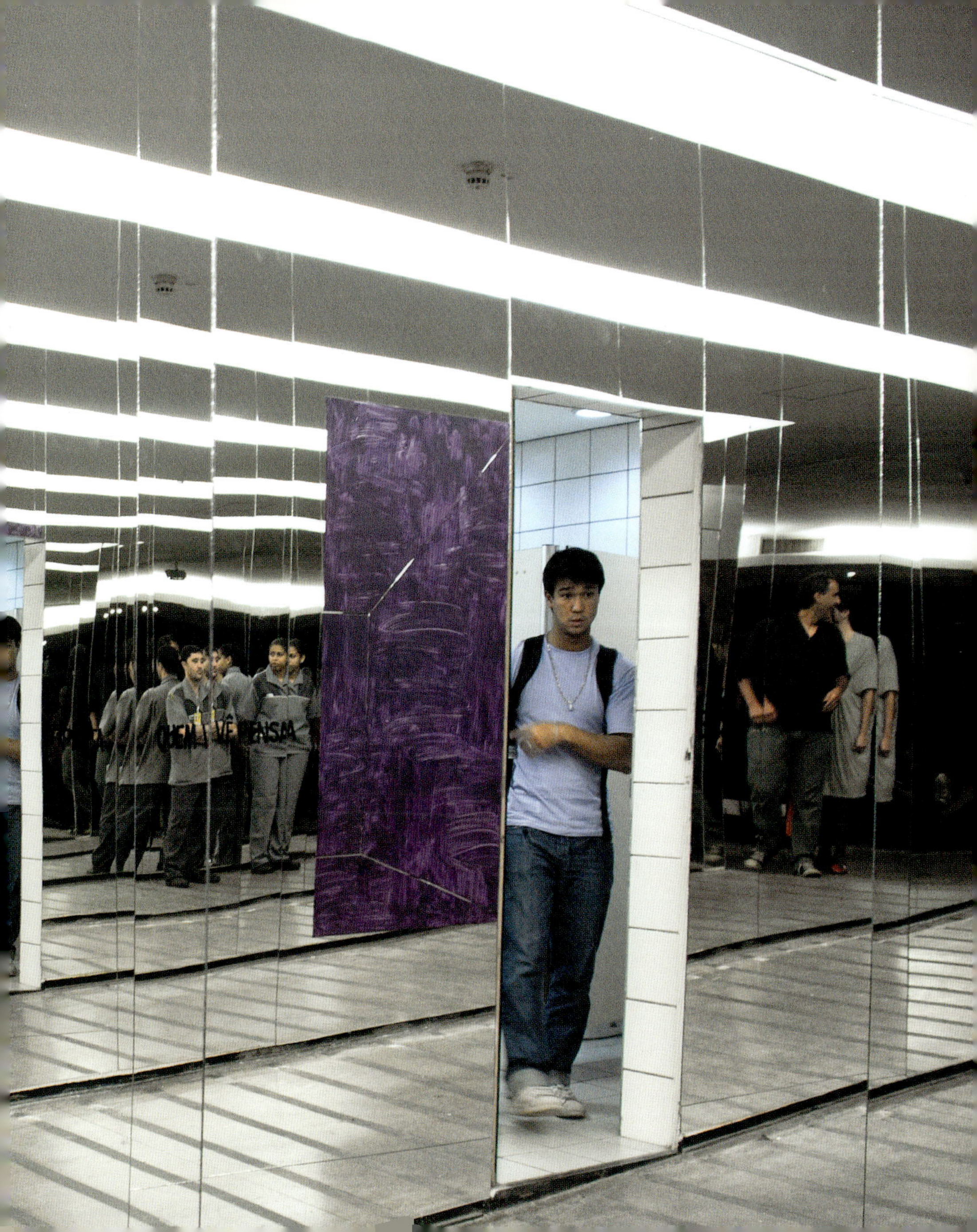

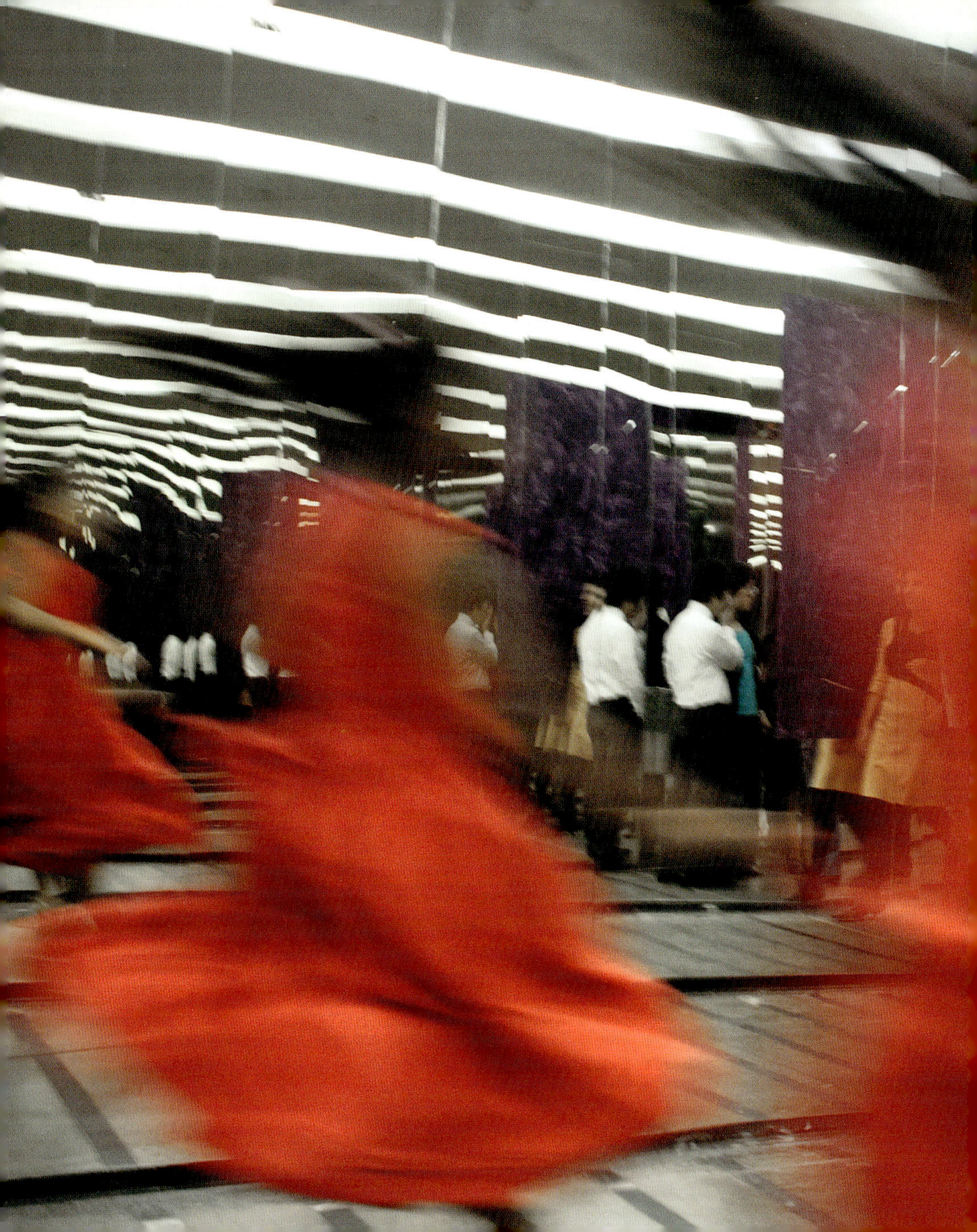

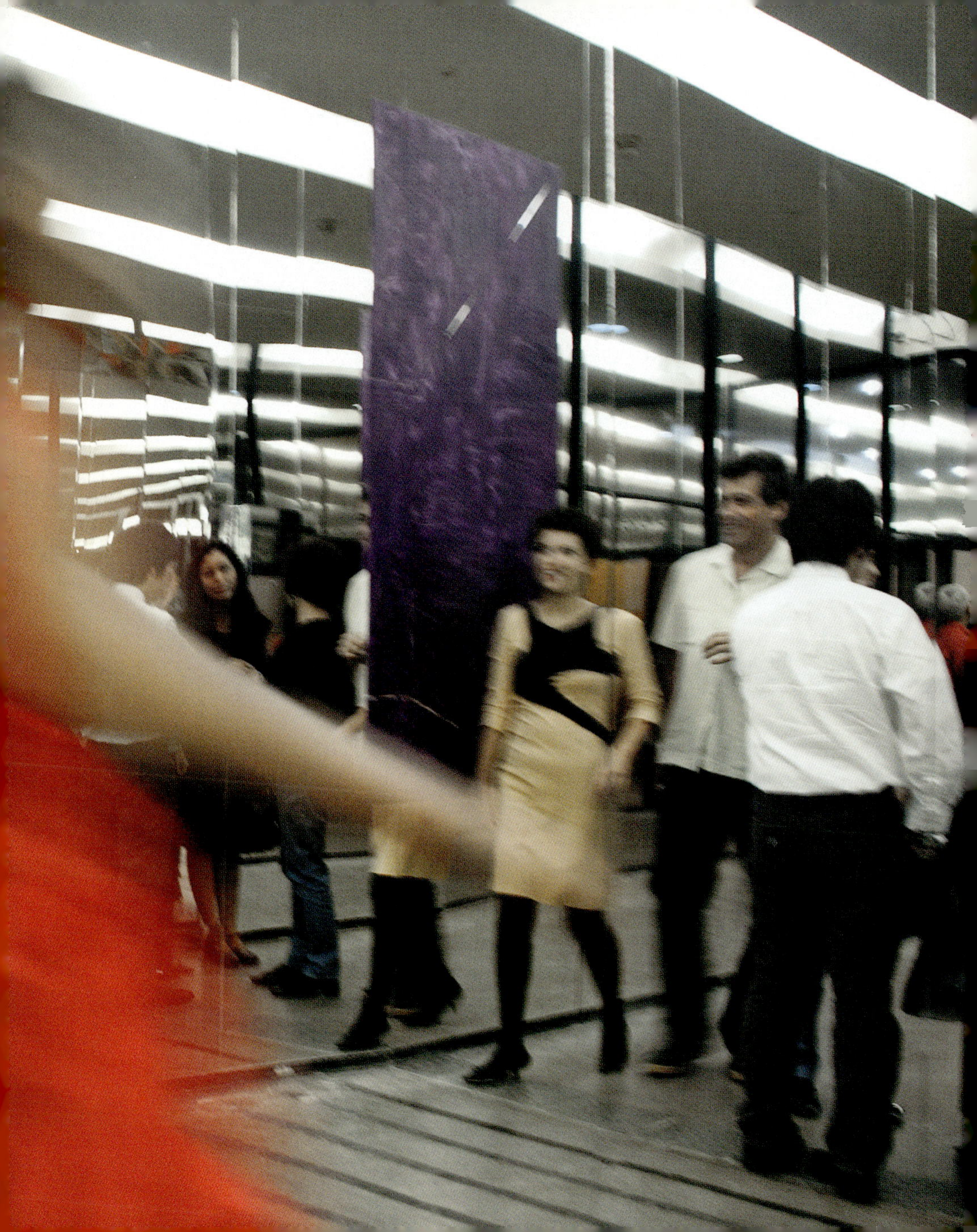

MEUS OLHOS

SOLAR DO BARÃO, CURITIBA, 2008
CURADORIA DE CRISTIANE SILVEIRA
4,3M ALTURA, 17 x 5M
TNT 20G. EM ~~[illegible]~~ 3 PEÇAS
LÂMPADAS T8, 32W, 4100°K
ALUMÍNIO, CABO DE AÇO, MICROFONE, ALTO-FALANTE

My Eyes

Solar do Barão, Curitiba, 2008

Curated by Cristiane Silveira
4.3m h, 17 x 5m,
TNT 20g. in 2 pieces
T8 lamps, 32w, 4,100°k
Aluminum, steel cables, microphone, loudspeaker

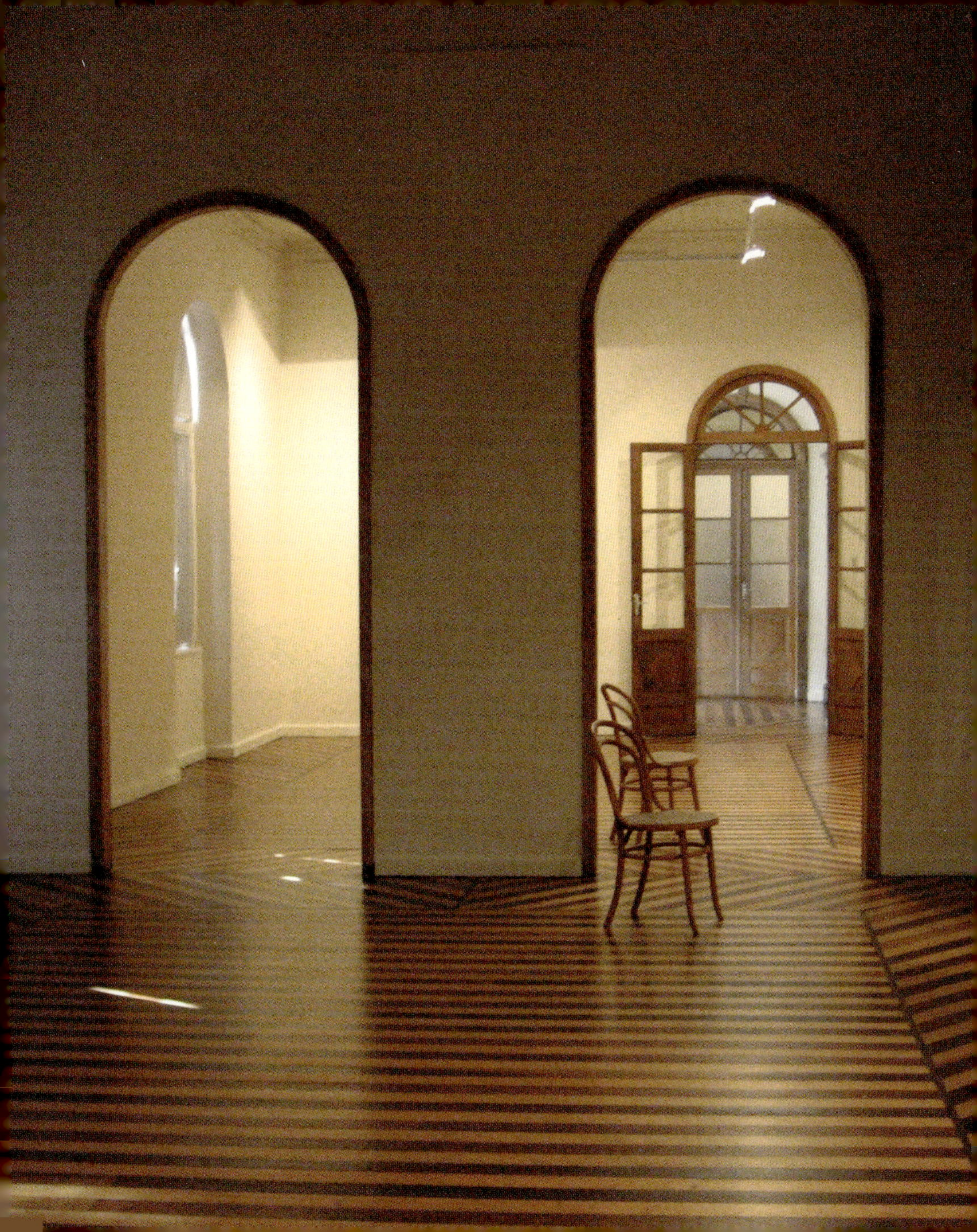

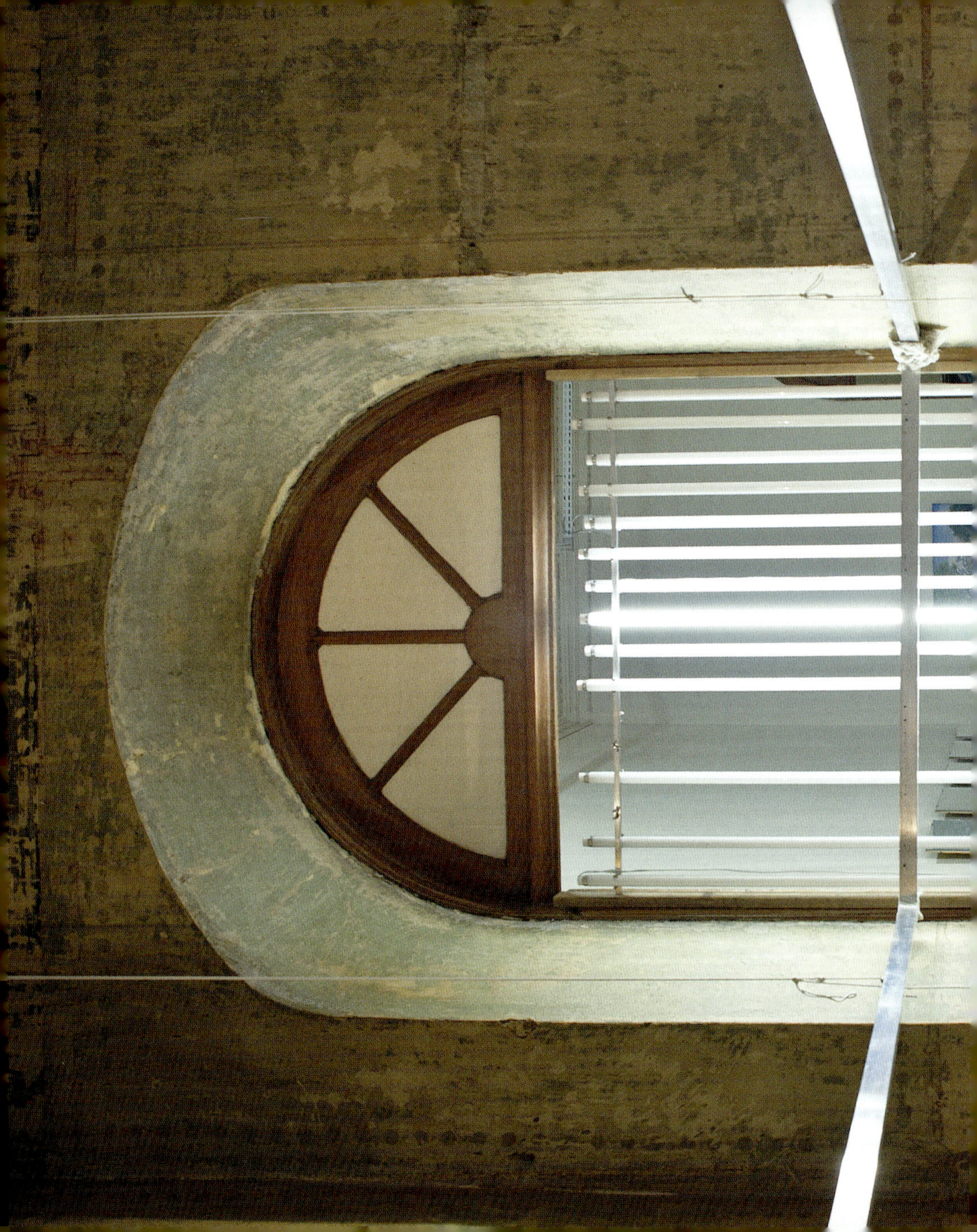

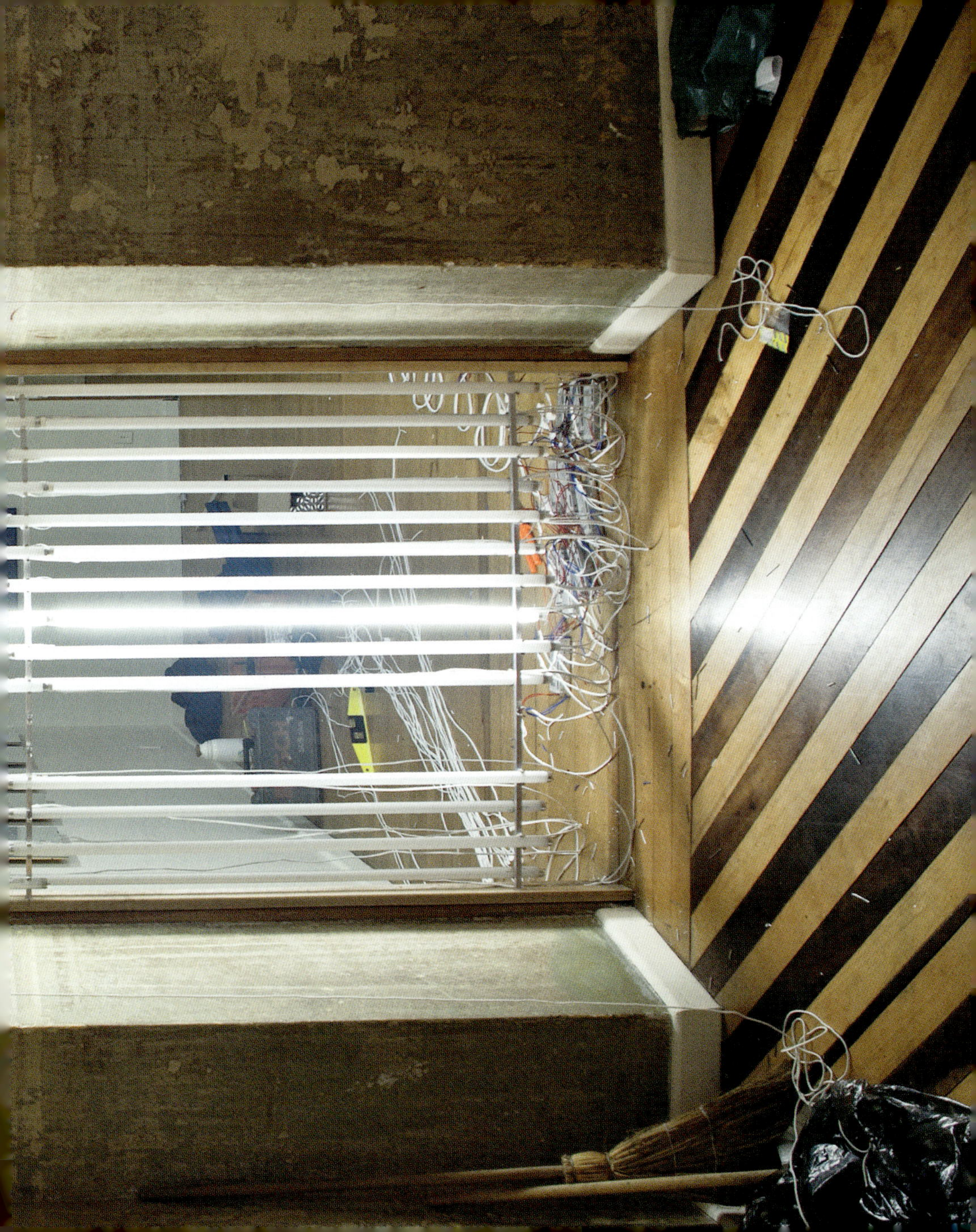

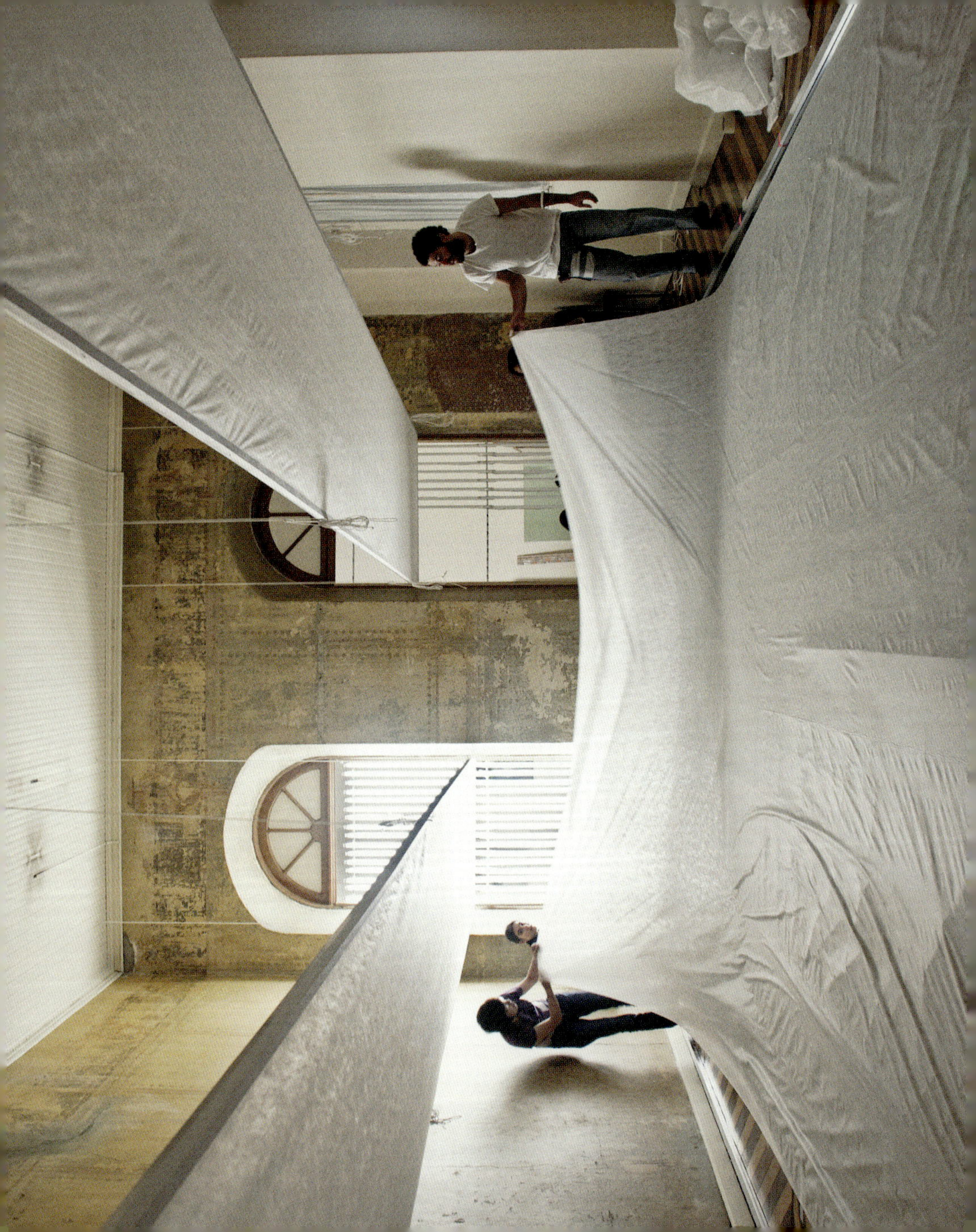

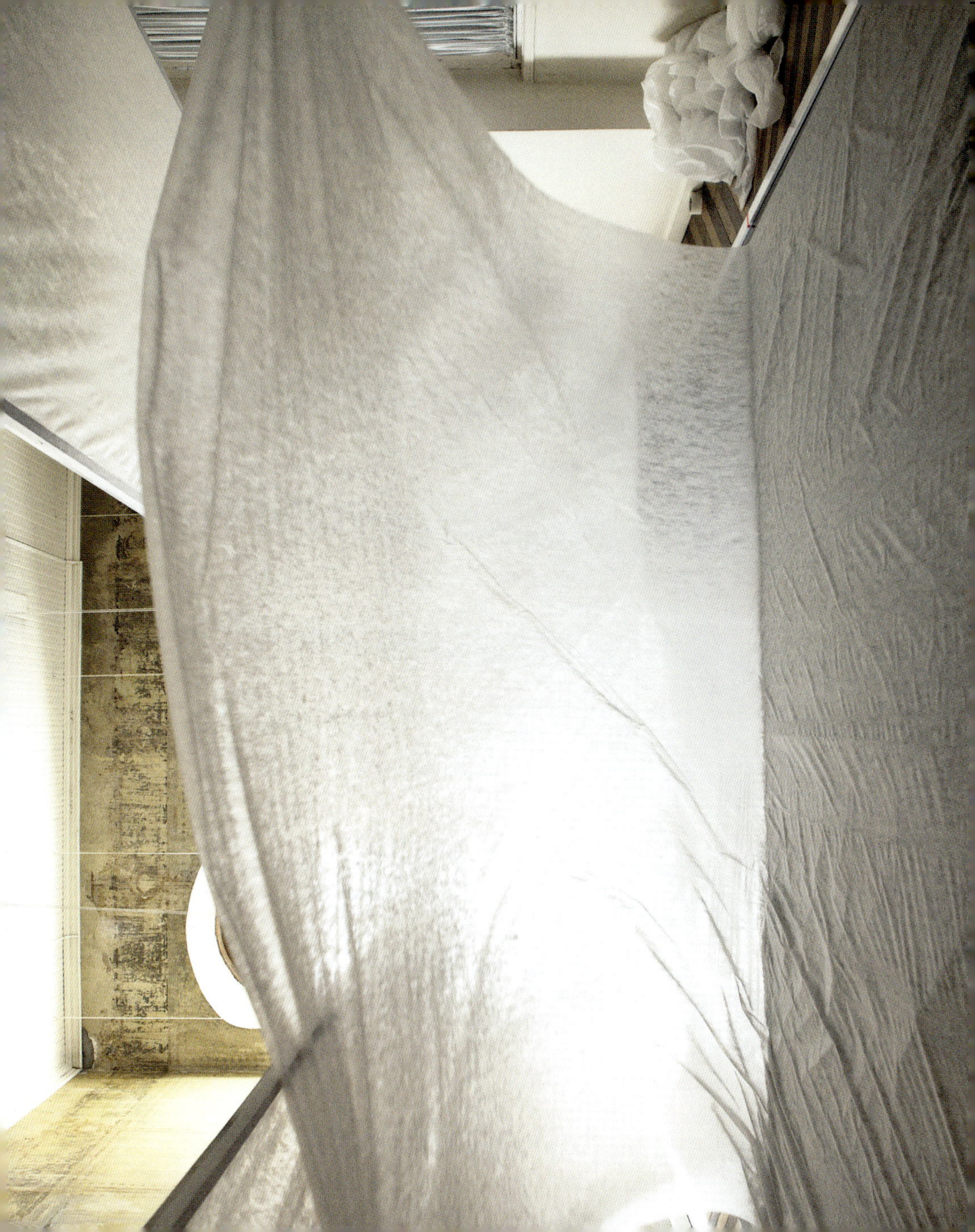

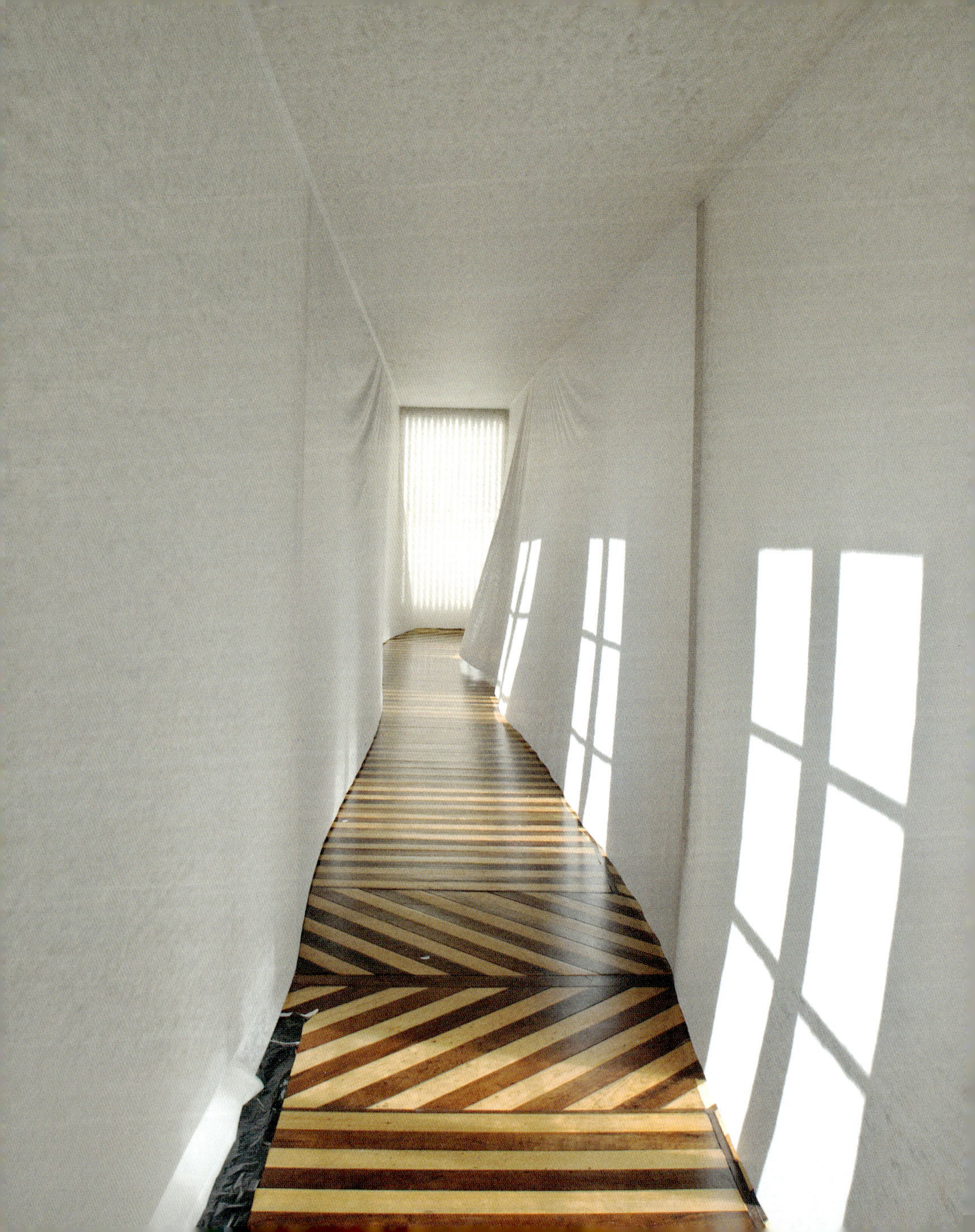

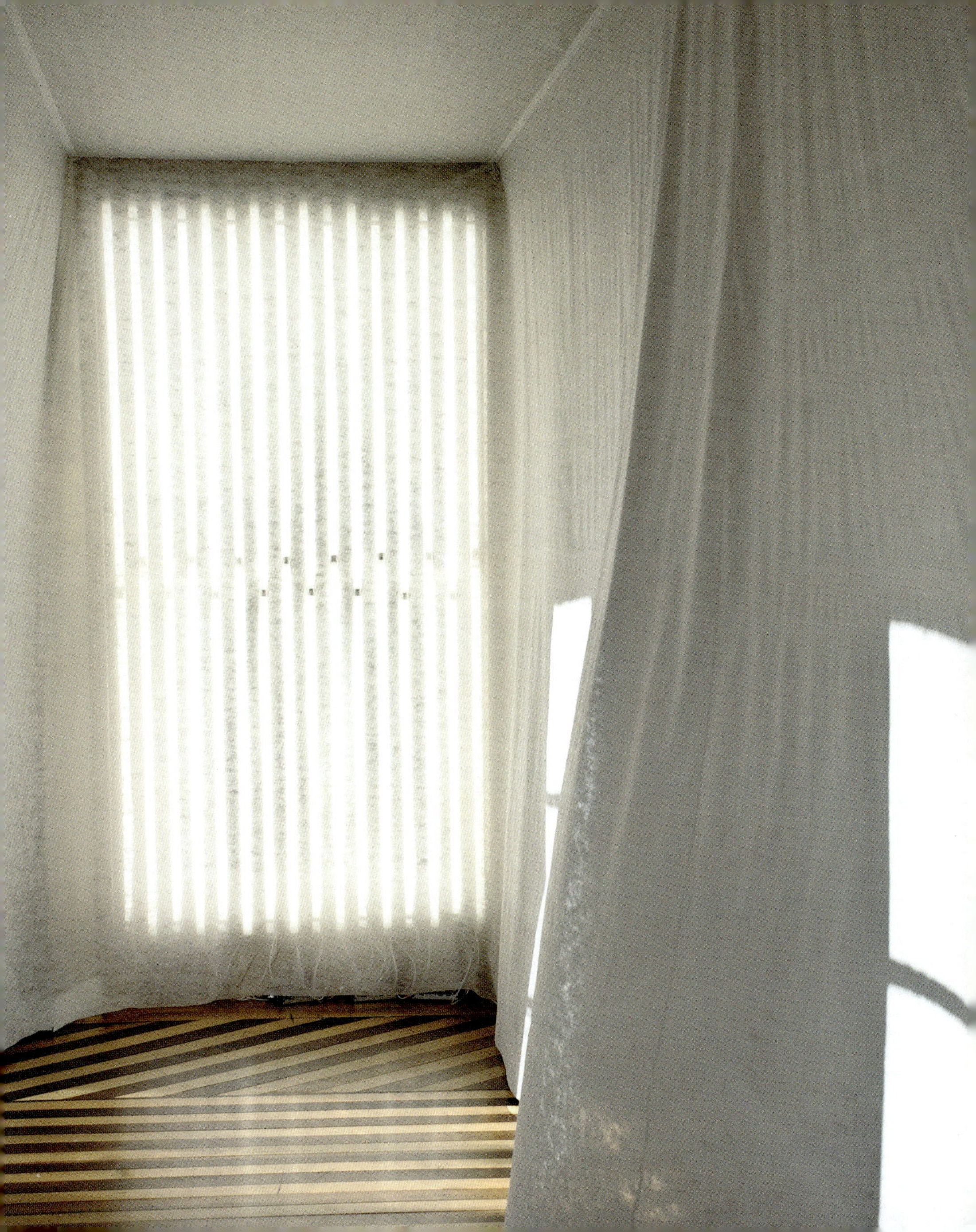

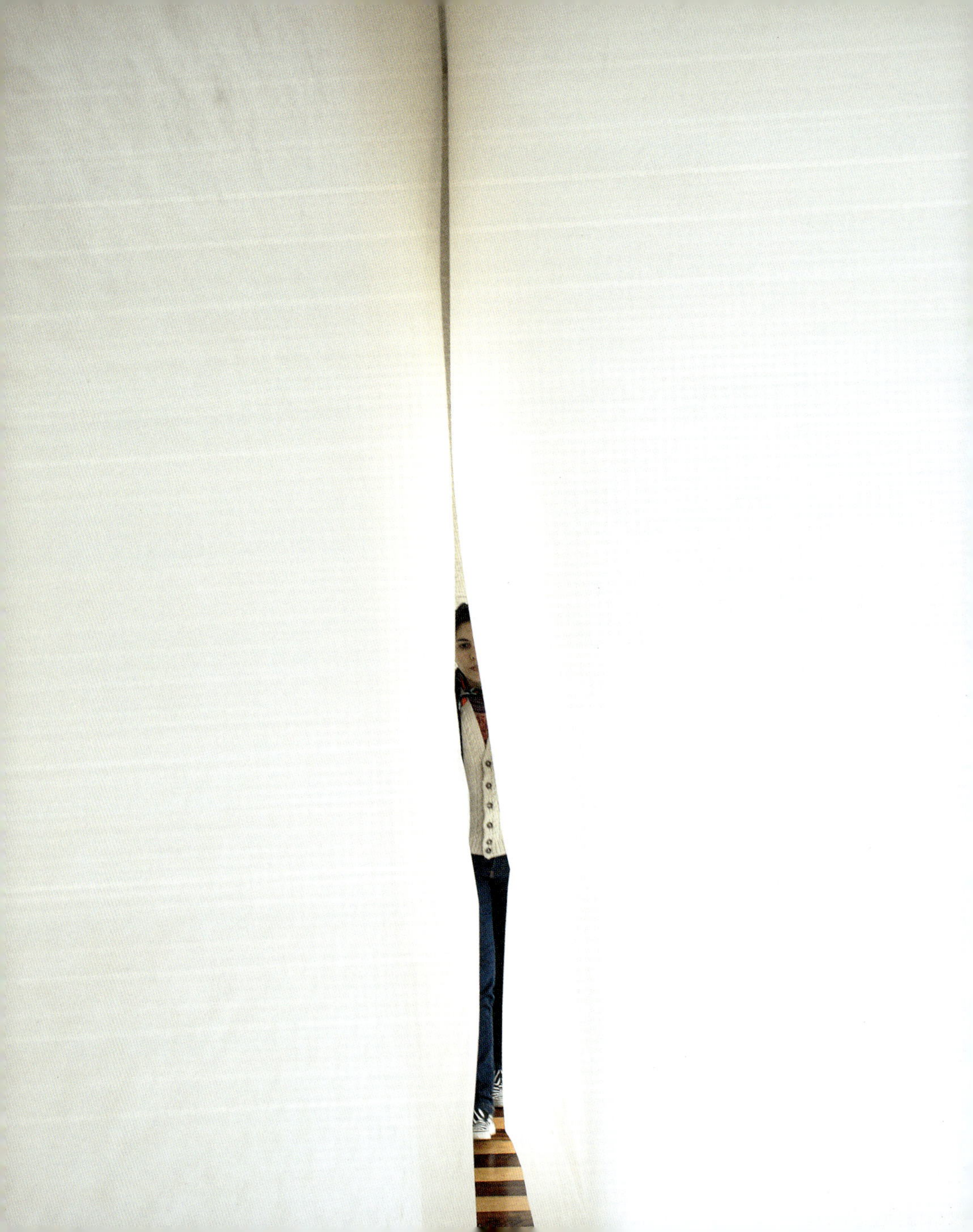

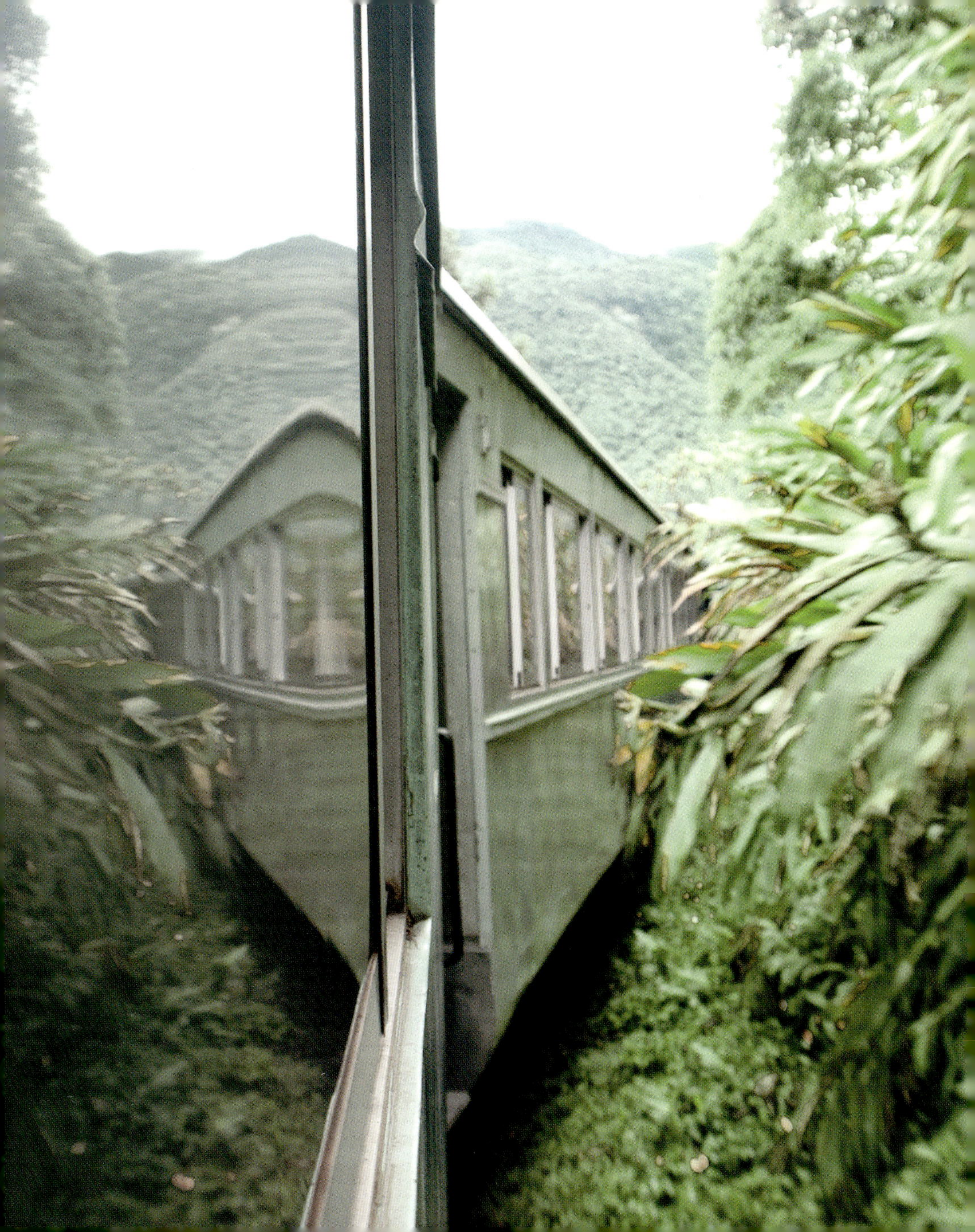

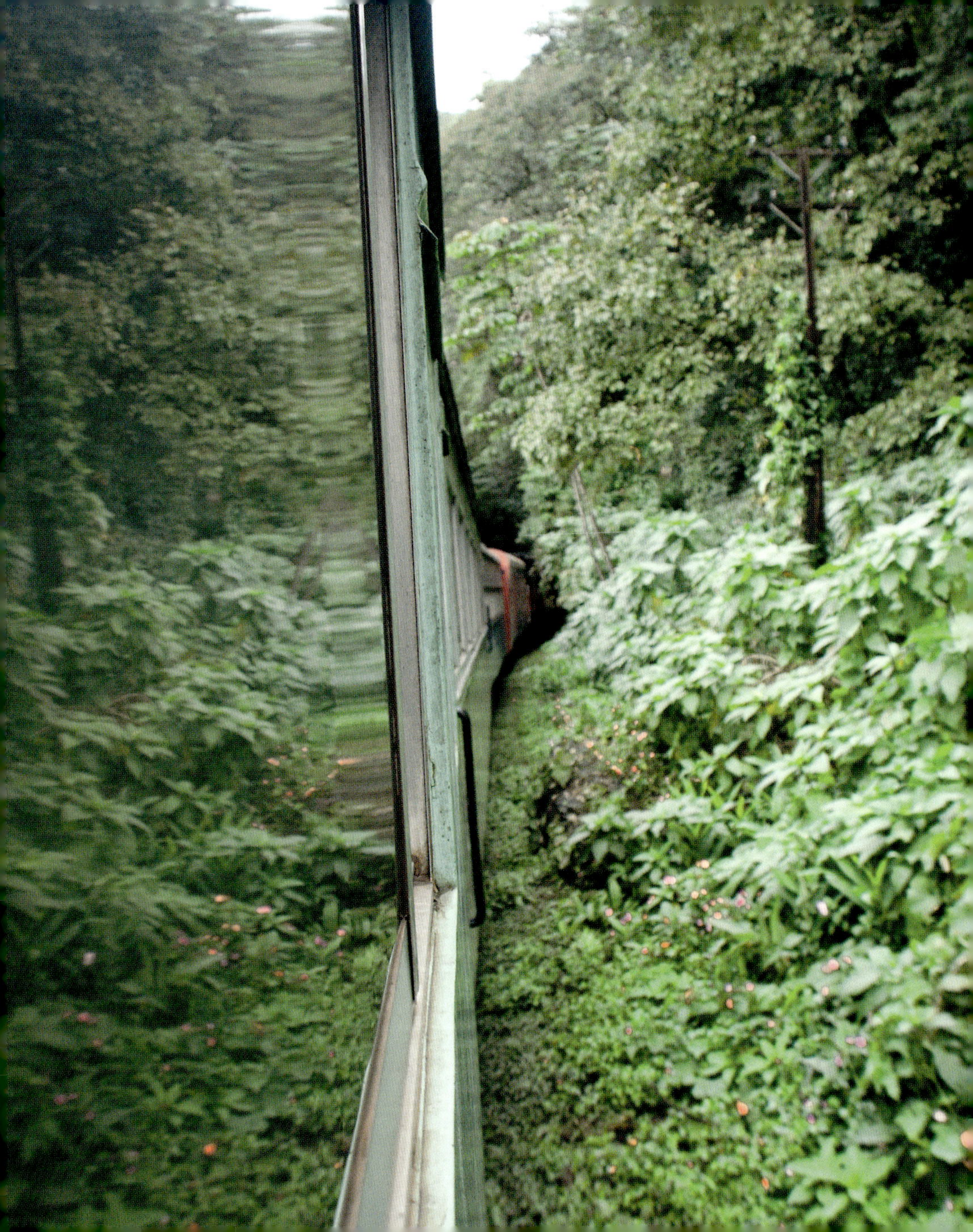

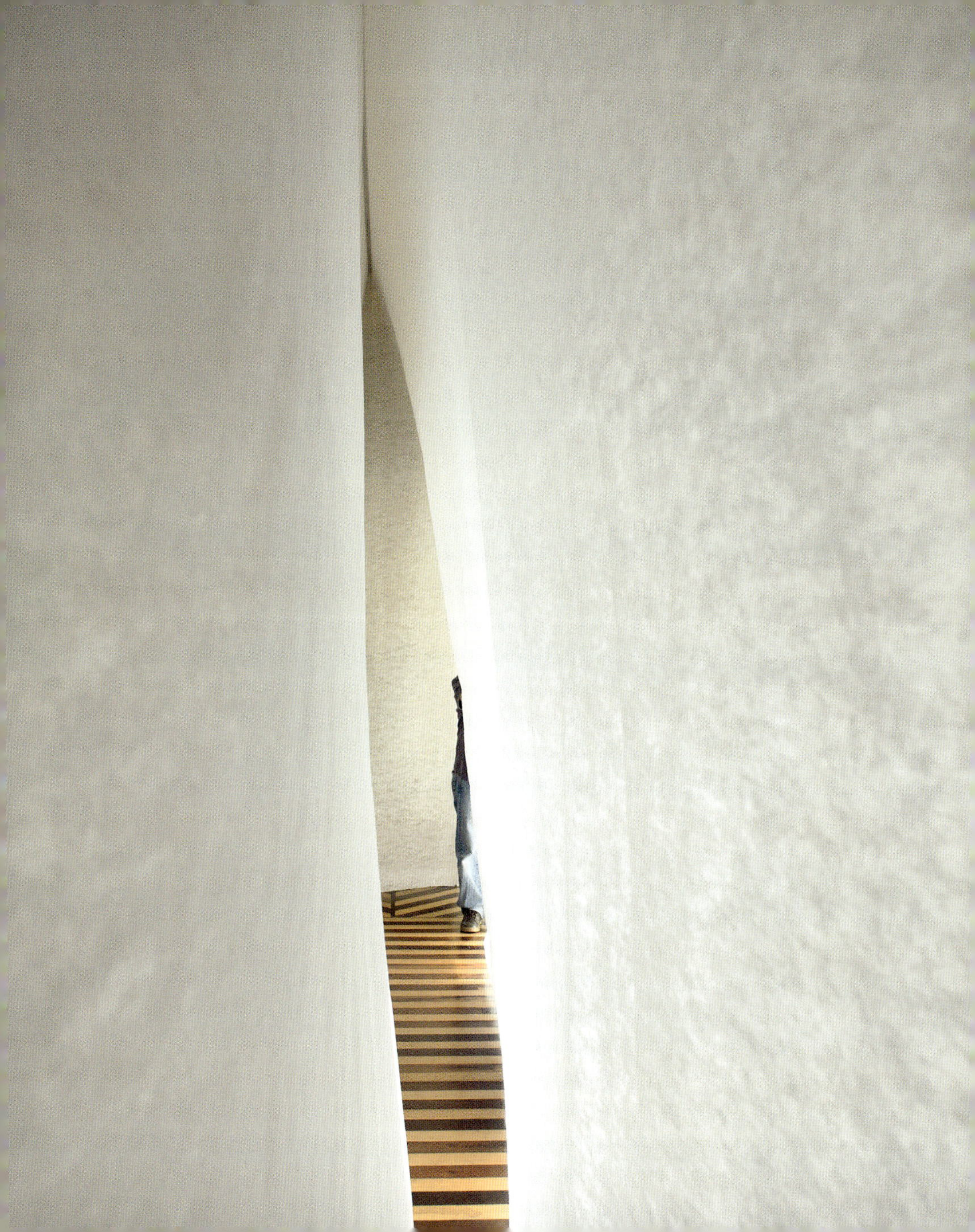

FAZ PARTE

GALERIA MILLAN E GABINETE DE ARTE RAQUEL ARNAUD
SÃO PAULO, 2008
EXPOSIÇÃO SIMULTÂNEA NAS DUAS GALERIAS
TNT, LÂMPADAS T8, MICROFONES, ALTO-FALANTES, LAPTOPS,
INTERFACE DE ÁUDIO, LENTES EM VIDRO ÓPTICO,
ESPELHOS, ESPELHOS NEGROS
O SOM GRAVADO À NOITE EM UMA GALERIA É
REPRODUZIDO SEPARADOS PELOS QUARTEIRÕES
ENTRE AS GALERIAS, TNT, LUZ, SOM E LENTES
REAPARECEM. OS ESPELHOS, NÃO

It Happens

Galeria Millan e Gabinete de Arte Raquel Arnaud, São Paulo, 2008

Simultaneous exhibitions in both galleries
TNT, T8 lamps, microphones, loudspeakers, laptops, audio interface, optical glass lenses, mirrors, black mirrors
The sound recorded overnight in one gallery is reproduced in the other during the day. Separated by city blocks between galleries, the TNT, light, sound and lenses reappear.The mirrors do not.

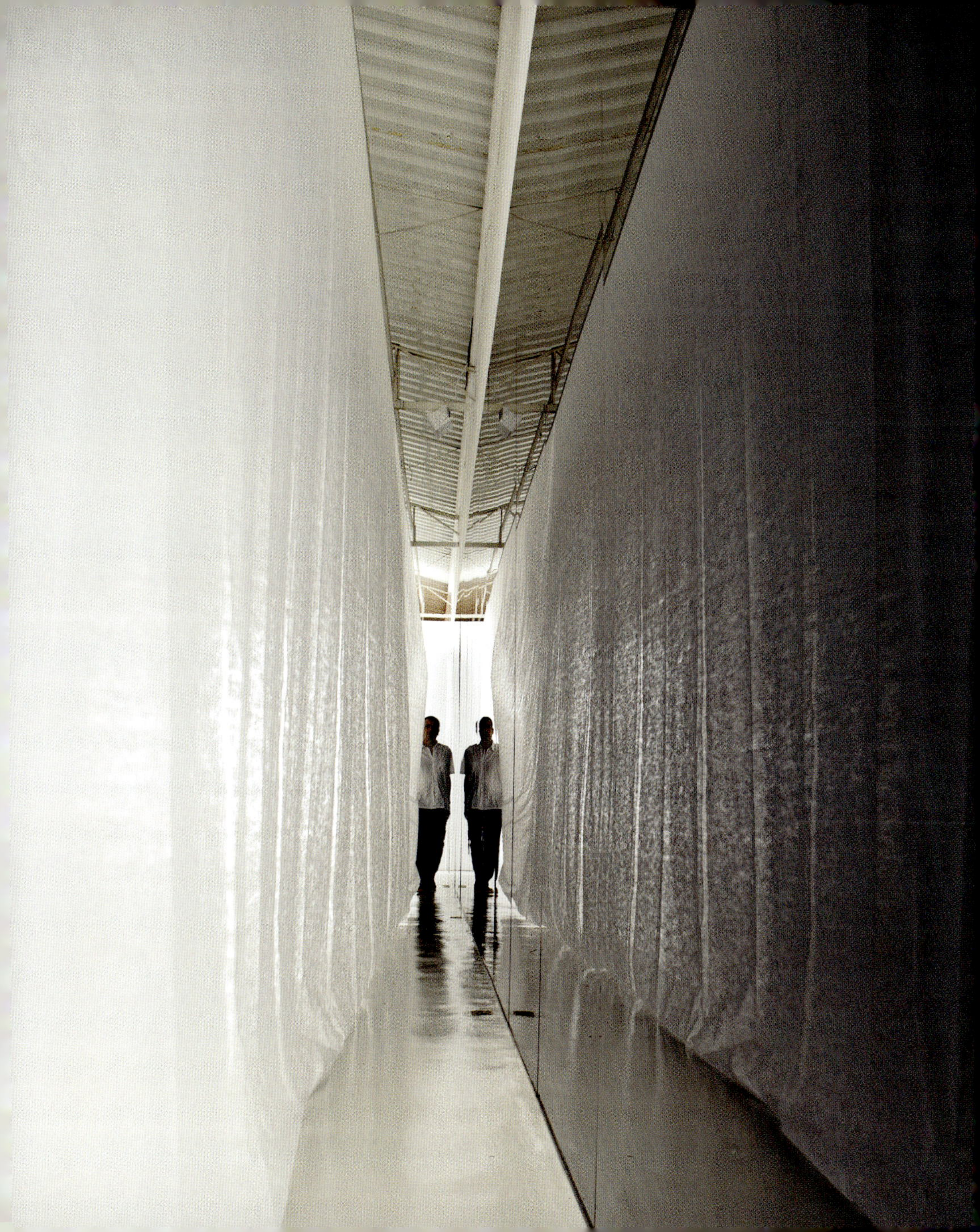

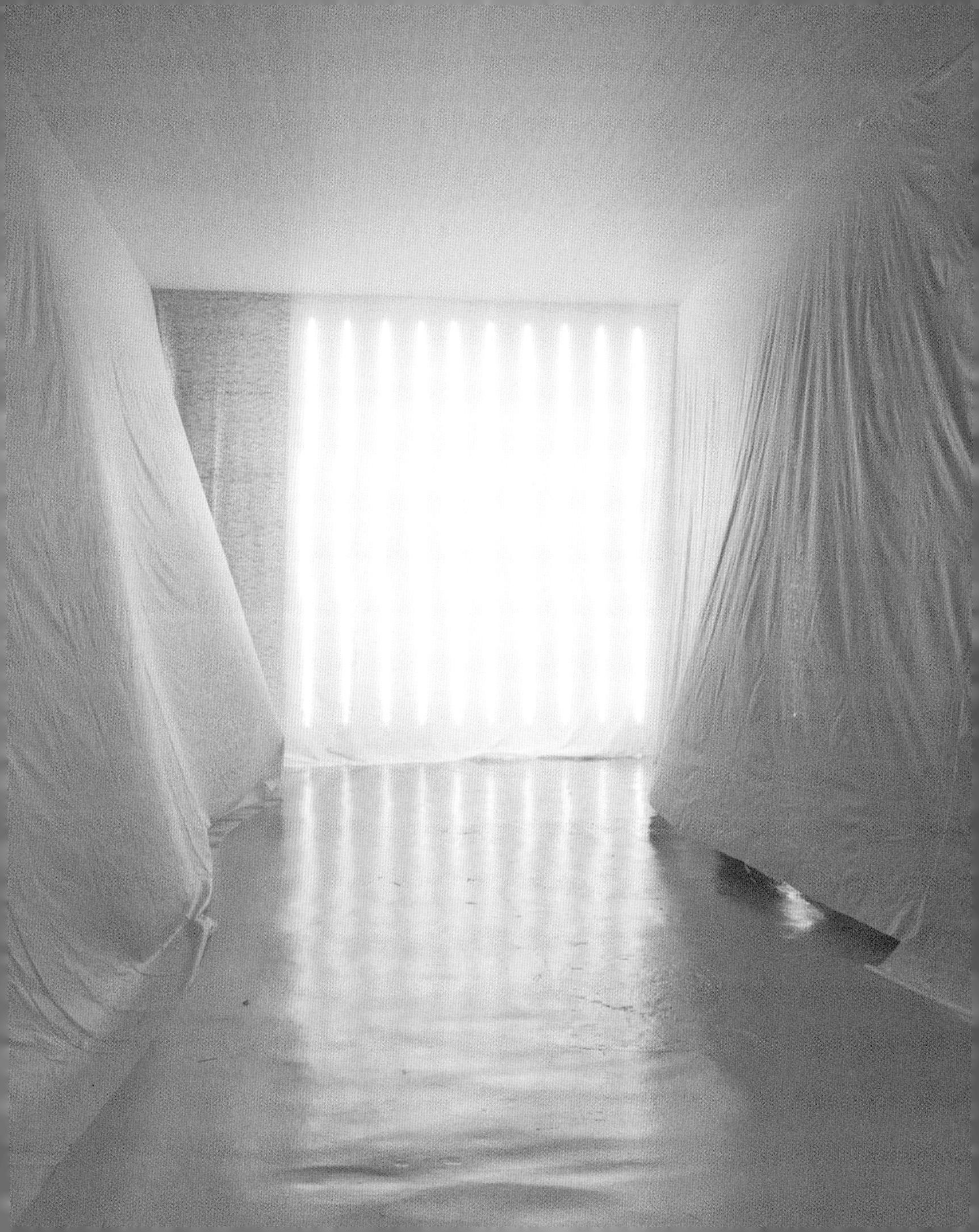

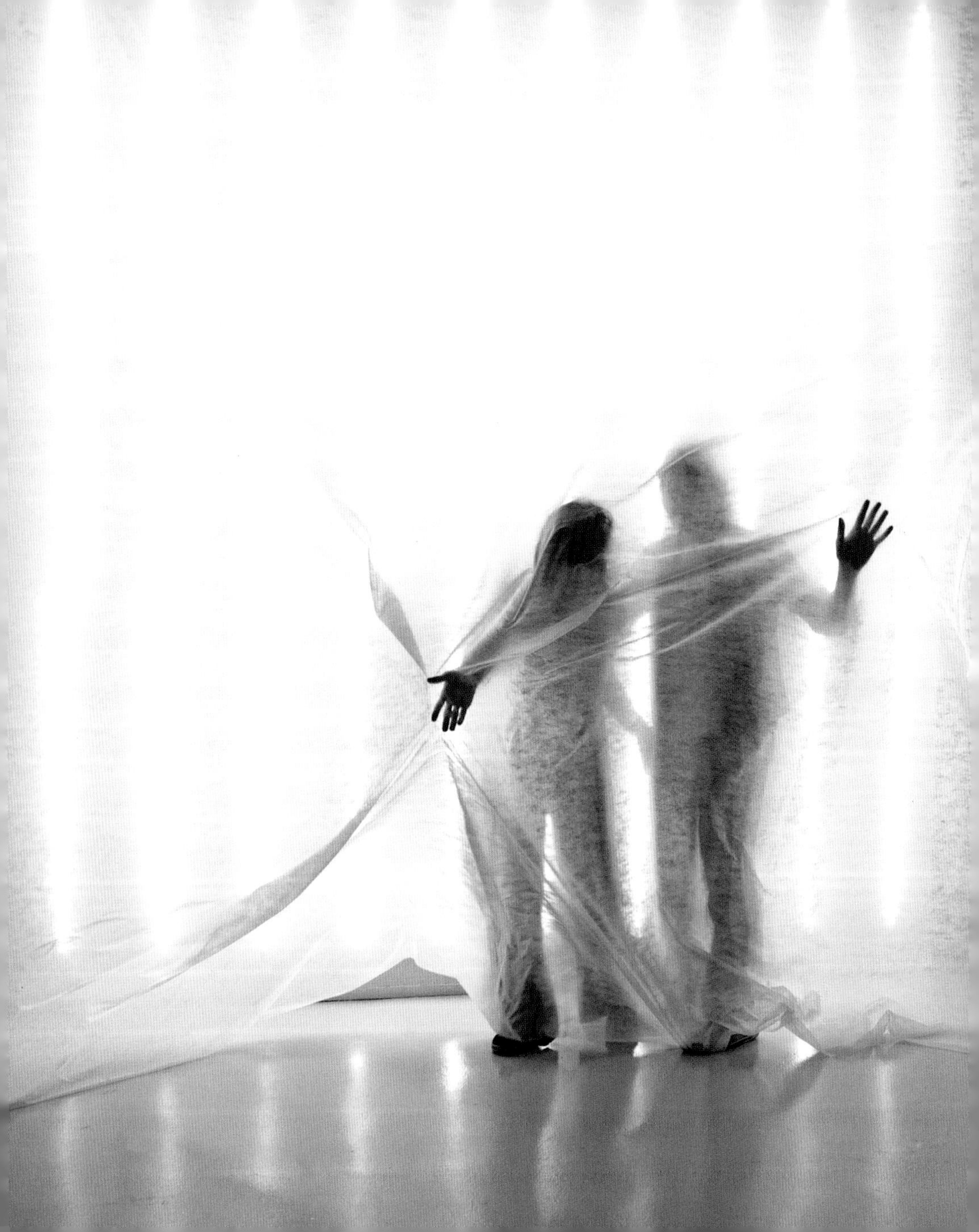

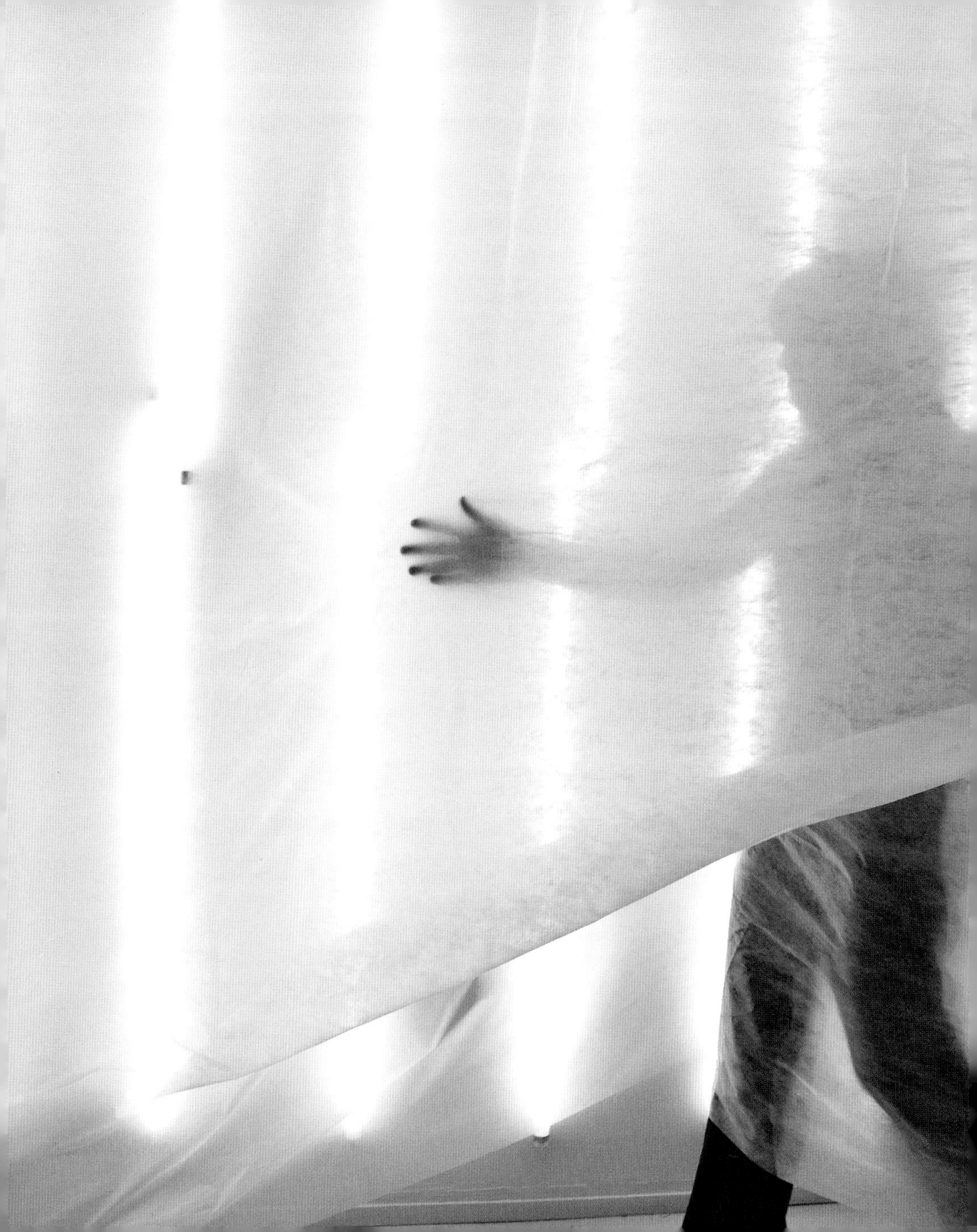

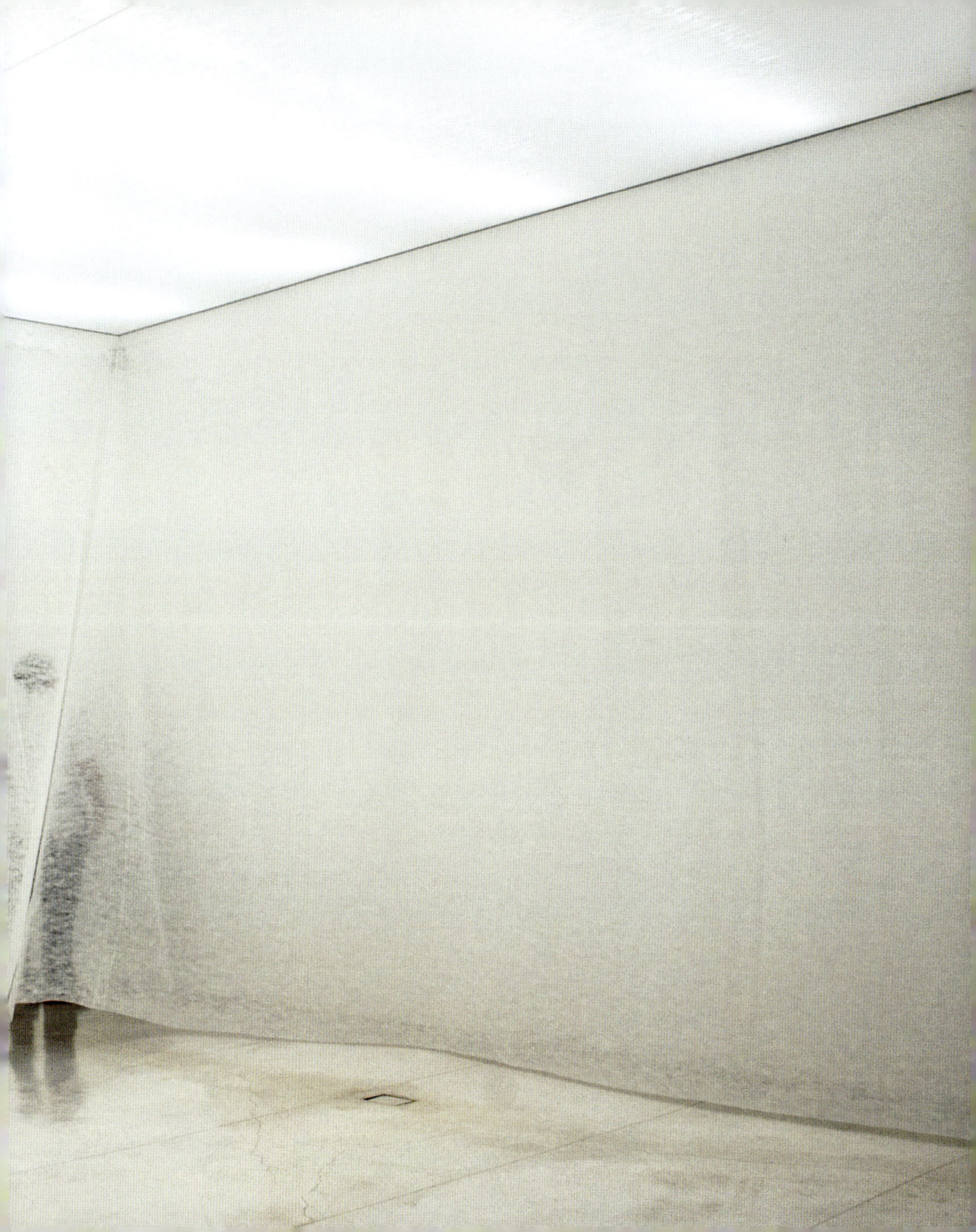

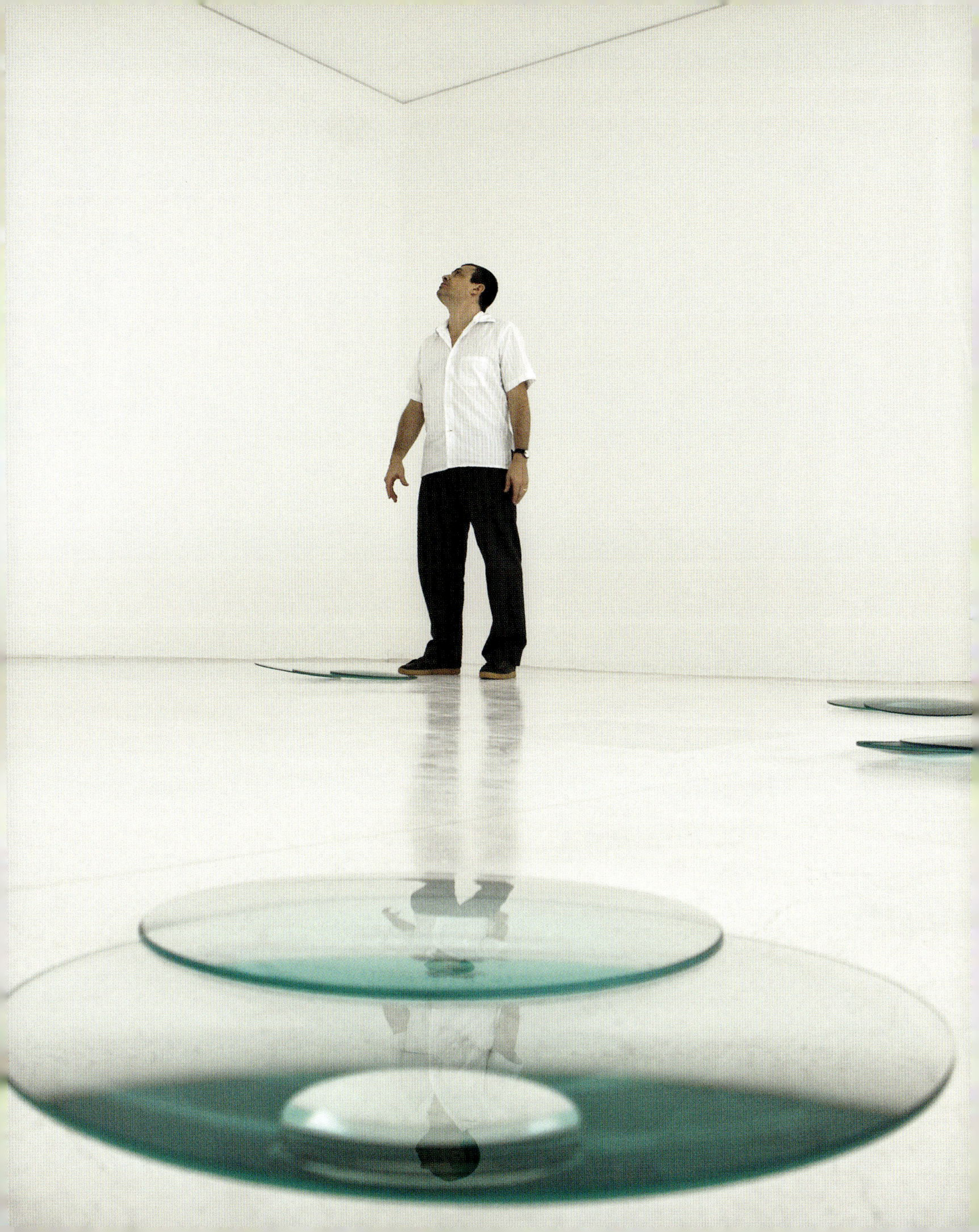

ESTOU LÁ

PAÇO IMPERIAL DO RIO DE JANEIRO, 2008
EDITAL ARTE E PATRIMÔNIO
TNT, LÂMPADAS T8, 32W, 4100 °K
5 PEÇAS. TOTAL 3,5M DE ALTURA. 35M X 10M
PERFORMANCE DE FLU, LEO MONTEIRO,
DANNY ROLAND, LAUFER E STEPHANE SAN JUAN
CADA MÚSICO, ISOLADO EM UM ESPAÇO, TOCA
SEM VER O RESTO DO GRUPO. O RETORNO
DO SOM É AO ACASO. O PÚBLICO ATRAVESSA AS
PEÇAS E VÊ O CONJUNTO. O PÚBLICO ESTÁ SÓ.

Estou Lá

Paço Imperial do Rio de Janeiro, 2008

Edital Arte e Patrimônio
TNT, T8 lamps, 32w, 4,100°k, 5 pieces
3.5m h, 35m x 10m
Performance by Flu, Leo Monteiro,
Danny Roland, Laufer and Stephane San Juan.
Each musician, alone in a space, plays without seeing
the rest of the group. The stage monitors are also random.
The public crosses the work and sees the space. The public is alone.

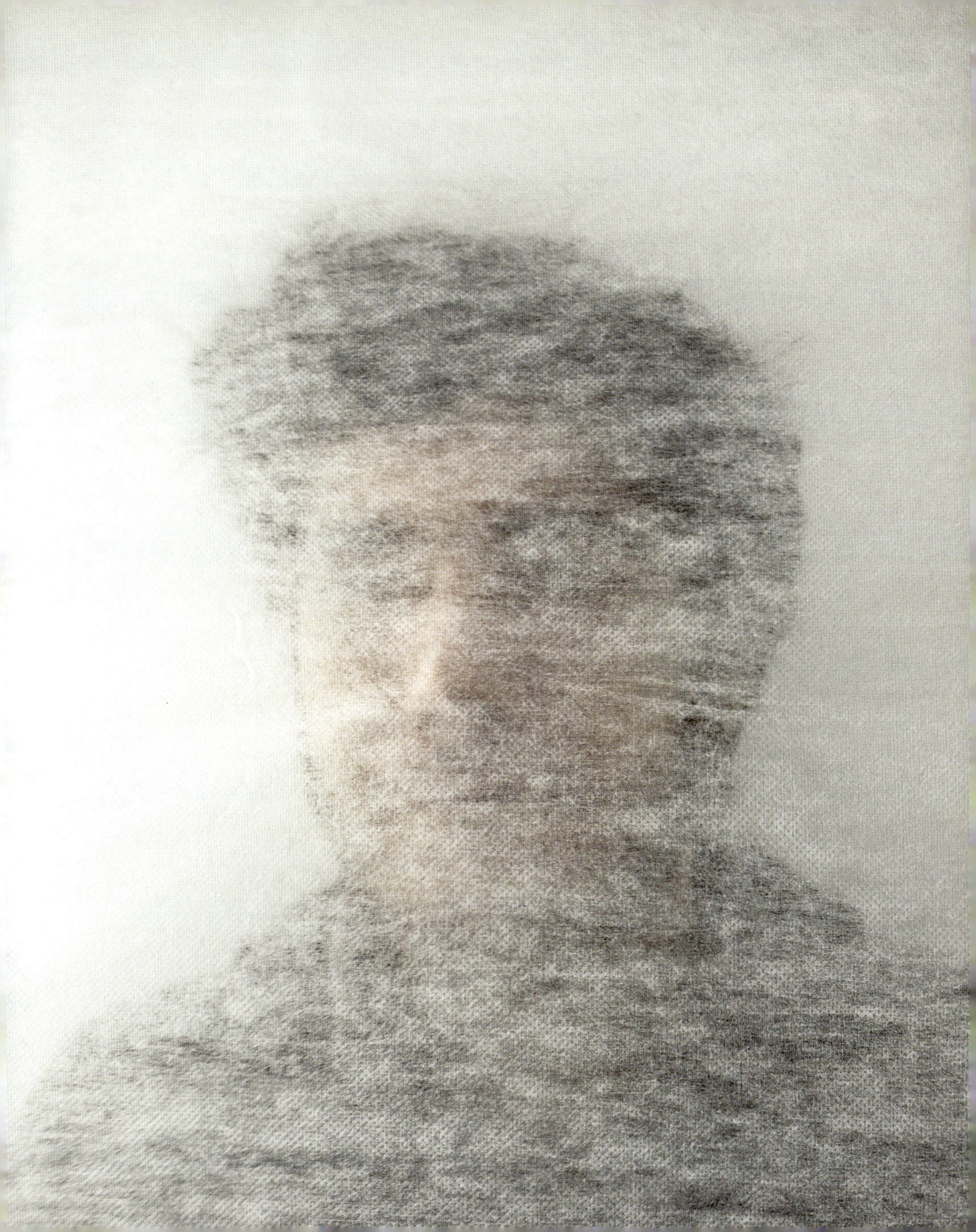

na exposição Estou L

os acendedores ataca

sua munição altame

maluco, sem noção, p

celebração neural-mu

Leo Monteiro_percs eletrônicas, máqu

laptop, sons viajantes e mixagens. Steph

cortados, mixagens. Laufer_baixo gra

sábado

20set08_16h30

de Carlito Carvalhosa,
o os apagadores com
e sonora! Aleatório,
soas reunidas pra uma
al. Veja os sujeitos:

barulhinhos em geral. Danny Roland_
e San Juan_maquinas indianas, loops
rave baixo. Flu_riff, sinths, mixagens

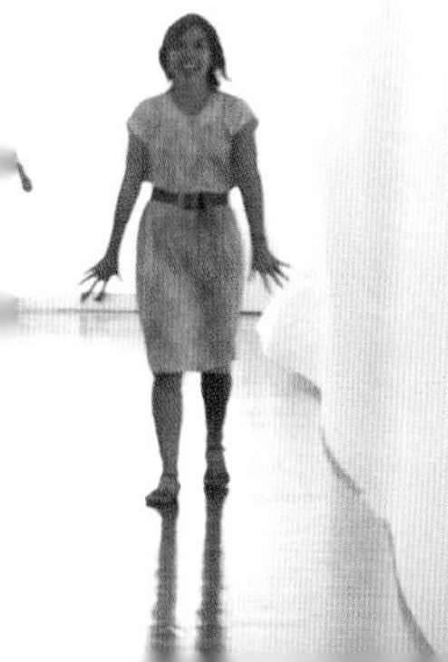

Paço Imperial

Praça XV_RJ

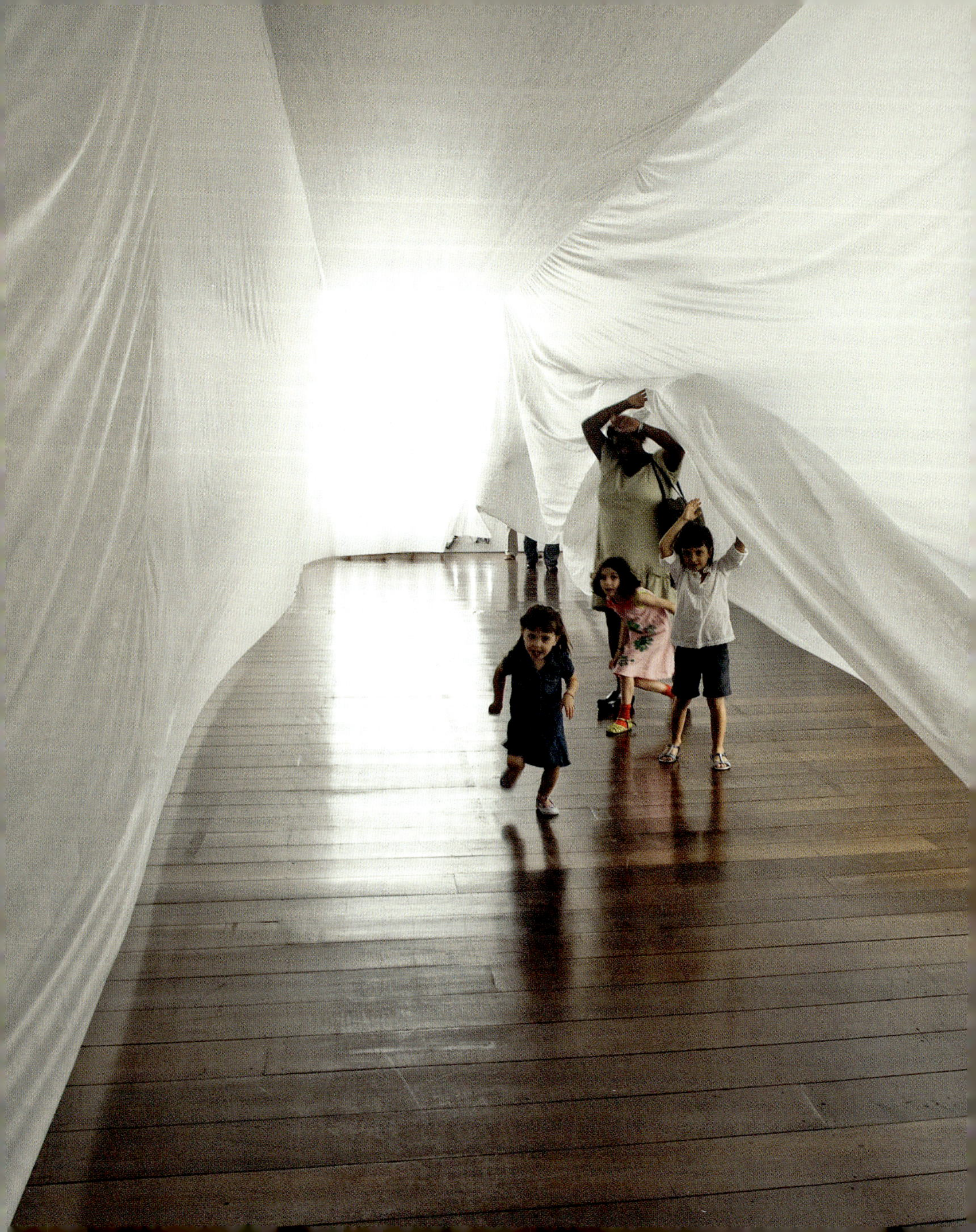

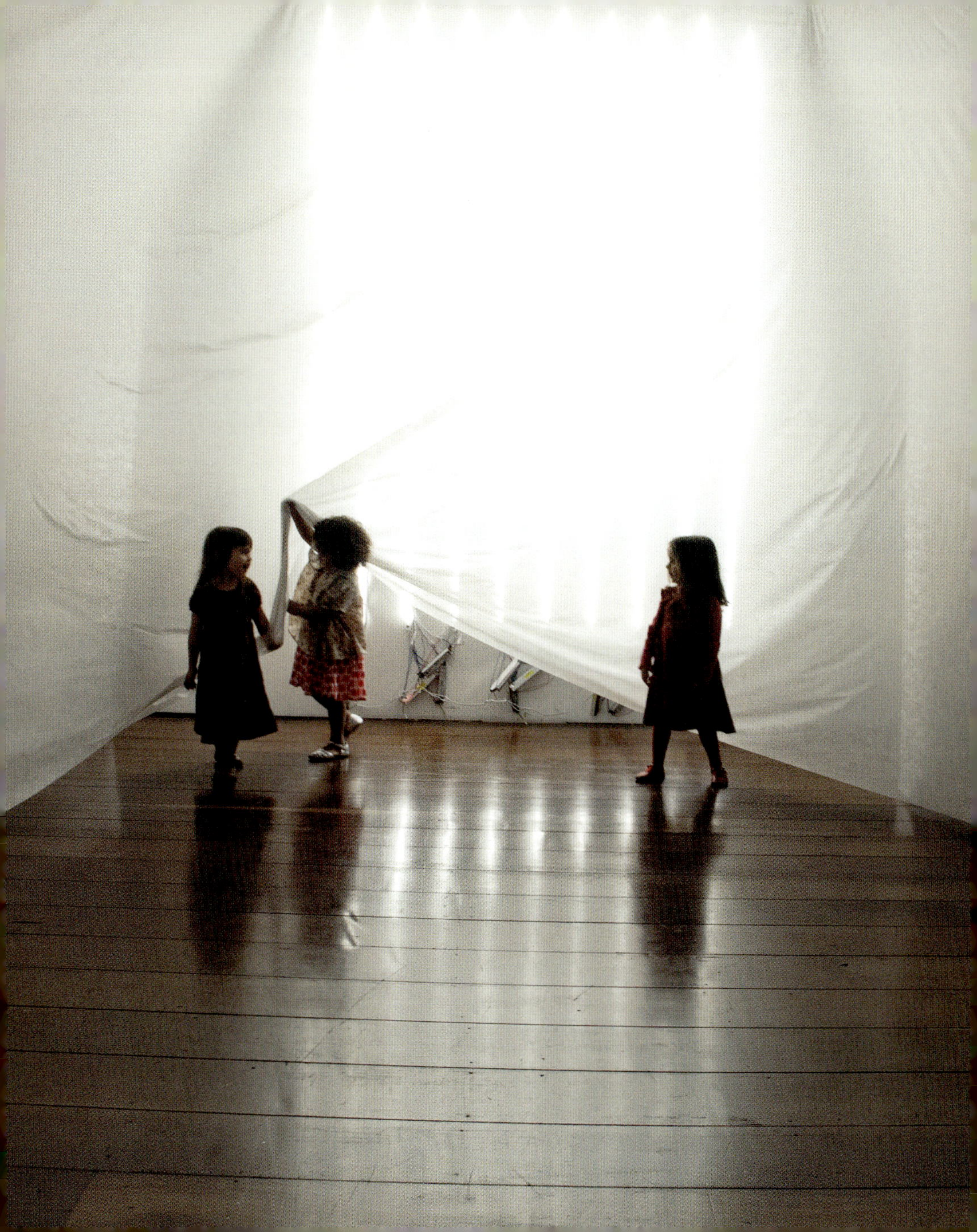

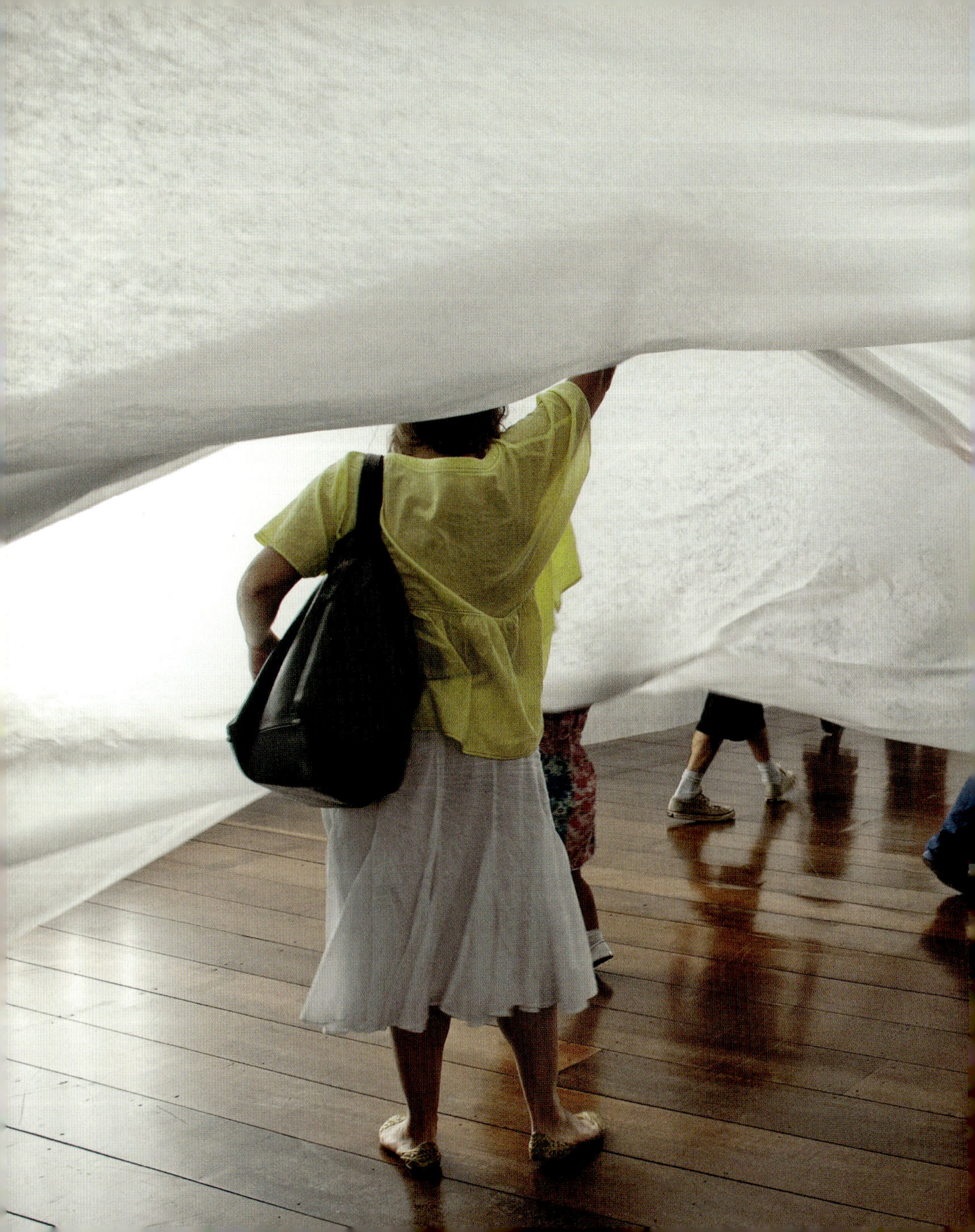

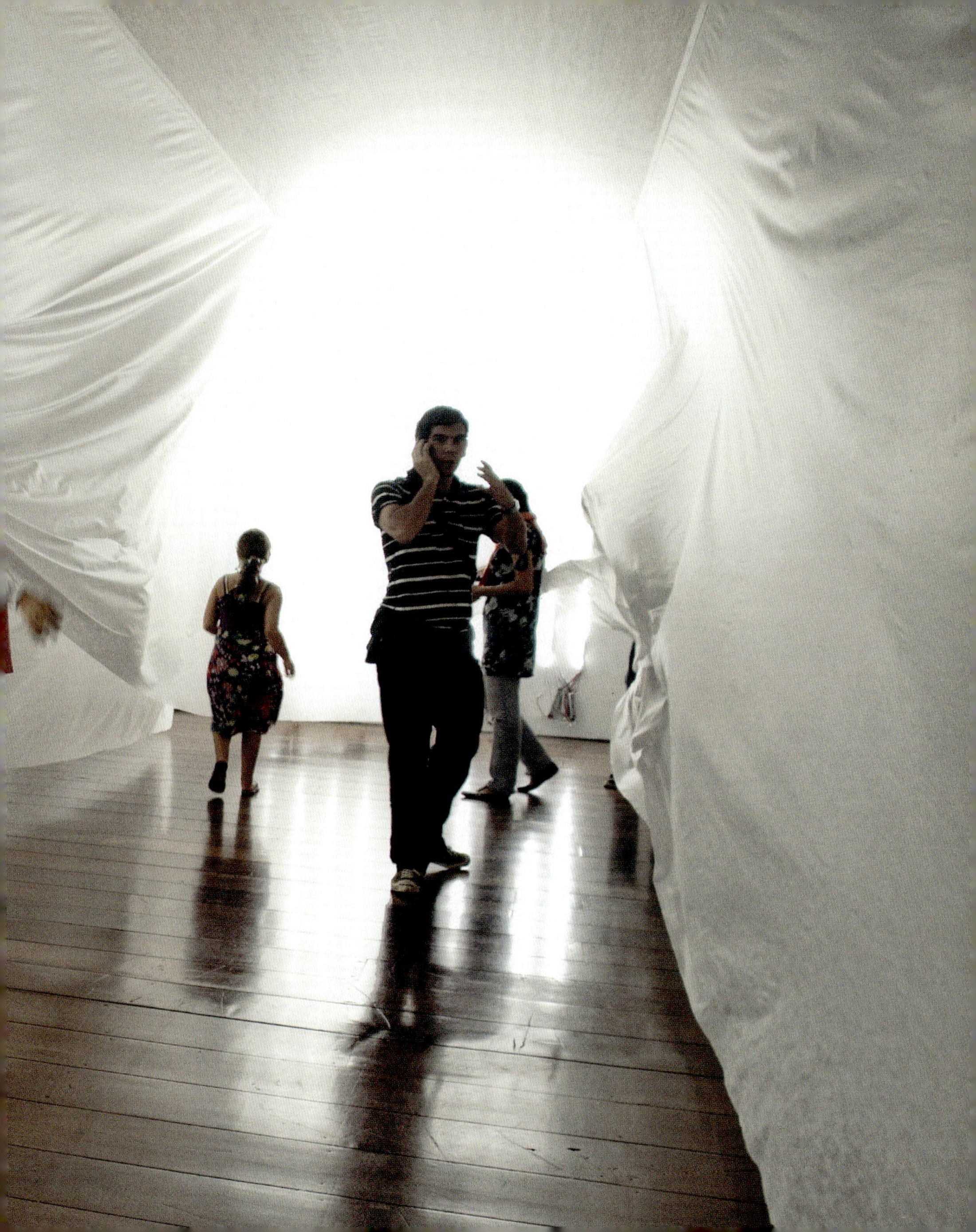

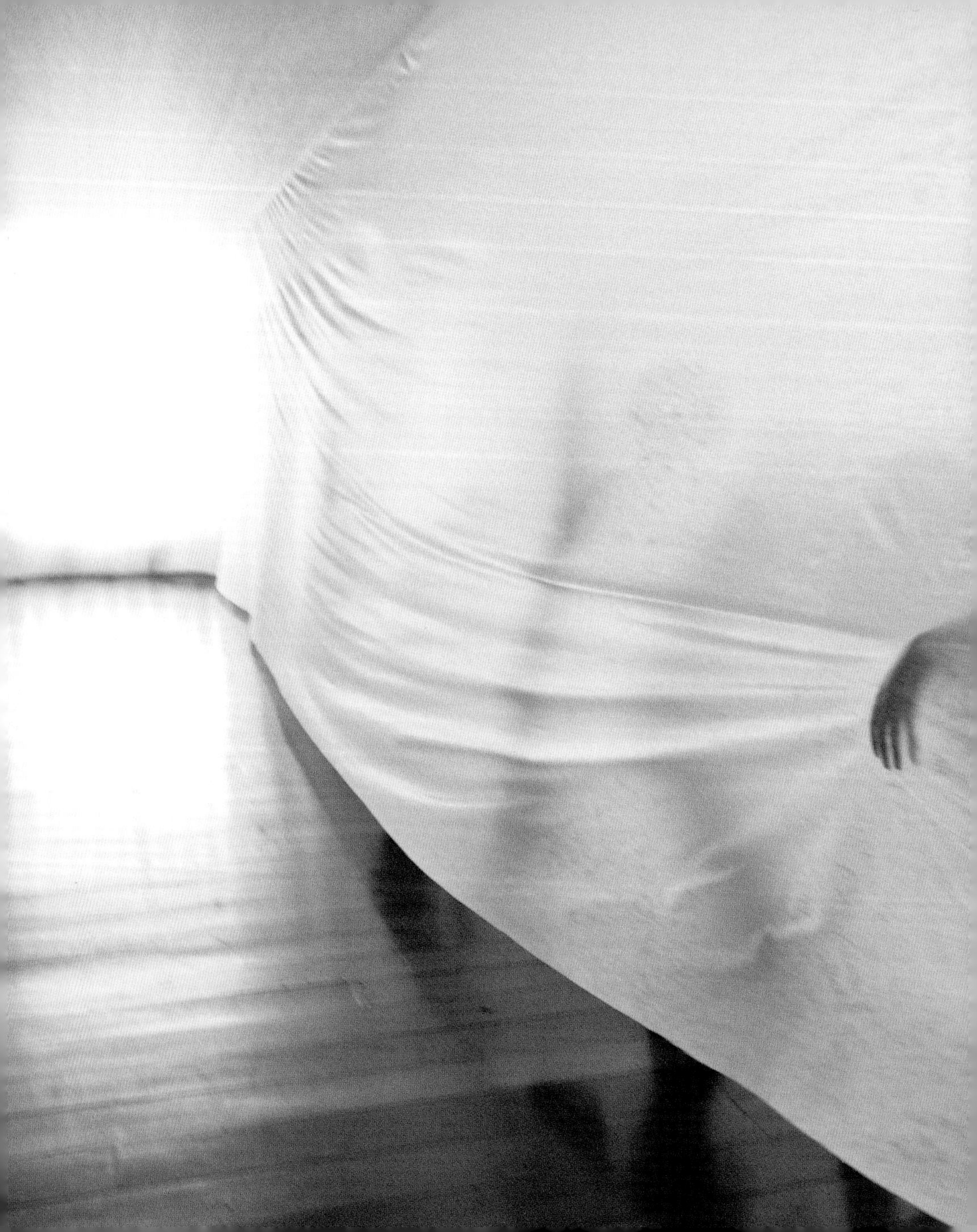

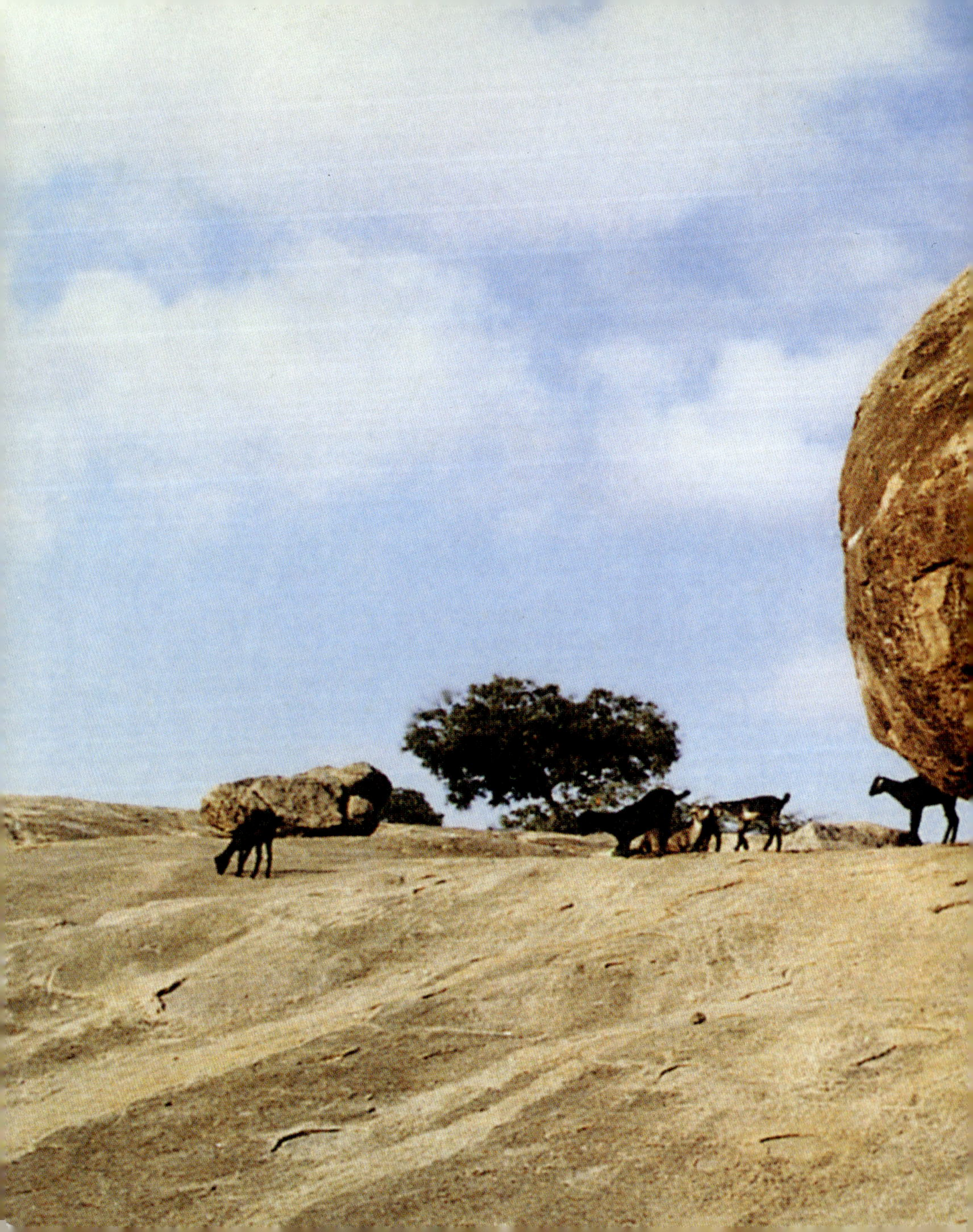